English Jackpot!

Teacher's Book 2

Michael Vince

Heinemann

Contents

Introduction	4
Contents map (Student's Book)	8
Teaching notes	Teacher's Book Unit 1
Songs	210
Wordlist	212
Grammar checkpoint	219
Tapescript	235
Progress tests	253
Progress tests: Answers	267
Key to Test Book	269
Workbook answers	276

Introduction

Who is the course intended for?
This course is intended for young learners of English. It takes learners from false beginner to intermediate level.

What are the course components?
Each level of the course has a Student's Book, a Workbook, a Teacher's Book, a Test book and a set of cassettes.

How long is the Student's Book?
In the Student's Book there are twenty-three main units, and three consolidation units, providing approximately eighty hours' work. Each main unit consists of three lessons of 45-60 minutes.

What is in each unit?
Each main unit contains three lessons. The first two lessons of one and a half pages each present new language in context. Each lesson contains between four and six activities which present and practise a new language item and also develop skills. There are three different types of third lesson, so that learners find variety in each unit.

1 Words in action

This lesson is based around either a specially written song, or a short text. This provides revision of grammatical points already learned. Song activities involve listening skills and speaking activities, with a strong focus on vocabulary development and pronunciation. Text activities include pre-activities, and promote effective reading skills, including dealing with vocabulary in context, and locating key information. Speaking activities are also included.

2 A story: *CHRIS*

This is a serial story with eight episodes. These lessons include reading, listening, speaking and writing activities, and are also designed to generate a general interest in reading. The reading text also includes items already learned, and acts as a means of recycling grammar and vocabulary. All the episodes of the story appear on the cassettes. Readers are involved actively in the story, by taking part in prediction and guessing activities.

3 Check up

This is a revision lesson. It gives learners the opportunity to practise grammatical points in a variety of exercise formats. The subject matter of these exercises often relates them to each other or they can be based around characters from earlier units. Each Check up lesson practises the new material from the previous three units.

These lessons are designed to recycle and combine what has been learned, and to make learners aware of what they have learned. They are not intended as formal test material. They can be used as a focus for revision before tests are given.

At three points in the book, there is an opportunity for further consolidation at greater length. Two-page consolidation units occur after units 8 and 16, and there is a final four-page consolidation unit at the end of the book, so that learners are aware of what they have learned in the course.

How easy is it to use the Student's Book?
Units are colour coded so they can be easily cross-referenced from the Contents map, and both the grammatical Helplines and the Consolidation lessons can easily be identified by colour coding also.

Units are clearly introduced with both thematic and grammatical headings. The lesson headings within a unit are thematic and they are not rigidly labelled 'Lesson 1', 'Lesson 2' etc so teachers can have some flexibility in lesson planning.

What kinds of topics are included?
The content of the course has been chosen to be both interesting and challenging for the age group, as well as enjoyable. There is a combination of humorous, fictional and real-life items, as these different kinds of materials motivate learners in different ways, and provide variety.

There is more emphasis on factual material in this level of the course. Helen and Nick, the reporters for their school magazine *Brilliant*, meet teenagers involved in a wide range of interesting activities. The Odds and the Normals are humorous cartoon characters. Learners also follow the Round the World Kids on their journey and find out about the countries they visit.

There is a higher proportion of longer texts as the course proceeds, and these are related to changing interests as learners grow older. Topic material has been matched with the interests of teenagers being taught in their own countries, and there is a variety of international contexts.

Are learners encouraged to speak?
New grammatical items are contextualised and practised through activities which encourage learners to use the language, and contribute their own ideas. The activities encourage learners to talk to one another or to the teacher.

Structural items are always presented so that learners associate them with specific functional uses. There are also opportunities to talk about topic material, and speaking activities related to the serial story. The illustrations are also designed to aid understanding and can be used as a focus for speaking activities.

The illustrated borders to the Check up, *CHRIS* and the Words in Action pages can be used to provide extra stimulus for speaking.

How is grammar dealt with?

There is a variety of approaches to grammar. The yellow Helpline boxes have a dual role. They give brief, on-the-spot help in dealing with grammatical points and they refer learners to the separate Grammar Checkpoint which is stored in the back cover pocket of the Student's Book. This is a reference grammar which helps learners to study grammar points presented in the main units. (GC in Helpline boxes = Grammar Checkpoint.)

The Grammar Checkpoint has been designed as a booklet so that learners can refer to grammatical points without losing their page in the Student's Book. It can be used by the teacher as a focus for preparation before learners use the unit activities, or learners can be encouraged to refer to it as a self-access resource during or after the activity.

In this way learners are encouraged to start dealing with grammatical problems on their own. Grammar is contextualised so that specific uses or functions are presented and practised.

The colour coding of the book makes it easy for the learners to find grammatical Helplines and Consolidation pages.

What is the approach to teaching and learning?

Although the Teacher's Book suggests procedures which can be used with the materials in each lesson, the course caters for different learning and teaching styles, so the materials can be used to suit learners and teachers in different situations. For example, there are numerous opportunities for pair and group work, but materials can also be used in situations where a teacher-focused activity is preferred. This allows for differences in teaching situations, such as class size, the level of independence of the learners, and the context in which they are learning.

The Check up and Consolidation pages provide opportunities for learners to think further about what they have learned, and to combine old and new learning. There are similar opportunities in the Grammar Checkpoint in which there are exercises which can be used for self-assessment. The Teacher's Book includes progress tests for more formal checking of learning. A test book is also available.

How are listening skills developed?

There are regular listening skill activities, with a variety of skill focus, and different types of format. The aim is to encourage learners to enjoy listening in the classroom and to develop skills appropriate to their level of learning. Learners are encouraged to listen for specific points, rather than to try to understand every word of the text. Activities include the use of illustrations and tables, and some are related to practice of grammatical points. The listening activities always occur within the context of other activities, and within a specific topic area, so that problems of understanding are reduced.

Specially written songs are included as listening activities. The Words in Action pages on which most songs appear have illustrated borders which give help with subject matter and lexical content.

Presentation and reading texts are also recorded, although these are not generally intended for use as listening skill activities. In this case, the cassette can be used to help learners make a link between written and spoken language. These recordings are intended to be played while the learners read the texts, as they usually contain new grammatical points, or a high density of information.

How are reading skills developed?

There is a variety of texts based on authentic types (eg letters, news articles, stories etc.), with complexity appropriate to the level. The type and amount of reading material varies with the stages of the course. Learners are encouraged to develop basic text skills, such as checking for main points and guessing vocabulary from context. At this level, learners are introduced to reading skills activities on Words in Action pages. The aim is to provide learners with the reading skills necessary for them to become independent readers.

The Teacher's Book suggests teaching procedures for lessons involving reading text, so that learners can become accustomed to approaching an unknown text in a productive and efficient way. Reading lessons can be based on silent reading or on reading of the text focused by playing the recording, or can be adapted to suit the teaching and learning context.

The serial story provides an interactive approach to reading, and the activities encourage learners to involve themselves with the story. The story material also includes listening, speaking and writing material, and is an approach to the integration of skills at this level. Learners discuss what might happen next, and take part in speaking or writing activities related to the story.

Learners should also be provided with a class library of Heinemann Guided Readers and New Wave Readers (see page 7) and be encouraged to continue extensive reading outside the classroom. There should be a variety of Readers chosen at the right level. It is possible to organize a library system, run by members of the class. The aim should be to develop a reading habit, rather than treat the text as something to be learned and tested.

How is pronunciation dealt with?

There are pronunciation activities directed at problem areas arising in language points, and as general background, with the aim of raising learners' basic awareness of how the sound system works. These are restricted to simple sound, stress and intonation areas, and some phonetic transcription where it will be helpful. The emphasis is on treating pronunciation as a manageable area of learning. By combining reading and listening as suggested in the use of presentation texts, learners may also increase their understanding of the relation between spoken and written language at a basic level. The teacher, of course, remains the most influential focus for the development of pronunciation.

How are writing skills developed?

The course assumes that writing is a skill, which has to be taught. There are regular writing activities, with different kinds of guidance on text type and content. Writing activities are related to grammatical level, and linked to other skills, such as speaking, reading or listening. Learners are encouraged to write short texts controlled to their level of achievement. The type and amount of writing material varies with the stages of the course. There are opportunities to develop writing activities in class, and to continue the activities as homework. In the Workbook writing is developed from sentence length tasks to paragraph length ones.

How is vocabulary taught?

Each unit includes topic material from two or three areas. It is assumed that for some activities, learners will need to use a wide range of lexical material, not all of which needs to be learned. A word list is provided for each unit. Each unit also has a Word Check box, containing key words from the unit. The Teacher's Book includes suggestions on how to use this material. Lexical activities are included in the Words in Action lessons, where the aim is to encourage learners to relate words, on the basis of meaning, or form, and to organize and consolidate what they have learned. Any of these activities can be used as a focus for dictionary work.

Are there Tests to accompany the course?

There are four photocopiable Progress tests in the Teacher's Book, one to follow each Consolidation unit and an end-of-book test. There is also a Test Book in which there are tests which can be used after each Check up and Consolidation in the Student's Book.

What is in the Workbook?

The Student's Workbook contains a variety of activities, which focus on both grammar and skills and provide consolidation and supplementary activities for each unit.

The Workbook can be used in the classroom for extra practice, or as a basis for homework. (NB There is no listening material in the Workbook.)

What is in the Teacher's Book?

The Teacher's Book is interleaved with the Student's Book pages so that the teacher can easily use the teacher's notes with the students' material. There are step-by-step lesson notes which include answers to the Student's Book activities. There are also suggestions for extra practice which further develop exercises in the Student's Book and there are optional activities which offer practice of the target language. These are not related to particular exercises in the Student's Book. Where it is appropriate the Teacher's Book gives cultural notes and it also includes practical advice on what aids teachers might need for a lesson, and also tapescripts, Progress tests and answers, and answers to Workbook activities and the tests in the separate Test book.

Heinemann Guided Readers and New Wave Readers

Here are some books which might be interesting as extensive reading for students studying this course. A Heinemann catalogue will tell you more about them.

New Wave Readers

Level 2 (16 pp)

Double Danger by Tony Hopwood
Escape from Castle Czarka by Alan C McLean
Kareteka by Sue Leather and Marje Brash
The House on the Moors by Paul Shipton
Kate's Revenge by Philip Prowse
Zargon Zoo by Paul Shipton

Level 3 (32 pp)

Born to Run by Alan C McLean
Dancing Shoes by Colin Granger
Murder at Mortlock Hall by Donald Dallas
One Pair of Eyes by Caroline Laidlow
Sheela and the Robbers by John Escott
The Smiling Buddha by Michael Palmer

Heinemann Guided Readers

Beginner Level (32 pp)

The Long Tunnel by John Milne
The Truth Machine by Norman Whitney
Death of a Soldier by Philip Prowse
Dangerous Journey by Alwyn Cox
Money for a Motorbike by John Milne
The Sky's the Limit by Norman Whitney
Marco by Mike Esplen
Newspaper Boy by John Escott
The House on the Hill by Elizabeth Laird
Anna and the Fighter by Elizabeth Laird
Rich Man Poor Man by T C Jupp
The Garden by Elizabeth Laird
Dear Jan ... Love Ruth by Nick McIver
The Wall by Stephen Colbourn
Winning and Losing by T C Jupp
L A Raid by Philip Prowse
The Night Visitor by R MacAndrew and C Lawday
This is London by Philip Prowse
This is New York by Betsy Pennink
This is San Francisco by Betsy Pennink

Elementary Level (64 pp)

The Runaways by Victor Canning, *retold by* F Peers
The Stranger by Norman Whitney
The Black Cat by John Milne
Don't Tell Me What To Do by Michael Hardcastle, *retold by* Phillip King
The Goalkeeper's Revenge and Other Stories by Bill Naughton
The Man With No Name by Evelyn Davies and Peter Town
Road To Nowhere by John Milne
The Promise by R Scott-Buccleuch
The Cleverest Person in the World by Norman Whitney
Z for Zachariah by Robert C O'Brien, *retold by* Peter Hodson
The Verger and Other Stories by W Somerset Maugham, *retold by* John Milne
The Red Pony by John Steinbeck, *retold by* Michael Paine
Frankenstein by Mary Shelley, *retold by* Margaret Tarner
Tales of Horror by Bram Stoker, *retold by* John Davey
Claws by John Landon
The Escape and Other Stories by W Somerset Maugham, *retold by* John Davey
The Woman in Black by Susan Hill, *retold by* Margaret Tarner
Tales of Ten Worlds by Arthur C Clarke, *retold by* Helen Reid-Thomas
The Boy who was Afraid by Armstrong Sperry, *retold by* Stephen Colbourn
Silver Blaze and Other Stories by Sir Arthur Conan Doyle, *retold by* Anne Collins
The Flower Seller by Richard Prescott
Room 13 and Other Stories by M R James, *retold by* Stephen Colbourn
The Narrow Path by Francis Selormey, *retold by* John Milne
The Hound of the Baskervilles by Sir Arthur Conan Doyle, *retold by* Stephen Colbourn
Riders of the Purple Sage by Zane Grey, *retold by* Florence Bell
The Canterville Ghost and Other Stories by Oscar Wilde, *retold by* Stephen Colbourn
Lady Portia's Revenge and Other Stories by David Evans
The Picture of Dorian Grey by Oscar Wilde, *retold by* F H Cornish
Treasure Island by Robert Louis Stevenson, *retold by* Stephen Colbourn
A Christmas Carol by Charles Dickens, *retold by* F H Cornish
Dr Jekyll and Mr Hyde by Robert Louis Stevenson, *retold by* Stephen Colbourn
Love by Design by Kieran McGovern
The Lost World by Sir Arthur Conan Doyle

Contents

		Grammar:	Functions/activities:
1 Happy holidays	1 Back again	Past simple, present simple, present continuous	Activities with go + ing Describing and asking about past events, habits and events happening now
	2 Holiday stories	Past simple, present simple	Describing and asking about past events and habits
	3 Words in action		Song: The aliens Verb and noun collocations Word choice
2 What happened?	1 Round the World 2 When the lights went out	Past simple and past continuous Past simple and past continuous While, when	Describing events in a narrative Narrating past events
	3 CHRIS 1		
3 Make your choice	1 Choosing a bike	Comparative and superlative adjectives Not as [adjective] as..., [adjective] than	Making comparisons
	2 The Odds and the Normals 3 Check up Units 1–3	Too [adjective], not [adjective] enough	Making comparisons
4 So far, so good	1 The Round the World Kids 2 What has he done?	Present perfect simple Ever, yet Present perfect simple [regular and irregular verbs] Just	Describing recent events Describing recent events
	3 Words in action		Reading: Volcanoes Lexical skills Comprehension skills
5 Time travellers	1 A visit to the past	Past simple and present perfect simple Since, ago, for	Contrasting definite and indefinite events
	2 Discoveries 3 CHRIS 2	Past simple and present perfect simple	Contrasting definite and indefinite events
6 What's it like?	1 The Round the World Kids	What's it like? Comparisons with adverbs	Describing and comparing places, things, people
	2 Born to shop 3 Check up Units 4–6	Order of adjectives	Describing things
7 Watch this space!	1 Space cadets 2 Space for peace	Could, couldn't Could, couldn't Was/were able to [achievement]	Describing past ability Describing past ability
	3 Words in action		Song: Have you ever? Verb and noun collocations The I've lost it game Countable and uncountable nouns
8 Home and away	1 Animal time	Question tags with present simple, be, can, have got	Checking information
	2 What happened? 3 CHRIS 3	Question tags with past simple	Checking information
Consolidation 1 Units 1-8			
9 Arranging the future	1 What's he doing on Monday? 2 Would you like to ...?	Present continuous: future use Present continuous future use Would like, I don't think so, I'm afraid I can't	Describing social arrangements Making and responding to invitations
	3 Words in action		Song: Would you like to sail ...? Making invitations Adjectives and nouns Tag questions Connecting nouns
10 Habits and home	1 Eating habits	Countable and uncountable nouns How much ...?, how many ...?, few, little	Asking and answering about quantity
	2 The Round the World Kids	Too much, too many Not enough + noun	Describing problems
	3 CHRIS 4		

			Grammar:	Functions/activities:
11	On the air	1 Stars of the small screen 2 Outside broadcast 3 Check up Units 9–11	Will, won't, going to Could you …?, Would you mind …?	Making predictions, promises, plans Describing definite future events Making requests Asking someone to do something
12	Follow the rules	1 School rules 2 The Round the World Kids 3 Words in action	Had to, didn't have to couldn't Had to, didn't have to couldn't	Describing obligation Describing obligation and inability Reading: Food through the ages Reference word skills Word field: food
13	Did you know?	1 Green corner 2 It's hard to believe 3 CHRIS 5	Present simple passive Past simple passive	Describing a system impersonally Describing events
14	Good advice	1 Emergency 2 Your letters answered 3 Check up Units 12–14	Should, shouldn't I think/I don't think + should	Giving advice Giving advice
15	Changes	1 Old and new 2 Turn over a new leaf 3 Words in action	Used to Used to, didn't use to	Contrasting past habits/everyday actions with habits/everyday actions in the present Contrasting past states with present states Song: You shouldn't do that Sentence stress Adjectives and adverbs The passive game
16	Be careful!	1 Safety first 2 Round the World problems 3 CHRIS 6	Could, might Could, might Gerund or infinitive after certain verbs	Describing possible events Describing possible events Giving warnings
Consolidation 2 Units 9-16				
17	Don't worry so much!	1 Not a care in the world 2 Worry, worry, worry! 3 Words in action	Real condition: if + present simple, + imperative Real condition: if + present simple, + will	Giving instructions about possible events Making predictions about possible events Reading: A Head for Heights Lexical skills Comprehension skills
18	In the rainforest	1 The Programme for Belize 2 A visit to Rio Bravo 3 CHRIS 7	Let's, why don't we?, how about? I'd rather	Making suggestions Expressing preferences
19	What have you been doing?	1 Life style 2 The bank robbery 3 Check up Units 17–19	Present perfect continuous For, since Present perfect continuous	Describing extended actions Narrating past events
20	Are you sure?	1 Spot the mistakes 2 Round the World album 3 Words in action	Can't be Can't be, must be	Describing certainty and uncertainty Describing certainty and uncertainty Song: I'd rather watch TV Word families Adjectives and activities Verb and noun collocations
21	Just imagine!	1 What would you do? 2 Changing places 3 CHRIS 8	Would, wouldn't Unreal condition: if + past tense, + would	Describing imaginary situations Describing imaginary situations
22	Difficult moments	1 How embarrassing! 2 The Round the World Kids 3 Check up Units 20–22	Definite/indefinite/zero article Verbs followed by infinitive or gerund	Narrating past events Describing events in a narrative
23	What did you see?	1 At the supermarket 2 All in the past 3 Words in action	Tense contrasts: past simple, past continuous present perfect simple	Describing events in a narrative Describing events in a narrative Talking about when things happen Reading: Finding a Fortune Lexical skills Comprehension skills
24	Final consolidation			

Songs — page 104
Wordlist — page 105
Grammar checkpoint — booklet

1 Happy holidays

revision: past simple, present simple, present continuous

Back again

1a 🔊 Practice

Hi, I'm Helen.

And I'm Nick. Do you remember us?

Yes, I did. I had a fantastic time.

I stayed for three weeks. It was great!

I went swimming every day and played beach tennis.

We usually stay with my uncle and aunt in Wales.

To the same place again. It was really good.

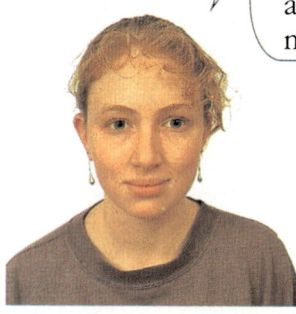

I went to Scotland and stayed with my penfriend.

It's the beginning of a new school year, so we interviewed people for our school magazine, *Brilliant*. We asked them about their summer holidays. Read their answers and make their questions.

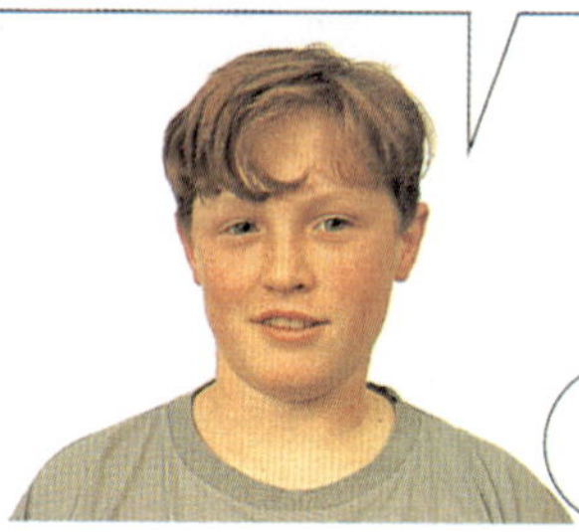

> **Helpline** – revision of past simple
>
> **regular verbs**   **irregular verbs**
> add -ed   go – went   have – had
> questions: use *did*
>   Where did you stay?   Where did you go?
>   → GC p2, 15

1b Practice

Check your questions from **1a** by matching these questions with the answers in **1a**.

1. Where do you usually go for your holiday?
2. Where did you go this year?
3. How long did you stay there?
4. Did you have a good time?
5. What did you do every day?
6. Where do you want to go next year?

Ask someone the same questions. Make some notes or remember their answers. Then tell a new partner about your first partner's holiday.

> **Helpline**
> – revision of present simple and present continuous
>
> We use present simple for everyday actions/habits with frequency adverbs:
>   Where do you usually go?
> We also use present simple with verbs that describe feelings:
>   Where do you want to go next year?
> We use present continuous for events which are happening now:
>   At the moment we are staying in Sydney.
>   → GC p2

Happy holidays 1

Unit 1		Functions	Grammar
Lesson 1	Back again	Activities with go + ing Describing and asking about past events, habits and events happening now	Past simple, present simple, and present continuous
Lesson 2	Holiday stories	Describing and asking about past events and habits	Past simple and present simple
Lesson 3	Words in action		

Word check

beach	holidays	piece
environment	lie (v)	remember
fantastic	magazine	rubbish
fire	mean (v)	sand
go sightseeing	penfriend	similar
		stay

Lesson 1 Back again

1a Practice

Aim: To revise the past simple (and present simple).
Summary: Ss ask and answer questions about their holidays.

Lead in

- Helen and Nick are characters from the first book. Ask Ss what they can remember about them. (They are at school and work as reporters for their school newspaper, *Brilliant*.)

Main activity

- Books open. Make sure Ss cover activity 1b.
- Explain that Helen and Nick have interviewed some students about their holidays. Ask Ss to read the students' answers and then write the questions which Helen and Nick asked.
- Ss work individually or in pairs. Go around the class and check Ss' work but do not ask for their questions – this is done in activity 1b.

Helpline – revision of past simple

- Ask Ss to tell a partner about the rules. Check by saying:
  I play basketball most days. Yesterday I …
  Ss complete the sentence:
  Yesterday I played basketball.
- Check that Ss remember that *-ed* is added to regular verbs. Ask:
  Can you remember some irregular verbs?
  Give some examples:
  buy - bought, ride - rode, put - put

- Tell Ss to ask questions about someone's summer holidays, eg: *Where did you go?*
- Check that Ss remember how to form the question in the past simple, ie with *did* and the root of the verb.
- Ask Ss to make some more questions about past time. Write some of their example questions on the board, eg: *What did you eat for breakfast?*

1b Practice

Aim: to practise the past simple (and present simple).
Summary: Ss check the questions they wrote in activity 1a and use these questions to talk about their summer holidays.

Main activity

- Ss confirm the questions they wrote in activity 1a by matching a list of six questions with the answers given in 1a and then checking with a partner. Ask individual Ss to read out the questions and answers.

Answers:
1. We usually stay with my uncle and aunt in Wales.
2. I went to Scotland and stayed with my penfriend.
3. I stayed for three weeks. It was great!
4. Yes, I did. I had a fantastic time.
5. I went swimming every day and played beach tennis.
6. To the same place again. It was really good.

- Ss use these questions to find out about a partner's holiday. They then change partners and exchange information in their new pairs about their first partner's holiday. Go around the class and help if necessary.
- Ss report back to the whole class about their first partner's holiday.

Helpline – revision of present simple and present continuous

- Tell Ss to explain the use of these two tenses.

Present simple
- Write some example sentences of the present simple on the board, eg:
  I sometimes forget to feed my dog but she always reminds me.
  Most people get up quite late at the weekend.
  My neighbour washes her car every weekend.
  Ask why we use this tense here. (In general, the present simple is used for everyday actions/habits.) It can also be used to describe feelings.

Present continuous
- Tell Ss to explain why we use this tense in the following sentences. (They describe events which are happening now.)
  I'm thinking about my summer holidays.
  Sally is looking out of the window.
  Some dogs are barking outside.

Teacher's Book Unit 1

1 Happy holidays

1c Writing

Aim: to read for missing information; to provide guided writing practice and revision of the past simple, present simple and present continuous.
Summary: Ss try to guess the missing words on the postcard.

Lead in
- Tell Ss that Helen has just got a postcard from San Francisco. What do they know about this city? (It has a famous bridge – the Golden Gate Bridge, it has earthquakes, it's in California on the Pacific coast of the USA.)

Main activity
- Explain that Helen cannot read some of the words on the postcard because the dog played with it after the postman brought it. Ask:
  What words are missing?
- Ss work individually. They then check answers with a partner. Ask individual Ss to read out sentences from the postcard and write the missing words on the board.

Answers:
Dear Helen
Here I am in San Francisco! All the family is here. We are staying with my father's friend, Tom. It's a beautiful city. Last week we went to see some old trees in the National Park. Then we had a boat trip and looked at the Golden Gate Bridge. Every day we go to the beach. The waves are very high here. We're having a great time. Did you have a good summer? Write me a letter!
Love from me
Annie

- Ss work in small groups (three or four) to discuss ideas for a similar postcard about a town in their country using the postcard in the SB as a model. Each group chooses a town and lists some of the local sights and things to do. (Set a time limit of 3 minutes.) Then ask for ideas and write some of Ss' suggestions on the board.
- Ss should write cards individually and try to use some of the expressions they found in Helen's card. Go around the class and help if necessary.
- Early finishers can read each other's cards and make suggestions for useful changes or additions.
- Ask Ss to bring from home (or draw) a picture to accompany their postcards. Postcards can then be displayed on a large piece of cardboard.

1d Practice

Aim: to practise the present simple describing habitual actions; to practise the lexical set *go + -ing*.
Summary: Ss talk about their habits when on holiday.

Main activity
- Ss work with a partner to talk about frequent holiday activities using *usually* or *sometimes*. Do some examples first with individual Ss, eg:

  - *Do you usually read a lot when you are on holiday?*
  - *No, I don't. How about you?*
  - *I sometimes read magazines if the weather is bad.*

- Use the Helpline to check that Ss understand *go + -ing* in the list of cues.

Helpline – go + -ing

This focuses on *go* + gerund to talk mainly about sports activities.

- Ask Ss to write four true sentences about themselves/their family/their partner using *go + -ing*, eg;
  I never go climbing.
  My mother often goes skiing.
  My brother sometimes goes dancing with his friends.
  My father often goes shopping on Saturdays.

- Ss work in pairs, using the list of cues. Go around the class and check that Ss are using the verb form correctly.
- Write some Ss' example sentences on the board. Tell Ss to copy them into their exercise books.

Extra activity
- Ask individual Ss to find out the most popular/least popular/most unusual holiday activities in the class.

Lesson 2 Holiday stories

2a Practice

Aim: to practise the past simple (affirmative, negative and question form).
Summary: Ss use pictures to roleplay conversations about holidays.

Lead in
- Books closed. Ask Ss about their ideal holiday. Ask for some ideas and offer some of your own.
- Books open. Ask Ss to describe the two places they can see in the pictures. Which do they prefer?

Main activity
- Give one student the part of Student A and you take the part of Student B. Ask A some questions about his/her picture:
  T: *Where did you go for your holidays this year?*
  S: *To a tropical island. It was fantastic.*
  T: *What did you do there? etc*
- Ss work with a partner. One takes the part of Student A and the other takes the part of Student B. First Student B asks Student A the questions about picture A and Student A talks about his/her holiday.
- Ss then exchange roles to talk about the other picture. Go around the class and help with vocabulary if necessary.

Extra activity
- Ss write three or four sentences about the holiday they have just described. Go around the class and check as they write.

1c Writing

Helen's French penfriend, Annie, sent her a postcard. Helen's dog played with the card when it arrived. What does the card say?

Write a similar postcard about a holiday in a town in your country.

1d Practice

What do you usually do when you are on holiday?

> go sightseeing   go swimming   lie on the beach
> play beach games   go fishing
> go to the cinema

Ask a partner. Then tell him or her your answers. Use *usually/sometimes*.

▶ A: *Do you usually go sightseeing when you are on holiday?*
   B: *No, I don't. How about you?*
   A: *I sometimes go sightseeing when the weather is bad.*

What are the most popular holiday activities in the class?

Helpline — go + -ing

Sports activities. You can:
   go swimming   go climbing   go sailing
   go skiing   go dancing   go fishing
And you can go shopping, but it's not a sport!

→ GC p2

Holiday stories

2a Practice

With a partner, choose a part, Student A or Student B.

Student A

You went to the place in picture A for your holiday. Talk about your holiday with Student B. Student B will ask you questions. Then ask Student B about his or her holiday. Use the questions below.

Student B

Ask Student A about his or her holiday. Use the questions. Then talk about your holiday. You went to the place in picture B. Student A will ask you questions.

> How long …?   Where …?   What … all day?
> What … eat and drink?   What … enjoy most?
> Do you want … next year?

2b Listening

Listen to three teenagers talking about their holidays. Fill in the details in the table.

	Colin	Maria	Tina
name of place	Manchester	Crete	Greenville
where?	north of England		
when?	September, a week	August	
who with?	other teenagers		
stayed?	with aunt, went to training ground every day	chalet	
activities	films, running, training, football matches		

2c Writing

Read the paragraph about Colin's holiday and write a similar paragraph about Maria or Tina. Use information from **2b**.

> This year Colin had a football holiday in Manchester. Manchester is in the north of England. He went for a week in September, with other teenagers, boys and girls. He stayed with his aunt and went to the training ground every morning. Every day he watched films, went running and did training. He also played in football matches. He liked his holiday very much.

2d Practice

What problems are there for the environment in holiday places? Discuss the problems in the picture before you read the article.

Eleni comes from Naxos, a Greek island. She asks, 'Are you a green tourist?' Read the article and decide which verbs are missing.

> Everyone enjoys a summer holiday, but when some people ..1.. home, their rubbish ..2.. behind. You ..3.. the people I mean. When they ..4.. a day at the beach, they ..5.. their rubbish on the sand. When they ..6.. by boat, they ..7.. things into the sea. Plastic bags and bottles are often dangerous for birds and fish, so please ..8.. them in a rubbish bin.
>
> Some people ..9.. fires in forest areas. This is very dangerous in summer. Others ..10.. bottles and don't clear up the pieces. So, tourists, please make sure that your rubbish ..11.. home with you. We ..12.. here and when you go home, we are still here!

2e Listening

Listen to Eleni and write the missing words in **2d**.

Word check

beach	lie [v]	remember
environment	magazine	rubbish
fantastic	mean [v]	sand
fire	penfriend	similar
go sightseeing	piece	stay
holidays		

Happy holidays   1

2b Listening

Aim: to listen for specific information; to talk about holidays using the past simple.
Summary: Ss listen and complete the information in a table.

Lead in

- Tell Ss to write down as many different kinds of holidays as they can think of and activities they might do. Then write some ideas on the board, eg:
  Holiday in the mountains (walking, climbing, skiing).
  Seaside holiday (water sports).
  Summer camp (sports).
  Holiday in a new country (sightseeing).
  Study holiday (learning, improving a foreign language).

Main activity

- Go through the table in the SB and the answers for Colin, so Ss understand what they must listen for. Tell Ss that you will play the cassette twice.
- Use the pause button between each speaker to give Ss plenty of time to write. Go around the class during pauses and check that Ss are completing the table. It does not matter if Ss do not get all the information for each answer.
- Play the recording a third time if necessary. Tell Ss to check their answers with a partner and then ask individual Ss for the answers.

Answers:

	Maria	**Tina**
Where?	large island in the Mediterranean, Greece	summer camp in the state of Maine, USA
When?	August, two weeks	July, two weeks
Who with?	her family (parents and brother)	two brothers
Stayed?	chalet (small house near beach)	wooden bungalow
Activities?	swimming, sightseeing, walking, reading	cooking, walking, playing games, dancing, singing, going on lake in a boat

- Ask Ss to use the information in the table to talk about each person's holiday.

Extra activity

- Play one of the taped extracts again from beginning to end. Then play it with pauses. Tell Ss to continue what the speaker is saying when you pause the cassette. It does not matter if they do not remember all the details.

2c Writing

Aim: to write a guided paragraph using the past simple.
Summary: Ss compare the notes in activity 2b and the paragraph about Colin; they then use their notes for Maria and Tina to write two similar paragraphs.

Main activity

- Ask Ss to read the paragraph about Colin silently and compare it with the notes from activity 2b. Deal with any new vocabulary at this point.
- Explain that Ss have to write two more paragraphs for Maria and Tina using their notes from activity 2b. Ss work individually. Early finishers exchange paragraphs to make suggestions for changes or corrections about each other's work. Go around the class and help if necessary.

2d Practice

Aim: to practise the present simple for habitual actions.
Summary: Ss guess missing words using context.

Lead in

- Books closed. Write the word ENVIRONMENT on the board and ask Ss to suggest any words that they associate with this word, eg: *clean air   rubbish   pollution   waste   cars   dirty water*
- Say: *Look at the picture in your books. What problems are there for the environment in holiday places?*
  Ss suggest problems, eg:
  rubbish on the beach, danger from fires

Main activity

- Give Ss one minute to read the article once through to get the main ideas. Tell them not to fill in the missing verbs. Ask individual Ss to say what the main ideas are: *People leave their rubbish behind them after holidays and they light fires in forest areas.*
- Tell Ss to read the article more slowly to fill in the missing verbs. They then check their answers with a partner. Do not ask for their answers yet – these will be found in activity 2e.

2e Listening

Aim: to listen for specific words.
Summary: Ss listen to the text from activity 2d and confirm their guesses.

Main activity

- Ask individual Ss for their answers to activity 2d but do not confirm. Play the cassette so that they can check their answers.
- Ask individual Ss to read sentences from the article and write the answers on the board.

Answers:

1 go	5 leave	9 light
2 stays	6 travel	10 break
3 know	7 throw	11 goes
4 spend	8 put	12 live

Optional activity

- Books closed. Ss work in pairs and write three or four pieces of advice for holiday-makers about looking after the environment. Ask Ss to find or make pictures to match their sentences for the next lesson. Use them to make a collage and display in class.

Word check
Ss check each other's spelling in pairs.

Teacher's Book Unit 1

Happy holidays

Lesson 3 Words in action

1

Aim: to revise the past simple, present simple and present continuous.
Summary: Ss guess the missing verbs and listen to confirm their guesses.

Lead in

- Books closed. Write these words on the board and tell Ss to predict the contents of the song:
  aliens   planet   sky   and   questions   books
  Listen to a variety of suggestions but do not confirm anything.
- Books open. Ask Ss to describe the picture.

Main activity

- Tell Ss to read the first part of the song and fill in the spaces with the verbs in the SB. They then compare their answers with a partner.
- Play the first part of the song twice. Ss listen and check their answers. Ask individual Ss for the answers and write them on the board.

Answers 1–9:

1 took	4 passed	7 saw
2 climbed	5 turned	8 went
3 waved	6 came	9 landed

- Tell Ss to guess the missing words (not just verbs now) before listening to the second part of the song. They then compare their ideas with a partner.
- Play the second part of the song twice and ask individual Ss for the answers and write them on the board.

Answers 10–15:

10 school	12 song	14 floor
11 street	13 light	15 small

- Tell Ss to guess what the aliens are doing. The first letter will help Ss guess. They then compare their answers with a partner.
- Play the chorus twice and ask Ss for the answers. Write the words on the board.

Answers:
They're running, jumping, climbing, falling, flying.
They're eating, dancing, singing, shouting, laughing in my face.

- Ss sing along with the song.

Optional activity

- Tell Ss to draw a picture of an alien. They then describe the alien to their partner without showing the picture. They can also talk about the differences between their alien and humans, eg:
  It doesn't eat food.
  It usually gets up at midnight.

2

Aim: to focus on frequent verb/noun collocations.
Summary: Ss make sentences using the words given.

Lead in

- Books closed. Write some of the nouns from activity 2 in SB on the board with part of the word missing:
  tr-p   f—tb-ll   f-re   -ountai-   son-   sand—ch   -uest-on
  Tell Ss to guess the words. They then check their answers in pairs and then in the SB.

Main activity

- Tell Ss to suggest verbs that could go with the nouns.

Suggested answers:

take a trip	light a fire
watch a football match	climb a mountain
eat a sandwich	answer a question
sing a song	drink a cup of tea

- Ss work with a partner to write a sentence for each verb using different time expressions (*today, next week, last year* etc) so they use a variety of tenses. Ask Ss for some examples before they begin, eg:
  Last month I took a boat trip to a beautiful island.
  He doesn't want to climb that mountain.
  She's lighting a fire.
- Go around the class and check Ss' sentences.

Extra activity

- Put Ss into two or three teams. Each team must choose some of the word combinations and prepare to mime them for the rest of the class, eg: *putting out a fire, making a sandwich*.
- Explain the scoring system. The team who is miming gets 2 points if someone from another team guesses the mime. The other teams get 1 point for guessing the action and 1 point for correct grammar.

3

Aim: to focus on words with similar meanings.
Summary: Ss choose from alternatives in sentences.

Main activity

- Ss work with a partner to choose the correct word for each sentence. Ask individual Ss for answers. Help them to explain their answers if necessary.

Answers:
a) stay (for a short time, temporary)
   lives (permanent)
b) speak (you 'speak a language' but 'say something in that language')
   talks (you 'talk to someone' but 'say something')
c) see (this describes the use of the eyes)
   watched (used about looking at something that is moving or about looking with a specific purpose)

WORDS in ACTION

1 🔊 Before you listen, use the verbs in the list to complete the first part of the song.

climb come go land pass
see take turn wave

The Aliens

One day they ..1.. a trip, they ..2.. into their ship,
And ..3.. their alien friends goodbye,
They ..4.. a thousand stars, ..5.. left at planet Mars,
And ..6.. down from the sky.

I ..7.. them from below and ..8.. to say hello
When they ..9.. outside one day.
They came inside for tea and now as you can see
They don't want to go away!

Before you listen, guess the missing words in this part of the song.

They come with me to ..10.., they make me feel a fool,
They answer all the questions wrong,
They follow me down the ..11.. and stamp upon my feet
And can't even sing this ..12..

They never sleep at night, they don't turn off the ..13..,
They drop books on the ..14..
They're very very ..15.., you can't see them at all
And here they come once more.

Listen to the song. Complete the list of the things the aliens are doing now.

They're running, j..., c..., f..., f...
They're eating, d..., s..., s..., l...

2 Make a sentence with a verb from list A and words from list B.

A take watch eat sing light climb answer drink

B a trip   a football match   a cup of tea
a fire   a mountain   a song
a sandwich   a question

▶ *You can take a trip to the seaside.*

3 Choose the best word for each sentence.

a) I usually *live/stay* with my cousins in the country in summer.
Bryan *stays/lives* in Manchester.
b) My sister can *speak/say* French very well.
Helen *says/talks* to lots of people for the school magazine.
c) My seat is at the back and I can't *see/watch* the blackboard.
The police *saw/watched* the house for a week.

7

2 What happened?

past simple and past continuous

Round the World

1a New language

Here is part of a magazine article about the Robinson family. They are sailing round the world. Read about their trip and answer the questions.

Alan and Jean Robinson
We had the idea for the trip while we were cleaning our house! We found an old book about a family that sailed round the world. At the time the children were learning to sail and they liked the idea of the trip. So we decided to use our savings and go! We are both teachers, so the children are doing their lessons with us.

Vicky
The first two days of the trip were difficult. When we started the trip it was raining. All our friends were waving goodbye and cheering as the boat left the harbour. I felt happy and sad at the same time!

George
Strange things happen too! We crossed the Atlantic and stopped on the island of Bermuda. We stayed there for a week and looked around. While we were walking around the town we met some friends from England. They were staying there on holiday!

1 When did Alan and Jean have the idea for the trip?
2 What were the children doing at that time?
3 How is the family paying for the trip?
4 Who is going to teach Vicky and George?
5 What were their friends doing as they left?
6 How did Vicky feel when they left?
7 What were they doing when they met their friends in Bermuda?
8 Why were their friends there?

Helpline – past continuous

past simple of *be* + *-ing* form

I/he/she/it   was sailing
you/we/they   were sailing

→ GC p2–3

What happened? 2

Unit 2		Function	Grammar
Lesson 1	Round the World	Describing events in a narrative	Past simple and past continuous
Lesson 2	When the lights went out	Narrating past events	Past simple and past continuous While, When
Lesson 3	CHRIS 1		

Word check

accident	go out	meet
ambulance	harbour	move
burglar	have a bath	pay for
ceiling	living-room	sad
chat		shell
cheer		star

Lesson 1 Round the World

1a New language

Aim: to present the past continuous (positive, negative and question form) and contrast it with the past simple.
Summary: Ss read a text and answer questions.

Lead in

- Books closed. Write the first sentence from the story in activity 1a on the board.
  We had the idea for the trip while we were cleaning our house!
- Tell Ss to predict what the story will be about.
- Use these questions to ask Ss to guess some more details:
  Where is the trip to? Did something in the house give them an idea?
- Now write this sentence on the board:
  All our friends were waving goodbye and cheering as the boat left the harbour.
- Use these questions to ask for more guesses:
  Why did all their friends come? What kind of boat was it?

Main activity

- Ask Ss to describe the picture and the map first.
- Write these focus questions on the board:
  Was the Robinsons' trip long or short?
  Where did they stop first?
  What are the names of the Robinsons' children?
- Ss read the magazine article silently to answer the focus questions. Ask individual Ss for the answers.

Answers:
It was a long trip because they sailed round the world.
They stopped at/on Bermuda first.
Their names are Vicky and George.

- Ss read the text again more slowly and write answers to the questions. Ss discuss their answers with a partner.

Answers:
1 They had the idea while they were cleaning their house.
2 They were learning to sail.
3 They are going to use their savings.
4 Their parents are going to teach Vicky and George.
5 They were waving and cheering as they left.
6 Vicky felt both happy and sad when they left.
7 They were walking around the town when they met their friends.
8 They were staying there on holiday.

Extra activity

- Ss decide on three personal things to take with them on a trip like this. They then work in small groups and explain their choices:
  A personal stereo because I like listening to music.

Helpline – past continuous

- Use the example in the SB to show that you form this tense using *was/were* (the past tense of *be*) + *-ing* form of the main verb.
- Write another verb on the board as an example. Tell Ss to copy it into their exercise books, eg:
  I/he/she/it/ was playing.
  We/you/they were playing.
  Were you playing? Was she playing?
  They weren't playing. I wasn't playing.
- Tell Ss to find six examples of the past continuous from the story in activity 1a. They then check with a partner:
  we were cleaning
  the children were learning
  it was raining
  all our friends were waving goodbye and cheering
  we were walking
  they were staying
- Help Ss to understand the difference between past continuous and past simple. Explain that the past continuous is often used in sentences with the past simple. When this happens the past continuous usually describes a continuing action or situation. The past simple usually describes a shorter action or event that happened in the middle of the longer one or interrupted it.
- Draw this time line on the board and write some more example sentences:

  I was playing with my computer
  ←――――――――↑――――――――→
  when my mum called me.

  She was watching cartoons when the television suddenly went off.
  Alex was helping his father in the kitchen when the phone rang.
  We were making sandwiches for a picnic when it started to rain.
- Ss make two true example sentences for themselves and then tell a partner. Write some of their examples on the board.

Teacher's Book Unit 2

2 What happened?

1b Practice

Aim: to contrast the past continuous and past simple.
Summary: Ss describe what was happening and what happened in the pictures.

Lead in
- Ss look at the pictures and guess what happened.

Main activity
- Read aloud the example sentence:
  While Alan and Jean were visiting the town, they left a camera in the café.
  Ask: *Which was the long action?* (Visiting the town – past continuous)
  What happened in the middle of their visit? (They left a camera – past simple)
- Ss look at the pictures and then write sentences. Ss check with a partner by reading their sentences aloud.
- Write some answers on the board.

Answers:
2 While they were having lunch, a dolphin jumped out of the water.
3 While George was fishing, he fell into the water.
4 While Vicky was swimming, she found a crab.

1c Practice

Aim: to practise the past continuous when used to contrast two simultaneous continuing actions.
Summary: Ss compare their own activities with those of Vicky and George.

Lead in
- Books closed. Ask Ss to imagine what Vicky and George do on a typical day, eg:
  They get up early and have a swim before breakfast.
- Books open. Focus on the timetable in the SB. Ss check if some of their ideas were right. Ask:
  What were Vicky and George doing at eight o'clock?

Main activity
- Individual Ss make example sentences comparing their day with Vicky and George's day, eg: *At five o' clock yesterday afternoon Vicky and George were playing basketball, but I was having an English lesson.*
- Check that Ss understand all the items in the timetable.
- Ss work with a partner to exchange information about their day yesterday. Go around the class and check that Ss are using the past continuous correctly. After 2-3 minutes tell Ss to close their books and continue practising from memory.

1d Writing

Aim: to practise the past continuous.
Summary: Ss make notes and then question other members of the class.

Lead in
- Tell Ss to make a list of their activities yesterday.
- Agree on the times to ask about or use the times from activity 1c. Draw a table on the board for Ss to copy.

	Me	S1	S2	S3
8.00				
10.00				
etc				

Main activity
- Ss take turns to answer questions; the other Ss make notes and complete their table.
- Ss work individually to write the report.

Lesson 2 When the lights went out

2a Listening

Aim: to practise the past continuous (question form) and *when …*
Summary: Ss guess the activity from context and make statements about it.

Lead in
- Ask Ss to close their eyes and day-dream for a few moments! Then clap your hands and say:
  Open your eyes. What were you thinking about when I clapped my hands? Tell your partner.
- Ask a few individual Ss for their thoughts, eg:
  I was thinking about my maths test when you clapped your hands.

Main activity
- Ask Ss to explain what a power failure is. If necessary, explain. Does it ever happen in their country? Why? Possible reasons include a storm, a strike, an accident.
- Say: *There was a power failure last night and now Helen is finding out what each friend was doing when it happened.*
- Explain that Ss will hear the sounds of someone doing something. Read aloud the sentence:
  Jim was having a bath when the lights went out.
- Ask Ss to guess what they will hear on the tape for Jim in the bath, eg: *water splashing, singing, sudden shout*
- Ask Ss to listen to each sound sequence and decide what each person was doing. Ss then write a similar sentence for each person.
- Play it again. Use the pause button to give Ss time to write. Ss check answers with a partner. Listen to their sentences.

Answers:
Luke was doing his maths homework when the lights went out.
Sally was watching television when the lights went out.
Paula was eating when the lights went out.
Mike was cooking when the lights went out.

1b Practice

Here are some pictures of things that happened on the trip. Match the words with the pictures and make sentences like this:

While … (past continuous), … (past simple)
▶ 1 *While Alan and Jean were visiting the town, they left a camera in the café.*

1 visit leave
2 have lunch jump out
3 fish fall in
4 swim find

1c Practice

Talk to a partner and compare your day yesterday with Vicky and George's day in Bermuda.

Vicky and George's day

Morning
8.00   swimming
10.00   science lesson: collecting shells on the beach

Afternoon
2.00   history lesson: visiting a museum
5.00   playing basketball

Evening
7.00   cooking supper
10.00   science lesson: watching the stars from the boat

▶ At eight o'clock yesterday morning Vicky and George were swimming, but I was getting ready for school.

1d Writing

Make a list of your activities yesterday. Then make a survey of a group of students in your class. Ask:
▶ *What were you doing at [say a time] …?*
Make some notes about their answers and write a report about your group.

> My activities yesterday
> 8.00 I was getting ready for school.
> 10.00 I was …
> Survey report
> At 8.00 two people were getting ready for school, three people were having breakfast and one person was sleeping.

When the lights went out

2a Listening

Last night there was a power failure. All the lights went out. Helen asked people in her class this question: *What were you doing when the lights went out?* Listen and decide what each person was doing. Write a sentence for Luke, Sally, Paula and Mike.

▶ Jim: *Jim was having a bath when the lights went out.*

2

Helpline – while and when

When refers to an exact time:
  Jim was having a bath when the lights went out.
While refers to something that happens in a period of time:
  While they were having lunch some dolphins jumped out of the water.

→ GC p3

2b New language

Helen asked some people to describe something dramatic that happened to them. She asked: *What were you doing when it happened? What did you do then?*

What did each person say? There are three sentences for each person.

2c The complete it game

One student begins a sentence:
Yesterday afternoon while I was walking home …

Another student finishes the sentence. Make the ending funny if possible: *… I saw a green elephant!*

2d Writing

Use ideas from **2b** to write a paragraph.

One day last year something very dramatic happened to me. While I was …. I had to think quickly. First I …. After that I …. Finally I …

Word check
accident
ambulance
burglar
ceiling
chat
cheer
go out
harbour
have a bath
living-room
meet
move
pay for
sad
shell
star

A very tall tree fell down and blocked the street.
Water started coming through our living-room ceiling.
There was an accident outside our school.

I was going shopping.
I was watching television with my parents.
I was chatting to my friend.

I started laughing because everyone was wet.
I went to help people move it.
I ran and phoned for an ambulance and the police.

Write a sentence beginning *While …* about each person and another sentence describing what he or she did.

What happened? 2

Helpline – while and when

- Write these sentences on the board to illustrate the difference between *while* and *when*:
  While the Robinsons were cleaning their house, they found an old book.
  The Robinsons were cleaning their house when they found an old book.
- Give Ss some more sentences with *while* and ask them to rephrase them with *when*, eg:
  While the Robinsons were walking around the town, they met some friends.
  While George was fishing, he fell into the sea.
  Then give then some sentences with *when* and ask Ss to rephrase them with *while*, eg:
  Vicky was doing her homework when the lights went out.
  She was shopping in Bermuda when she lost her money.
- Explain that *when* can also be used to talk about two events, one of which happened after the other, eg:
  When George fell into the sea, he got wet.
  When the lights went out, Vicky stopped writing.
  Ask Ss to give some example sentences.

2b New language

Aim: to practise *when* and *while* + past continuous to describe an interrupted action in the past.
Summary: Ss match sentences to pictures and then combine pairs of sentences.

Lead in

- Ask Ss to give a short description of each picture, eg:
  In picture 1 there's a big tree across a road.

Main activity

- Take the role of Helen and give the role of Colin to a student. Act out this dialogue:
  Helen: *I believe something dramatic happened to you last month. What were you doing when it happened?*
  Colin: *I was going shopping when a very tall tree fell down and blocked the street.*
  Helen: *What did you do then?*
  Colin: *I went to help people move it.*
- Ss work in pairs to practise the mini dialogues, exchanging roles so they practise each piece twice. They should try to add a few more details. Go around the class to correct and make suggestions if necessary.
- Ask different pairs to practise their dialogues for the whole class.
- Ss then write sentences with *While* for each person.

Extra activity

- Tell Ss to think of something dramatic that happened to them. (They can invent something if they want.) Ask them to talk about it with a partner. Then ask individual Ss to tell the class what happened to their partner, eg:
  George was cycling to school. Suddenly a dog ran across the road. George fell off his bike and all his books fell out of his bag.

2c The complete it game

Aim: to practise *while* + past continuous to describe an interrupted action in the past.
Summary: Ss complete sentences started by other Ss.

Lead in

- Explain that Ss are going to play the game in teams. Team members each take a turn either to complete a sentence or to begin another one. Teams score a point for completing or beginning a sentence correctly. If they are completing a sentence, they can score an extra point if the sentence is funny. They can also score an extra point for correcting another team's sentence if it contains a mistake. Point out that the teacher's decision is final!

Main activity

- Divide the class into three teams. Give two minutes for teams to think of some funny ideas and then start the game. Make sure that everyone takes a turn.

Extra activity

- Write some of the best sentences on the board. Ss vote for the funniest sentence.

2d Writing

Aim: to write a short narrative paragraph using the past continuous and past simple.
Summary: Ss use ideas from activity 2b and continue/complete the paragraph.

Lead in

- Books closed. Ask Ss to remember what happened to Colin, Maria and Tony in activity 2b. Tell them to use some of these ideas to write a paragraph about themselves. Ask Ss to find the joining words in the model in SB, eg: *First, After that, Finally.*
- Remind Ss that they can also use *Next* and *Then*.

Main activity

- Ss work individually. Early finishers exchange paragraphs and make suggestions for changes or corrections. Go around the class and help if necessary.

Extra activity

- Ss find pictures at home or draw pictures to accompany their paragraphs. Stick them on cardboard and display in class.

Word check

- Divide the class into two teams. Tell Ss that they are going to make up a story going around the class.
- The first team begins with this sentence: *There was an accident outside my house last week.* Then each team takes a turn to make a sentence which follows on from the previous one. Each S in the team must take a turn at making the next sentence of the story using a word from the Word check box.
- The teams get one point for each sentence.

2 What happened?

Lesson 3 CHRIS Episode 1

Aims: to read for gist and specific information; to listen for specific information; to revise uses of past simple and past continuous.

Lead in

- Write the following types of story on the board:
  comedy detective adventure mystery romance science fiction
- Ask Ss what type of stories they prefer.
- Explain that this is a mystery story.

a

Extra activity

- Ask Ss to read section a and find the names of three people. Check answers:
  Sandy, Chris, Peter
  Ask Ss what they know about the three people:
  Sandy is a girl.
  Peter is her twin brother.
  Sandy and Peter go to school.
  Chris is their elder brother.
  He works with computers.

1

Main activity

- Ss read section a again and answer the questions in activity 1. They then check their answers with a partner.
- Ask individual Ss for the answers.

Answers:
a) She drank some milk and went to see her elder brother, Chris.
b) Suggested answer: I do my homework, I watch television.
c) Chris works with computers and writes computer programs.
d) Suggested answers: Computers can play a game of chess, guide a spacecraft, check fingerprints, draw maps. Today's computers are much smaller than the first computers of the 1940s.

b

Extra activity

- Write the names *Mrs Jackson* and *CHRIS* on the board. Ask Ss to read the rest of the text and find information about Mrs Jackson and CHRIS. Then check the answers.

Answers:
Mrs Jackson lives next door to the twins. She sometimes looks after them when Chris is not there.
CHRIS is the name of a computer program. The letters in CHRIS stand for Computer Help: Reporting Information Service.

2

Main activity

- Look at activity 2 with the class. Make sure that everyone understands that the man in the checked shirt is Chris. Ss work with a partner and tell a story for each picture, eg:
  The man with Chris in picture 1 is a scientist. He has some important information for Chris. He cannot speak to Chris on the telephone. He has come to the house to meet him. Chris has gone out with the man.

Extra activity

- Books closed. Write these sentences on the board:
  When Sandy ... (knock) at Chris's door
  no one ... (answer).
  When Sandy ... (go) into Chris's room, Peter ... (stare) at a computer on his desk.
  Mrs Jackson ... (clean) the windows when Peter ... (come) home.
  When Peter .... (turn) on the computer, he ... (see) a message on the screen.
  Ss complete the sentences with the past simple or past continuous. Check answers.

Answers:
When Sandy knocked on Chris's door, no one answered.
When Sandy went into Chris's room, Peter was staring at a computer on his desk.
Mrs Jackson was cleaning the windows when Peter came home.
When Peter turned on the computer, he saw a message on the screen.

3

a)

- Ss suggest questions that Sandy and Peter ask CHRIS, eg:
  Where's Chris? Is he safe?

b)

- Play the cassette twice. Pause the cassette between each listening to give Ss time to write the questions.
- Ss check with a partner. Ask Ss for the four questions.

Answers:
Where is Chris?   Why did he leave?
Where did our brother Chris go?   When will he be back?

4

- Ss work with a partner to read the computer's coded message. If they have problems with the code, tell them to add some of the following letters: *a e i o u*. Ask different Ss to spell out the words and write the message on the board.

Answer:
Chris is safe. Don't worry. Read my messages. Then you can find your brother.

Episode 1

CHRIS

▶ a

There was nothing special about Friday. Sandy got home from school, went into the kitchen, opened the fridge as usual, drank some milk and went to see her elder brother, Chris. Chris worked with computers. He wrote computer games programs, and his office was on the ground floor of the house. She knocked at the door, but he wasn't there. Her twin brother, Peter, was sitting at Chris's desk, staring at a computer. There was a piece of paper on it that said, 'For Sandy and Peter'.

Sandy wasn't very interested in computers then. She did not like computer games, and she thought computers were boring. This is the story of how she changed her mind.

1 Answer these questions.
a) What did Sandy do when she got home?
b) What do you usually do when you get home from school?
c) What does Chris do?
d) What do you know about computers? What do they do? Do you like them?

▶ b

Sandy sat down at the desk next to Peter. 'Where's Chris?' she asked.

'I don't know. I asked Mrs Jackson. She was cleaning the windows when I came home. But she didn't know.'

Mrs Jackson lived next door to the twins and looked after them when Chris was not there.

'He doesn't usually disappear without leaving a note,' said Sandy.

'And there is something else,' said Peter. 'I found this computer when I came home. It wasn't here this morning. I turned it on. Look at the screen.'

2 Why did Chris leave the house? Look at the three pictures at the bottom of the page. There are three different ideas. Tell the story for each one.

3 a) Before you listen, what questions do you think Sandy and Peter asked CHRIS?
b) Now listen and write down the questions. Were you right?

4 Here is the first message from the computer. It is in code. Can you understand it?

chrs s sf/dnt wrry/rd my mssgs/thn y cn fnd yr brthr

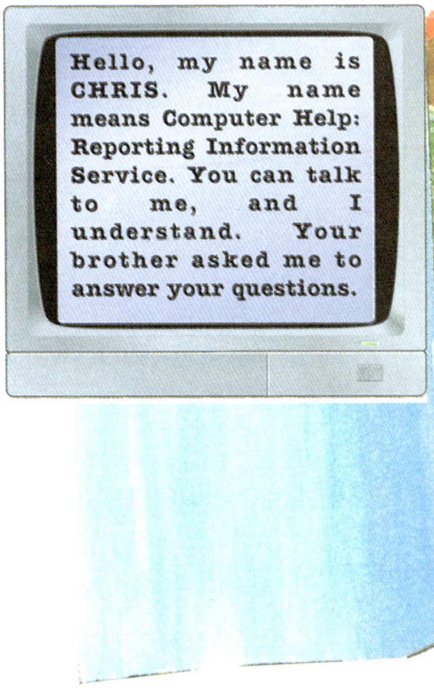

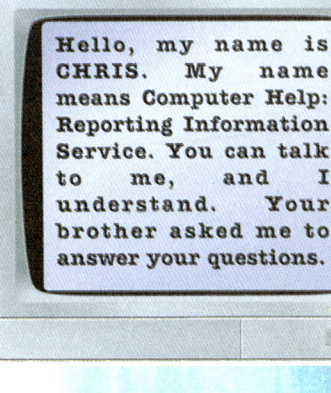

Hello, my name is CHRIS. My name means Computer Help: Reporting Information Service. You can talk to me, and I understand. Your brother asked me to answer your questions.

3 Make your choice

comparative and superlative adjectives, ... than; not as ... as; too, not enough

Choosing a bike

1a New language

Nick wrote this quiz for *Brilliant*. Do the quiz with a partner.

KNOW YOUR BIKES *True or False*

1. A mountain bike is faster than a racing bike. *True or False*
2. A roadster is lighter than a mountain bike. *True or False*
3. A mountain bike is more expensive than a roadster. *True or False*
4. A racing bike has larger wheels than a roadster. *True or False*
5. A racing bike has thicker tyres than a mountain bike. *True or False*
6. A mountain bike has a more comfortable saddle than a racing bike. *True or False*
7. A mountain bike is stronger than other bikes. *True or False*
8. A mountain bike has more powerful brakes than other bikes. *True or False*

roadster

racing bike

mountain bike

1b Listening

Listen to Nick and Helen talking about the quiz and check your answers.

Helpline — comparatives

Add *-er* to short adjectives:
   fast → *faster*

Use *more* + adjective for long words:
   expensive →
         more expensive

We can change the order of the sentence and use:
   not as + adjective + *as*
   A racing bike is not as fast as a mountain bike.

→ GC p3

Make your choice 3

Unit 3		Function	Grammar
Lesson 1	Choosing a bike	Making comparisons	Comparative and superlative adjectives Not as [adjective] as ..., [adjective] than
Lesson 2	The Odds and the Normals	Making comparisons	Too [adjective], not [adjective] enough
Lesson 3	Check up Units 1–3		

Word check

carry		parent
comfortable	heavy	powerful
damage	kind (n)	size
dirty	light (adj)	thick
fast	noisy	tyre
get on well with		wheel

Lesson 1 Choosing a bike

1a New language

Aim: to present the comparative form of adjectives; to compare and contrast similar products (bikes).
Summary: Ss complete a questionnaire.

Lead in

- Ask:
  Have you got a bike? Can you name the parts of a bike in English?
- Books closed. Draw a simple picture of a bike and put lines to certain features.
- Ask Ss to copy the picture and label the parts. They then check with a partner. While Ss are labelling their drawings, write a few questions about bikes on the board, eg:
  How old were you when you learnt to ride a bike?
  Where do you ride your bike?
  What kind of bike is best for the roads in your area?
  Was your bike a present?
- Ss work in pairs and ask the questions on the board. Tell them to ask more questions if they can.

Main activity

- Ss work in pairs and do the True/False quiz. Do not check answers yet – this is done in activity 1b.

1b Listening

Aim: to listen for specific information; to practise the comparative form of adjectives and *as ... as*.
Summary: Ss listen and check their answers from activity 1a.

Lead in

- Explain that Ss will hear the conversation between Helen and Nick twice.

Main activity

- Play the cassette twice. Pause between each listening to give Ss an opportunity to think about and make changes to their own answers.
- Ask Ss if their answers are the same as Helen and Nick's. Check answers and the reasons for them. Point out that some answers are a matter of opinion.

Answers:
1 F *(Mountain bikes are strong but not as fast as racing bikes.)*
2 T
3 T *(All mountain bikes are very expensive.)*
4 T
5 F *(Racing bikes need thin tyres.)*
6 T *(Racing bikes usually have thin saddles but mountain bikes must have comfortable ones.)*
7 T
8 T *(Mountain bikes must have good brakes.)*

Extra activity

- Ask Ss to find the adjectives in the quiz. Write them on the board.
- Books closed. Ss work with a partner and use the adjectives to ask the quiz questions again.

Helpline – comparatives

- Ask Ss to explain the rules for making the comparative form of adjectives. (We add *-er* to short words and *more* before longer words.)
- Write some examples on the board and ask Ss to suggest others, eg:
  Bikes are cleaner than cars.
  Cars are more expensive than bikes.
  Motor bikes are more dangerous than bicycles.
- Explain that we can also make comparatives using *not as ... as*, eg:
  Cars are not as clean as bikes.
  Bikes are not as expensive as cars.
  Bikes are not as dangerous as bicycles.
  Buses aren't as fast as trains.
  Planes aren't as cheap as buses.

3 Make your choice

1c Practice

Aim: to introduce the superlative form of adjectives.
Summary: Ss choose the best form of transport for a specific situation.

Lead in

- Ask these questions:
  What is a rally?
  (a kind of competition, a car race often on public roads)
  What different forms of transport do competitors use?
  (bikes, motorbikes, but usually cars)
  Are there any rallies in your country?
  (internationally famous ones, eg Monte Carlo Rally, Paris-Dakar Rally)

Main activity

- Read the introduction to the activity with the class. Ss look at the photos and make sentences about the four different kinds of transport, eg:
  A camper van is comfortable.
  A camel is very slow.
- Ask questions, eg:
  Which kind of transport is the fastest?
  Which one is the slowest?
  Ss answer your questions.
- Ss work in pairs and ask and answer questions. Go around the class and help if necessary. Ss then decide which kind of transport is best for the Across Africa Rally. Invite individual Ss to say which kind of transport is best, eg:
  I think an off road vehicle is best. It's the safest. You can drive it across deserts and in the mountains. A hot air balloon is faster but it isn't as safe.
- Ask Ss to suggest other kinds of transport for the rally.

Extra activity

- Ss say which of the different kinds of transport are best for their country, eg:
  The best kind of transport is the hot air balloon because you can see everything from the sky.

Helpline – superlatives

- Ask Ss to explain the rules for making the superlative form of adjectives. (We add *-est* to short words and *most* before longer words.)
- Write a few examples on the board, eg:
  That watch is the most expensive in the shop.
  This is the most exciting computer game.
  That is the funniest cartoon on television.
  .... is the highest building in our city.
- Ask Ss to suggest further examples.
- Point out that a superlative adjective compares one thing with all the other things in a similar group.

1d Writing

Aim: to write a short paragraph which practises superlative adjectives.
Summary: Ss compare different forms of transport.

Lead in

- Ask some of these questions:
  What is the usual form of transport in our cities?
  Are there any traffic problems? Why?
  Can we do anything about this situation?
  You might like to mention that the average speed in London today is 18 kilometres an hour – about the same as it was a century ago!

Main activity

- Ask Ss about the advantages and disadvantages of bikes, eg:
  They don't use petrol so they don't pollute the air.
  They aren't very fast.
  Then ask about buses and cars.
- Ss work in pairs and decide which kind of transport is the best for travelling in a big city. They then work individually and write a paragraph. Go around the class and help if necessary.
- Ask a few Ss to read out their paragraphs to the class. Do other Ss agree with their choice and reasons?

Lesson 2 The Odds and the Normals

2a New language

Aim: to provide a context for introducing *too* and *enough* in activity 2b.
Summary: Ss guess answers to questions.

- Ss look at the picture in the SB. Ask them to find at least three unusual things about the Odd family and their house, eg:
  The house is a strange colour.
  The son is wearing roller skates.
  They have a pet kangaroo.
  The daughter is wearing flippers and not shoes.
  They are all holding noisy musical instruments.
- Ask Ss to guess the answers to the questions. Accept all answers at this point, as Ss have to match these questions with their answers in activity 2b.

1c Practice

This is a puzzle from *Brilliant*. Talk about it with a partner.

> You and your friends want to go on the Across Africa Rally. The rally is a long and difficult trip across mountains and deserts. How do you want to travel? Discuss these different kinds of transport. Which one is best?

A camper van · A camel

A hot air balloon · An off road vehicle

Which one is: the fastest? the slowest? the strongest? the safest? the quietest? the most expensive? the most comfortable? the most dangerous?

Which other kinds of transport are useful for the rally and why?

Helpline – superlatives

Add *-est* to short adjectives:
 strong → *strongest*

Use *most* + adjective for long words:
 dangerous → *most dangerous*

→ GC p3

1d Writing

Complete the paragraph.

> I think the best way of travelling in a big city is to use a ... [choose: bike/bus/car. Compare the one you choose with the other two]. I think this is the best because ...

The Odds and the Normals

2a New language

The Odds and the Normals live next door to each other. An interviewer is talking to the Odds. Guess the answers to the questions.

1. Why does Ozzy sleep in the bath?
2. Why have you got a pet kangaroo?
3. Why are you wearing roller-skates?
4. Why is Olive wearing flippers?
5. Why don't you get on well with your neighbours, the Normals?

2b New language

Match these answers with the questions in **2a**.

a) His bed is not big enough. And he likes to be first in the bathroom in the morning!
b) Her shoes are too small.
c) The bus isn't fast enough! And it doesn't stop outside the house.
d) We don't like dogs and cats. They are not friendly enough.
e) We are very good friends, but I think we are too noisy for them!

> **Helpline** – too and enough
>
> *Too* goes before the adjective: *too small*
> *Enough* goes after the adjective: *… big enough*
> → GC p4

2c Practice

Look at the picture and find some problems! Use ideas from the list.

too heavy   too small   too big   too dirty
not big enough   not strong enough
not old enough

Make some statements about the picture. Use these verbs:

see   carry   ride   walk

▶ *Ozzy can't see well because his glasses are too dirty.*

2d Writing

What did the policeman say to Olive and Ozzy? Complete the paragraph.

> Ozzy, you can't ride that bike. First of all it isn't … and your glasses are … . As well as that, the basket isn't … . Olive, don't try to ride the motorbike. First of all you aren't … and it is … . As well as that, your hat is … and your bag is …

2e The too and not enough game

Think of comments for these situations. Use *too* and *not enough*, and these adjectives:

dangerous   expensive   large   long   old
small   tall   warm

1. You want to see a horror film at the cinema. The manager stops you at the door.
   ▶ *You can't see this film. You aren't old enough.*
2. You want to be in the basketball team but you have a problem!
3. Your teacher asks you to read a book with 500 pages for homework tonight.
4. You want to go swimming but then you put your feet in the water …!
5. You want to buy a bike but it costs a lot of money.
6. Two hundred students are waiting outside your classroom and want to come in.
7. Someone buys a pair of shoes for your birthday but they are the wrong size.
8. You want to go skateboarding but your parents won't let you.

Word check

carry	light (adj)
comfortable	noisy
damage	parent
dirty	powerful
fast	size
get on well with	thick
heavy	tyre
kind (n)	wheel

Make your choice 3

2b New language

Aim: to present *too* (adjective) and *not* (adjective) *enough*.
Summary: Ss match answers with the questions in activity 2a.

- Ask Ss to find the answers to the questions about the Odds in activity 2a.
- They then check with a partner. Ask individual Ss for the answers.

Answers:
1 a   2 d   3 c   4 b   5 e

Helpline – too and enough

- Explain that *too* goes before the adjective when it makes the adjective stronger or more emphatic, eg: *She can't win the race because she's too slow.*
- Explain that *enough* goes after the adjective, eg: *She can't win the race because she isn't fast enough.*
- Point out that *too* and *not ... enough* both have negative meanings.
- Ask Ss to find examples of *too* and *enough* from activity 2a.

2c Practice

Aim: to practice *too* (adjective) and *not* (adjective) *enough*.
Summary: Ss describe some problems illustrated in a picture.

Lead in
- Ask Ss to name and describe the people in the picture.

Main activity
- Ss work with a partner to find the problems in the picture. Ask individual Ss to make example sentences, eg: *Ozzy's bike is too small.*
- Go around the class and check that Ss are using *too* and *enough* correctly. Ask individual Ss for their answers.
- Tell Ss to write some sentences about the picture using the verbs and example in SB.
- Ask individual Ss for their answers and write them on the board.

Suggested answers:
Olive can't see well because her hat is too big.
Ozzy can't carry the kangaroo on his bike because the basket is too small/isn't big enough.
Olive can't carry her school bag because it's too heavy.
Ozzy can't ride his bike well because it isn't big enough/is too small for him.
Ozzy can't walk well because his shoes are too small/aren't big enough.
Olive can't ride the motor bike because she's too young/isn't old enough.

Extra activity
- Books closed. Write some of the adjectives from activity 2c on the board. Ask Ss to tell their partner about their own family using *too* or *enough*.

2d Writing

Aim: to give guided writing practise of *too* and *enough*.
Summary: Ss complete a paragraph based on the picture in activity 2c.

Lead in
- Books closed. Ask Ss to guess what the policeman says to Olive and Ozzy.

Main activity
- Ss work individually. They then check answers with a partner.
- Ask individual Ss for their answers and write them on the board.

Answers:
Ozzy, you can't ride that bike. First of all it isn't big enough and your glasses are too dirty. As well as that, the basket isn't big enough. Olive, don't try to ride the motorbike. First of all, you aren't old enough and it's too fast. As well as that, your hat is too big and your bag is too heavy.

2e The too and not enough game

Aim: further practice of *too* (adjective) and *not* (adjective) *enough*.
Summary: Ss comment on specific situations.

- Explain the game and the scoring system to the class. Ss work in small groups. Group members write appropriate comments for the situations in the list. Groups score one point for choosing an appropriate adjective and another point for making an appropriate comment.
- Divide the class into groups. Ss read the situations and write their comments. Group members then take turns to read out their sentences. The winning group is the group with the most points.

Suggested answers:
2 *I'm too small/not tall enough.*
3 *It's too long.*
4 *It's not warm enough.*
5 *It's too expensive.*
6 *It's too small/not large enough.*
7 *They're too small/not large enough.*
8 *It's too dangerous.*

Word check
- Divide the class into two teams. Choose seven words for each team from the Word Check box or use more words from the rest of the unit. Hold a spelling quiz. If one team fails to spell a word correctly, the opposite team has a chance to spell the same word.

Teacher's Book Unit 3

3 Make your choice

Check up Units 1-3

1

Aim: to revise the present simple, present continuous, past simple and past continuous; to use context to choose an appropriate tense.

Lead in

- Books closed. Ss say what they know about the Odds and the Normals.

Main activity

- Ss read the text and put the verbs into a suitable tense.
- Ss check their answers with a partner. Ask individual Ss for the answers and write them on the board.

Answers:

1 live	4 were having	7 was painting	
2 do	5 heard	8 were painting	
3 try	6 was sitting	9 are you doing	
		10 are doing	

2

Aim: to revise contrasting uses of the past simple and past continuous.

Lead in

- Write this sentence on the board:
  While we ... (have) an English class yesterday the lights ... (go) off.
- Ask Ss to complete the sentence and explain the use of the past continuous (for a longer action) and the past simple (for an action which interrupts or comes in the middle of the longer one).

Main activity

- Ss complete the sentences individually. They then check their answers with a partner.

Answers:

a)	was washing	started
b)	began	decided
c)	were carrying	damaged
d)	left	went
e)	came down	sat down
f)	was sitting	came
g)	ran	jumped
h)	was jumping	broke

3

Aim: to revise the present simple for habitual actions.

Lead in

- Ss work in pairs and use the questions in the SB to talk about an average family.

Main activity

- Ss work in pairs to write answers to the questions. Write some of the funniest answers on the board.

4

Aim: to revise the comparative form of adjectives and *as ... as*.

Lead in

- Write the following example on the board:
  Ozzy's bike/Nigel's bike (strong)
  Ask Ss to make two sentences:
  1 *Nigel's bike is stronger than Ozzy's.*
  2 *Ozzy's bike isn't as strong as Nigel's.*

Main activity

- Ss write sentences individually. They then check their answers with a partner. Ask Ss for the answers.

Answers:

a) *Nigel Normal's face is cleaner than Ozzy Odd's face.
Ozzy's face isn't as clean as Nigel Normal's face.*
b) *Natalie Normal's brother is more normal than Olive Odd's brother.
Olive Odd's brother isn't as normal as Natalie Normal's brother.*
c) *Natalie's room is tidier than Olive's room.
Olive's room isn't as tidy as Natalie's room.*
d) *Nigel's bike is faster than Ozzy's bike.
Ozzy's bike isn't as fast as Nigel's bike.*
e) *Olive's school bag is heavier than Natalie's school bag.
Natalie's school bag isn't as heavy as Olive's school bag.*
f) *Ozzy's French is worse than Nigel's French.
Nigel's French isn't as bad as Ozzy's French.*

Extra activity

- Ss write their own comparisons between the two families.

5

Aim: to revise *too* and *not ... enough*.

Lead in

- Books closed. Make some sentences with *too* and *not ... enough*, eg:
  This book is too short.   It's not hot enough.
- Ask Ss to rephrase the sentences.

Main activity

- Ss write sentences individually. They then check their answers with a partner. Ask individual Ss for the answers and write them on the board.

Answers:

a) *She was too cold.*
b) *It was too short.*
c) *She wasn't warm enough.*
d) *It was too low.*
e) *It wasn't small enough.*

- Ss each think of three changes to the room. They then exchange ideas in small groups and write their suggestions. Groups then report back to the whole class. Go around the class and help if necessary.

UNITS 1-3

CHECK UP

1 Put each verb in brackets into a suitable tense. Use the present simple, present continuous, past simple or past continuous.

This is the story of two families. They ..1.. (live) next door to each other, but they are not the same. The Normals always ..2.. (do) the same as everyone else. The Odds ..3.. (try) to be different. For example, last week while the Normals ..4.. (have) breakfast they ..5.. (hear) strange noises outside. Mr Odd ..6.. sitting on the roof holding a bucket of water. Mrs Odd ..7.. (paint) all the furniture in the garden. The Odd children ..8.. (paint) the outside of the house pink and yellow. 'What on earth ..9.. (you do)?' called Mr Normal from the window.
  'We ..10.. (do) our spring cleaning. Do you want to help?'

2 Put each verb in brackets into the past simple or the past continuous.

a) While Mr Odd … (wash) the roof, it … (start) raining.
b) When the rain … (begin), Mrs Odd … (decide) to take the furniture inside the house.
c) While the children … (carry) the furniture inside, they … (damage) two chairs.
d) They … (leave) the damaged chairs in the garden and … (go) inside the house.
e) When Mr Odd … (come down) from the roof, he … (sit down) on one of the chairs.
f) While he … (sit) in the rain on the broken chair, the kangaroo … (come) outside.
g) It … (run) to Mr Odd and … (jump) up and down on his head.
h) While it … (jump) on him, the chair … (break) into a thousand pieces.

3 What do you think the Normals and the Odds do every day? What do they eat? What time do they do things? What do they wear?

4 Make some comparisons between the Odd children and the Normal children. Use the word or words in brackets. Write two answers for each sentence, one with a comparative form and one with *not as … as*.

a) Ozzy Odd's face/Nigel Normal's face   (clean)
b) Olive Odd's brother/Natalie Normal's brother   (normal)
c) Olive's room/Natalie's room   (tidy)
d) Ozzy's bike/Nigel's bike   (fast)
e) Olive's school bag/Natalie's school bag   (heavy)
f) Ozzy's French/Nigel's French   (bad)

5 Olive decided to change her room. Give an explanation for each action, using the adjective given and *too* or *not … enough*.

a) Olive put more blankets on her bed. Why?   (cold)
b) She made her bookshelf longer. Why?   (short)
c) She turned on two electric fires. Why?   (warm)
d) She made longer legs for her chair. Why?   (low)
e) She cut her desk in half and put half in the garden. Why?   (small)

Suggest some changes for the room you are in now and give explanations.

▶ *We can make the windows bigger. They are too small.*

4 So far, so good

present perfect simple

The Round the World Kids

1a 📼 New language

The Round the World Kids have left Bermuda and now they are in Mexico. Today they are talking on the radio to their friends in England. Look at the map. Where have they been?

Vicky: Sorry we haven't talked to you before. We've been very busy!

George: We've sent you all postcards. Have they arrived?

Vicky: We've had a great time and we've visited lots of places.

George: It really has been an interesting trip! We can tell you about some of the things we've done so far. We've …

Look at the pictures from their trip. Continue the conversation between Vicky and George and their friends, and describe what Vicky and George have done. Use these verbs:

visit/visited   meet/met   speak/spoken
see/seen   catch/caught   eat/eaten

Helpline – present perfect simple

	have/has + past participle	
I/you/we/they	have ('ve)	visited
he/she/it	has ('s)	visited

past participles
regular — same as past simple
irregular — have – had   do – done

→ GC p4, 15

16

So far, so good 4

Unit 4		Function	Grammar
Lesson 1	The Round the World Kids	Describing recent events	Present perfect simple Ever, yet
Lesson 2	What has he done?	Describing recent events	Present perfect simple regular and irregular verbs] Just
Lesson 3	Words in action		

Word check		
busy	fix	send
carpet	get up	so far, so good
curtain	hope	take down
explanation	ladder	tasty
fall off	necessary	tidy (v)
feed		travel

Lesson 1 The Round the World Kids

1a New language

Aim: to introduce the present perfect simple 1st and 3rd persons plural (affirmative, negative and question form).
Summary: Ss use pictures to decide what Vicky and George have done so far.

Lead in

- Ask Ss some questions to see what they can remember about the Robinsons:
  Who are the Robinsons?
  What are they doing?
  How did they decide to make this journey?
  What island (beginning with B) have they visited?

- Point to the map in the SB and say:
  Where are the Robinsons now? They're in Mexico. They aren't in Bermuda any more – they've left Bermuda.

Main activity

- Read aloud the introduction to the mini dialogue in the SB. Tell Ss to read Vicky and George's dialogue silently. Write these focus questions on the board:
  Why haven't Vicky and George talked to their friends before?
  What have they sent their friends?
  Has it been a good trip?
- Ask individual Ss for their answers.
- Ask Ss to look at the pictures of Vicky and George and describe where they are and what they are doing.
- If necessary, explain that people speak Spanish in Mexico (picture C) and that the men in picture D are limbo dancers, who dance under a low pole.

- Then tell Ss to work in pairs and continue the conversation between Vicky and George and their friends. Explain that they can choose what they want to say, using the verbs to help. Go around the class and help Ss with the new tense.
- Ask individual Ss to make a sentence about each picture and write the sentences on the board.

Suggested answers:
A *We have visited a Wild West Museum.*
B *We have caught a big fish.*
C *We've eaten Mexican food.*
   We've spoken to a Mexican waiter.
D *We've seen a West Indian dancer.*
   We've met local people.

Extra activity

- Books closed. Remove the verbs from the sentences on the board. Ss recall the missing information.

Helpline – present perfect simple

This introduces Ss to the form of this tense.
- Tell Ss that you form the present perfect tense with the auxiliary verb (helping verb) *have* + past participle. Write another verb on the board for Ss to copy, eg:
  I/you/we/they have ('ve) talked
  he/she/it has ('s) talked
  Have you talked? You haven't talked
  Has she talked? They haven't talked
- We often use this tense when we do not say when the action happened, eg:
  The Robinsons have left Bermuda.
- Point out that the past participles of regular verbs have the same form as the past simple. Some irregular verbs, eg *have*, have participles with the same form as the past simple; others, eg *do*, have different forms.

4 So far, so good

1b Listening

Aim: to practise the present perfect simple.
Summary: Ss listen and tick the things Vicky and George have done.

Lead in

- Tell Ss to look at the list of things in the SB. They work with a partner and guess which things Vicky and George have done so far. Ask for some suggestions but do not confirm answers, eg:
  I think they've spoken Spanish.
  I don't think they've met any Mexican teenagers.

Main activity

- Tell Ss that they will hear the cassette twice. Pause between the first and second listening. Ss compare answers with a partner. Ask Ss for the answers:
  1 ✗   2 ✓   3 ✗   4 ✓   5 ✓   6 ✓   7 ✗   8 ✓
- Ask individual Ss to make sentences about what Vicky and George have and haven't done.

1c Practice

Aim: to practise the present perfect simple (1st and 2nd person singular).
Summary: Ss talk about their own personal experiences.

Lead in

- Write the verbs from activity 1b on the board:
  visited   eaten   spoken   had   taken   written   met   fallen
- Check that Ss understand the meaning of the irregular verbs by asking for the infinitive form, *spoken - speak*.
- Ask individual Ss a few questions using the verbs on the board, eg:
  Have you ever eaten rabbit?
  Have you ever written with your left/right hand?
  Ss give short answers.
- Tell Ss to think of questions to ask you. When they can form the questions correctly tell them to work with a partner. Go around the class and check that Ss are asking and answering the questions correctly.
- Write some of the best questions on the board for Ss to copy.

Helpline – ever and yet

- Explain that *ever* means *at any time*. Tell Ss that we use it in questions and we put it before the main verb.
- Write some more examples on the board for Ss to copy, eg:
  Has he ever fallen into the sea?
  Have you ever talked to an animal?
- Explain that *yet* means *so far, up till now*. We put it at the end of negative sentences and questions. Write some more examples on the board for Ss to copy, eg:
  Have you met your new teacher yet?
  I haven't finished the exercise yet.
  We haven't visited the museum yet.

1d Writing

Aim: to practise the present perfect simple in writing.
Summary: Ss write a guided postcard describing personal experiences.

- Ss complete the postcard individually. They then compare answers with a partner.

Suggested answers:
Dear…
Now we're in … So far we've visited Bermuda and Texas. We've taken lots of photos of different places and people. The food is great! We've eaten Mexican food. It was very tasty. And we've also been to a Wild West Museum. We haven't spoken any…yet but we're hoping to meet some …teenagers tomorrow.
Love from both of us
Vicky and George

- Ss work individually and write their own postcard based on the model in the SB. Go around the class and help if necessary.

Lesson 2 What has he done?

2a New language

Aim: to practise the present perfect simple 3rd person singular.
Summary: Ss talk about things Mr Odd *has* and *hasn't* done.

Lead in

- Books closed. Tell Ss that you are going to decorate your living room. Ask for advice. What must you do before you begin? Help with any vocabulary.

Main activity

- Tell Ss to cover the picture and read the note Mrs Odd wrote at nine o'clock.
- Tell Ss to guess what Mr Odd has done so far. Listen to a few suggestions and then tell Ss to look at the picture.
- Ss work with a partner to describe what Mr Odd has and hasn't done.
- Write answers on the board.

Answers:
He hasn't put on some old clothes.
He hasn't painted the walls blue.
He hasn't covered the furniture with newspaper.
He hasn't given the children a safe and easy job.
He hasn't taken down the curtains.
He hasn't painted the door green.
He hasn't put the carpet outside.
He hasn't fixed the broken windows.
He hasn't put the piano in the corner.
He hasn't fed the kangaroo.

Extra activity

- Tell Ss that Mr Odd now remembers to look at his wife's note. Ss work in pairs to decide what he says, eg:
  Oh, dear! I haven't put on my old clothes.

1b 🎧 Listening

Listen to Vicky and George talking about their trip so far. Tick ✓ the things they have done.

1 visited Brazil ✗
2 eaten Mexican food ✓
3 spoken Spanish ☐
4 had Spanish lessons ☐
5 taken photos ☐
6 written postcards ☐
7 met Mexican teenagers ☐
8 fallen in the sea ☐

▶ *They haven't visited Brazil yet. They've eaten Mexican food.*

1c Practice

Ask a partner questions with the verbs from **1b**.

▶ *Have you ever visited …* [Mexico? Italy? France? Egypt? other places?]
Have you ever eaten … [Chinese food? Italian food? other kinds of food?]
Yes, I have./No, I haven't.

Helpline – ever and yet

ever = at any time
  Have you ever visited Italy? Yes, I have.
not … yet = not so far

→ GC p4

1d Writing

Imagine that Vicky and George are in your country. They are writing postcards to their friends in England. Complete this postcard.

Dear …
Now we're in … . So far we've visited … and … .
We've taken lots of photos of … and … . The food is great! We've eaten … . It was very tasty. And we've also … . We haven't … yet but we're hoping to … tomorrow.
Love from both of us
Vicky and George.

You are travelling with Vicky and George. Write a postcard to a friend about your trip.

What has he done?

2a New language

Mrs Odd has gone out for the day because Mr Odd has decided to decorate the living room. She wrote this note for Mr Odd at nine o'clock. It tells him what to do.

Now it's two o'clock. Before you look at the picture, what do you think Mr Odd has done so far? What hasn't he done?

Now look at the picture and check. Were you right?

▶ *He hasn't covered all the furniture with newspaper.*

Put on some old clothes.
Paint the walls blue.
Cover all the furniture with newspaper.
Give the children a safe and easy job.
Take down the curtains.
Paint the door green.
Put the carpet outside.
Fix the broken windows.
Put the piano in the corner.
Feed the kangaroo.

4

2b 🎧 Listening

Mrs Odd phones Mr Odd to ask him what he has done. She hears some strange noises. Listen to each noise and decide what has happened. Write the letter for each noise next to an explanation.

1 Ozzy has just fallen off the ladder.
2 The kangaroo has just bitten Mr Odd.
3 Olive has just dropped the paint on Mr Odd's head.
4 A cat has just jumped through the window into the room.
5 Mrs Normal has just walked through the door.

> **Helpline** – just
>
> *Just* describes very recent actions.
>
> *Ozzy isn't here. He has just left the room.*
> → GC p4

2c Practice

Here is your list of Good Intentions for this week. You wrote it on Monday. Today is Friday. Put a tick ✓ on the list for each thing you have done.

> This week's Good Intentions:
>
> read a good book
> study English every day
> help my parents at home
> get up earlier
> do lots of homework
> tidy my room
> eat healthy food only
> be nice to everybody

Ask a partner about the list.

▶ *Have you read a good book this week?*
– *Yes, I have./No, I haven't.*

2d Writing

You are Ozzy or Olive Odd. Complete this short note to your penfriend. Explain what you have done so far this week. Use the words in the list and any other necessary words.

clean   fix   wash   paint

> Dear …
>
> I'm sorry I haven't written to you for a long time but I have been very busy this week. I am helping with some decorating at home. We haven't finished yet but so far we have …
>
> I'll write to you again when we have finished! That's all for now.
> Best wishes
> …

Word check

busy	ladder
carpet	necessary
curtain	send
explanation	so far, so good
fall off	take down
feed	tasty
fix	tidy [v]
get up	travel
hope	

18

So far, so good   4

2b Listening

Aim: to practise the present perfect simple 3rd person singular.
Summary: Ss deduce the activity from the sounds they hear.

Lead in
- Tell Ss to predict some terrible things which can still happen to Mr Odd and his children while they are painting. Ask for suggestions but do not confirm answers.

Main activity
- Read aloud the introduction to this activity. Ss read the sentences silently.
- Tell Ss that you will play the sound sequences twice. Ss match the sounds and the sentences. They then compare their answers with a partner.
- Ask individual Ss to read out the correct sentence.

Answers:
Noise a) 4   Noise b) 5   Noise c) 1   Noise d) 3   Noise e) 2

Optional activity
- Ss work with a partner and ask about similar disasters or bad experiences, eg:
Has an animal ever bitten you?
Have you ever dropped a tin of paint/a bottle of water?
Have you ever fallen off a ladder/a bike?

Helpline – just
- Explain that we use *just* to describe very recent events. We put it before the main verb. Write some more examples on the board for Ss to copy, eg:
My football team has just bought a new player.
Mrs Odd has just phoned her husband.
Vicky and George have just spoken to their friends on the radio.

2c Practice

Aim: to practise the present perfect simple short answers.
Summary: Ss check whether they have carried out their good intentions.

Lead in
- Books closed. Write the words *Good Intentions* on the board. Explain that these are things which you plan and hope to do. Give an example for yourself, eg:
tidy my desk
- Tell Ss to think of three good intentions and then exchange ideas with a partner. Ask for suggestions and write them on the board.

Main activity
- Books open. Ss compare their good intentions with the list in the SB. They tick the items in the SB list that they have done in the last week.
- Ss ask a partner about the list. They should try to ask an extra question if the answer is *Yes*, eg:
Have you helped your parents at home?
Yes, I have.
What have you done?
I've put the plates away.
- Ss change partners and tell their new partner what their first partner has/hasn't done, eg:
She hasn't read any good books this week but she's studied English most days.

2d Writing

Aim: to write an informal note using the present perfect simple.
Summary: Ss complete the note using suggested vocabulary.

Lead in
- Books closed. Ss tell you what Olive and Ozzy have done this week.

Main activity
- Tell Ss to imagine they are Olive or Ozzy. They are going to write a note to a friend using the words in the list in the SB.
- Remind Ss to use the present perfect simple because the action is not complete – the Odds haven't finished decorating yet.
- Ss write their note individually. They then compare their notes with a partner. Go around the class and help if necessary.

Word check
- Put the following anagrams on the board:
  PRACET   (carpet)
  DRALED   (ladder)
  TRUINAC   (curtain)
  SYTAT   (tasty)
  URALET   (travel)
- Explain that the letters of each word are in the wrong order and ask Ss to find the words.
- Write these sentences on the board:
  a *I need a _____ to clean the high window.*
  b *If you close the _____ the television picture will be better.*
  c *My father made me a really _____ pizza.*
  d *We sometimes _____ by train but we usually go by car.*
- Ask Ss to use each word to complete the sentences. Tell them that one of the words is not used.

Teacher's Book Unit 4

4 So far, so good

Lesson 3 Words in action

1

Aim: to arouse interest in a topic; to read for specific information.
Summary: Ss guess the answers to questions before they read and then read to confirm their guesses.

Lead in

- Books closed. Write this anagram on the board:
  CANOLOV
- Tell Ss to guess the word. When they guess it, ask them a few general questions about volcanoes, eg:
  What does a volcano look like? (a mountain with a large opening at the top/without a top)
  Do you know the names of any famous volcanoes? (Etna and Vesuvius in Italy, Surtsey in Iceland)
  Have any volcanoes erupted in the last few years? (Yes, in Japan and in the Philippines in the early 90s)

Main activity

- Tell Ss to cover the reading text and try to predict the answers to the three multiple choice questions about volcanoes. Ask for some ideas but do not confirm.
- Tell Ss to read the text silently and quickly to check their answers to the three questions. They should not worry about some of the more technical vocabulary which is dealt with in the next activity.

Answers:
a 600 volcanoes   b Hawaii   c the earth

2

Aim: to guess meaning from context.
Summary: Ss make guided guesses about the meanings of words from the text.

Lead in

- Ask if anyone has read an encyclopedia in their own language. Do Ss know what sort of language an encyclopedia uses? Simple or more difficult words? Are some of the words technical words?

Main activity

- Tell Ss that some of the words in this text are technical words. The writer has used them to describe volcanoes in the most accurate way.
- Ss look at the five questions. They scan the text and locate the words first. They then work out the answers. Discourage the use of fingers or rulers while reading.
- Ss check their answers with a partner.

Answers:
a It was too hot outside and my ice cream melted.
b the outside
c dormant
d erupts
e magma

Optional activity

- Tell Ss to draw an active volcano and label the following words on the volcano:
  the surface   magma   hot rocks   gases cracks in the rock
- Interested students might like to find books in English or L1 about volcanoes and bring them to the next lesson. See activity 3 below.

3

Aim: to read for detailed information.
Summary: Ss read more carefully for detail.

Main activity

- Tell Ss to read silently but more slowly to find the answers to the questions. They then compare their answers with a partner. Ask individual Ss for the answers.

Answers:
a 1000 degrees C
b magma
c about 300
d hot rocks and gases
e 4168 metres
f 150 times

Extra activity

- Focus on tenses. Tell Ss to read the text again and to look for examples of the following:
  a) something that is happening now (present continuous)
     (the volcano is actually erupting, hot rocks and gases are coming out)
  b) something that often happens (present simple)
     (it moves like water, the magma comes up, the rock forms a small hill, many volcanoes stay dormant)
  c) something that happened some time in the past but we do not know when (present perfect)
     (the rock here has melted, Mount Etna has erupted,)

Optional actvity

- Ss work with a partner to write a short report about a volcano. Ss should look in encyclopedias in the school or town library and ask their parents or older brothers and sisters. The report should include (a picture if possible and) the following information:
  Where is it?
  Is it active or dormant?
  When did it last erupt?
  Any other interesting information about volcanoes, eg:
  What did the Ancient Greeks and Romans say about volcanoes? (They were the chimneys of the underground forge of the fire god. The Roman name for this god was Vulcan and this is where we get the word volcano from.)
  The finished projects can be displayed in the classroom.

WORDS in ACTION

1 🎧 Vicky and George learnt about volcanoes when they were in Mexico. What do you know about volcanoes?

Make some guesses before you read.

a) How many volcanoes are there on earth?
   i) about 150   ii) about 600
   iii) about 900
b) Where is the largest volcano?
   i) Sicily   ii) Iceland   iii) Hawaii
c) What makes volcanoes hot?
   i) the earth   ii) the sun   iii) water

What is a volcano? About 50 kilometres below the surface of the earth the temperature is hotter than 1000 degrees C. The rock here has melted and it moves like water. It is called magma. Sometimes the magma comes up to the surface through cracks in the rock. Then the rock forms a small hill, a volcano.

There are more than 600 active volcanoes on earth. About half of these are in the area of the Pacific Ocean and there are two hundred in Iceland. 'Active' means that the volcano is actually erupting and hot rocks and gases are coming out of it. Only about thirty volcanoes are active all the time and most volcanoes are dormant. Many volcanoes stay dormant for hundreds of years. The largest active volcano on earth is Mauna Loa in Hawaii, which is 4168 metres high. Mount Etna in Sicily has erupted about 150 times in the last 3500 years.

2 The text in **1** is from an encyclopedia. It contains some technical words. Answer the questions about some of these words.

a) Which of these examples of the verb 'melt' gives the best explanation?
   ▶ *I can't play football because my shoes have melted.*
   I haven't done my homework because my pen melted.
   It was too hot outside so my ice cream melted.
b) The 'surface' of the earth is:
   the outside?   the hottest part?
   another word for 'magma'?
c) The opposite of 'active' is [adjective] …
d) When a volcano is active it [verb] …
e) The name of the rock under the earth is [noun] …

3 Answer these questions about volcanoes.

a) What is the temperature 50 kilometres below the surface of the earth?
b) What is the melted rock called?
c) How many volcanoes are there in the area of the Pacific Ocean?
d) What comes out of a volcano?
e) How high is the largest volcano on earth?
f) How many times has Mount Etna erupted in the last 3500 years?

5 Time travellers

present perfect simple and past simple

A visit to the past

1a 📼 New language

Nick talked to Young Archeologist, Sheila Moorhead. Read Nick's article about Sheila. What did she tell him? Put four more events in each list.

> An event and the time when it happened
> 1 I started helping some archeologists when I was thirteen.

> An event with no stated time (an indefinite event)
> 1 I've learnt a lot about the Romans on this dig.

I started helping some archeologists when I was thirteen. When I was younger, I didn't like history at school. Then a few years ago I read about this Roman villa in the local paper. I came here one Saturday afternoon and they gave me some easy jobs to do.

I've learnt a lot about the Romans on this dig. I haven't found anything exciting yet. Most of the work is routine. I've helped with the records - we make drawings of things we find and write about them. So far we've found coins, broken pots and the walls of the villa. I've taken photos and made cups of tea! The most exciting moment was in 1993 when two of the team found a beautiful mosaic floor.

Now match Nick's questions with information in the article.

1 Have you found any exciting objects?
2 Did you like history lessons at school?
3 What jobs have you done on the dig?
4 When did you learn about this dig?
5 What have the archeologists found on this dig?
6 What was the most exciting moment?

Work with a partner. One of you is Nick and one of you is Sheila. Cover the article. Use Nick's questions to roleplay his interview with Sheila.

Helpline – since, ago, for

since + date/time + present perfect

Since 1990 I have visited the villa twice.

length of time + *ago* + past simple

They discovered the villa twenty years ago.

for + length of time + present perfect/past simple

Jill has been an archeologist for ten years. She worked on that dig for two years.

→ GC p5

20

Time travellers 5

Unit 5		Functions	Grammar
Lesson 1	A visit to the past	Contrasting definite and indefinite events	Past simple and present perfect simple Since, ago, for
Lesson 2	Discoveries	Contrasting definite and indefinite events	Past simple and present perfect simple
Lesson 3	CHRIS 2		

Word check

ancient	discover	interesting
birth	exciting	library
bone	farmer	map
building	find out	owner
burn	huge	past
coin		

Lesson 1 A visit to the past

1a New language

Aim: to contrast the use of the past simple and present perfect simple; to introduce *ago* with the past simple.
Summary: Ss match interview questions with information in the text; they then roleplay the interview.

Lead in

- Ask questions to introduce the topic:
  Has anyone ever found something old outside? Where?
  How did you find it?
  There are special people who look for old things. What do we call these people? (archeologists)
  Do you know any places in our country where archeologists have found ancient buildings?
  Have you visited any of these places?
  What information do we find out from these places? (how people lived in the past)

Main activity

- Introduce the text. Ask Ss to read silently and find the answers to these simple focus questions:
  Where does Sheila help the archeologists?
  What does Sheila do there?

- Draw a chart with two columns on the board. Copy the headings *An event and the time when it happened* and *An event with no stated time (an indefinite event)* at the top of the columns. Look at the two examples with the class. Check that Ss are able to tell the difference between the two types of sentences. Ask Ss to complete the columns using sentences from the text. When Ss finish tell them to underline the time expressions in the sentences in the first column. Ask individual Ss for the answers.

Answers:
1st column
2 *When I was younger*, I didn't like history at school.
3 Then *two years ago* I read about this Roman villa in the local paper.
4 I came here *one Saturday afternoon* and they gave me some easy jobs to do.
5 The most exciting moment was *in 1993* when two team members found a beautiful mosaic floor.

2nd column
2 I haven't found anything exciting yet.
3 I've helped with the records.
4 We've found coins, broken pots and the walls of the villa.
5 I've taken photos and made cups of tea!

- Ask Ss to read Nick's questions and find the answers in the article. Ss check their answers with a partner.

Answers:
1 I haven't found anything exciting yet.
2 When I was younger, I didn't like history at school.
3 I've helped with the records – we make drawings of things we find and write about them. I've taken photos and made cups of tea.
4 Two years ago I read about this Roman villa in the local paper.
5 We've found coins, broken pots and the walls of the villa.
6 The most exciting moment was in 1993 when two team members found a beautiful mosaic floor.

- Ask Ss to cover the article. They work in pairs and act out the interview between Nick and Sheila.

Helpline – since, ago, for

- Explain that *since* is used to give the starting point of a period of time that continues up to the present. It is used with the present perfect simple and never with the past simple. Draw a time line on the board and an example, eg:
  Since last month I've visited my grandmother three times.
  ←――――――――――――――――――――→
  Last month   Now
  Then ask: *Do you know when exactly I visited my grandmother? (No.)*
  Write some more examples on the board for Ss to copy, eg:
  I've read about six books since September.
- Explain that *ago* means *in the past* and tells us how long before the present something happened. It always goes after the time expression. It is used with the past simple and never with the present perfect simple. Ask Ss: *Do we know when the Saxon pirates burned the villa? (Yes, 1500 years ago.)*
- Write some more examples on the board for Ss to copy, eg: *You started English lessons three years ago.*
- Explain that *for* is used to talk about the length of a period of time. We can use it to talk about the past, present or future. We can use it with both the present perfect simple and past simple. Write some examples on the board for Ss to copy, eg:
  You've studied English for three years.

Teacher's Book Unit 5

5 Time travellers

1b Practice

Aim: to contrast the use of the past simple and the present perfect simple; to introduce *since* with the present perfect simple.
Summary: Ss use the table to make statements using either the past simple or the present perfect simple.

Lead in

- Write some sentences about yourself on the board using both tenses, eg:
  I've met some archeologists.
  I visited the Acropolis in Athens in 1990.
  I've never discovered an ancient coin.
  I learnt to speak Italian when I was younger.
  Tell Ss to say which sentences do not say when the event happened.
- Tell Ss to make some sentences about themselves with either the past simple or the present perfect simple. Correct the sentences if the tense is wrong. Write some example sentences on the board.

Main activity

- Ask Ss to look at the poster in the SB and the two example sentences. Ss then prepare sentences about the other events in the poster. Ss compare their sentences with a partner. Go around the class and correct the tenses if necessary. Ask individual Ss for their sentences and write them on the board.
  In 1985 a farmer found pieces of a Roman pot in the field.
  In 1988 archeologists made a map of the area and began a dig.
  Since 1990 members of the team have taken hundreds of photos.
  Since 1990 over 5000 visitors have come to see the villa.
  In 1993 two archeologists discovered a mosaic floor.
  In 1994 a small museum opened at the dig.
  Since 1994 archeologists have uncovered a Roman road near the villa.
  Since 1994 many articles about the villa have appeared in magazines and newspapers.

Extra activity

- Books closed. Say or write a few key words on the board and ask Ss to make correct sentences about the dig, eg:
  Saxon pirates   a Roman pot   map
  twelve small buildings   hundreds of photos
  mosaic floor   museum   Roman road
  magazines and newspapers

1c Practice

Aim: to practise using the past simple and the present perfect simple.
Summary: Ss ask each other questions using the present perfect simple and the past simple.

Lead in

- Ask some of the questions in the SB to make sure that Ss understand what they must do. Tell Ss to ask you some questions.

Main activity

- Ss work with a partner to find out about his or her history. Go around the class and help if necessary. Tell Ss to report back to the whole class with information about their partner.

Extra activity

- Ss write a short report about their partner's history.

Lesson 2 Discoveries

2a New language

Aim: to contrast the use of the past simple and the present perfect simple.
Summary: Ss read about three people and divide the events in their lives into two lists – those with dates (past simple) and those without (present perfect simple).

Lead in

- Read the introduction. Look at the pictures in the SB with the class. Tell Ss to guess what interesting things the three teenagers learnt about the past. Do not confirm their predictions yet.

Main activity

- Ss read the texts silently and make two lists in their exercise books: List 1 is for the things the teenagers and other people did, with the exact times (past simple), List 2 is for the things the teenagers and other people have done (present perfect simple). Ss check lists with a partner. Ask individual Ss for their answers and write them on the board.

Answers:
List 1
Last summer Maria went to the local library one Saturday and looked at old newspapers.
Last year Colin started to find out about the history of his house. Every Friday for a month he went to the library and he looked at old maps.
He found the names of all the people who have lived in his house.
Tina found a dinosaur eight years ago.
She saw a huge bone in a rock (eight years ago).
List 2
Maria has discovered some interesting information about the year of her birth.
Since 1982 she has made an album with pictures of people, cars, singers and other things.
Colin has found the names of all the people who have lived in his house since 1861.
Tina has found other small things called ammonites and trilobites.

- Tell Ss to read the texts again silently and carefully to complete the sentences. They then check their answers with a partner. Ask individual Ss for the answers.

Teacher's Book Unit 5

1b Practice

Look at the poster about the dig at the Roman villa. Say what happened (with the date) and what has happened.

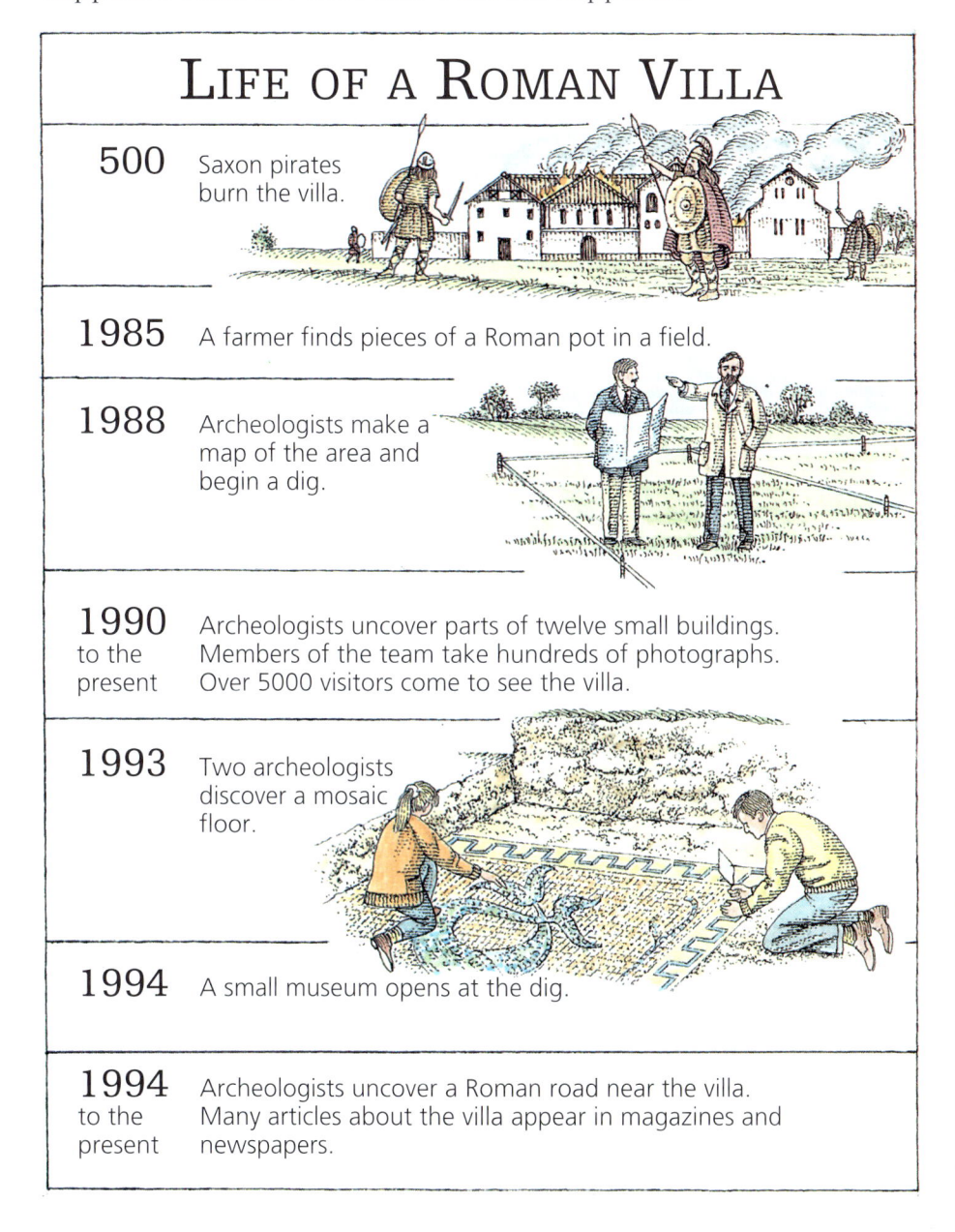

LIFE OF A ROMAN VILLA

500	Saxon pirates burn the villa.
1985	A farmer finds pieces of a Roman pot in a field.
1988	Archeologists make a map of the area and begin a dig.
1990 to the present	Archeologists uncover parts of twelve small buildings. Members of the team take hundreds of photographs. Over 5000 visitors come to see the villa.
1993	Two archeologists discover a mosaic floor.
1994	A small museum opens at the dig.
1994 to the present	Archeologists uncover a Roman road near the villa. Many articles about the villa appear in magazines and newspapers.

▶ *In 500 Saxon pirates burned the villa.*
Since 1990 archeologists have uncovered parts of twelve small buildings.

1c Practice

Ask a partner some questions about his or her own history.

▶ *How long have you been at this school? When did you start here? Have you ever visited ... [name a place in your country]? When did you go there?*

Discoveries

2a New language

Meet three teenagers on this page and the next page who have learnt about the past. Make two lists: List 1: Things they and other people did, with the times, List 2: Things they and other people have done.

> List 1
> ... went to ... one Saturday

> List 2
> ... has discovered ...

Maria I have discovered some interesting information about the year of my birth. I have investigated the year 1982. Last summer I went to the local library one Saturday and looked at old newspapers. And since then I have made an album with pictures of people, cars, singers, and other things.

5

Colin We live in an old house and last year I started to find out about its history. Every Friday for a month I went to the library and I looked at old maps and plans. I found the names of all the people who have lived there. Now I know the names of all the owners of the house since 1861.

Tina When I was six my dad said, 'Come on, let's go and find a dinosaur.' And I did. I saw a huge bone in the rock. It was a bone from a stegosaurus, which was 175 million years old. That was eight years ago. Since then I've found other small things called ammonites and trilobites.

Find the person or people who …

1 … has found out about his or her past.
2 … found something a few years ago.
3 … found something interesting in the library.
4 … has found things with strange names.
5 … has collected things in a book.
6 … found something with his or her father.

2b Practice

Ask a partner the questions.

Have you ever visited a museum or an ancient building? When? Who did you go with?

What have archaeologists discovered in your country? Which famous people lived in your country in the past? What did they do?

2c Listening

This is a metal-detector. You can use it to find things under the ground. Think of interesting things you can find.

Listen to a radio programme about an archeological discovery. Are the statements true or false?

1 David and Paul found thousands of coins.   True/False
2 The boys showed the coins to other people.   True/False
3 Since the end of last month, archeologists have found more coins.   True/False
4 Everyone knows where the boys found the coins.   True/False
5 Other people have found coins before in the same place.   True/False
6 Yesterday the boys told their story on television.   True/False

Retell the story in your own words.

2d Writing

David is telling the story in **2c**. Choose a tense for the verbs.

I ..1.. (have) my metal detector for a year. My parents ..2.. (give) it to me when I ..3.. (be) fifteen. Paul and I ..4.. (go) into the field because it is near Paul's house. We ..5.. (ask) the farmer for permission first. We ..6.. (find) ten coins very quickly and we ..7.. (decide) to phone the museum. So far the archeologists ..8.. (find) more than five thousand coins.

Write a similar paragraph about some teenagers who found something old and valuable. Use the notes.

Names?   Things found?   When and where?
What has happened since they found these things?

Word check

ancient	discover	interesting
birth	exciting	library
bone	farmer	map
burn	find out	owner
building	huge	past
coin		

Time travellers 5

Answers:
1 Colin 2 Tina 3 Maria and Colin 4 Tina 5 Maria
6 Tina

Optional activity

- Ss suggest other sentences for completion, eg:
  Find someone who ...
  ... has slept outside.
  ... spoke to someone in English on the phone last year.
  ... has been to a zoo.
  ... has made ice cream.
  ... made his or her bed this morning.
  ... has never borrowed anything.
  ... has broken a bone.
  They then move around the class, asking and answering questions in order to complete their sentences.

2b Practice

Aim : to practise using the present perfect simple and the past simple.
Summary: Ss ask each other about visits to museums or ancient buildings.

- Ss work with a partner and ask each other the questions in the SB. Go around the class and help if necessary.

Optional activity

- Find out which are the most popular museums or archeological sites in your class. Which one have most Ss visited?

2c Listening

Aim: to listen for specific information.
Summary: Ss listen and decide if statements are true or false.

Lead in

- Look at the picture in the SB with the class. Ask Ss to guess what the boy has got. Find out if Ss know what a metal-detector can find. (Coins, jewellery, weapons, tools, containers etc.)
- Point out that in many countries metal detectors are illegal and that it's not a good idea to dig for old things, as an archeologist can do this better than you!

Main activity

- Ask Ss to read the true/false statements. Play the radio programme about an archeological discovery twice. Ss then check their answers with a partner. Ask individual Ss for the answers and their reasons.

Answers:
1 F (The boys found ten coins.)
2 T (They only showed them to people at the museum.)
3 F (The programme says since then but does not say when exactly.)
4 F (The boys and the museum have kept the place a secret.)
5 F (Other people have found them in the same area but not exactly the same place.)
6 F (The boys spoke to journalists.)

- Books closed. Ss work with a partner to retell the story in their own words. Go around the class and help if necessary.

Extra activity

- Play the cassette again but pause before every verb. Ss continue the sentence eg *Two boys with a metal detector ...*

2d Writing

Aim: further practice of the present perfect simple and the past simple.
Summary: Ss complete a paragraph with the present perfect simple and past simple form of verbs.

Main activity

- Ask Ss to read the paragraph silently and quickly to understand the general sense. They then read silently but more slowly to choose the right tense. Ss check their answers with a partner. Go around the class and help if necessary. Ask individual Ss for the answers:

Answers:
1 have had   3 was   5 asked   7 decided
2 gave   4 went   6 found   8 have found

- Ss work with a partner to think of some ideas for their paragraph before they write. They then write their paragraphs individually. Go around the class and correct tenses if necessary. Early finishers exchange paragraphs and make suggestions for changes and corrections.

Word check

- Write these sentences on the board:
  a My dog likes <u>glasses</u>.   (bones)
  b You can borrow books from a <u>supermarket</u>. (library)
  c What an <u>awful</u> book! Can I borrow it? (interesting)
  d She took some <u>buttons</u> out of her pocket and paid for the chocolate.   (coins)
  e <u>Doctors</u> work in the fields.   (farmers)
  f This is my bike, I'm the <u>information</u>.   (owner)
- Tell Ss that each of these sentences has a wrong word. Ask Ss to write the sentences again, changing the underlined word for a correct word from the Word check box.

Teacher's Book Unit 5

5 Time travellers

Lesson 3 CHRIS Episode 2

Aims: to read for specific information; to guess coded information from context; to listen for specific information; to predict how the story will continue.

Main activity

The story so far:
- Ss work in pairs and tell each other what they remember about Chris, CHRIS, Sandy and Peter.

Answers:
Chris is a scientist. He writes computer games programs. He has disappeared. No one knows where he is. He often goes away. CHRIS is a computer and the letters mean Computer Help: Reporting Information Service.
Sandy and Peter are Chris's younger sister and brother. They are twins. Mrs Jackson often looks after them.

1

Lead in
- Ask Ss if they can remember CHRIS's first message.
- Write this question on the board:
  Who understands CHRIS's second message?
- Ask Ss to read section A of the story and find the answer to the question. Make sure that everyone agrees that Peter understands the message.

Main activity
- Ask for suggestions about the coded message but do not confirm yet. Tell Ss not to worry if they can't get the message as it will be easier to understand later.

2

Extra activity
- Write these True/False statements on the board:
  a They opened the envelope in Sandy's room. (F)
  b Peter put the map on the floor. (F)
  c Sandy thinks the map is from her older brother. (T)
  d The twins try to find NT on the envelope. (F)
  Ss read section B silently and decide if the statements are true or false. They then check with a partner. Ask individual Ss for the answers.

3

Main activity
- Ss guess the answer to the question *Where did they find the envelope?* Do not confirm the answer yet.

4

Main activity
- Play the cassette once but pause after each question to give Ss a chance to suggest an answer. Then play the cassette again without pausing.

Extra activity
- Tell Ss to work with a partner and retell this part of the story. They should begin: *Sandy and Peter heard a noise at the door and ...*

5

Main activity
- Ss look at the map in the SB and find the NT (the National Theatre).

Extra activity
- Write these questions on the board:
  a What is NT?
  b When did Chris go there?
  c Why does Sandy want to go there?
- Tell Ss to find the answers to the questions as they read the next part of the story.

Answers:
1 NT is the National Theatre.
2 He went there last week.
3 She wants to go there so that they can look for Ann or Alan, the mysterious A.

- Ss should now be able to de-code the message at the beginning of the episode:
  Find NT and go to the person with A.

6

- Ss work in small groups and discuss what they think has happened to Chris. Ask groups to report their ideas to the whole class.

Extra activity
- Ss roleplay this episode with a partner. Student A is Sandy and Student B is Peter. They then exchange roles.

Episode 2

CHRIS

The story so far:

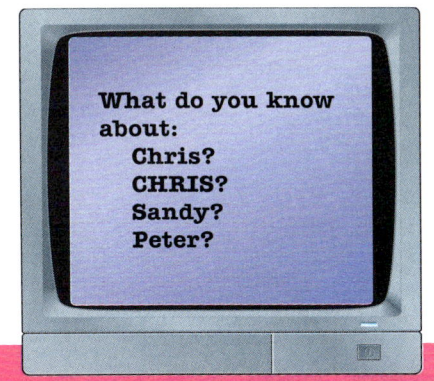

```
What do you know
about:
    Chris?
    CHRIS?
    Sandy?
    Peter?
```

1 Read the story and work out the message.

find/and/the NT/with A/the person/Go to

▶ **a**

Sandy and Peter looked at the computer screen. 'What on earth does it mean? We want an easier clue please, CHRIS!' said Peter.
   Some different words appeared and CHRIS said, 'This is my second message.'
   'It's another code,' said Sandy. 'Where has our brother gone? Just tell us that.'
   But the computer was silent.
   'I know this message,' said Peter. 'It's easy.'

2 Read this part of the story.

▶ **b**

   They took the envelope back to Chris's room and Sandy opened it.
   'What's inside?' asked Peter.
   In the envelope was a map of London. Sandy unfolded the map and put it on the desk.
   'Chris has sent us this map, I'm sure of it,' said Sandy. 'He's trying to help us. Where is the NT? That's the problem.'
   The twins started looking at the map very carefully.

3 Guess the answer to this question: Where did they find the envelope?

4 Listen to the missing part of the story. As you listen, answer the questions you hear. Were you right about the envelope?

5 Look at the map. Can you find the NT? Read the next part of the story.

▶ **c**

   'I've found it, Peter,' said Sandy. 'NT - it's the National Theatre. Chris went there last week I think. Come on, we can go there on the bus.'
   'What for?' said Peter.
   Sandy replied, 'We can look for this person, Ann or Alan. The mysterious A.'
   'It doesn't say that his or her name is A, Sandy,' said Peter. 'It says "the person with A". It's a difficult puzzle!'

6 Make some guesses about the story. What has happened to Chris?

a) Have some gangsters kidnapped him?
b) Has he lost his memory?
c) Has he become a spy?

6 What's it like?

what's it like?; comparisons with adverbs; order of adjectives

The Round the World Kids

1a New language

Vicky and George are now in Melbourne, in Australia. Their friends have written to them and asked them lots of questions. Match the questions with the replies that Vicky and George wrote.

1 What's Australia like?

2 What are the people like?

3 What's Melbourne like?

4 What's the food like?

5 What's the weather like at the moment?

a) It's tasty. Some is the same as English food, but there is lots of seafood and Chinese and Vietnamese food. There are lots of Greek restaurants too.
b) It's one of the largest cities in the country, with over three million people. Most people live in houses with gardens, but there are some big office blocks in the centre. The river is really lovely.
c) They're friendly, but we can't always understand their accents! They seem to come from all over the world too.
d) It's cold in July and warm in January. The weather changes very quickly. Yesterday it was sunny and today it's windy and chilly. In fact, it's nearly the same as in England.
e) The cities are crowded and busy and there are lots of big cars. We've sailed along the coast and we went to Brisbane and Sydney before we came here. The trees and flowers everywhere are really beautiful.

> **Helpline** – what's it like?
>
> We use *what's ... like?* when we want to know someone's opinion.
>
> It does not mean the same as 'Do you like?'
>
> → GC p5

Ask a partner questions about towns, countries, people, food and the weather.

▶ Have you ever been to/eaten/met/visited …?   What's it like?
What are the people like?   What's the weather like?
What's the food like?

What's it like? 6

Unit 6		Functions	Grammar
Lesson 1	The Round the World Kids	Describing and comparing places, things, people	What's it like? Comparisons with adverbs
Lesson 2	Born to shop	Describing things	Order of adjectives
Lesson 3	Check up Units 4–6		

Word check

blouse	impression	silk
chilly	late	take something seriously
cotton	leather	traditional
dress (v)	plate	try on
early	river	windy
fit (v)	short-sleeved	

Lesson 1 The Round the World Kids

1a New language

Aim: to ask about and describe a country; to present *What's it like?*
Summary: Ss match questions and answers.

Lead in

- Books closed. Tell Ss to guess which country the Round the World Kids visit next from the following clues:
  It's a very big country (almost as big as the USA without Alaska) but it has a small population (about 15 million).
  There is a huge desert in the middle of the country.
  There are some unusual animals there, eg kangaroos, koalas, wombats. They carry their babies in pouches or pockets.
  It is both a continent and a country.
  The capital city is Canberra. Other well-known cities are Sydney and Melbourne.
  The people living there before Europeans arrived are called Aborigines or native Australians.

Main activity

- Books open. Ss look at the map and find Melbourne.
- Tell Ss to read the questions that Vicky and George's friends have asked them. They then match the questions with Vicky and George's replies. Ss check with a partner. Ask individual Ss for the answers.

Answers:
1 e   2 c   3 b   4 a   5 d

- Deal with any new vocabulary after Ss have done the matching activity. Ss may find the expression *What ... like?* difficult to understand. Explain that we use it mainly when we ask about people, things and the weather. Write some more examples on the board for Ss to copy, eg:
  What's Sydney like?
  What are the beaches in Australia like?
  What's the summer like?
  What are the animals like?

- Books closed. Ask individual Ss questions about Australia, eg:
  What's the winter in Australia like?
  What are the houses like?
  What's the food like?
  What are the cars like?

- Ss work with a partner to ask questions about towns, countries, people, food and weather. Ask one pair to do an example for the whole class as a model:
  S1: *Have you ever been to Spain?*
  S2: *Yes, I have.*
  S1: *What's it like?*
  S2: *It's really beautiful.*
  S1: *What's the food like?*
  S2: *Very tasty. They eat a lot of paella.*

- Go around the class and help if necessary. Ask individual Ss to give information about the country or place their partner described.

Optional activity

- Books closed. Ss work in pairs and roleplay a radio conversation Vicky or George has with a friend in Britain. The friend asks a lot of questions about Australia using *What ... like?*

Helpline – What's it like?

- Ask Ss to make as many questions as they can with the expression *What ... like?*

6 What's it like?

1b New language

Aim: to present comparisons with adverbs.
Summary: Ss look for differences in Vicky and George's letters. Ss compare two different countries.

Lead in
- Ask Ss to guess what differences Vicky and George find between life in Australia and life in England.

Main activity
- Ask Ss to read Vicky's letter silently and find the differences between life in Australia and life in England.

Answers:
English kids work harder at school.
Australian kids dress more casually.
They take things less seriously.
They spend most of the time swimming or playing tennis.
They go to bed later.

- Ask Ss to read part of George's letter silently to find out if he says the same as Vicky.

Answers:
Australian kids get up earlier. (Vicky does not say this.)
They work harder at school. (Vicky says that English kids work harder.)
They spend more hours at school. (Vicky does not say this.)

- Ask Ss: *What differences will Vicky and George find if they visit your country?*
- Ss work with a partner and make sentences about young people and other things in England and their country. Ask individual Ss to make sentences, eg:
In our country people finish work later.
Then ask Ss to make a sentence about England, eg:
In England people finish work earlier.

Helpline – comparisons with adverbs

- Ask Ss to name some adverbs, eg:
hard, casually, seriously, late, early, smartly
- Ss make comparisons with these adverbs, using *-er than*, *more ... than*, *less ... than* and *not as ... as*.
- Explain: short adverbs such as *fast, soon, early, late, hard, long* have comparative forms with *-er*, eg:
Australians get up earlier than English people.
Our lessons begin later than their lessons.
Most adverbs, however, make their comparative form with *more*, eg:
He speaks more quietly than his sister.
Italian people dress more smartly than English people.
We can also use *less ... than* to say the opposite, eg:
English people dress less smartly than Italian people.
We can also make comparisons using *(not) as ... as* when we say that two things are different or the same in some way, eg:
Vicky swims as fast as George.
I don't think Australians dress as smartly as us.

- We can also make comparisons with some frequency adverbs, eg:
Australians go to see films more often than us.

1c Writing

Aim: to practise the comparative form of adverbs.
Summary: Ss write an informal postcard.

Lead in
- Tell Ss to write about a country which they know quite well. They can use some ideas from the previous activity but their postcard must include some comparisons, eg:
The cities are cleaner than at home but the traffic moves more slowly.

Main activity
- Ss write their postcards individually but exchange them when they finish.

Lesson 2 Born to shop

2a Listening

Aim: to focus on the order of adjectives.
Summary: Ss listen and tick the things Vicky bought.

Lead in
- Ask Ss what kind of souvenirs they might take home from another country, eg:
Clothes, eg T shirt
Leather things, eg wallet, bag
Glass things, eg vase, bowl
Wooden things, eg box, knife
Posters and pictures
- Books open. Ss name the things in the pictures.

Main activity
- Play the cassette twice. Ss tick the things that Vicky bought. Ask individual Ss to say which pictures they have ticked.

Answers:
(small glass) bowl   (small traditional) bag   (green silk) shirt

- Write the normal order of adjectives on the board:
SIZE   COLOUR   TYPE   MATERIAL
- Ask Ss to match the words in the SB with the different categories. Ss then work with a partner and write descriptions of the things in the pictures.

Answers:
a small glass bowl   a long red skirt
a large blue plate   a small traditional bag
a green silk shirt   a large white shopping bag

Teacher's Book Unit 6

1b 🔊 New language

This is part of Vicky's letter. How many differences does she find between life in Australia and life in England?

We are staying with some friends of my dad's and the children are nearly the same age as George and me. I think that we work much harder at school in England! Australian kids dress more casually and take things less seriously. They spend most of the time swimming or playing tennis! They go to bed later than us too.

Here is part of George's letter. Does he say the same as Vicky? Find the differences.

We're staying with a family and there are two kids nearly the same age as us. They get up earlier than we do and they work harder at school. They spend more hours at school than us, for a start. I think that the kids at our school dress more smartly.

Vicky and George have just arrived in your country. They compare your country with their country. Guess what they will say about these things. Look back at **1a** and **1b** before you begin.

Young people:
- speak more quickly/more slowly?
- go to bed earlier/later?
- talk more quietly/more loudly?
- start work or finish work earlier/later?
- are more friendly/less friendly?
- study harder/not as hard?
- take school more seriously/less seriously

Other things:
- the traffic moves more quickly/more slowly
- it rains more often/less often

Helpline – comparisons with adverbs

Use: -er, more … than, less … than, not as … as

We can also make comparisons with frequency adverbs:

They eat more often than we do.

→ GC p5

1c Writing

Write a postcard from Vicky and George. You can choose which country they are visiting. Use ideas from **1a** and **1b**.

Born to shop

2a 🔊 Listening

Vicky went shopping with her Australian friends. Listen and tick ✓ the things she bought.

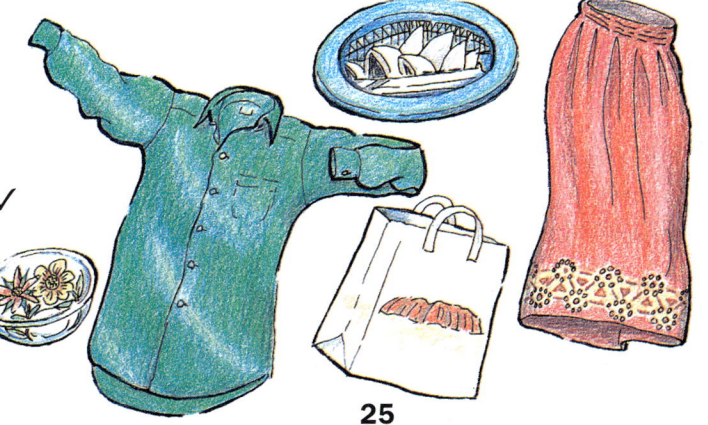

Describe all the things in the pictures. Use these words:

plate bowl small
large long blue
green skirt shirt
glass silk traditional
red white bag

6

2b 🔊 Practice

Vicky wanted to buy some clothes too. She went back to the shops with her mother. Put a number in each of the empty speech bubbles to make a dialogue.

1. It looks really great.
2. It's $95.
3. Yes, I'd like to try on that long blue coat in the window.
4. It fits me nicely. Do you like it, Mum?
5. Can I help you?
6. How much is it?
7. Does it fit you? Or is it too big?

Helpline

– order of adjectives

size   colour   type   material

a large red plate
a traditional cotton bag

→ GC p5

2c Practice

Describe the things in the shop window.

silk
wool
leather
cotton
plastic

▶ There's a purple short-sleeved silk blouse.

Practise the dialogue in **2b** with two partners, but shop for things in the window.

2d Writing

You went shopping and bought presents for your friends or family. Choose two things from **2a** and two from **2c** and complete the extract from your diary.

When I was in... [name a place] I went shopping. I bought two souvenirs ... [describe two things from 2a] for ... [say the names of friends or family]. I also bought some clothes for myself. I bought ... [name two things from 2c]. I tried on the ... [say which things] but ... [describe a problem from 2b].

Word check

blouse	impression	silk
chilly	late	take something seriously
cotton	leather	traditional
dress (v)	plate	try on
early	river	windy
fit (v)	short-sleeved	

What's it like? 6

Helpline – order of adjectives

- Point to the categories already on the board. Write some jumbled descriptions on the board. Ss work with a partner to put the adjectives in the right order, eg:
  a box (large, wooden)
  a poster (small, red)
  a pullover (big, woollen)
  a diary (black, leather)
  a ballerina (small, glass)

2b Practice

Aim: to practise the order of adjectives; to practise the language of shopping.
Summary: Ss match words to pictures and make a dialogue.

Lead in

- Tell Ss to look at the pictures but to cover the words. Ss work with a partner to guess what the people are saying. Ask for some suggestions but do not confirm.

Main activity

- Tell Ss to listen to the dialogue twice and to put a number in each speech bubble. Ask Ss to read their dialogues with a partner to see if it sounds right. Ask one pair to read their dialogue aloud for the whole class to check their answers.

Answers:
5   3   7   4   1   6   2

2c Practice

Aim: to practise describing clothes; to practise the language of shopping.
Summary: Ss describe the clothes in the picture and roleplay a shopping dialogue.

- Ask Ss to work with a partner to describe the things in the shop window. Go around the class and check that they are putting the adjectives in the correct order. Ask individual Ss for the answers:

Answers:
a purple short-sleeved silk blouse
blue plastic sandals
a green woollen pullover
red cotton shorts
a black leather jacket

- Ss work in groups of three and practise the dialogue in activity 2b, using the clothes in the pictures. Ask one group to practise aloud for the whole class as a model. Go around the class and help if necessary.

2d Writing

Aim: to practise the order of adjectives in a written text.
Summary: Ss complete a diary extract.

Lead in

- Ss tell a partner what presents from activities 2a and 2c they bought for friends or family and what they bought for themselves. Go through the diary extract to check that Ss understand what they must write, eg:
  When I was in Cairo I went shopping. I bought two souvenirs, a white cotton shirt and ...

Main activity

- Ss work individually and complete the diary extract. Early finishers read out their extract to a partner.

Optional activity

- Ss write an extract from Vicky or George's diary describing some of their impressions of Australia and the things they have bought.

Word check

- Divide the class into two teams. Each S chooses two words from the Word check box and uses them (singular or plural) to make a sentence, eg:
  This T-shirt is cotton.
  Ss may help one another.
- Teams take it in turns to say their sentences. Score one point for each correct sentence.

6 What's it like?

Check up Units 4-6

1

Aim: to practise the present perfect simple and past simple.

Lead in

- Ask Ss if they ever do any cooking or help with the cooking. Have they ever had any problems? Ask them to describe (or make up) a disaster they have had in the kitchen, eg:
  There was a power cut while I was cooking some meat in the oven.

Main activity

- Write these three sentences on the board:
  1 Ozzy cooks a lovely meal.
  2 Ozzy makes a mess in the kitchen.
  3 Ozzy's mother knows what he is doing.
  Tell Ss to read the whole paragraph silently but quickly and choose the sentence which best describes the story.

- Ask for Ss' choice (probably 2) and then tell them to read more slowly and put the verbs in brackets into either the present perfect simple or the past simple. Ss check their answers with a partner.

Answers:

1 went shopping	5 has fried	8 has not told
2 bought	6 has prepared	9 told
3 borrowed	7 has made	10 has not come
4 has put		

2

Aim: to practise the present perfect simple.

Lead in

- Ask Ss for suggestions of meals that they might make for their friends. Write a few ideas on the board.

Main activity

- Ss work with a partner to write a list of the things they have done so far, eg:
  So far I've cooked the rice and put the fish in the oven.
- Ss compare sentences with another pair. Ss make a sentence and write some of them on the board.

3

Aim: to practise time words and phrases.

Lead in

- Tell Ss that these sentences complete the story in activity 1. Ask:
  What terrible mistake has Ozzy made?
- Ss read the sentences and find the answer. Make sure that everyone agrees that *Ozzy hasn't taken the chicken out of the plastic bag.*

Main activity

- Ss read each sentence more slowly and put a suitable time word into each space. They then check their answers with a partner. Ask individual Ss to read out their answers.

Answers:

a) just   b) yet   c) since   d) ever   e) yet
f) ago   g) for   h) yet

4

Aim: to practise *What's it like?*

Lead in

- Ask individual Ss a few questions using *What ... like?* Encourage them to use more than one adjective and comparative forms, eg:
  What's your bedroom like?
  It's small but light. It isn't as big as my parents' room.

Main activity

- Ss work with a partner to ask about the things in the SB. Go around the class and help if necessary. Write a few more things on the board for Ss to ask about, eg:
  school, teachers, bikes/toys, pet animals.

5

Aim: to practise the comparative form of adverbs.

- Ask Ss to complete the sentences with three different endings and then compare their sentences with a partner.
- Write a few more sentences on the board for Ss to complete and ask them to make up some of their own, eg:
  I go to bed later when ...
  I ride my bike more slowly when ...
  I go out more often when ....
  I play basketball/tennis better when ...
  I watch television less when ...

6

Aim: to focus on the relation between sound and spelling.

- Tell Ss to work with a partner to find the pairs of words with the same sounds. Play the cassette and then ask individual Ss for the answers.

Answers:

done, fun	(won, son, sun, gun)
boat, wrote	(coat, goat, note)
meet, eat	(cheat, meat, heat, seat)
on, gone	(John, shone)
give, bit	(sit, live, fit, hit)

- Tell Ss to add some extra words to the pairs.

UNITS 4-6
CHECK UP

1

Put each verb in brackets into either the present perfect or the past simple.

Today Ozzy decided to do some cooking. He ..1.. (go shopping) this morning, and is still busy in the kitchen now. This morning he ..2.. (buy) a chicken, and ..3.. (borrow) a recipe book. So far he ..4.. (put) the chicken in the oven, and ..5.. (fry) some chips in olive oil. He ..6.. (prepare) some salad too. Unfortunately he ..7.. (make) a lot of mess on the floor. He ..8.. (not tell) his mother yet, because he wants the meal to be a surprise. He ..9.. (tell) her he was doing the washing up. His mother ..10.. (not come) into the kitchen yet.

2

You have decided to make a meal for your class. You haven't finished yet. Make a list of the things you have done so far.

3

Put one of the time words or phrases into each space. You can use a word more than once.

ago   ever   for   just   since   yet

a) Ozzy's mother came into the kitchen and said, 'Your friend Nigel Normal has … phoned.'
b) 'He left this message – Have you done your maths homework …?'
c) Ozzy said, 'Of course not. I've been at work … eight o'clock this morning.'
d) 'Have you … seen a chicken as delicious as this?'
e) His mother asked, 'Has it finished cooking … ?'
f) Ozzy replied, 'I don't know. I put it in the oven three hours …'
g) His mother said, 'Oh dear! You've cooked it … three hours!'
h) Ozzy said, 'Yes, and it isn't ready. The plastic packet hasn't disappeared …'

4

What's it like? Ask a partner about these things:

their part of town   their best friend
a place [say which one]   a book or film

5

Complete these sentences and make some true statements.

a) Time goes more quickly when you are …
b) I study harder when …
c) I dress more casually when …

6

Find pairs of words which have the same sound underlined.

d<u>o</u>ne   b<u>oa</u>t   m<u>ee</u>t   <u>o</u>n   g<u>i</u>ve
b<u>i</u>t   c<u>a</u>t   wr<u>o</u>te   g<u>o</u>ne   f<u>u</u>n

27

7 Watch this space!

could/couldn't; be able to

Space cadets

1a New language

Read Helen's interview with two space cadets and find things that Carol and Tom could and couldn't do.

LIFE IN SPACE
ON THE GROUND!

Teenagers in the USA, in Japan and in Belgium have discovered a new kind of holiday – space camp. I asked two space cadets to tell us about 'Space on Earth'.

Carol
It was a really interesting week! We lived in a building just like a space station. It was called Space Habitat. I lived with five other girls in a 'sleep station'. We could use computers there and we could do special exercises too. So it was the same as living in space. One day three of us stayed for an hour inside an Apollo space capsule. It was really small. We couldn't stand up!

Tom
We wore spacesuits too. I couldn't walk at first, but later on it was easier. We also directed a space shuttle mission – not a real one of course! We could see pictures of the Earth on the TV screens and we could talk to the astronauts in our shuttle.

Helpline

– could and couldn't

We use *could* and *couldn't* as the past tense of *can* and *can't*.

present: *Now I can swim very well.*
past: *When I was six I couldn't swim.*

pronunciation: we do not say the *l* in could /kʊd/

→ GC p5–6

1b Practice

Make some suggestions about the things Carol and Tom could and couldn't do.

– use computers to practise flying a space shuttle
– talk to aliens on the radio
– build a small rocket
– practise walking in spacesuits
– sit inside a real space shuttle
– walk in space

1c Listening

Listen to Carol and Tom and check your guesses from **1b**.

Watch this space! 7

Unit 7		Functions	Grammar
Lesson 1	Space cadets	Describing past ability	Could, couldn't
Lesson 2	Space for peace	Describing past ability	Could, couldn't
			Was/were able to [achievement]
Lesson 3	Words in action		

Word check

easily	of course	repair
fail	possible	rocket
hide	practise	room (= space)
keep	project (n)	send a message
later on	receive	successful
make a telephone call	real	whole

Lesson 1 Space cadets

1a New language

Aim: to present *could* and *couldn't* to talk about past ability.
Summary: Ss make guesses about what space cadets could and couldn't do.

Lead in

- Write the word SPACE in the middle of the board. Tell Ss to think of as many ideas as they can think of which they connect with space. Ask for suggestions in L1 and make a *network*, eg:

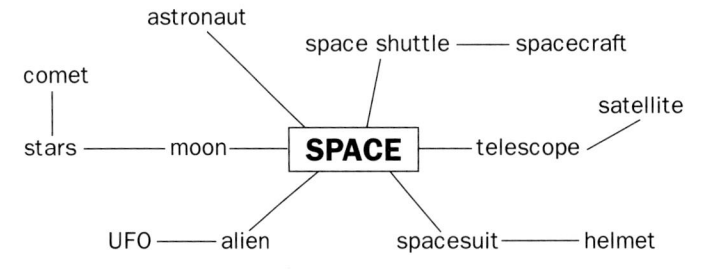

```
       astronaut
              space shuttle —— spacecraft
comet                                  satellite
   stars —— moon —— [SPACE] —— telescope
       UFO —— alien    spacesuit —— helmet
```

- Tell Ss that two children, Carol and Tom, went to a kind of summer camp where they discovered what it is like to live in space. Ss guess two things that the children did at the summer camp. Write some of their ideas on the board.

Main activity

- Ss silently read Helen's interview with Carol and Tom to find the things they could and couldn't do at the space camp. They then check their answers with a partner. Ask individual Ss for the answers.

Answers:
They could use computers.
They could do special exercises.
They couldn't stand up in the Apollo space capsule.
They couldn't walk at first in the spacesuits.
They could see pictures of the Earth on the TV screens.
They could talk to the astronauts in their shuttle.

Helpline – could and couldn't

- Explain that we use *could* as the past tense of *can* to talk about general ability, eg:
Carol could use the computers at the space camp.
They could see pictures of the Earth.
- Ask Ss:
What could and couldn't you do when you were five?
Individual Ss make suggestions, eg:
I could dress myself.
I could talk.
I couldn't read or write.
I couldn't speak any English.
I couldn't ride a two-wheel bike.
- Point out that we do not pronounce the sound /l/ in *could* /kʊd/ and /kʊdnt/.
Tell Ss to think of other words they know with silent letters, eg: *know   scissors   what*

1b Practice

Aim: to practise using *could* and *couldn't*.
Summary: Ss make guesses about other things the cadets could and couldn't do.

Lead in

- Ask Ss what they would most like to do in space. Write a list on the board, eg:
I would like to walk on the moon.
I'd like to look at the earth from a spacecraft.
Ask if the Ss think that Carol and Tom could do these things at the space camp.

Main activity

- Ss read the list of things in the SB. Ask for guesses but do not confirm yet as these are confirmed in activity 1c.

1c Listening

Aim: to listen for specific uses of *could* and *couldn't*.
Summary: Ss listen and confirm the guesses they made in activity 1b.

Lead in

- Explain that Ss will listen to an interview with Carol and Tom, and that they will hear things in a different order from the list in activity 1b.

Main activity

- Play the cassette twice. Pause the cassette after Carol finishes speaking to give Ss time to read and tick things in the list. Ss check their answers with a partner.

Answers:
They couldn't go into space in a real space shuttle.
They could eat space food.
They could use computers.
They couldn't talk to aliens.
They could build a small rocket.
They could practise walking in spacesuits.
They could sit inside a real space shuttle.
They couldn't walk in space.

Teacher's Book Unit 7

7 Watch this space!

1d Practice

Aim: to practise *could* and *couldn't*.
Summary: Ss compare space flight now with space flight in the 1960s.

Lead in

- Books closed. Give Ss this space quiz. Read the questions and possible answers twice.
  1. When did people first use telescopes?
     a) a century ago   b) two centuries ago
     c) four centuries ago
  2. What was the first animal in space?
     a) a dog   b) a monkey   c) a mouse
  3. The Americans landed on the Moon in
     a) 1963   b) 1969   c) 1971
  4. What does the word planet mean? It comes from the ancient Greek meaning:
     a) bright star   b) ball   c) wanderer
  5. Why does the moon shine?
     a) it reflects the light of the sun   b) it burns at night
     c) it reflects the light from many stars
  6. How far can you see if you look up into space?
     a) 3 kilometres   b) 10 kilometres
     c) millions of kilometres
  7. What does the word astronaut mean?
     a) sailor of the stars   b) traveller of space
     c) explorer

  Ss choose their answers.

Answers:
1 c   2 a   3 b   4 c   5 a   6 c   7 a

- Ask Ss to predict some of the changes for astronauts since the early days of space travel. Write their ideas on the board. Ask SS if they can name the astronaut in the picture. If necessary, tell Ss that *he is Yuri Gagarin, he was the first astronaut, a Russian, who went into space in 1961 – he flew round the earth once in Vostok I.*

Main activity

- Books open. Ask Ss to read the eight sentences about the early days of space silently. Ask Ss these questions to check comprehension and to practise *could*:
  How long could astronauts stay in space?
  How many astronauts could a spacecraft carry?
  Could the main spacecraft land?
  Could astronauts take off their suits?
  How could they talk to Earth?

- Ask Ss to read sentences a – f silently and match them with sentences from *EARLY DAYS OF SPACE FLIGHT*. Ss check their answers with a partner. Ask Ss for the answers:

Answers:
1 e   2 a   3 c   4 d   5 f   6 b

- Ss work with a partner to make comparisons between then and now. Use the example in the SB as a model. Go around the class and help if necessary.

Optional activity

- Ss draw a spacecraft and astronaut and label them.

Lesson 2 Space for peace

2a New language

Aim: to present *was* and *were able to*.
Summary: Ss read and find successes and failures in the texts about space exploration.

Lead in

- Write these focus questions on the board:
  What did the Apollo spacecraft do?
  How have space satellites helped life on Earth?
  When did the Russian Mir space station go into space?
  Ss read the texts and find the answers. They then check their answers with a partner. Ask individual Ss for the answers.

Answers:
1. They went to the moon.
2. We receive information about the weather and it is possible to make telephone calls more easily.
3. It went into space in 1986.

Main activity

- Ss use the information in the three paragraphs to say what people or things *are*, *were*, and *weren't able to do*. Ask individual Ss to give examples before Ss work with a partner. Go around the class and help if necessary. Check with the whole class at the end of the activity.

Suggested answers:
Apollo 13 was not able to land.
Apollo 13 was able to return to earth safely.
Thanks to space satellites we are able to receive information about the weather.
Thanks to space satellites we are able to make telephone calls more easily.
Astronauts were able to repair the giant Hubble telescope in 1993.
Many astronauts of different nationalities were able to visit the Mir space station between 1986 and 1992.
Two astronauts were able to stay there for a whole year.

Teacher's Book Unit 7

1d Practice

Find things that astronauts couldn't do in the early days of space flight, but can do now.

EARLY DAYS OF SPACE FLIGHT
1960s

1 Astronauts stayed in space for only 10 to 12 days.
2 Spacecraft carried only two or three astronauts.
3 Main part of a spacecraft stayed behind in space and only a small part landed.
4 Astronauts kept their suits on all the time.
5 Astronauts talked to the earth by radio.
6 Things sometimes went wrong – and there was no one to rescue the astronauts.

SPACE FLIGHT NOW

a Space shuttles have room for eight astronauts.
b Russian and US astronauts plan to work together in emergencies.
c The shuttle lands on earth like a normal plane.
d Inside the shuttle astronauts live and work in normal clothes.
e Astronauts stay in space for a year or more.
f There is a live television link between the spacecraft and earth.

▶ In the early days of space flight, astronauts couldn't stay in space for a long time. Now they can stay in space for a year or more.

Space for peace

2a New language

Read about three space projects. Which parts were a success? Which parts failed?

LANDING ON THE MOON

Seven Apollo spacecraft visited the moon between 1969 and 1972. One, Apollo 13, went wrong and it was not possible for the astronauts to land. Luckily it was possible for them to return to earth safely.

SATELLITES

Thanks to space satellites we receive information about the weather and it is possible to make telephone calls more easily. In 1990 the space shuttle put the giant Hubble telescope into space. It did not work well at first and in 1993 the shuttle returned to the telescope and astronauts repaired it.

7

SPACE STATIONS

The Russian Mir space station went into space in 1986. Between 1986 and 1992 it was possible for many astronauts, men and women, to visit it. They came from countries such as Japan, Hungary, Syria, India, France and Britain. Two astronauts stayed there for a whole year.

Use the information in **2a** and say what people or things are able to do, were able to do or were not able to do.

▶ *Six spacecraft were able to land on the moon. One, Apollo 13, was not able to land on the moon.*

Helpline – be able to

We can use *be able to* instead of *can* and *could*:

Astronauts are able to (= can) walk in space.

They were able to (= could) see the earth clearly.

We usually use *was/were able to* instead of *could* for something that someone could do and did do:

Astronauts were able to repair the telescope.

→ GC p6

2b Practice

You and your partner have just returned from your first mission in space. Here is your mission checklist. Tick ✓ three successful activities and put a cross ✗ next to three unsuccessful ones.

```
repair the TV satellite              ✗
talk to the astronauts in the Mir space
station                              ✓
walk in space for two hours          ☐
look at Mars with the space telescope ☐
check the forest fires in Greece and Italy ☐
take photographs of the earth        ☐
collect dangerous space rubbish      ☐
send TV messages to our friends on earth ☐
```

Work together and decide what to say to your boss.

▶ *We weren't able to repair the TV satellite. We were able to talk to the astronauts in the Mir space station.*

2c Writing

Use your answers from **2b** and write your report.

Space flight Number 1 from … [date] to… [date]. On this flight five activities were successful. We were able to … . Unfortunately five activities were unsuccessful. We weren't able to …

2d Listening

Have you seen the film *ET The Extra Terrestrial*? Listen to the story and answer the questions.

1. Why wasn't ET able to leave the earth?
2. Where was ET able to hide?
3. How was ET able to send a message to his friends?
4. How were the children able to take him to meet the spacecraft?

Word check

easily	of course	repair
fail	possible	rocket
hide	project [n]	room [= space]
keep	practise	send a message
later on	real	successful
make a telephone call	receive	whole

Watch this space! 7

Helpline – be able to

- Explain that we use *be able to* to talk about a specific ability (that is, when we do something on one occasion). This is especially true for past time, eg: *After travelling for many hours Armstrong and Aldrin landed on the moon. They were able to leave their spacecraft and do experiments on the moon. How many times were astronauts able to land on the moon?*
- Books closed. Write some key words on the board: *Apollo spacecraft   satellites   Mir space station*
- Ask Ss to work with a partner to make sentences using *be able to*.

2b Practice

Aim: to practise *be able to*.
Summary: Ss complete a check list and comment on what they *were* and *weren't able to* do.

- Ask Ss to read the mission checklist in the SB silently. Ss then work with a partner and check the activities that were successful and the activities that were unsuccessful. Ss must decide what they will say to their boss back on earth. Read aloud the examples in the SB as models. Go around the class and help if necessary.

2c Writing

Aim: to practise *be able to*.
Summary: Ss write a short report using information from activity 2b.

Main activity

- Ss write their reports individually. Go around the class and help if necessary.

Extra activity

- Ss extend their list with other ideas based on the verbs in activity 2b and write a second report.

2d Listening

Aim: to listen for detailed information.
Summary: Ss listen and answer questions using *able to*.

Lead in

- Ask Ss if they have seen *ET The Extra Terrestrial*. Then ask what other space films they have seen. Ss tell a partner about the best film they have seen.

Main activity

- Ss read the questions about the story silently. Play the cassette twice but pause after the first time to give Ss time to write their answers. Ss compare their answers with a partner. Ask individual Ss for the answers.

Answers:
1 *ET's spacecraft took off while he was walking in the woods.*
2 *He was able to hide in the bedroom of some children who become his friends.*
3 *He was able to make a radio.*
4 *They took him on their bikes.*

Optional activity

- In small groups, Ss write down some ideas for a film called *The Return of ET*. After 4 – 5 minutes ask groups for their ideas and write a few suggestions on the board.
  Ss write a short paragraph for homework.

Word check

- Write these sentences on the board:
  a Don't _____ those shoes in the rain.   (wear)
  b Bryan's TV doesn't work well, so he is _____ it. (repairing)
  c The cat is _____ behind the tree.   (hiding)
  d The Apollo 13 space project _____   (failed)
  e I don't _____ my car in a garage.   (keep)
- Ask Ss to find all the verbs in the Word check box: *(fail, hide, keep, practise, receive, repair, wear)*
- Tell the Ss to complete the sentences using the correct forms of these verbs.

7 Watch this space!

Lesson 3 Words in action

1

Aim: further practice of the present perfect simple.
Summary: Ss guess the missing words and then listen to the song to confirm their guesses.

Lead in

- Ss work with a partner to guess the missing words in each line. Ask for some suggestions but do not confirm.

Main activity

- Ss listen to the song twice and fill in the missing words. They then check their answers with a partner. Ask Ss for the answers.

Answers:
1 walked home in the
2 travelled on
3 climbed an apple
4 made a cup of
5 swum in a swimming pool
6 been late for
7 dropped your pen on the
8 sung this song

- Play the song again. Ss sing with it.

Extra activity

- With a partner Ss, write new words for the song, eg:
Have you ever swum in the sea in the rain?
Have you ever taken a photo of an express train?

2

Aim: further practice of the present perfect simple.
Summary: Ss to match words that go together and make phrases.

Ss match the words in lists A and B. Check answers.

Answers:
have a great time or have lots of money
take a photo
leave my books at home
spend lots of money
go to a football match

Ss work with a partner and choose phrases to write complete sentences. Go around the class and help if necessary. Ask individual Ss for the answers:

Answers:
a) I've left my books at home.
b) I've spent lots of money.
c) I've had a great time.
d) I've taken a photo.
e) I've been to a football match.

Extra activity

- Ss either think of other ways to end the sentences or complete the sentences with these phrases:
just come from the dentist.
lent my dictionary to my sister.
never danced so much before!
forgotten to buy any bread.
bought lots of postcards.

3

Aim: further practice of the present perfect simple.
Summary: Ss give reasons why they *can't do* things using *I've lost*.

- Explain the rules of the game. Team members take turns to begin sentences. The first team has 20 seconds to make up a sentence beginning, eg:
I can't find my shoes ...
The second team has 20 seconds to complete the sentence, eg:
because the dog has taken them.
Teams score one point for completing a sentence successfully. If a team member is not able to complete the sentence successfully (or in the time allowed), then the team who began the sentence, score one point.

- Play the *I've lost it game* for about 8 – 10 minutes. Make sure that everyone has a turn.

4

Aim: to revise nouns with unusual singular or plural forms.
Summary: Ss complete sentences.

- Ss work individually but compare answers with a partner. Ask individual Ss for the complete sentences.

Answers:
a) 3   b) 4   c) 5   d) 1   e) 2

- Ask Ss to tell you about the two types of words. If necessary, explain that the words *people* and *police* may look singular but they are, in fact, plural words. The words *information*, *weather* and *food* are singular and uncountable in English (but they may not be in other languages). Other examples of this type of word are *advice, furniture, spaghetti, fruit*, eg:
The fruit is on the table.

Extra activity

- Tell Ss to work with a partner to complete the sentences with different endings, eg:
The information you need is on the map.

WORDS in ACTION

1 Before you listen to the song, guess the missing words in each line.

Oh, have you ever … ?
Oh, have you ever … ?
Oh, have you ever … ?
Have you ever .1. rain?
Have you .2. an express train?
Have you ever .3. tree?
Have you ever .4. tea?
Have you .5. pool?
Have you ever .6. school?
Have you ever .7. floor?
Have you ever .8. before?
Oh, have you ever … ?
Oh, have you ever … ?

Listen to the song and write the missing words. Listen to the rest of the song. Then sing the song.

2 Make a phrase with a verb from list A and words from list B.

A have   take   leave   spend   go to
B lots of money   a photo   a great time   my books at home   a football match

Use each phrase to complete one of these sentences. Put the verb in the present perfect.

a) I can't do the exercise. I've …
b) I've just been shopping. I've …
c) Thanks for inviting me to the party. I've …
d) Now we'll remember this trip for ever. I've …
e) I'm sorry I'm late. I've …

3 **The I've lost it game**   The class plays in two teams. A member of Team A says a sentence beginning:

▶ *I can't …*

A member of Team B completes the sentence with:

▶ *… because I've lost …*

Team A: *I can't do my homework …*
Team B: *… because I've lost my book.*

4 Complete each part sentence with one of the endings.

a) All the people …
b) The information you need …
c) The weather …
d) The food for lunch …
e) The police …

1) … is in the fridge.
2) … are coming soon.
3) … are waiting in a queue.
4) … is in this book.
5) … in this country is very good.

8 Home and away

tag questions: present simple, past simple, be, can, have got

Animal time

1a 📼 New language

Helen's class had a quiz in their biology class. Before the quiz, Helen checked her knowledge of animals with Nick. Match the dialogues with the pictures.

> **Helpline**
> **– tag questions for checking**
>
> Positive statement + negative tag:
>
> It *lives* in China, *doesn't it*?
> – Yes, that's right./No, it doesn't.
>
> Negative statement + positive tag:
>
> They *don't talk, do they*?
> – No, they don't./Yes, they do.
>
> be   You *are* ready, *aren't you*?
>   It *isn't* white, *is it*?
>
> have got   It's *got* one hump, *hasn't it*?
>   They *haven't got* feathers, *have they*?
>
> can   It *can't* fly, *can it*?
>   It *can* run fast, *can't it*.
>   → GC p6

1 It lives in China, doesn't it?   Yes, that's right.
2 It runs very fast, doesn't it?   Yes, it does. At 70 km an hour!
3 They don't live at the North
  Pole, do they?   No, they don't.
4 They don't talk, do they?   No, they don't.

1b Practice

Check the facts with a partner by asking a positive or negative tag question.

1 A camel has got only one hump.
2 An African elephant is larger than an Indian elephant.
3 Ostriches put their heads in the sand when they are afraid.
4 Swans are always white.
5 The hummingbird is the smallest bird.
6 Giraffes can sleep standing up.
7 Bats have got feathers.
8 Most whales sing very loudly.

Home and away 8

Unit 8		Functions	Grammar
Lesson 1	Animal time	Checking information	Question tags with present simple, be, can, have got
Lesson 2	What happened?	Checking information	Question tags with past simple
Lesson 3	CHRIS 3		

Word check

afraid	dustbin	lock (v)
ask the way	feather	loudly
as usual	giraffe	tap
bring	invitation	turn off
catch a bus	key	whale
disaster	knowledge	

Lesson 1 Animal time

1a New language

Aim: to present question tags with the present simple.
Summary: Ss check facts about animals using question tags.

Lead in

- Tell Ss to look at the photos and name the animals and birds. What do they know about the animals and birds?

Some information:
Giant pandas live in the bamboo forests of China and there are not many left.
Penguins are swimming birds. They can't fly as their wings are like flippers.
Chimpanzees are mammals that belong to the same group of animals as humans.
Ostriches are the largest living bird. They live in herds in Africa. The females lay large white eggs in a nest dug in the sand. They can live to be 50 years old.

- Explain that Helen is going to have a biology quiz. She has asked her friend, Nick, to ask her questions.

Main activity

- Tell Ss to look at the photos and match them with the questions and answers.

Answers:
1 panda   2 ostrich   3 penguin   4 chimpanzees

- Say that Helen is nearly sure that she knows the information but she is checking with Nick. Read Helen's tag questions (with level/falling not rising intonation) and tell Ss to repeat them together and individually.
It lives in China, doesn't it?
It runs very fast, doesn't it?
They don't live at the North Pole, do they?
They don't talk, do they?

- Ss practise the questions and answers with a partner.

Helpline – tag questions for checking

- Explain the form, meaning and intonation.

Form: The question tag contains *be*, *have* or a helping verb + personal pronoun, eg:
can't you?   is it?   haven't they?
If the sentence is positive, the tag is negative, eg:
Helen's got a biology quiz, hasn't she?
If the sentence is negative, the tag is positive, eg:
They don't live in Spain, do they?
The tag question uses the same verb as the verb in the main part of the sentence, eg:
I haven't got a lot of time before the test, have I?
You can climb up dormant volcanoes, can't you?
If the main part of the sentence includes *be*, the tag questions uses *be*, eg: *Your computer is fast, isn't it?*
But note: *I'm early, aren't I?*
If the sentence does not include *be*, *have* or a helping verb, we use the helping verb *do* in the tag question, eg:
Ostriches run very fast, don't they?
Meaning: To ask for confirmation of something we are not sure about or to ask for agreement. A tag question means something like: *Is this true?* or *Do you agree?*
Intonation: With level or falling intonation the sentence is more like a statement, not a question, eg:
You know Helen, don't you?
With rising intonation, the sentence is like a real question, eg: *You haven't got my grammar book, have you?*

1b Practice

Aim: to practise tag questions.
Summary: Ss check more facts about animals.

Lead in

- Write these animals on the board:
  camel   African elephant   swan   hummingbird
  giraffe   bat   whale
  Ask Ss what they know about them.

Main activity

- Tell Ss to read all the sentences silently first and to think about the correct tag question for each one. Ask two Ss to do the first sentence as an example, eg:
  S1: *A camel has got only one hump, hasn't it?*
  S2: *No, not always.*

- Ss continue to check the facts with a partner.

- Play the cassette so that Ss can check their tag questions (and the correct intonation).

Answers:
1 *hasn't it?*   no
2 *isn't it?*   yes
3 *don't they?*   no
4 *aren't they?*   no (some swans are black)
5 *isn't it?*   yes
6 *can't they?*   yes
7 *haven't they?*   no
8 *don't they?*   yes (or at least, they make a singing noise underwater)

Teacher's Book Unit 8

8 Home and away

1c The yes/no game

Aim: further practice of tag questions.
Summary: Ss play a game in which questions must be formed with tags, and answers must not contain *yes* or *no*.

- Explain the rules of the game. Team A asks a player from Team B up to ten tag questions; the player must answer without saying *yes* or *no*.
  Team B then asks a player from Team A up to ten tag questions.
  Teams score one point if their player does not say *yes* or *no* after ten tag questions. If the player does say *yes* or *no*, then the other team scores one point.

- Before you start the game, tell everyone to prepare some questions. Everyone should ask at least one question during the game.

- Play the game for about 8 – 10 minutes.

1d Listening

Aim: to listen for gist.
Summary: Ss identify the main topic of each dialogue.

Lead in

- Tell Ss to guess what some of the tag questions in each dialogue will be. Do not confirm their guesses.

Main activity

- Ask Ss to listen to the dialogues twice and match the explanations to the dialogues. Pause after each dialogue. Ss check their answers with a partner. Ask individual Ss for the answers.

  Answers:
  a - 4
  b - 5
  c - 2
  d - 1
  e - 3

- Play the cassette again but pause before the tag questions for Ss to say the tag.

Optional activity

- Write the following first lines of some dialogues on the board:
  1 *Excuse me, this is the way to the ...*
  2 *You haven't seen my ...*
  3 *Chris! That is you, ...*
  Ss continue them (orally) with a partner. Tell them to use at least two tag questions in each dialogue. They then write the dialogues for homework.

Lesson 2 What happened?

2a New language

Aim: to present tag questions in past simple sentences.
Summary: Ss use pictures to make guesses about three stories involving the Odds.

Lead in

- Tell Ss to complete these sentences about the Normals with tag questions:
  The Normals don't do strange things, ... ?
  The Normals haven't got a kangaroo, ... ?
  Nigel Normal doesn't play with Ozzy Odd, ... ?
  Mr Normal has never washed his roof, ... ?
  The Normals are very boring people, ... ?
  Nothing funny happens to them, ... ?

Main activity

- Ask Ss to look at the pictures of the Odd family. They work with a partner and try to guess the rest of each story. Ask for some suggestions, eg:
  1 They left the hotel and forgot to pay their bill.
  2 They forgot to take extra petrol on the boat.

- Read the dialogue aloud. Ask:
  Which picture does it match and why?

- Make sure that everyone agrees that the dialogue comes from story 3. Ask Ss to practise the dialogue with a partner.

- Books closed. Write a few key words and phrases on the board:
  good time   lock door   windows   beach
  Ask Ss to practise the dialogue from memory.

Helpline – past simple tag questions

- Ask Ss to tell you when we use tag questions. Make sure that everyone agrees that we use them to check some information, eg:
  You didn't give Peter my ball, did you?

- Explain that the rules for forming the tag question in the past simple are the same as for the present simple, that is, with the helping verb *do* in the past tense (*did*), eg:
  Helen interviewed some children about a space holiday camp, didn't she?
  Nick made a terrible mess in the kitchen, didn't he?
  You didn't leave your school bags on the bus, did you?

- Remind them that with some verbs we use the same verb in the tag as in the statement, eg:
  She wasn't at school today, was she?
  He could swim when he was eight, couldn't he?

1c The yes/no game

You mustn't say yes or no. One player asks tag questions and you must answer *That's right/That's correct* or *That's wrong/That isn't correct*. When you say yes or no you are out of the game. Use these questions and think of questions of your own.

▶ *Your name's ..., isn't it?   You like/don't like ...
You've got/You haven't got ...*

1d Listening

Listen to each dialogue and decide what it is about. Write the letter for the dialogue next to one of the explanations.

1 asking the way in the street
2 meeting an old friend from school
3 looking for the right coat
4 catching a bus in a strange town
5 meeting a friend's family for the first time

What happened?

2a New language

Lots of strange things have happened to the Odds. Here are pictures from three stories. Make some guesses about the rest of the story for each picture.

Read the dialogue and decide which story it comes from.

Mr Odd: Right, let's go. We're going to have a really good time.
Mrs Odd: You locked the door, didn't you dear?
Mr Odd: Yes.
Mrs Odd: And you didn't leave the windows open, did you?
Mr Odd: No, of course I didn't. Don't worry about the house. Let's enjoy our day at Funworld.

Helpline
– past simple tag questions

You *locked* the door, *didn't you*?

You *didn't leave* the windows open, *did you*?

→ GC p6

2b Practice

Here are some more things that Mrs Odd told members of the family to do before they left the house. Did they do them? Look at picture 3 in **2a** and check with a partner by asking tag questions.

1 Turn the lights off in all the rooms.
▶ *Mr Odd didn't turn the lights off, did he?*
  – *No, he didn't.*

2 Put the rubbish in the dustbin.

3 Bring the key with you.

4 Turn off the taps in the bathroom.

5 Take the kangaroo next door.

2c Practice

Here are some more disasters. Ask your partner a check question for each situation. Use positive or negative tags.

1 It's beginning to rain. Ask your partner about the umbrella. (bring)
▶ *You brought the umbrella, didn't you?/You didn't bring the umbrella, did you?*
  Sorry, I forgot!
2 Nobody has arrived at your party yet. Ask your partner about the invitations. (send)
3 You and your partner are waiting outside his/her house. The door is locked. Ask your partner about his/her keys. (forget)
4 You are on holiday. You have taken lots of photos. Something is wrong with the camera. Ask your partner about the film. (put)
5 You are in a queue for tickets at the cinema. Ask your partner about money. (bring)
6 You are lost in the mountains. Ask your partner about the map. (remember)

2d Writing

Here are some notes about the Odds' house disaster. Use them to write a paragraph about what happened.

> Mrs Odd tells the family to do some things – they don't do them – they go to Funworld – the Odds enjoy themselves – they arrive home – all the lights are on – water on the floor – rubbish bags – the kangaroo

Write a similar paragraph about another disaster.

Word check

afraid	dustbin	lock [v]
ask the way	feather	loudly
as usual	giraffe	tap
bring	invitation	turn off
catch a bus	key	whale
disaster	knowledge	

Home and away 8

2b Practice

Aim: to practise tag questions in past simple sentences.
Summary: Ss use pictures to check whether the Odds did certain things.

Lead in

- Write on the board: *Going away for the weekend*. Ask Ss what they and their parents must remember to do before they go away. Write some of Ss' ideas on the board.

Main activity

- Ss look at the pictures and read Mrs Odd's instructions Ask:
  Did the Odds do the things?
  Ss check with a partner by asking a tag question as in the example in the SB, eg:
  Olive didn't put the rubbish in the dustbin, did she?
- Go around the class and check that Ss are forming the tag questions correctly. Ask Ss for the answers:

Answers:
2 Olive didn't put the rubbish in the dustbin, did she?
3 Mr Odd didn't bring the key with him, did he?
4 Ozzy didn't turn off the taps in the bathroom, did he?
5 Olive didn't take the kangaroo next door, did she?

Extra activity

- Books closed. Say a key word from each sentence. Individual Ss say the whole sentence and tag question, eg:
  T: *kangaroo*
  S: *Olive didn't take the kangaroo next door, did she?*

2c Practice

Aim: to practise positive and negative tag questions in past simple sentences.
Summary: Ss make check questions for situations.

Lead in

- Books closed. Write on the board: *More disasters*. Ask Ss to describe some disasters that have happened or could happen to them.

Main activity

- Tell Ss to read the sentences in the SB and see if the disasters are similar to the ones they talked about.
- Ss work with a partner and take turns to ask questions for the situations. Go around the class and help if necessary. Ask pairs of Ss to roleplay the situations.

Possible answers:
2 You did send the invitations, didn't you?
  You didn't send the invitations, did you?
3 You forgot your keys, didn't you?
  You didn't forget your keys, did you?
4 I/you put the film into the camera correctly, didn't I/you?
  I/you didn't put the film into the camera correctly, did I/you?
5 You brought some money, didn't you?
  You didn't bring any money, did you?
6 You remembered the map, didn't you?
  You didn't remember the map, did you?

- The second version, negative main clause and positive tag, sounds more accusing.

2d Writing

Aim: to write a short guided story using the past simple.
Summary: Ss use notes to write a paragraph.

Lead in

- Tell Ss to work with a partner and exchange some ideas for their paragraphs. Ask some Ss for their ideas and write a few suggestions on the board.

Main activity

- Ss work individually but exchange paragraphs with a partner when they finish. Their partner can make suggestions for changes and additions. Go around the class and help if necessary.
- After you have dealt with any problems, Ss write a similar story using their own ideas. They may need help with vocabulary.

Optional activity

- Ss write about or record their own disaster stories. Ss can then read or listen to each other's disaster stories.

Word check

- Ask Ss to find all the nouns in the Word check box: (*disaster, dustbin, feather, giraffe, invitation, key, knowledge, tap, whale*)
- Tell Ss to think of an adjective to go with each of the nouns, eg:
  terrible disaster
- Ask Ss to write five sentences using their adjective + noun pairs.

8 Home and away

Lesson 3 CHRIS Episode 3

Aims: to match sentences with visual clues; to listen for specific information; to read for general understanding; to fill in missing information using context.

The story so far:

Main activity

- Ss work in pairs and answer the questions. Ask individual Ss for the answers.

Answers:
1 Go to the NT and find the person with A.
2 The twins received an envelope with a map inside it.
3 They are going to the National Theatre.

1

Lead in

- Tell Ss to cover the words and look only at the pictures. Ask them where Sandy and Peter are and who they are talking to. Ss then try to guess what the people are saying. Do not confirm yet.

Main activity

- Ss match the lines of dialogue with the speech bubbles. Ask individual Ss for the answers.

Answers:
Picture 1: Peter - d, Anna - f
Picture 2: Peter - e, Anna - b
Picture 3: Sandy - a, Anna - c

Extra activity

- Ss work in groups of three and practise the dialogue. They should then cover the lines of dialogue and practise the dialogue again.

2

Lead in

- Tell Ss to read the four possible answers in the SB. Ask them to predict what Sandy and Peter decide to do.

Main activity

- Play the conversation between Sandy and Peter twice. Ss then check the answer with a partner. Tell Ss to put up their hands if they think the answer is a). Repeat this procedure with b), c) and d). Play the cassette again if a third or more of the class have not yet found the right answer c).

Optional activity

- Write the following True/False statements on the board:
1 Peter and Sandy are not sure if Anna is telling the truth. (F)
2 The name of one of the plays is Arms and the Man. (T)
3 They went to a restaurant called Patricia's on Sandy's birthday. (F)
4 CHRIS helps them find the answer. (T)
5 Cleopatra's Needle is in Egypt. (F)
- Ss decide if the statements are true or false. Play the tape again if necessary.

3

Lead in

- Books closed. Tell Ss to predict what Sandy has written in her diary about the story so far. Do not confirm any ideas yet.

Main activity

- Ask Ss to read the whole paragraph silently before they fill in the missing information. They then read it again and fill in the missing words. Ss check answers with a partner. Ask individual Ss for the answers.

Answers:
1 Friday   5 computer   10 map
2 school   6 clues   11 National Theatre
3 Chris   7 questions   12 A
4 there   8 answers   13 three
              9 envelope   14 Cleopatra's Needle

Extra activity 1

- Ss work with a partner to roleplay a conversation about the story so far. Student A is Sandy or Peter and Student B is a friend of theirs. They talk about what has happened in the story so far.

Extra activity 2

- Books closed. Ss tell a partner everything they can remember about Chris, Mrs Jackson, Anna, Patricia's and Cleopatra's Needle.

CHRIS

Episode 3

The story so far:

1. What did the second message say?
2. What did the twins receive?
3. Where are they going?

1 Match the lines of dialogue to the empty speech bubbles.

a) Do you know this man? He's our brother, Chris. And he's disappeared.
b) My name's Anna. But why do you want to know?
c) Sorry, I've never seen him before.
d) What's on at the theatre this week?
e) Excuse me, but what's your name?
f) There are two plays on this week: Arms and the Man and Anthony and Cleopatra.

2 Sandy and Peter go home and talk about the puzzle. Listen to them talking. What do they decide? Tick ✓ the answer.

a) Anna is the person they are looking for.
b) They are looking for a man, but they don't know his name.
c) They find the answer and it is the name of a place.
d) The person they are looking for is called Patricia.

3 Do you remember the story so far? Look back if necessary. Then fill in the missing information in Sandy's diary.

It all started on ..1.. when I came home from ..2.. I went to see ..3.. as usual but he wasn't there. Peter was ..4.. and he showed me a ..5... It spoke to us and gave us some ..6... We asked it ..7.. and it told us the ..8.., but they were difficult to understand. Then an ..9.. arrived with a ..10.. inside it. We decided to go to the ..11.. to look for someone called ..12... We found ..13.. possible answers so we went home to think about it. In the end the answer wasn't a person at all. Tomorrow we are going back to the river to visit ..14...

CONSOLIDATION 1

1 Ask a partner to complete the questionnaire.

a) Where did you go on holiday last summer?
b) What did you spend most of the time doing?
c) What did you do every morning, afternoon and evening?
d) Was it a good holiday?
e) What did you enjoy doing most?
f) Did you meet any interesting people?
g) Did you visit any interesting places?
h) Why was it interesting?
i) Describe something that happened to you.

2 Write two paragraphs using the information from your partner's answers. Use this outline.

> Last summer [write a name] ... spent most .... In the morning he/she usually ... and in the afternoon .... In the evening he/she .... It was a good holiday and he/she enjoyed .... He/she also met ... called ... and visited .... This place was interesting because .... One day ...
> [describe what happened]

3 Complete each dialogue.

a) **A:** Why didn't you bring your book today?
   B: I ...
   A: Did you look everywhere for it?
   B: Yes, but it has disappeared.
b) **A:** What ... at eight o'clock last night?
   B: I was listening to the radio at home.
   A: And which programme ...?
   B: I can't remember.
c) **A:** Do you like swimming?
   B: Not in winter! The water isn't ...
   A: I agree. It's too ... for me too.
d) **A:** Thanks for lending me that book.
   B: ... yet?
   A: No, I haven't. I ... half of it so far.
   B: Can you bring it back next week?

4 Put each verb in brackets into either the past simple or past continuous.

Last week, while I ..1.. (walk) to the shops near my house, I ..2.. (see) an old man. He ..3.. (stand) at the side of the road and he ..4.. (carry) a heavy bag. There was a lot of traffic and it was difficult to cross the road. I ..5.. (decide) to help him. I ..6.. (pick up) his bag and ..7.. (start) to help him across the road. Just then a bus ..8.. (stop) near us. The old man ..9.. (not want) to cross the road! He ..10.. (wait) for the bus!

5 Put the verb in brackets into the past simple or the present perfect.

a) How are you? I ... (not see) you since the summer.
b) When ... (you buy) your new skateboard?
c) ... (the kangaroo/eat) its dinner yet?
d) I ... (just buy) a new CD.
e) Nick ... (start) at this school five years ago.
f) Could you help me, please? I ... (lose) my bus ticket.
g) Nick ... (know) Helen for five years and they are good friends.
h) Where ... (you/be) last night at seven o'clock?

Consolidation 1 Units 1–8

1

Aim: further practice of the past simple.
Summary: Ss ask and answer questions in pairs.

Main activity

- Books closed. Ask Ss to predict the questions someone might ask them in a questionnaire about holidays. Write some of Ss' questions on the board.
- Ss read the questions and compare them with their guesses. They then ask each other the questions in the SB and write short answers. Early finishers change partners.

2

Aim: written practice of the past simple.
Summary: Ss write a paragraph about their partner's holiday.

Main activity

- Ss work individually to write a guided paragraph about their partner's holiday using the information from the questionnaire in activity 1. Ss show their partner the paragraph for changes or corrections. Go around the class and help if necessary. Early finishers can write a paragraph about their own holiday.

3

Aim: revision tenses.
Summary: Ss complete dialogues.

Main activity

- Ask Ss to read each dialogue before they complete the missing parts. They then check their answers with a partner. Ask individual Ss for the answers and write some of their suggestions on the board.

Possible answers:
a) B: I've lost it./I couldn't find it.
b) A: What were you doing at eight o'clock last night? And which programme were you listening to?
c) B: The water isn't warm enough. A: I agree. It's too cold for me too.
d) B: Have you finished it yet? A: I've only read half of it so far.

Extra activity

- Ask Ss to practise reading the dialogues with a partner.

4

Aim: further practice of the past simple and the past continuous.
Summary: Ss complete a paragraph with the appropriate forms of verbs.

Lead in

- Ask Ss to read the paragraph silently and quickly to get the gist of the story. Ask individual Ss to say briefly what happens.

Main activity

- Ss read the paragraph more slowly and put the verbs into the correct tense. They then check their answers with a partner. Ask individual Ss for the answers and write them on the board.

Answers:
1 was walking   5 decided   8 stopped
2 saw   6 picked   9 did not want
3 was standing   7 started   10 was waiting
4 was carrying

Extra activity

- Ask Ss to re-tell the story from the point of view of the old man or a passer-by.

5

Aim: further practice of the past simple and present perfect simple.
Summary: Ss complete sentences with the appropriate forms of verbs.

Main activity

- Ask Ss to read each sentence carefully to decide if they should use the past simple or the present perfect simple. They then check their answers with a partner. Ask individual Ss for the answers and write them on the board.

Answers:
a) I haven't seen   e) Nick started
b) did you buy   f) I've lost
c) Has the kangaroo eaten g) has known
d) I've just bought   h) were you

Optional activity

- Ask Ss to make a list of words that we usually find with the past simple and words we use with the present perfect simple (some are in the activity), eg:
past simple: ago, yesterday, last night etc
present perfect simple: just, so far, yet, since, for

Teacher's Book Consolidation 1 Units 1–8

Consolidation 1 Units 1–8

6

Aim: further practice of the comparative and superlative forms of adjectives.
Summary: Ss rewrite sentences.

Main activity

- Ss rewrite the sentences using the words given at the end of the sentences in the SB.

Answers:
a) Ozzy isn't as tall as Olive.
b) The last record was better than this one.
c) You are too young to watch this film.
d) This bike is the cheapest./This is the cheapest bike.
e) I'm not tall enough.
f) This team is the worst. This is the worst team.

Extra activity

- Ss make some true sentences using some of the comparative and superlative adjectives from the activity, eg:
Our teacher isn't as tall as Christine.

7

Aim: further practice of the present perfect simple.
Summary: Ss write sentences about what Helen has and hasn't done.

Main activity

- Ss write a sentence for each thing in Helen's list. They then check their sentences with a partner. Ask individual Ss for the answers and write them on the board.

Answers:
b) She hasn't been to the library.
c) She hasn't checked Nick's article.
d) She has bought some writing paper.
e) She hasn't cleaned her room.
f) She has made some sandwiches.
g) She hasn't written a letter to Vicky.
h) She has phoned Nick.

Optional activity

- Ask Ss to write sentences about what they have done so far today and what they haven't done (but want to do), eg:
I've spoken to the Maths teacher about the test tomorrow.
I haven't returned my library books yet.

8

Aim: further practice of *be able to*.
Summary: Ss rewrite sentences.

Main activity

- Ask Ss to read the sentences silently and to rewrite them using *was/were able to* or *wasn't/weren't able to*.

Answers:
a) The table was heavy and I wasn't able to lift it.
b) Luckily I was able to get two tickets for the concert.
c) The police weren't able to find the missing boy.
d) After the play I was able to speak to some of the actors.
e) We weren't able to climb the pyramids that day.

9

Aim: further practice of question tags.
Summary: Ss complete sentences with question tags.

Main activity

- Ask Ss to read the sentences silently and to complete them with question tags. Ss then check tags with a partner. Ask individual Ss for the answers and write them on the board.

Answers:
a) haven't you?
b) aren't you?
c) didn't you?
d) aren't you?
e) didn't you?
f) don't you?

Optional activity

- Ss write five sentences with question tags to ask a partner, eg:
You're coming to the basket ball match on Saturday, aren't you?

10

Aim: further practice of adjective order.
Summary: Ss order words and make sentences.

- Ss work with a partner to reorder the words and make sentences. Ask different pairs for the answers and write them on the board.

Answers:
a) I have seen lots of large French towns.
b) I think French people speak more quickly than English.
c) I forgot to take my black leather jacket.
d) Most people here eat earlier than us in the evening.
e) I have bought a fantastic pair of white cotton trousers.

Extra activity

- Ss write two or three jumbled sentences (containing more than one adjective) for their partner to reorder.

6 Rewrite each sentence so that it contains the word or words given.

a) Olive is taller than Ozzy. (not as)
b) This record is not as good as the last one. (better)
c) You can't watch this film. You are not old enough. (young)
d) All the other bikes are more expensive. (cheapest)
e) I can't reach that shelf. I am too short. (enough)
f) All the other teams are better than this one. (worst)

7 This is Helen's list of things to do today. It is now lunchtime. She has ticked the things she has done. Write a sentence for each list, saying what she has done so far and what she hasn't done.

a) take the dog for a walk	✓
b) go to the library	
c) check Nick's article	
d) buy some writing paper	✓
e) clean my room	
f) make some sandwiches	✓
g) write a letter to Vicky	
h) phone Nick	✓

▶ *She has taken the dog for a walk.*

8 Rewrite each sentence using *was/were able to* or *wasn't/weren't able to*.

a) The table was heavy and it was impossible for me to lift it.
b) Luckily I managed to get two tickets for the concert.
c) The police tried to find the missing boy but they were unsuccessful.
d) After the play I managed to speak to some of the actors.
e) It wasn't possible for us to climb the pyramids that day.

9 Helen's mother talked to her before she went to stay with her penfriend, Annie. Write a question tag at the end of each sentence.

a) You've got your passport, …?
b) You're leaving on Saturday, …?
c) You wrote down Annie's address, …?
d) You're taking your camera, …?
e) You phoned Annie, …?
f) You want to go on this trip, …?

10 Helen wrote a letter from France. Put each set of words in order so that it makes a sentence.

a) of towns seen French have lots I large
b) quickly English more people I speak than think French people
c) black to I jacket forgot take my leather
d) earlier us evening most eat than people here the in
e) white bought pair have of trousers fantastic cotton I a

9 Arranging the future

present continuous: future use; invitations; would like;
I don't think so, I'm afraid I can't

What's he doing on Monday?

1a New language

Bryan Gibbs is Nick and Helen's favourite footballer. They want to interview him, but it is difficult to find him! What does Bryan's manager tell them? What is Bryan doing on Monday, Tuesday and Wednesday next week?

Helen: Can we interview him on Monday morning?
Manager: I'm sorry, but he's opening the new Sports Superstore in Bristol on Monday morning.
Nick: And what's he doing on Monday afternoon?

Monday morning
Open new Sports Superstore

Monday afternoon
Drive home to Manchester

Tuesday morning
Football training

Tuesday afternoon
Make a TV programme

Wednesday morning
Visit the Children's Hospital

Wednesday afternoon
Give an interview on the radio

> **Helpline** – present continuous: future use
>
> We can use the present continuous for the future when we describe a definite arrangement:
>
> What is Bryan doing on Monday morning?   He's opening the Sports Superstore in Bristol.
>
> → GC p7

38

Arranging the future 9

Unit 9		Functions	Grammar
Lesson 1	What's he doing on Monday?	Describing social arrangements	Present continuous: future use
Lesson 2	Would you like to ...?	Making and responding to invitations	Would like, I don't think so, I'm afraid I can't
Lesson 3	Words in action		

Word check

accept	give an interview	politely refuse
arrangement	go out on a trip	reply (v)
excuse (n)	hairdresser's	rest
explain	hospital	study for
factory	in secret	
future	keep trying	

Lesson 1 What's he doing on Monday?

1a New language

Aim: to present the present continuous for future use for a definite arrangement.
Summary: Ss roleplay an interview in which they try to make an appointment.

Lead in

- Show Ss pictures of well-known sportsmen and women. Ask:
  What do they do when they are not training or doing their sport?

Main activity

- Books open. Ss look at the picture of Bryan Gibbs. Read or play the introduction. Write these focus questions on the board:
  Why do Helen and Nick want to interview Bryan Gibbs? (For 'Brilliant' and because he is their favourite footballer.)
  Why isn't this easy? (He's very busy.)
- Ask:
  T: *What's he doing on Monday morning?*
  S: *He's opening the new Sports Superstore in Bristol.*
  Emphasize that *Monday morning* is in the future, ie next Monday.
- Ss look at the pictures. Ask a pair of Ss to ask and answer a question about Monday afternoon:
  S1: *What's he doing on Monday afternoon?*
  S2: *He's driving home to Manchester.*
  Continue in this way for all the pictures.

Helpline – present continuous: future use

- Say:
  Bryan's making a TV programme on Tuesday afternoon. Tuesday afternoon is in the future. We can sometimes use the present continuous to talk about the future. We often use it for a definite arrangement or an appointment, ie: Bryan has made an appointment with the TV studio for Tuesday afternoon.

- Ask Ss to look at the pictures again but to cover the words. Ss work with a partner to say what Bryan is doing next week.

Teacher's Book Unit 9

9 Arranging the future

1b Practice

Aim: to practise the present continuous for future use.
Summary: Ss continue the questions from activity 1a using Bryan's diary.

Lead in

- Books closed. Ask:
  What other things is Bryan doing on the other days next week?
  Ss guess.

Main activity

- Books open. Ask Ss to read the other information about Bryan's plans for next week. Emphasise again that this refers to the future. Ss work with a partner to continue the dialogue in activity 1a; S1 is Helen or Nick and S2 is Bryan's manager. Ss then change roles and practise the dialogue again. Go around the class and help if necessary.

Extra activity

- Books closed. Ss make True/False sentences about Bryan for their partners, eg:
  S1: Bryan's visiting a sportswear factory on Monday morning.
  S2: No, he isn't. He's opening a Sports Superstore.

1c Practice

Aim: further practice of the present continuous for future use.
Summary: Ss roleplay an interview with a famous person and ask about his/her arrangements.

Lead in

- Take out your diary. Tell the class that they must find a time when you are free for an interview with their school newspaper, eg:
  S1: Can we interview you on Monday morning?
  T: No, I'm sorry but I'm teaching all morning.
  Make up excuses using the present continuous tense, eg:
  going to the dentist   meeting a friend
  visiting your parents etc

Main activity

- Ask for the names of famous people and write some suggestions on the board. Ss may then choose to be one of these or another famous person. Draw a page of a diary with all the days of the week on the board.
- Ask Ss to write detailed plans for every day (morning and afternoon) next week. They must not show their diary to any other Ss. They then work with a partner and take turns to interview each other about the coming week. Early finishers find another partner to interview or write some sentences about their partner's week.

Extra activity

- Individual Ss read out some of their appointments to the class. Other Ss try to guess what the famous person does and, if possible, who it is.

1d Listening

Aim: further focus on the present continuous for future use.
Summary: Ss listen and decide what each person is doing on Saturday.

Lead in

- Ss guess what the four children are doing on Saturday.

Main activity

- Ask Ss to listen to the three conversations twice. Ss write a sentence for each conversation to say what the children are doing. They then check their answers with a partner. Ask individual Ss for the answers.

Answers:
Nick's visiting his cousins (and uncle and aunt).
Helen's studying or revising for tests.
Vicky and George are going to an (Australian) beach party.

Lesson 2 Would you like to ...?

2a New language

Aim: to present *Would you like to ...?* for making invitations.
Summary: Ss match invitations with events.

Lead in

- Books closed. Ask:
  What kind of things do you invite friends to do with you? Do you go to the cinema? Do you play basketball?
- Write a few of Ss' suggestions on the board.

Main activity

- Ss read the invitations in the SB silently and match them with the mini dialogues. They then check with a partner. Ask individual Ss for the answers.

Answers:
1 b)   2 c)   3 a)

- Ask Ss to read the mini dialogues again to see if the person accepts the invitation (says *yes*/agrees to go) or refuses (says *no*/cannot go). Ask:
  How does the friend accept or refuse?
- Ask Ss to find the exact words.

Answers:
a) accepts – 'Good idea.'
b) accepts – 'I'd love to!'
c) refuses – 'I'm afraid I can't. I'm going out with my family.'

Helpline – inviting

- Ask Ss to find the questions in the three dialogues which are invitations. Ask:
  What language do the speakers use?
  Make sure that everyone agrees that the speakers ask
  Would you like to ...?

1b Practice

Read the information about next Thursday and Friday. Continue the dialogue in **1a**.

```
Thursday morning   9.00
   visit sportswear factory and
   try on new kit
Thursday afternoon   2.30
   train in secret for
   Saturday's match
Friday morning   10.30
   return to Manchester
Friday afternoon   3.00
   meet photographers for a
   photo session
   rest at home
```

1c Practice

You are a famous person from your country. Write your programme for each day next week, in the morning and the afternoon.

With a partner, choose a role, Student A or Student B.

Student A
You want to interview the famous person. Ask what he or she is doing on different days of the week.

Student B
You are the famous person. Use the details you wrote and reply to the questions.

1d Listening

Listen and decide what these people are doing on Saturday.

Nick   Helen   Vicky and George

Would you like to …?

2a New language

Match the invitations with the events.

1. Romeo and Juliet
By William Shakespeare,
Saturday 14th February 7:30

2. Barrow Road School
Sports Day
Feb 14th 2.00

3. Park Road Concert Hall - National Youth Orchestra
Sat 14th Feb 8.30

a) **A:** Are you doing anything on Saturday evening?
   B: I don't think so. Why?
   A: Would you like to go to a concert? The National Youth Orchestra is playing.
   B: Good idea.
b) **A:** Would you like to see a play on Saturday?
   B: I'd love to. What time does it start?
c) **A:** Would you like to come to our sports day on Saturday?
   B: I'm afraid I can't. I'm going out with my family.

Helpline – inviting

We can use *Would you like to …* to make an invitation. *I'd* = I would.

pronunciation: we do not say the *l* in would /wʊd/

→ GC p7

9

Helpline – invitations
You can accept an invitation (say yes) or refuse it (say no).
Are you coming on Saturday?
I think so. (= I think I will come, but I'm not certain.)
I don't think so. = (I think I won't come, but I'm not certain.)
I'm afraid I can't. (= I'm sorry, but I can't.)
→ GC p7

2b Practice

With a partner, choose a part, Student A or Student B. Practise ways of inviting, accepting and refusing from **2a**.

Student A
You want to meet your friend after school one day this week. Invite him/her on Monday and then keep trying other days!

Student B
This is your diary for this week. You can't meet your friend this week. Explain to Student A what you are doing each day.

Monday	go to the hairdresser's
Tuesday	write an article about clothes
Wednesday	take the dog for a walk
Thursday	study for the maths test
Friday	play tennis

2c The excuses game

With a partner, choose a part Player A or Player B. The idea of the game is to make excuses and politely refuse all invitations. Use ideas from the lists and use ideas of your own.

Player A
Make an invitation for each day of the week. Ask about your partner's arrangements for different times. Don't give up! Try another day!

come to a party   go to the cinema   play (tennis/basketball etc)
listen to music   go to (name a place)   go shopping

▶ *Are you doing anything on [Monday] [afternoon/evening]? Would you like to …?*

Player B
Keep refusing politely and say what you are doing on each day.

go out   stay at home because …   visit (say who)   go to (say where)   someone (say who) is coming to your house

▶ *Sorry, but I'm …   I'm afraid not. I'm …   I'd like to come but I'm afraid I'm … on [day].   Sorry, I don't really like …*

2d Writing

Complete this note to a friend.

> Dear …
> I tried to find you at school, but you weren't there on Friday. I'm … *[say what you are doing]* next … *[give a day and a time]*. Would you like to come? I'm sure we'll have a good time.
> *[your name]*

Write a short reply, explaining that you can't come because you are doing something that day.

Word check
accept
arrangement
excuse (n)
explain
factory
future
give an interview
go out (on a trip)
hairdresser's
hospital
in secret
keep trying
politely
refuse
reply (v)
rest (v)
study for

Arranging the future 9

Helpline – invitations

- Explain that there are many ways to accept and refuse invitations and these can be found in the mini dialogues.
- Point out that when we refuse an invitation, we usually give a reason. Ask Ss to find the reason that the speaker gives in dialogue c), and to suggest some other reasons.

2b Practice

Aim: to practise ways of inviting, accepting and refusing.
Summary: Ss roleplay a conversation based on a diary.

Lead in

- Ask Ss what they usually do after school. Write a few suggestions on the board. Practise a dialogue with individual Ss, eg:
  T: *Would you like to meet me after school on Monday?*
  S: *I'm afraid I can't. I'm visiting my grandmother.*
  T: *What about Tuesday?*
  S: *I'm afraid I can't. I'm going to my computer club on Tuesday.*

Main activity

- Ss work with a partner and make and respond to invitations. They change roles. They can also talk about their own plans. Go around the class and help if necessary.

2c The excuses game

Aim: to practise refusing invitations politely.
Summary: Ss continue inviting someone who keeps refusing the invitations.

- Ss work in pairs or small groups of two pairs. Everyone prepares invitations and refusals for each day of the week. They can use ideas from the SB and their own ideas. Players score one point for each correct invitation and one point for each correct refusal and excuse.
- Go around the class and help if necessary. Ask early finishers to work with a different partner.

Extra activity

- Ask Ss to tell you their most interesting invitations and the most unusual excuses!

2d Writing

Aim: to practise writing and replying to an informal invitation.
Summary: Ss complete a note and write a short reply.

Lead in

- Books closed. Ask:
  Do you ever write notes to friends inviting them to do something? When? Why?

Main activity

- Give Ss a partner who is sitting on the other side of the class. Ss complete the note. Collect and deliver the notes to appropriate Ss. They then reply with a refusal and an excuse.

Extra activity

- Make a collage of the invitations and refusals. Display it on the classroom wall so that Ss can match the invitations and refusals.

Word check

- Write these sentences on the board:
a *I can't go to the cinema on Thursday. I'm _____ a test at school.* (study for)
b *My favourite teacher always _____ the difficult parts of the lesson.* (explains)
c *They make shoes at that _____* (factory)
d *My friend didn't tell me they were going to the swimming pool. They went _____* (in secret)
e *She didn't answer her phone at first but I _____ _____* (kept trying)
f *Some people _____ in the afternoons in my country.* (rest)

- Ask Ss to choose a word or phrase from the Word check box to complete the sentences. Remind them to change the form of the words if necessary.

9 Arranging the future

Lesson 3 Words in action

1

Aim: further focus on invitations.
Summary: Ss guess the missing verbs before listening, and then listen to the song to confirm their guesses.

Lead in

- Ss work with a partner to guess the missing verbs. Listen to Ss' ideas but do not confirm.

Main activity

- Play the song twice and ask Ss to write in the missing verbs. Ask individual Ss for the answers.

Answers:
1 come 2 sail 3 have 4 hear 5 swim 6 go

Extra activity

- Books closed. Ss work with a partner to recall the words of the seven invitations in the song.

2

Aim: further practice of making invitations.
Summary: Ss use verb cues to make invitations.

Lead in

- Ask Ss to suggest an idea for each verb, eg:
  Would you like to fly to Mount Olympus with me?

Main activity

- Ss write their invitations using the verbs on the page. They then work with a partner to make and reply to the invitations.

3

Aim: further practice of tag questions.
Summary: Ss make sentences using words from lists, and adding tag questions.

Lead in

- Say a sentence with a tag question, eg:
  It's a very cold day today, isn't it?
- Ask Ss to make some sentences with tag questions. Write a few examples on the board.

Main activity

- Ss make sentences with tag questions using the words from lists A and B in the SB. They then look at and check a partner's sentences. Go around the class and check sentences too. Write some of Ss' sentences on the board.

4

Aim: to make connections between words.
Summary: Ss make connections between pairs of words from two lists.

Lead in

- Ask Ss to look for logical and unusual connections between a word in list A and a word in list B, eg:
  We sometimes wash curtains in the bath.

Main activity

- Ss work with a partner to write the sentences. Go around the class and help if necessary.

Extra activity

- Ask Ss to write some of their unusual sentences on the board.

WORDS in ACTION

1 🎧 Before you listen to the song, guess the missing verbs.

Would you like to sail around the world?

Would you like to ..1.. with me
On a trip across the sea?
Would you like to ..2.. away
For an ocean holiday?
Would you like to ..3.. some fun
On tropical islands in the sun?

Would you like to sail around the world?

Would you like to slowly float
On our little sailing boat?
Would you like to ..4.. the cry
Of the sea-birds in the sky?
Would you like to ..5.. below
Where the playful dolphins ..6..?
Would you like to sail around the world?

Would you like to sail around the world?

Listen and write the missing verbs.

2 Make some invitations with the verbs.

stay with   have a (?)   go out   visit
try on   fly

3 How many sentences can you make with one word from each list? Use a tag question at the end of each sentence.

A amazing   boring   tasty   tight
favourite   busy   strange   comfortable

B dinner   chair   day   friend   trousers
smell   weather   film

▶ *This is a very tasty dinner, isn't it?*

4 Make a connection between each word in A and a word in B.

A curtain   food   rubbish   bus   tap   cat
bird   milk

B window   dustbin   cooker   bath
feather   fridge   stop   pet

▶ *curtain and window = There are usually curtains in front of windows.*

41

10 Habits and home

much, many; countable and uncountable nouns; little, few; not enough, too much, too many

Eating habits

1a 📼 New language

Read these strange food stories. Ask a partner five *How much ...?* and five *How many ...?* questions about them.

Michel 'Mangetout' Lotito, a Frenchman, eats metal things! Since he was 16 he has eaten seven bicycles, seven televisions, a supermarket trolley and a small plane. He eats about a kilo of metal every day. He cuts the metal into tiny pieces first!

In Spain in 1987 Josep Gruges made a giant paella, a Spanish dish. It contained 3700 kilos of rice, 3000 kilos of meat and fish, 1400 kilos of beans and onions, along with 200 kilos of garlic and 400 litres of olive oil. Forty thousand people ate it for lunch!

In seventy years of life the average British person eats 420 chickens, 3500 loaves of bread, 4000 kilos of potatoes and 2000 kilos of vegetables. He or she also drinks 93 000 cups of tea.

Helpline

– countable and uncountable

how many + countable nouns (plural *s*):

How many bicycles has he eaten?

how much + uncountable nouns:

How much metal does he eat?

→ GC p8

1b 📼 New language

Read about the eating habits of these animals. Match the description with the picture.

1

This animal eats only leaves from eucalyptus trees. There are 350 kinds of leaves, but it eats very few of them – only five kinds! It also drinks very little water because the leaves contain all the water it needs.

42

Habits and home 10

Unit 10		Functions	Grammar
Lesson 1	Eating habits	Asking and answering about quantity	Countable and uncountable nouns How much ...?, How many ...?, few, little
Lesson 2	The Round the World Kids	Describing problems	Too much, too many Not enough + noun
Lesson 3	CHRIS 4		

Word check

average	half	salt
breathe	hole	share
contain	hungry	tiny
cupboard	leaf	wait for
dig (v)	metal	
dust	plane	

Lesson 1 Eating habits

1a New language

Aim: to present *how much* and *how many* + countable and uncountable nouns; to revise cardinal numbers (*hundreds, thousands*).
Summary: Ss ask questions about three texts with *How much ...?* and *How many ...?*

Lead in

- Revise large cardinal numbers. Write the following on the board:
  100   750   1600   3000   50,000   88,000
  Point to numbers in turn and ask individual Ss to say them. Add extra numbers if Ss need more practice.
- Ask Ss to predict the following information before they open the SB:
  What's the strangest thing (not food) that a person could eat?
  Someone made a very big paella (a Spanish dish). How many people ate it? (100, 1000 or 40,000)
  How many cups of tea does a British person drink in a lifetime? (83,000, 93,000 or 103,000)

Main activity

- Ss read the three texts silently and check their guesses.

Answers:
metal   forty thousand people   ninety-three thousand cups of tea

- Practise a few *How much ...?* and *How many ...?* questions with individual Ss, eg:
  T: Lisa, ask George a question with 'much' or 'many' about televisions.
  S1: How many televisions has Lotito eaten?
  S2: He's eaten seven televisions.

- Ss work with a partner and ask five *How much ...?* and five *How many ...?* questions.

Extra activity

- Books closed. Ss ask T or each other questions about the four texts.

Helpline – countable and uncountable

- Explain that we use *How many...?* with plural countable nouns, eg:
  How many chickens does a British person eat?
  We use *How much...?* with uncountable nouns, eg:
  How much meat did the paella contain?
- Point out that some uncountable nouns can be used with countable measurements in front of them:
  How much rice did the paella contain?
  How many kilos of rice did it contain?
  How much metal does Lotito eat a day?
  How many kilos of metal does he eat a day?
- Explain that some names of food can be countable or uncountable, depending on how they are used, eg:
  How much chicken do you want?   (cooked food)
  How many chickens have you got?   (animals)

1b New language

Aim: to present *few* and *little*.
Summary: Ss match descriptions with pictures and make questions about the animals.

Lead in

- Books open. Ss cover the texts. They look only at the pictures and try to name the animals. Make sure that everyone agrees that they are a) *whale*, b) *koala bear* and c) *toad*.
- Ask Ss to say what they know about each of these animals.

Main activity

- Ss read the three texts and match them with the correct pictures. Ask individual Ss for the answers.

Answers:
1 koala bear   2 toad   3 whale

- Read out the example question in the SB:
  How many kinds of eucalyptus leaves does this animal eat?
  Very few!
- Ss work with a partner and ask five questions. Questions must being with *How much...?* and *How many...?*

Possible questions and answers:

How much water does the koala drink?	Very little.
How much water do eucalyptus leaves contain?	A lot.
How much does a whale eat?	A lot.
How much does a human eat compared to a whale?	Very little.
How many animals live in the desert?	Very few.
How many months can this animal wait for rain?	A lot.

Teacher's Book Unit 10

10 Habits and home

Helpline – few and little

- Explain that we use *few* with countable nouns and *little* with uncountable nouns, eg:
  Very few animals live in the desert.
  Koalas drink very little water.
- Point out that we often use *very* before both *few* and *little*.

1c Practice

Aim: to practise *much* and *many* and *few* and *little*.
Summary: Ss ask each other about their eating and drinking habits.

Lead in

- Books closed. Draw two columns on the board with the headings:
  How many ...?   *How much ...?*
- Write these words on a different part of the board:
  bread   cans of fizzy drink   packets of crisps
  milk   oranges   water
- Ask Ss to copy the words in the correct column in a chart in their exercise books. Check answers. Remind Ss that the things in the *How many ...?* column are countable and the things in the *How much ...?* column are uncountable. Write the words in the appropriate columns. Ask:
  T: *How much bread do you eat a day?*
  S: *About a quarter of a kilo.*
  T: *How many cans of fizzy drink do you drink a week in summer?*
  S: *Three or four.*

Main activity

- Books open. Ask Ss to work with a partner and ask questions with *How much...?* and *How many ...?* about food and drink. Ask individual Ss to tell the whole class about their partner's eating and drinking habits, eg:
  Mary eats six plates of spaghetti a week.
  Paula eats very little bread.
  George drinks about 3 litres of milk a week.
- Ask Ss to name different kinds of food and drink that they like and dislike. Find out which of these they eat and drink every day. Write some of their ideas on the board.
- Ss work individually to write a short paragraph about their eating habits. Go around the class and help if necessary.

Extra activity

- Ss read a partner's paragraph silently. They then write three or four sentences comparing their own eating habits with their partner's, eg:
  I eat a lot of spaghetti compared to X.
  X drinks very little milk compared to me.

Lesson 2 The Round the World Kids

2a New language

Aim: to present a context for later practice of *not enough*, *too much* and *too many* + noun.
Summary: Ss read texts and identify Vicky's problems.

Lead in

- Look at the introduction to the activity in the SB and ask:
  Where are the Round the World Kids now?   (Indonesia)
  Which continent is that in?   (Asia)
  Where have they just come from?   (Australia)
  What else can you remember about their trip so far?
- Ss cover the text and look at the picture of Vicky in her cabin. Ask them to predict what sort of problems she has living on a boat. Write a few ideas on the board but do not confirm.

Main activity

- Ss read the text in the SB silently and check their guesses. Ask individual Ss to say what Vicky's problems are. They can use her words at this stage – this involves reading out most of Vicky's letter to Denise.

Helpline

– few and little

with countable nouns:
There are *not many* fish here. = there are *very few* fish

with uncountable nouns:
There *isn't much* food here. = there is *very little* food

→ GC p8

2 There is little to eat and drink in deserts and so very few animals live there. However, this animal digs a hole and waits for rain. It can stay in its hole for eleven months of the year!

3 Compared to this animal, humans eat very little! In one day it can eat the same as a person eats in one year.

1c Practice

Ask a partner about his or her eating habits.

▶ *How much/many … do you eat/drink a day?*

– *A lot. About two bottles/ glasses/boxes/plates a day. Not many. Very few.*

Write a paragraph about your eating habits. Use names of food from **1a** and **1b**.

Make five questions. Each question must have one of these answers:

Very few. Very little. A lot.

▶ *How many kinds of eucalyptus leaves does this animal eat?*
  – Very few!

The Round the World Kids

2a New language

The Round the World Kids are in Indonesia now. Read Vicky's letter to her friend, Denise. What problems has Vicky got?

One problem of living on a boat is space. You bump into things all the time! I keep a lot of my things in a box under my bunk bed. It's my fault because I brought lots of clothes and books and they won't fit in my cupboard.

George and I share a cabin. I have half and he has the other half. He is impossible. He has a radio and plays it loudly all the time. He hasn't got any earphones and I can't sleep.

10

2b New language

Write a comment on each of the things Vicky mentions in **2a** using *isn't enough/aren't enough* or *too much/too many*.

*space   cabins   cupboards
noise   clothes/books*

▶ *There isn't enough space, so she bumps into things all the time.*

Helpline

– too much/many and not enough

I can't eat it all. – There are *too many* potatoes./There is *too much* meat.

We can't sit here. – There *aren't enough* chairs./There *isn't enough* room.

→ GC p8

2c Listening

Listen to the Round the World family talking about their problems. Which comment finishes each conversation? Write the letter for the conversation next to the comment.

1 There isn't enough space.
2 There are too many potatoes.
3 There aren't enough plates.
4 There is too much salt in it.
5 There isn't enough time now.

2d Practice

Denise wrote back to Vicky and described her family's holiday. Look at the pictures and talk about their problems. Use the words in the boxes and make sentences.

1   2

3   4

| noise   food   people   chairs   space   insects   rubbish
tables   dust and smoke   water |

There weren't enough	... in the dining-room.
There wasn't enough	... on the beach.
There was too much	... in their room.
There were too many	... in the town.

2e Writing

Now write Denise's letter to Vicky.

We had a terrible holiday. The hotel was awful. First of all we couldn't sleep because ... and .... We were hungry all the time because .... The town was awful too. We couldn't breathe because there ... and .... To make things worse, the beach was really overcrowded. We couldn't sunbathe because ...

Word check

average	hungry
breathe	leaf
contain	metal
cupboard	plane
dig (v)	salt
dust	share
half	tiny
hole	wait for

Habits and home   10

2b New language

Aim: to practise *not enough*, *too much* and *too many* + noun.
Summary: Ss make comment about Vicky's problems.

- Use the example in the SB to comment on one of Vicky's problems. Invite individual Ss to make sentences about the other things Vicky mentions in activity 2a. Remind them that *space* and *noise* are uncountable nouns. Ss then work individually and write comments about the things Vicky mentions. Go around the class and help if necessary.

Suggested answers:
There aren't enough cabins, so Vicky must share one with George.
There aren't enough cupboards and Vicky brought too many clothes and books.
Vicky can't sleep because George makes too much noise with his radio.

Extra activity 1

- Ask Ss to suggest problems with houses, schools, towns etc using *not enough*, *too much* and *too many*.

Extra activity 2

- Ss work with a partner and roleplay a conversation between George and his mother. He is complaining about Vicky. Ss could mention these problems in their conversation:
She has too many things.
She doesn't like listening to the radio.

Helpline – too much/many and not enough

- Explain that *too* (*much* and *many*) usually has a negative meaning in English, eg:
Vicky is untidy because she has too many clothes.
The Normals think that the Odds make too much noise.

- Point out that *not enough* means that you need more of something, eg:
There aren't enough drawers on the boat.
There isn't enough space for Vicky's things.

- Ask Ss to write some true example sentences for themselves, eg:
We have too much homework.
We don't have enough free time.
There aren't enough sports centres in our town.

2c Listening

Aim: further focus on *not enough*, *too much* and *too many* + noun.
Summary: Ss listen and decide which comment finishes each conversation.

Lead in

- Ask Ss to read the five comments which finish the conversations. Ss predict what each conversation is about. Do not confirm yet.

Main activity

- Ask Ss listen to each conversation twice. They write the letter of the conversation next to the comment. They then check their answers with a partner. Ask individual Ss for the answers:

Answers:
a) 3   b) 5   c) 2   d) 1   e) 4

- Books closed. Play the conversations again and pause before the final comments. Ss say the final comment in each case.

Extra activity

- Ss work with a partner to roleplay one or more of the conversations. It is not important to remember the exact words.

2d Practice

Aim: further practice of *not enough*, *too much* and *too many* + noun.
Summary: Ss describe problems shown in the pictures.

Lead in

- Books closed. Write these two kinds of holiday on the board:
Travelling around in a small boat with not much space.
Going to a hotel near a beach.
Find out which holiday Ss would prefer. Ask for their reasons.

Main activity

- Books open. Ss cover the words and look only at the pictures. Ask individual Ss to say what problems there were on Denise's holiday.
- Ss uncover the words. They work with a partner to write ten sentences about Denise's holiday. They must use *not enough* and *too much* and *too many*. Go around the class and help if necessary.

Optional activity

- Ss tell a partner about any problems they have had on holiday.

2e Writing

Aim: further practice of *not enough*, *too much* and *too many* + noun.
Summary: Ss complete Denise's letter.

- Remind Ss to use the information from activity 2d to complete Denise's letter. Ss write individually but exchange letters when they have finished. Go around the class and help if necessary.

Word check

- Ss test each other's spelling in pairs.

Teacher's Book Unit 10

10 Habits and home

Lesson 3 CHRIS Episode 4

Aim: to read for specific and detailed information; to listen for specific information.

The story so far:

Main activity

- Ss work with a partner to answer the questions. If they cannot remember the answers, they may look at the last episode. Ask individual Ss for the answers.

Answers:
1. The twins talked to Anna.
2. There were two plays on that week. They were 'Arms and the Man' and 'Antony and Cleopatra'.
3. They are going to Cleopatra's Needle.

1

Main activity

- Ss read the conversation between the twins and CHRIS and find the answers to the two questions. Ask individual Ss for the answers.

Answers:
Can the police help us?
Are we doing the right thing?
What will we find at Cleopatra's needle?
CHRIS can't help them because he needs the password first.

Extra activity

- Ss work with a partner to roleplay the conversation between the twins and the computer. S1 closes his/her book and takes the role of the computer. S2 reads Sandy and Peter's part from the SB. Ss then exchange roles.

2

Lead in

- Ss work with a partner and decide what the password might be. Write some of their ideas on the board but do not confirm.

Main activity

- Play the cassette twice. Ask Ss to listen to the conversation between the twins and CHRIS. Ss guess the password when there is a pause at the end of the conversation. They should only give their answer after the second listening. Make sure that everyone agrees that the password is *London*.

Extra activity

- Play the cassette again. Ask Ss to listen for the four wrong guesses that the twins made about the password. Make sure that everyone agrees that they are *Cleopatra's Needle, letter, map* and *NT*.

3

Lead in

- Ss cover Chris's letter. They then read the three questions and predict the answers. Listen to some guesses but do not confirm.

Main activity

- Ss read Chris's letter silently and answer the questions. Ask individual Ss for the answers.

Answers:
a) He wants them to work hard before they find him.
b) He needed a holiday.
c) He wants the twins to have fun with CHRIS and do some sightseeing in London.

- Ask Ss to predict the information that the computer is going to give them.

Extra activity 1

- Ss write Sandy's diary entry for today. They should begin *We had another puzzle today …*

Extra activity 2

- Books closed. Write these sentences on the board:
  a) The p … for the computer is not 'map' or 'letter'. (password)
  b) The computer can only p … Chris's letter if the twins give it the right word. (print)
  c) Who is the p … with 'A'? (person)
  d) The twins have to find the answer to another p …. (puzzle).
- Explain that all the missing words from these sentences begin with *p* and they are in this episode. Ss complete the sentences.

CHRIS

Episode 4

The story so far:

1. Who did the twins talk to at the National Theatre?
2. How many plays were on that week? What were their names?
3. Where are they going next?

1 Read the next part of the story. What do the twins ask CHRIS? Why can't he help them?

▶ **a**

Sandy: CHRIS, this is Sandy. We're going to Cleopatra's Needle tomorrow. Are we doing the right thing? Can the police help us?

CHRIS: Hello, Sandy. This is CHRIS, the Computer Help Reporting Information Service. Can I help you?

Peter: We need some help, CHRIS. What will we find at Cleopatra's Needle?

CHRIS: I am not able to answer your questions this time. Please give me the password first.

Sandy: Password? What password? Oh dear, another puzzle!

CHRIS: Your brother Chris gave you the password …

2 Listen to Sandy and Peter talking to CHRIS. When there is a pause, guess the password. Then listen to the end of the conversation. Which word is the password?

3 Read the next part of the story. Answer the questions.

a) Why doesn't Chris say much in his letter?
b) Why has he disappeared?
c) What does he want the twins to do?

▶ **b**

I have some information for you. I am going to print it now. Please turn on my printer.

```
Dear Sandy and Peter

Well done! You've understood my
messages so far, so I expect you
are going to 'the person with A'
next. I am not going to say much
in this letter because I want
you to work hard before you
find me!

I have disappeared for a few
days. I hope that Mrs Jackson is
looking after you well. I needed
a holiday, and I want you to
have some fun with CHRIS, and do
some sightseeing in London. I've
left lots of clues for you, so
good luck! Please think about
the information very carefully.
CHRIS will help you, but he
doesn't know all the answers.
Enjoy the puzzle! I hope it
teaches you that computers
are fun!

Chris
PS Before you go to visit 'the
person with A', ask CHRIS for
some more information.
```

11 On the air

*will and going to; making requests with could;
asking someone to do something*

Stars of the small screen

1a New language

This week a TV company is coming to Nick and Helen's school. They are going to interview some students for a programme about teenage sports. Nick and Helen wrote a letter to the director, Nina Taylor. What questions did they ask? Read Nina Taylor's reply and complete Nick and Helen's letter.

Nina Taylor

Sue Parks

Mike Bell

Barrow Road School,
London
March 2nd

Dear Nina Taylor
Thanks for your letter about the interviews. We have a few questions. First, when exactly …? How long … ? How many …? Will you … with the interviews? And what about the programme? Will … live, or will we … of the programme? We are also a bit worried about one thing. Will … questions?

We are looking forward to meeting you.

Helen Adams

Nick Porter

SCOOP TELEVISION
Ridgeway House, Western Road, London W1

Nick Porter and Helen Adams
Barrow Road School
London
March 14th

Dear Nick and Helen
Thanks for your letter. We'll arrive at the school on Friday 18th March at 11.00. The interviews will probably take about two hours. There will be three of us in the team: myself, my assistant, Mike Bell, and Sue Parks, the camera operator. We'll need your help with the interviews. This won't be a live programme, so we'll show you the video of the interviews on the same day. I promise that we won't ask any difficult questions! We'll see you on Friday.
Best wishes
          Nina Taylor
          Nina Taylor

Helpline – will and won't

We use *will/won't* for:

predictions about the future: *The programme will probably take two hours.*

definite future events: *We'll arrive at the school on Friday.*

promises: *We won't ask any difficult questions.*

→ GC p8

On the air 11

Unit 11		Functions	Grammar
Lesson 1	Stars of the small screen	Making predictions, promises, plans Describing definite future events	Will, won't, going to
Lesson 2	Outside broadcast	Making requests Asking someone to do something	Could you ...? Would you mind ...?
Lesson 3	Check up Units 9–11		

Word check

assistant	in the way	probably
change (n)	last (v)	promise
director	look forward to	repeat
exactly	organize	take part
help (n)	phone box	worried

Lesson 1 Stars of the small screen

1a New language

Aim: to present *will*.
Summary: Ss read a letter and decide what questions the letter answers.

Lead in

- Ss look at the photos and say what the people are doing. Ask:
  What do film directors do? (They give everyone instructions.)
  Where do they work? (In film studios and outside.)
  Is it difficult to use a video camera? Have you ever tried? Has anyone ever videoed you? What were you doing?

- Read out the first two sentences of the introduction:
  This week a TV company is coming to Nick and Helen's school. They are going to interview some of the students for a programme about teenage sports.
- Ask Ss to predict the questions that the TV company will ask. Write a few ideas on the board but do not confirm.

Main activity

- Read the introduction aloud again. Make sure that Ss understand that they must read both letters in order to complete the questions in Nick and Helen's letter. Ask Ss to read the two letters silently and carefully.
- Ss write the questions in their exercise books. Go around the class and help if necessary. Ask individual Ss for the answers and write them on the board.

Answers:
When exactly will you arrive?
How long will the interviews take and will you disturb any classes?
How many people will come?
Will you need our help with the interviews?
Will they be live, or will we see the video of the programme?
Will you ask any difficult questions?

Extra activity

- Books closed. Ask Ss to imagine that Nick or Helen did not write a letter to Nina Taylor. One of them phoned her. Ss use the questions in their exercise books and other questions to roleplay the conversation between Nina and Helen or Nick.

Helpline – will and won't

- Explain the three uses of *will/won't*.
  1 Predictions about the future, eg:
    Sandy and Peter will probably find their brother, Chris.
  2 Definite future events, eg:
    We'll go to Cleopatra's Needle tomorrow.
  3 Promises, eg:
    'We won't do anything dangerous,' said Peter.

- Ss look in Nina's letter for more examples of these uses of *will/won't*. Ask individual Ss to read aloud the sentences.

Answers:
1 We'll need your help with the interviews.
  We'll see you at 11.00 on Friday.
2 There'll be three of us in the team.
  This won't be a live programme.
3 We won't disturb any classes.
  We'll show you the video of the interviews on the same day.

11 On the air

1b Listening

Aim: to practise *going to* for future plans.
Summary: Ss listen and decide what each person is going to do.

Lead in

- Write the names *Nina, Sue* and *Mike* on the board and ask Ss what their jobs are. Ask Ss to look at the list of eight activities and predict who is going to do each one.
- Play the cassette twice. Ss write the name next to each activity. They then check their answers with a partner. Ask individual Ss for the answers.

Answers:

| 1 Nick | 3 Mike | 5 Nina | 7 Sue |
| 2 Helen | 4 Helen | 6 Sue | 8 Nina |

- Ask Ss to work with a partner and say what each person is going to do.

Optional activity

- Books closed. Ask Ss to imagine that Nina had to go back to the film studio suddenly and Mike is going to finish the programme. Unfortunately, he did not hear what Nina said and he gives the wrong instructions! Ss work with a partner to roleplay the conversation between Mike and either Helen or Nick, eg:
Mike: *I'm going to interview the tennis players.*
Helen: *No, Nick's going to interview the tennis players.*

Helpline – going to

- Explain that we use *going to* for plans for the future, eg:
The Robinsons are going to visit Egypt.
- Ask Ss to write about their own plans, eg:
I'm going to have lunch with my friends.
My brother and I are going to play tennis after school.

1c Practice

Aim: further practice of *going to*.
Summary: Ss plan their own TV programme.

Lead in

- Tell Ss that they are going to make a TV programme about an interesting place or person. Ss make some suggestions. Write their ideas on the board.

Main activity

- Ask Ss to read the questions in the SB silently and to add one more question to the list. Ss then work with a partner and plan a TV programme. Go around the class and help if necessary. Ask Ss to report back to the whole class about their programme.

Extra activity

- Ss use their answers to the questions to write a report about their TV programme. They should begin:
This programme is going to be about …
- Ss bring a picture or drawing to accompany their report. Display the reports in class.

Lesson 2 Outside broadcast

2a New language

Aim: to present *Would you mind …?* and *Could you …?* for making requests.
Summary: Ss match requests with items on a list. They then make more requests using the list.

Lead in

- Books closed. Ask Ss to suggest some interesting things for the tennis players and athletes to do for the TV programme. Write some of their ideas on the board, eg: *practise a long jump.*

Main activity

- Read out the examples in the SB and repeat each request using both forms:
Could you tell me your name?
Would you mind telling me your name?
Would you mind repeating your answer?
Could you repeat your answer?
- Ask Ss to match the questions with the ideas on Mike's list.

Answers:

| Could you tell me your name, please? | Ask him/her to tell you his/her name. |
| Would you mind repeating your answer? | Ask him/her to repeat his/her answer. |

- They then use Mike's ideas to write a list of Nick and Helen's questions. Each question must begin with *Would you mind … ?* or *Could you … ?*
- Go around the class and help if necessary.

Optional activity

- Tell Ss that they are going to interview the school basketball team. They prepare a list of ideas for the interview and use it to ask their partner questions.

Teacher's Book Unit 11

1b 🎧 Listening

Before the interviews begin, Nina Taylor talks to Nick and Helen. What is each person going to do? Listen and write the name next to the activity.

Nina   Sue   Mike   Nick   Helen

1 talk to the tennis players
2 talk to the people on the sports field
3 organize the order
4 say the number of the interview
5 help when we do the real interview
6 stand next to the interviewer
7 say when to start
8 watch the video playback

Tell a partner your answers.

▶ *Nick is going to talk to the tennis players.*

> **Helpline** – going to
>
> We use *going to* for plans for the future:
> *Nick is going to talk to the tennis players.*
>
> → GC p8

1c Practice

Plan a TV programme with a partner. Think about these questions:

What are you going to film? [places? people?]
How many people are going to take part?
Are you going to have any interviews?
When are you going to make the programme?
How long is it going to last? [time? day?]

Outside broadcast

2a 🎧 New language

Mike Bell, the director's assistant, wrote a list of ideas for Nick and Helen's interviews. Match the two questions Nick and Helen ask with ideas on Mike's list. Then make similar questions for the other ideas. Use *Would you mind ...?* or *Could you ...?*

▶ *Could you tell me your name, please?*
Would you mind repeating your answer?

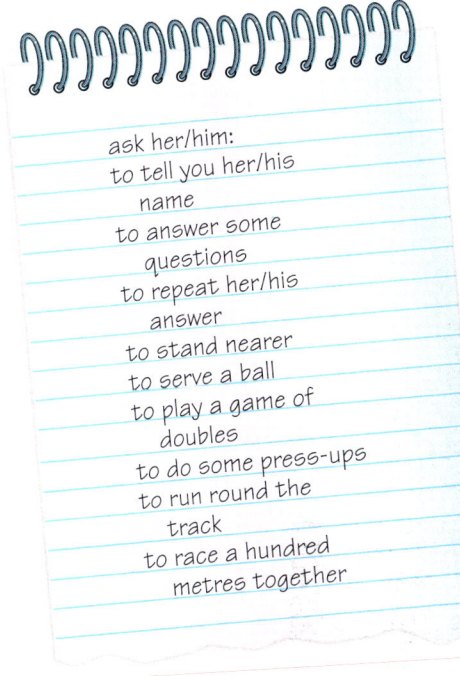

ask her/him:
to tell you her/his name
to answer some questions
to repeat her/his answer
to stand nearer
to serve a ball
to play a game of doubles
to do some press-ups
to run round the track
to race a hundred metres together

11

Helpline – making requests

We can use *could* or *would you mind* + *-ing* form:

   Could you open the window, please?

We usually answer: *Yes, of course.* or *Sorry but …* (= No.) with an explanation.

   Would you mind opening the window?

We usually answer: *No, of course not.* (= Yes, I'll open it.) or *Sorry but …* (= No.) with an explanation.

→ GC p9

2b Practice

Complete the speech bubbles.

We can't see your face. Could you look this way, please!

Now write an answer for each of the other people. Then practise the dialogues.

2c Practice

You are making a film. Read about some situations and make some requests. You are talking to strangers, so begin *Excuse me …* .

1. You are interviewing a woman. Ask for her name.
2. You can't use your video-camera because a group of very old people is standing in the way. Ask them to move.
3. You have to phone your director from a phone box but you haven't got the right money. Ask someone for change.

2d Writing

Complete Helen's note.

> Dear David
> … help me? They … [show] our programme on television next Wednesday at 2.30 but Nick and I haven't got a video. … record it for us? It's on Channel 6 and it lasts about twenty minutes. … buying a tape too? We'll pay you back on Thursday.
> Thanks a lot, Helen

Jim is Helen's friend. Write a note from Jim to Helen asking to borrow the video. Jim's uncle and aunt want to see the video and they are visiting him next weekend. Ask Helen to bring the video to Jim's house.

Word check

assistant	organize
change (n)	phone box
director	probably
exactly	promise
help (n)	repeat
in the way	take part
last (v)	worried
look forward to	

On the air 11

Helpline – making requests

- Explain that we use *Could you...?* or *Would you mind + -ing?* to make requests, eg:
  Could you turn on the computer?
  Could you close the door?
  Would you mind cleaning the board?
  Would you mind carrying this bag?
- Explain that we answer *Yes, of course* or *Sorry but ... +* explanation to requests with *Could you ...?*
- Explain that *No, of course not* in response to a request with *Would you mind ...?* means *yes, I'll do it*; *Sorry but ... +* explanation means *no, I won't do it*. Ss are often confused by the fact that the negative-looking answer to requests with *Would you mind ...?* means *I'll do it*.
- Write some more requests on the board:
  Would you mind taking these dictionaries to the library?
  Could you turn off your radio please?
  Would you mind tidying your room?
  Could you put the books on that shelf?
  Would you mind taking this message to Nina Taylor?
  Ask Ss to practise requests and replies with a partner.

2b Practice

Aim: to practise making requests with *Could you ...?* and *Would you mind ...?*
Summary: Ss complete the speech bubbles and then practise making dialogues.

Lead in

- Books closed. Ask Ss to predict the problems that happen during filming, eg:
  People speak too quietly during an interview.

Main activity

- Ss work with a partner to complete the speech bubbles. They then practise the dialogues. Go around the class and help if necessary. Ask pairs of Ss to read out their answers.

Suggested answers:
a) Would you mind looking at the camera?
   Oh, no, of course not.
b) Would you mind holding this light?
   No, of course not.
c) Could you explain this question please?
   Yes, of course.

Optional activity

- Ask Ss to suggest requests that a stranger who is visiting their school might make, eg:
  Excuse me, could you tell me the way to the library?

2c Practice

Aim: to practise making requests.
Summary: Ss make requests for different situations.

- Ask Ss to read the situations first. Make sure that they understand them.
- Ss work with a partner and think of a request and a possible response. Ask for ideas for each situation. Some Ss might like to perform their dialogues for the class.

2d Writing

Aim: written practice of requests.
Summary: Ss complete a letter and make requests.

Main activity

- Ss work individually to complete Helen's note. Go around the class and help if necessary. Ask individual Ss for their answers and write them on the board.

Answers:
Could you help me?
Could you record it for us?
Would you mind buying a tape too?

- Ss write Jim's note to Helen. Early finishers can exchange notes and make suggestions for changes. Go around the class and check.

Optional activity

- Explain that Ss have to imagine that the class is going on a school trip tomorrow. Ask Ss to write a note to someone in the class. They have to make three requests and give reasons for their requests in the note.

Word check
- Put these anagrams on the board:
  IMPROSE   (promise)
  TSASTISAN   (assistant)
  CAXYELT   (exactly)
  BLYPBRAO   (probably)
  PRETAE   (repeat)
  ZNEIROG   (organize)
  RDEIWRO   (worried)
  GENACH   (change)
- Explain that the letters of each word are in the wrong order and ask the Ss to find the words.
- Write these sentences on the board:
  a Could you _____, please?   (repeat)
  b The train journey will _____ take two hours. (probably)
  c The time is _____ five o'clock.   (exactly)
  d Fiona is _____ . She has got a difficult English test at school tomorrow.   (worried)
  e Can you _____ the food for the party?   (organize)
- Ask Ss to use five of the words to complete the sentences.

Teacher's Book Unit 11

11 On the air

Check up Units 9-11

1

Aim: further practice of the present continuous with future reference.
Summary: Ss complete a paragraph with suitable verbs.

- Ask Ss to read the paragraph silently and decide on a suitable verb for each space. (If necessary, tell Ss that all the verbs are in the present continuous tense.) Go around the class and check. Ask individual Ss to read aloud a sentence each and write the missing verbs on the board.

Answers:
1 interviewing   5 going
2 visiting   6 studying/revising
3 taking   7 going
4 writing   8 meeting

Extra activity 1

- Books closed. Say one day of the week and ask what Nick is doing on that day.

Extra activity 2

- Ss tell a partner what they are doing each day of next week.

2

Aim: further practice of *a few, a little, not enough*.
Summary: Ss complete sentences and then make sentences of their own.

Lead in

- Books closed. Write the word *Omelette* on the board. Ask Ss if they have ever made one or watched someone make one. Ask:
  What do you need to make an omelette?

Main activity

- Ask Ss to look at the picture in the SB and complete the sentences with one of the three words. Ask individual Ss for their answers.

Answers:
a) eggs   b) butter   c) milk

- Ss make similar sentences for the other three things.

Optional activity

- Read out the ingredients for a traditional dish, eg *moussaka, paella*. Ss say why you can't make it, eg: *There are only a few potatoes.*

3

Aim: further practice of *too much, too many* and *not enough*.
Summary: Ss write sentences explaining why Vicky and George couldn't do certain things.

Main activity

- Ask Ss to use *too much, too many* and *not enough* with the words in brackets to write an explanation for each situation. Ask individual Ss for their answers.

Answers:
a) They didn't have enough money.
b) They had/ordered too much food.
c) They didn't have enough room.
d) They had too many exercises.
e) They didn't have enough time.

Optional activity

- Ask Ss to write three true sentences about themselves using *too much, too many* and *not enough*.

4

Aim: further practice of *going to* for future plans.
Summary: Ss work with a partner and talk about their holiday plans.

Lead in

- Invite Ss to ask you five questions about your holiday plans.

Main activity

- Ss work with a partner and ask about his or her holiday plans. They use the questions in the SB and any other questions they can think of.

Extra activity

- Ss write a short paragraph about their own or their partner's holiday plans.

5

Aim: to focus on the relation between spelling and pronunciation.
Summary: Ss pronounce words with silent letters and words in which the written vowel sound is not pronounced as it is written.

Main activity

- Ask Ss to work with a partner and practise saying the words in the SB. Play the cassette twice for Ss to check. Then ask individual Ss to say the words.

UNITS 9-11
CHECK UP

1 Put a suitable verb in each space.

Nick has a very busy week next week. On Monday he's playing tennis and is ..1.. two teachers for *Brilliant*. On Tuesday he is ..2.. the museum and ..3.. some photos. On Wednesday he is ..4.. an article for *Brilliant* and ..5.. running. On Thursday he is ..6.. for a test. On Friday he is ..7.. to the dentist and ..8.. Helen at the cinema.

2 Vicky wanted to make an omelette, but she couldn't. What did she find in the kitchen on the boat? Use the words in the list to complete the description.

butter   eggs   milk

a) There were only a few ... and the family needed them for breakfast.
b) There was only a little ... and there wasn't any margarine.
c) There wasn't enough ... because the family needed some for tea.

Here are some more things she couldn't make. Explain why.

chips   cheese sandwiches   a salad

3 Explain why Vicky and George couldn't do these things. Use the words in brackets and *too much/too many/not enough* to complete their explanations.

a) They couldn't buy any souvenirs in Mexico. (money)
b) They couldn't finish the meal they had in the restaurant. (food)
c) They couldn't play tennis on the boat. (room)
d) They couldn't do all their homework. (exercises)
e) They couldn't see all the sights in Australia. (time)

4 Ask a partner about his or her holiday plans.

a) What are you going to do this summer?
b) Where are you going to stay?
c) What are you going to do every day?
d) What are you going to do every evening?
e) Are you going to do any school work?

5 How do we say these words? Be careful of the letters underlined.

should   would   could   listen   science
castle   thought   high   weigh   front
brother   love

Now listen and repeat.

49

12 Follow the rules

have to, don't have to; had to, couldn't

School rules

1a New language

Nick interviewed two teenagers. Sue goes to school in a small village, but David does his lessons at home. Find what each of them has to do and doesn't have to do. Use these headings.

Uniform   Travel   Starting and finishing
Lessons   Tests   Other things?

Sue goes to school in a village. 'The school is next door to my house, so there isn't any travelling. We can't wear just any clothes – we wear a blue top and black trousers or skirt. School starts at 9.00. We have a lot of lessons and some of them are difficult. There are tests every week and we do extra work at lunchtime when our marks are bad. And we have lots of homework! On Wednesday afternoon there aren't any lessons and we go for trips or do sports. And we can choose some extra subjects. I'm learning the guitar and I do painting.'

David Aitken learns at home with his parents. Some school children in Britain do this. 'I left my school two years ago and now I don't have any school rules. I can start my lessons and finish them when I want. I don't wear a uniform and I can work on one subject for a day or a week! I have some lessons with teachers, but they visit the house. I can do projects in the countryside or in the town library, or I can work on my computer. I still do sports with other kids, but at weekends.'

▶ *Uniform*
Sue has to wear a uniform.
David doesn't have to wear a uniform.

Helpline – have to

We use *have to* to describe a rule:
   Sue has to wear a uniform.

We also use *have to* to describe what is necessary:
   I have to get up early to go to school.

→ GC p9

Follow the rules 12

Unit 12		Functions	Grammar
Lesson 1	School rules	Describing obligation	Had to, didn't have to, couldn't
Lesson 2	The Round the World Kids	Describing obligation and inability	Had to, didn't have to, couldn't
Lesson 3	Words in action		

Word check

adventure	countryside	instead of
ask the way	deck	learn by heart
canal	extra	meal
candle	free	uniform
change money	give permission	wedding
	housework	

Lesson 1 School rules

1a New language

Aim: to present the use of *have to* for rules.
Summary: Ss read two texts and find out what people *have to* and *don't have to* do.

Lead in

- Books closed. Write the title of the lesson on the board: *School rules*
Ask Ss to think of at least two school rules. Write a few of the rules on the board.

Main activity

- Read the introduction to activity 1a. Ask Ss to copy the headings from the SB into their exercise books. Ss then read the two paragraphs silently and write notes under each heading. They then compare notes with a partner. Go around the class and help if necessary. Write the headings on the board and ask individual Ss for the answers. Ss should use *have/has to* or *don't/doesn't have to.* **They can use the sentences in the book as examples.**

Suggested answers:

Uniform
Sue has to wear a uniform.
David doesn't have to wear a uniform.
Travel
Sue and David don't have to travel to school.
Starting and finishing
Sue has to start lessons at 9.00.
David doesn't have to start or finish at a special time.
Lessons
Sue has to do a lot of lessons.
David doesn't have to follow a timetable.
He has to do some lessons with teachers.
Tests
Sue has to do tests every week.
We don't know if David has to do tests.
Other things
Sue doesn't have to do lessons on Wednesday afternoons.
David has to spend a lot of time with his parents (because they are his teachers).
Sue has to work at lunchtimes sometimes.
Sue has to do a lot of homework.

Helpline – have to

- Explain that we use *have to* to describe:
  a) rules, eg:
     Policewomen have to wear uniforms.
  b) what is necessary, eg:
     Sandy has to use the correct password.
- Emphasize the use of *don't/doesn't have to* as some Ss may try to say *haven't/hasn't to.*

12 Follow the rules

1b Practice

Aim: to practise *have to* to talk about rules.
Summary: Ss ask and tell each other what they have to do and don't have to do at school and at home.

Lead in

- Books closed. Ask Ss to say some of the things they usually have to do at home. Ask them some – but not all – of the questions from activity 1b. Make sure that Ss use short answers:
  Do you have to wear a uniform?   *Yes, I do/No, I don't.*

Main activity

- Ss work with a partner and ask each other questions. Ask them to make notes about their partner's answers. Ss form new pairs and tell their new partner about their previous one, eg:
  John has to wear a uniform at school. He doesn't have to do lots of homework.
- Ask Ss to add other ideas, eg:
  I have to catch the school bus at 7.30.
  I don't have to make my bed.

1c Practice

Aim: further practice of *have to*.
Summary: Ss describe what people *have to do* and *don't have to do* in certain jobs.

Lead in

- Books closed. Write the word *Teacher* on the board. Then draw two columns with the headings *has to* and *doesn't have to*. Ask Ss to think of two things a teacher has to do and two things that a teacher doesn't have to do. Write some of their ideas in the appropriate columns.

Main activity

- Ss look at the pictures. They work with a partner to make sentences for each job. Ask individual Ss for the answers.

Suggested answers:
a teacher has to
read lots of books   work long hours   like children
a police officer has to
wear a uniform   be good at talking to people
work late at night
a footballer has to
run very fast   practise every day

Optional activity

- Write some more jobs on the board. Ask Ss to write a sentence for each using *has to* or *doesn't have to*, eg:
  engineer   astronaut   air steward   cook

1d Writing

Aim: further practice of *have to/don't have to*.
Summary: Ss write two paragraphs using ideas from activity 1b.

Lead in

- Books closed. Ask Ss to say some of the 'rules' they have at school and at home.

Main activity

- Ss work individually to write two paragraphs about themselves.

Lesson 2 The Round the World Kids

2a New language

Aim: to present *couldn't* to describe inability to do something; to present *had to*.
Summary: Ss read Vicky's diary and make comments about the family's problems.

Lead in

- Tell Ss that the Robinsons are now in Egypt and are going to sail through the Suez Canal. Ask Ss what they know about the Suez Canal.
- Tell Ss that you are going to read some statements. Ask them to say if they are true or false. If they are false, ask Ss to give the correct answer if possible.
  1 A French company built the Suez Canal. (T)
  2 They completed it 100 years ago. (F – They completed it in 1869.)
  3 Ships use it as a quicker way between Africa and Europe. (F – They use it between Europe and Asia. It saves them from sailing 9650 kilometres around southern Africa.)
  4 It is the longest canal in the world. (T and F – It is the longest canal that big ships can use. It is 160 kilometres long and 60 metres wide.)

Main activity

- Read or play the introduction to Ss. Ask Ss to read the extracts from Vicky's diary silently to find out what problems the Robinsons have had recently.

Answers:
The air conditioning isn't working.
The cabin lights aren't working.
A lot of ships were passing through the Suez Canal.
The banks were closed when they wanted to change money.

- Read aloud the example in the SB. Ss read the extracts again. Ss make sentences using *couldn't* and *had to*.

Answers:
They couldn't see anything in their cabin because the lights didn't work, so they had to use candles and a torch.
They couldn't go through the Suez Canal because there were a lot of ships passing through it, so they had to wait all day in Lake Timsah.
They couldn't change any money in Alexandria because they arrived late at night, so they had to eat spaghetti on the boat again.

1b Practice

Ask a partner about rules at school and at home.

▶ *At school do you have to …*
    wear a uniform?   do tests?
    do lots of homework?
    learn things by heart?

▶ *At home do you have to …*
    do the washing up?
    help with the housework?
    go to bed before 9.00?
    go shopping?

Think of other things and tell your partner.

▶ *School*
  I don't have to sit in the same seat every day.
  Home
  I have to look after my baby brother.

1c Practice

What do these people have to do? What don't they have to do? Use ideas from the list. There is more than one answer!

read lots of books   wear a uniform   be good at talking to people
run very fast   work long hours   practise every day
work late at night   like children

▶ *A teacher has to read lots of books, but he or she doesn't have to wear a uniform.*

1d Writing

Write two paragraphs about yourself.

1 Things you have to do and don't have to do at home.
2 Things you have to do and don't have to do at school.

The Round the World Kids

2a New language

The Round the World Kids have reached Egypt and are sailing through the Suez Canal. Read the extracts from Vicky's diary. Decide what the family couldn't do and what they had to do.

▶ *They couldn't sleep in their beds because the air conditioning didn't work, so they had to sleep on deck in their sleeping bags.*

Guess other things that Vicky and George had to do on their trip.

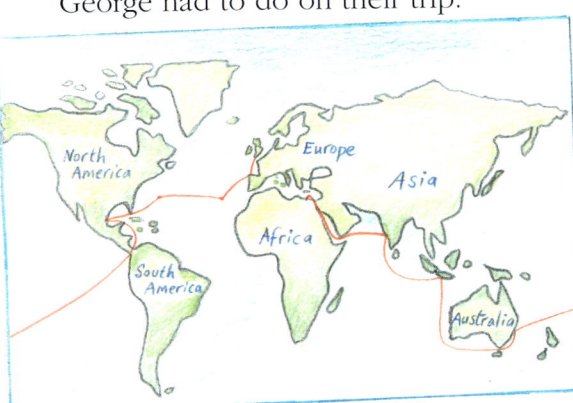

Monday 7th
The air conditioning stopped working and it was very hot last night. It was impossible to sleep in the cabin. We slept on deck in our sleeping bags.

Thursday 10th
Now the lights in the cabin don't work. It was impossible to see a thing. We lit some candles and I used my torch.

Sunday 13th
There are a lot of ships passing through the canal. Today we waited all day in Lake Timsah, because the canal was too busy.

Tuesday 22nd
We arrived in Alexandria late last night. We needed to change some money but the banks were closed so no shopping and no restaurant! We stayed on the boat and ate spaghetti - again!

12

> **Helpline** – couldn't, had to/didn't have to
>
> *couldn't* (negative of *could* in the past) = being unable to do something:
>   They couldn't sleep in their cabin.
>
> *had to* = past of *have to*
>   They had to eat spaghetti.
>   *didn't have to* = negative
>
> → GC p9

2b Listening

Look at the pictures of Vicky and George and decide what they couldn't do and what they had to do.

Listen to Vicky and George talking about the situations. Were you right?

2c Practice

Read another extract from Vicky's diary. Find five things Vicky and George didn't have to do.

> On Wednesday we had a free day – no lessons! We walked around the city in the morning. We now have a map so it wasn't necessary to ask people the way all the time!
>
> George and I visited the old castle, which was the site of the ancient lighthouse, the Pharos. It wasn't very far away, so we walked instead of taking a bus. While we were there, we met some students. There was no need to use the phrasebook because they spoke English. One of them invited us to his brother's wedding party that evening.
>
> Mum and Dad gave us permission to stay out late and we had a great time. There was dancing and singing and it was really interesting. We stayed here on Thursday too, so there was no need to get up early in the morning.

▶ They didn't have to do any lessons on Wednesday.

2d Writing

Write Vicky's diary, describing the situations in **2b**.

> So far we have had some interesting adventures here. First … and so … . Unfortunately … and so … . Then we found a restaurant but we had another problem. … so we … . We had a lovely meal and after we left the restaurant we got a taxi back to the boat.

Continue the diary with ideas of your own.

Word check

adventure	deck	instead of
ask the way	extra	learn by heart
canal	free	meal
candle	give permission	uniform
change money	housework	wedding
countryside		

52

Follow the rules 12

Helpline – couldn't, had to/didn't have to

- Explain that *couldn't* means *was /were unable* to do something. It is the negative of *could* in the past, eg:
  In the beginning Sandy and Peter couldn't find the password.
  Chris couldn't speak to the twins because strangers were following him.

- Explain that *had to* is the past of *have to*. Point out that *must* has no past form, we usually express past obligation with *had to*, eg:
  The Robinsons had to use candles.
  They didn't have to eat spaghetti on Wednesday.
  The twins had to find the password.
  Did Chris have to hide his computer program?

2b Listening

Aim: further practice of *couldn't* and *had to*.
Summary: Ss predict problems using the pictures and then listen to confirm their predictions.

Lead in

- Books closed. Ask Ss to predict what the Robinsons are going to do on Wednesday 23rd, eg:
  I think they'll go to the bank and change some money.

- When Ss have made some suggestions, ask what problems the Robinsons may have. (They don't speak the language, they don't know their way around the city.)

Main activity

- Books open. Ss look at the pictures and decide what Vicky and George couldn't do and what they had to do. Listen to some suggestions but do not confirm.

- Play the cassette twice. Pause the cassette at intervals to allow Ss time to compare their predictions with the conversation. Ask Ss to compare their answers with a partner and then ask individual Ss for the correct answers.

Answers:
1 They couldn't find their way so they had to ask a man.
2 Vicky and George couldn't speak Arabic (and the people couldn't speak English), so they had to show the man in the market the words in a phrase book.
3 They couldn't understand the menu in the restaurant, so they had to go into the kitchen and point to things.

- Ask Ss to make some guesses about other problems Vicky and George had that day. Write some cues on the board if necessary, eg:
  pay for the meal/no money/do the washing-up
  walk back to the harbour/too far/take a bus
  pay for the ticket/no money/go to the police station

Extra activity 1

- Ask Ss to write a sentence for each pair of pictures using *couldn't* and *had to*.

Extra activity 2

- Ss work with a partner to roleplay a conversation between Vicky or George and a friend. They talk about their adventures in Alexandria.

2c Practice

Aim: to practise *didn't have to*.
Summary: Ss read Vicky's diary and then rephrase parts of it.

Main activity

- Ss read the extract from Vicky's diary and find six things Vicky and George didn't have to do on that day.

Answers:
They didn't have to do lessons.
They didn't have to ask the way all the time.
They didn't have to take a bus to the old castle.
They didn't have to use their phrase book when they talked to some students.
They didn't' t have to go to bed early on Wednesday.
They didn't have to get up early on Thursday.

- Ask Ss to expand the sentences above by giving a reason, eg:
  They didn't have to do lessons on Wednesday because they had a free day.

Extra activity 1

- Ss tell a partner three things they didn't have to do last weekend, eg:
  I didn't have to go to school.

Extra activity 2

- Ask Ss what else they know about Alexandria. (Some information: Alexander the Great founded this city in 332 BC. It had a large, impressive library which was destroyed by fire around the time of Julius Caesar. The Pharos (Lighthouse), 120 metres high and built in about 280 AD, was one of the Seven Wonders of the World but it was destroyed in 1280. Today Alexandria is the second largest city in Egypt and has a busy port.)

2d Writing

Aim: more practice of *couldn't* and *had to/didn't have to*.
Summary: Ss use ideas from activity 2b to complete Vicky's diary.

Lead in

- Ask Ss to look at the pictures in activity 2b again and tell a partner what happened.

Main activity

- Ss work individually to continue Vicky's diary. Go around the class and help if necessary. Early finishers draw a picture to accompany one of her adventures.

Word check

Ss test each other's spelling in pairs.

Teacher's Book Unit 12

12 Follow the rules

Lesson 3 Words in action

1

Aim: to make predictions and then read for specific information.
Summary: Ss predict the answers to questions and then check them in a text.

Lead in

- Books closed. Write the title of the project on the board:
  Food through the ages.
  Ask Ss to make some guesses about what information this project might contain.
- Books open, text covered. Ask Ss to read the three questions in the SB and to guess the answers. Do not confirm yet.
- Ask Ss to read the text silently to check their answers to the questions. Ask individual Ss for their answers.

Answers:
a) in salt   b) America   c) 1810

2

Aim: to identify reference words in the text.
Summary: Ss decide what words in the text refer to.

Main activity

- Ask Ss to read the text again to decide what the words underlined in the text in 1 refer to. Go through the example with the whole class. Ss check answers with a partner. Ask individual Ss for the correct words.

Answers:
them – animals
it – meat
there – America
it – tinned food

- Explain to Ss that potatoes and tomatoes come from South America and that chocolate comes from Mexico.

Extra activity

- Books closed. Ss work with a partner to remember three things connected with food that people had to do in past times, eg:
  The earliest people had to spend nearly all their time looking for food.

3

Aim: focus on lexical sets.
Summary: Ss divide food words into four groups.

Lead in

- Books closed. Ask Ss to think of different types of food categories. Suggest one category, eg *meat*, if Ss seem to have no ideas.

Main activity

- Books open. Write the four categories in the SB on the board. Ask Ss to put the words in the right categories.
- Ss then work with a partner to add more words to each category. Ask individual Ss for the answers.

Answers:
Things you can drink: milk, water, tea, coffee
Kinds of fruit: apple, orange, banana
Kinds of vegetable or salad: tomato, bean, potato, onion
Things we put in food for flavour: sugar, garlic, salt, pepper

Extra activity

- Ask Ss to think of different milk products. (These include butter, cheese, yogurt, ice cream and cream.)

WORDS in ACTION

1 David Aitken wrote a project about food. How much do you know about the history of food? Make some guesses before you read David's project.

a) How did people keep food before they had refrigerators?
   in salt   in ice   in oil
b) Where did potatoes first come from?
   Egypt   Ireland   America
c) When did tinned food first appear?
   1710   1810   1910

Food through the ages

The earliest people, before the age of farming, spent nearly all their time looking for food. The men hunted and the women and children collected nuts, leaves, roots and insects. There wasn't <u>enough</u> in one place, and people had to move around.

Thousands of years later, food was still a problem. In the middle ages (1000-1500), farmers had to kill all their animals in the autumn, because there wasn't enough food for <u>them</u> in the winter. They had to put salt with the meat to preserve <u>it</u>, and the cooks had to make lots of tasty sauces when they cooked the meat.

In the 1600s, explorers from Europe found new kinds of food in America. Potatoes, tomatoes and chocolate all came from <u>there</u>.

In 1810 a Frenchman invented tinned food, and after the 1850s <u>it</u> became more common. Also, special ships carried cheap frozen meat from Australia and South America to Europe. Then people did not have to buy fresh food every day.

2 What do the words underlined in the text in **1** refer to?

enough
a) enough people   b) enough food
   = *enough food*
them
a) farmers   b) animals
it
a) meat   b) salt
there
a) America   b) Europe
it
a) tinned food   b) frozen meat

3 Divide the list of food into four different types. Can you add any more words to your lists?

Things you can drink
Kinds of fruit
Kinds of vegetable or salad
Things we put in food for flavour

milk	banana	potato	salt
apple	tomato	tea	pepper
water	bean	garlic	onion
orange	sugar	coffee	

53

13 Did you know?

present simple passive; past simple passive

Green corner

1a Practice

Nick's friend Tony told *Brilliant* about SORT. SORT is a project for using rubbish. SORT stands for Separate Out Recyclables Today. This is what Tony said. Match some of the information with the pictures.

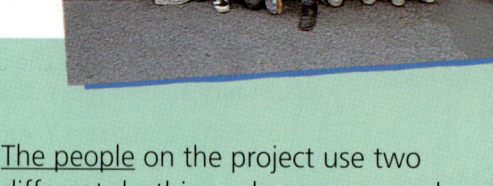

The people on the project use two different dustbins, a brown one and a green one.
They put different types of rubbish into each bin. The brown bin has two sections.
They use the front part for organic waste, like fruit and vegetables.
They use the other section for things which are not suitable for recycling.
They fill the green bin with recyclable things.
They take glass bottles to the bottle bank.
People collect the rubbish as usual. At the SORT plant people separate the types of rubbish from the green bin.
They divide the rubbish into eighteen different types of paper, plastics, metals and textiles.

Helpline

– present simple passive

is/are + past participle

The front part *is used* for organic waste.

Different types of rubbish *are put* into each bin.

→ GC p10

Did you know? 13

Unit 13		Functions	Grammar
Lesson 1	Green corner	Describing a system impersonally	Present simple passive
Lesson 2	It's hard to believe	Describing events	Past simple passive
Lesson 3	CHRIS 5		

Word check

alive	destroy	nowadays
bury	divide	pollution
chest	electricity	section
cleaner (n)	lift (n)	separate (v)
cut down	metal (n)	waste

Lesson 1 Green corner

1a Practice

Aim: to present a context in which the passive can be used.
Summary: Ss match information with pictures.

Lead in

- Books closed. Read the first part of the introduction:
Nick's friend, Tony, told 'Brilliant' about SORT. SORT is a project for using rubbish. SORT stands for ...
Ask Ss to guess what each word of this acronym is. Accept some guesses and then write the answer on the board:
Separate Out Recyclables Today
- Ask Ss to mention some things which we can recycle. Write a few ideas on the board.

Main activity

- Books open. Ask Ss to match some of the information with the pictures. Point out to Ss that they can guess some of the words in the text by using the pictures.
- Ss check their answers with a partner. Ask individual Ss for the answers.

Answers:
From the top clockwise:
The people on the project use two different dustbins, a brown one and a green one.
The brown bin has two sections. They use the front part for organic waste, like fruit and vegetables. They use the other section for things which are not suitable for recycling.
At the SORT plant people separate the types of rubbish from the green bin.

Extra activity

- Ss cover the sentences and describe what the people in the pictures are doing.

Helpline – present simple passive

- Point out that in a description of a project or a process, we are usually more interested in the steps than in who carries them out. We use the present simple passive to describe such steps.
- Explain that we form the present simple passive with is/are + past participle, eg:
Bottles are taken to the bottle bank.
Is the front part used for organic waste?
- Explain that one use of the passive is when we are more interested in events and processes, ie in what happens and not in the people who make these things happen, eg:
Our rubbish is collected twice a week
NOT
The refuse collectors collect our rubbish twice a week.
- Point out that only verbs that have an object [transitive verbs] can be made passive. Some languages use the passive form of a verb when English does not use the passive. This may be a problem for some students. Point out also that some passive sentences mention the person who performed the action if this is important.

Our rubbish is collected twice a week.	*(We know who collects the rubbish.)*
Our dustbins are provided by the local council.	*(We want to know who provides the dustbins.)*

13 Did you know?

1b Practice

Aim: to present and practise the present simple passive.
Summary: Ss rewrite the information in activity 1a using the present simple passive.

Lead in

- Remind Ss that when Nick writes about the project he does not want to talk about the people on the recycling project. The interesting information is what and how they recycle.

Main activity

- Read aloud the first sentence from the information in activity 1a and then read the first sentence from Nick's article in activity 1b. Point out that Nick has not used the underlined words from activity 1a.
- Read aloud the rest of Nick's article. Ask Ss to continue the article with a partner. Go around the class and check that Ss are using the present simple passive. Ask individual Ss to say a sentence each from the article. Then ask Ss to write the article.

Answers:
The green bin is filled with recyclable things.
Glass bottles are taken to the bottle bank.
The rubbish is collected as usual.
At the SORT plant the types of rubbish from the green bin are separated.
The rubbish is divided into eighteen different types of paper, plastics, metals and textiles.

Extra activity

- Ss use the pictures from activity 1a to make sentences using the present simple passive.

1c Listening

Aim: further practice of the present simple passive.
Summary: Ss listen and identify what the things in the pictures are made from.

Lead in

- Ask Ss if they have ever made anything from rubbish or found anything useful in the rubbish.

Main activity

- Play the cassette twice. During the second listening pause after each description to give Ss more time to write. Ask Ss to write their answers and compare them with a partner. Ask individual Ss what the things are made from.

Answers:
1 cans
2 metal foil cartons (the kind you get from takeaway food shops)
3 (recycled) plastic bottles
4 (recycled) newspapers

Extra activity

- Play the cassette again. Ask Ss to identify the things in the pictures. They then say what they are made from and give any extra information they can remember.

1d Practice

Aim: further practice of the present simple passive.
Summary: Ss match endings to beginnings and make true sentences.

Lead in

- Books closed. Write these words on the board:
  ducks   fish   burn   bury   smog   exhaust fumes
- Ask Ss to guess how they are connected to the environment. Listen to some suggestions but do not confirm.

Main activity

- Ss work with a partner to match the beginnings and endings of the sentences. Ask individual Ss for the answers.

Answers:
1 d)   2 a)   3 e)   4 b)   5 f)   6 c)

Optional activity

- Write these four verbs on the board:
  is/are burned   is/are produced   is/are used   is/are found
- Ask Ss to make four new sentences about the environment with these phrases.

Lesson 2 It's hard to believe

2a New language

Aim: to present the past simple passive.
Summary: Ss complete a quiz.

Lead in

- Ask Ss:
  What is the strangest thing that has happened in your city or country?
  Be ready with an anecdote if Ss cannot think of anything.

Main activity

- Ask Ss to read the amazing stories silently and guess the correct answers. Ss compare their answers with a partner. Ask individual Ss to read out the answers as in the example.

Answers:
1 b)   2 b)   3 c)   4 b)   5 a)   6 b)

Extra activity

- Books closed. Write these key words on the board:
  the highest mountains   sandwiches   an Indian
  the walk   the numbers   one of the Seven Wonders
  city council
- Ask Ss to make sentences using the past simple passive.

Teacher's Book Unit 13

1b Practice

Nick wrote an article about SORT. Continue his description of SORT so that Tony's underlined words in **1a** are not in the article.

> Two different dustbins, a brown one and a green one, are used on this project. Different types of rubbish are put into each bin. The brown bin has two sections. The front part is used for organic waste, like fruit and vegetables. The other section is used for things which are not suitable for recycling …

1c Listening

Look at the pictures and listen to the radio programme. What are the things in the pictures made from?

1d Practice

How much do you know about the environment? Match the endings to the beginnings and make true sentences.

1 In parts of China, ducks …
2 Most newspapers are not …
3 Nowadays many large cities …
4 Pollution from British factories …
5 Ninety per cent of all rubbish …
6 In Edmonton, England, rubbish …

a) … made from trees that are cut down. Recycled paper is used.
b) … is carried by the wind and damages fish and plants far away in Sweden.
c) … is burned and used to produce electricity.
d) … are used instead of chemicals to control insects in rice fields.
e) … are covered with poisonous smog, caused mainly by car exhaust fumes.
f) … is buried in big holes in the ground called landfill sites.

It's hard to believe

2a New language

Read these amazing stories. Which are the correct facts? Make some guesses!

1 In 1835 an Indian was locked into a chest and the chest was buried under the ground. The chest was dug up … later and the man was alive and well.
   a) 10 days   b) 40 days   c) 52 days
2 The numbers used today in Europe were invented in … 1500 years ago.
   a) Greece   b) India   c) Rome
3 In 1959 a … was elected to the city council in São Paulo, Brazil.
   a) horse   b) monkey   c) rhinoceros
4 Between 1868 and 1876, the highest mountains in the Alps were climbed by …
   a) three children.   b) a dog.   c) a cyclist.
5 Sandwiches were invented by the Earl of Sandwich. They were served when he …
   a) was playing cards.   b) was riding his horse.
   c) was writing letters.
6 Only one of the Seven Wonders of the World is still standing. This was built in …
   a) Greece.   b) Egypt.   c) Italy.

▶ *I think the Indian was dug up 10 days later.*

13

> **Helpline** – past simple passive
>
> was/were + past participle:
>
> The Indian was locked in a chest.
>
> Sandwiches were invented by the Earl of Sandwich.
>
> → GC p10

2b Practice

Yesterday you had lots of homework, but you did not do it! Think of five unusual excuses. Use ideas from the pictures and ideas of your own.

▶ I'm afraid my homework was eaten by my pet crocodile. This is what happened. Last night I finished my homework and …

2c Listening

The Empire State Building is an amazing building! Before you read, guess the missing information.

1 The Empire State Building was finished in …
2 It was built by … workers in …
3 The building is visited by … every year.
4 People are carried to its … floors by … lifts.
5 Every evening the offices inside are cleaned by … cleaners.
6 On 28th July 1945 the building was damaged by …

Now listen and complete the sentences. Were your guesses correct?

2d Writing

Is there an amazing building in your country? Write a paragraph about it. Use the sentences in **2c** to help you and use these verbs:

build   start/finish
damage/destroy   visit

Word check
alive
bury
chest
cleaner (n)
cut down
destroy
divide
electricity
lift (n)
metal (n)
nowadays
pollution
section
separate (v)
waste

Did you know? 13

Helpline – past simple passive

- Explain that we form the past simple passive with *was/were* + past participle, eg:
  Present-day numbers were invented in India.
  The pyramids were built in Egypt.

2b Practice

Aim: further practice of the past simple passive.
Summary: Ss make up excuses for not doing their homework.

Lead in

- Ask Ss what excuses they usually give when they do not do their homework.
  I left my exercise book at home.
  I had to visit the doctor/the dentist/my grandmother.
  I couldn't understand the exercise.

Main activity

- Read the introduction and the example. Ask Ss to work in small groups. They use the pictures in the SB and their own ideas to invent some more amazing excuses. One member of the group must keep notes. Go around the class and help if necessary. Ask a member from each group to give their excuses. The class can vote on the best excuse.

Suggested answers:
My notebook was stolen by a burglar.
My notebook was thrown into the dustbin.
My notebook was burnt.

2c Listening

Aim: further practice of the past simple passive with an agent.
Summary: Ss guess missing information about the Empire State Building and then listen and check.

Lead in

- Books closed. Show Ss the picture for activity 2c in your own book and ask them to identify the building. (It is the Empire State Building.) Ask Ss to say what they know about it, but do not confirm.

Main activity

- Ask Ss to read the sentences about the Empire State Building and guess the missing information. Ask for guesses and write them on the board.
- Play the cassette twice. Ss complete the missing information. Tell them to write numbers and not words for the figures they hear. Ss compare their sentences with a partner. Ask individual Ss for the answers.

Answers:
1 1931
2 3000 workers/15 months
3 2 million tourists
4 102 floors/73 lifts
5 150 cleaners
6 a plane

Extra activity

- Books closed. Write these words on the board:
  begin   finish   build   visit   clean   damage
  Ask Ss to work with a partner to write three or four sentences about the Empire State Building with the present or past simple passive.
- This extra information about the Empire State Building can be used as a dictation:
  It was sold / for 42 million dollars / in 1991 / and this / was considered / cheap! / About 1800 people / work there / and they are visited / by 20,000 more people / who do business / with the jewellers, / shoemakers, / dentists and doctors /who work there. It is said / that you never need / to leave the building / as it has everything / you need./ It is like a street / that goes up / to the sky.

2d Writing

Aim: further practice of the present and past simple passive.
Summary: Ss write about an amazing building in their own country.

Lead in

- Ask Ss for suggestions of amazing or interesting buildings in their country. Write some names on the board and ask for useful information about each, eg:
  The Great Pyramid – was built about 2600 BC, was used as a tomb.
  The Eiffel Tower – was built in 1889, was nearly destroyed by the Germans at the end of the Second World War.
  Theatre at Epidaurus – was built in 400 BC.

Main activity

- If this activity is done outside class Ss can consult encyclopedias and other people for extra information.
- Ss work individually to write a paragraph about a particular building. Early finishers exchange paragraphs. Go around the class and help if necessary.

Optional activity

- Tell Ss to imagine that they live in the year 2099 and write a similar paragraph about an imaginary building. They can illustrate their text if they wish.

Word check

- Ss test each other's spelling in pairs.

13 Did you know?

Lesson 3 CHRIS Episode 5

Aim: to read for specific information; to revise making questions using the past simple passive; to listen for specific information.

The story so far:

Main activity

- Ss work with a partner to answer the questions. Ask individual Ss for the answers.

Answers:
1 London.
2 He needed a holiday.
3 Chris wants them to have fun with the computer and to see some interesting places in London.

1

Lead in

- Ss look at the picture and say what they can see. Ask them what they know about Cleopatra's Needle and Egypt.
- Ask Ss to read the text once and find the answers to these questions:
  a) What is shown in the picture?
  b) Where did it come from?
  c) Where is it now?
  d) How did it get there?
- Ask individual Ss for the answers.

Answers:
a) Cleopatra's Needle
b) Egypt
c) London
d) On a special ship called 'Cleopatra'.

Main activity

- Ask Ss to underline all the passive verbs in the text. Write these on the board.
- Ss read the text a second time and make questions for the answers given below the text. Ask individual Ss to read aloud their questions.

Answers:
a) Who was Cleopatra's Needle made for?
b) When was it brought to London?
c) How much (money) was collected to pay for it?
d) Where was it loaded onto the special ship?
e) Where was it placed?

Extra activity

- Ask Ss to close their books and use the list of passive verbs on the board to recall the main points in the text.

2

Lead in

- Ss look at the picture and say what they think will happen next.

Main activity

- Ss read the next part of the story and find out what happens. Ask individual Ss to tell the class.

Extra activity

- Play the recorded version of the conversation. Ss work in groups of three and read the conversation. They then roleplay it. Groups can record their roleplay if they wish.

3

Lead in

- Ask Ss to predict what Inspector Wendy Harman tells the twins.

Main activity

- Play the cassette and ask Ss to listen for what the inspector says about Chris and the computer game. Ss work with a partner and discuss what she says. Play the cassette a second time. Then ask individual Ss to give the answers. Do not ask Ss to use the passive.

Answers:
Chris has stolen a new computer game.
He is going to sell it to a foreign company.

Extra activity

- Books closed. Ss work in groups of three to roleplay the conversation between the twins and Wendy Harman. Tell them that they need not try to remember the exact words.

CHRIS

Episode 5

The story so far:

1. What was the computer password?
2. Why has Chris disappeared?
3. What does Chris want the twins to do?

1 Read this part of the story and make the questions to go with the short answers.

CHRIS printed this information for the twins.

a

Cleopatra's Needle. This is an Egyptian obelisk and is over 3500 years old. It was made for the Pharaoh, Thotmes III. It was brought to London in 1878. £15000 was collected from people in Britain to pay for it. A special ship, called 'Cleopatra', was built. The obelisk was loaded onto the ship in Alexandria and the 'Cleopatra' was pulled by another ship. The 'Cleopatra' nearly sank in a storm in the Bay of Biscay, but finally arrived in London in January 1878. The obelisk was placed beside the Thames in London as a memorial to the war with Napoleon which ended in 1815. A similar obelisk was given to France and still stands in the Place de la Concorde in Paris.

Short answers

a) ...   For Thotmes III.
b) ...   In 1878.
c) ...   £15000.
d) ...   In Alexandria.
e) ...   Beside the Thames.

2 Read the next part of the story.

b

Sandy: Well, this is it Peter. What do we do now?
Peter: We look for the next clue, I suppose.
Woman: Hello, are your names Peter and Sandy?
Sandy: Yes, they are! But how did you know? Are you a friend of Chris's?
Woman: Not exactly. My name is Wendy Harman, Inspector Wendy Harman. I'm from the police. We are trying to find your brother. Do you know where he is?
Peter: No, we don't. We're looking for him too. But why do you want him?
Woman: Come over here and sit down, and I'll tell you.

3 Listen to the ending of this episode. What does Inspector Harman tell the twins about Chris and the computer game?

14 Good advice

should, shouldn't; I think, I don't think

Emergency

1a New language

Helen is writing a project about earthquakes. Helen's penfriend Alexandros sent her some information from Greece.

EARTHQUAKES

Good things to do

You should shelter under a table or stand in a doorway.

Bad things to do

You shouldn't panic and rush out into the street.

What do you think about these suggestions? Give some advice using should or shouldn't.

– listen to the news on the radio
– use the lift
– stand outside near the walls of houses
– practise leaving the school in an emergency
– go back into your house straight after the earthquake
– stand outside in an open space
– keep a bag at home with useful things for an emergency

Helpline – should and shouldn't

We use *should* and *shouldn't* for good or bad ideas. We often use them when we give advice.

Pronunciation: we do not say the *l* in should /ʃʊd/

→ GC p10

Good advice 14

Unit 14	Functions	Grammar
Lesson 1	Emergency	Giving advice	Should, shouldn't
Lesson 2	Your letters answered	Giving advice	I think/I don't think + should
Lesson 3	Check up Units 12–14		

Word check

advice	glue	straight
battery	it doesn't matter	suggestion
bored	make notes	the news
earthquake	panic	try
emergency	relax	whistle (n)
		worry

Lesson 1 Emergency

1a New language

Aim: to present *should* and *shouldn't* as a recommendation or as advice.
Summary: Ss choose items of good advice and bad advice from a list.

Lead in

- Write the word *Emergency* on the board and ask Ss to give examples of emergencies or crisis situations, eg:
  car accident   volcanic eruption   hurricane

Main activity

- Ask Ss to read the information that Alexandros sent to Helen about earthquakes. Then ask one or two Ss to repeat the advice.
- Ask Ss to read the suggestions in the list and decide, with a partner, which are good ideas and which are bad ideas. Ask individual Ss to give advice.

Answers:
You should listen to the news on the radio.
You shouldn't use the lift.
You shouldn't stand outside near the walls of houses.
You should practise leaving the school in an emergency.
You shouldn't go back into your house straight after the earthquake.
You should stand outside in an open space.
You should keep a bag at home with useful things for an emergency.

Extra activity

- Books closed. Ask Ss to give their partner advice about earthquakes. They should use the ideas in the SB and their own ideas.

Helpline – should and shouldn't

- Explain that *should* is used for something which is a good idea and *shouldn't* is used for something which is a bad idea. We often use *should* and *shouldn't* when we give advice, eg:
  You should find an open space.
  You shouldn't stand near a tall building.
- Point out that we do not pronounce the *l* in *should* and *shouldn't*.
  Other similar words are *could* and *would*.

Teacher's Book Unit 14

14 Good advice

1b Practice

Aim: further practice of *should* and *shouldn't*.
Summary: Ss choose items for an emergency bag.

Lead in

- Books closed. Ask Ss to suggest some things that would be useful for an emergency. Write some ideas on the board.

Main activity

- Ask Ss to look at the list in the SB. They work with a partner and choose some of the things. They must give a reason for their choices as in the example. Ask individual Ss for suggestions. Then ask:
What other things should you have in your emergency bag?
Tell Ss that they must agree on only two other things.

1c Listening

Aim: further practice of *should* and *shouldn't*.
Summary: Ss predict advice given in a radio programme and then listen to confirm.

Lead in

- Ask Ss to look at the list in the SB and decide what they should not do with these things. Listen to some ideas but do not confirm.

Main activity

- Play the cassette twice. Ss make notes about what you shouldn't do and why. Pause the cassette during the second listening to give Ss time to write. Ss check their notes with a partner. They may need to hear the piece a third time in order to find the reasons for not doing certain things.
- Ask individual Ss for complete answers – the advice + the reason.

Answers:
You shouldn't put heavy things on shelves because they might fall on your head during an earthquake.
You shouldn't put plants in heavy pots on windowsills or balconies because they might fall on people in the street.
You shouldn't jump out of windows or run out of doors because people are injured in this way.
You should open the doors when you feel an earthquake because after an earthquake it can be difficult to open them.

Extra activity 1

- Use part of the last paragraph of the listening as a dictation:
Sometimes we know / that an earthquake is coming / or we can feel it / beginning./ Some people / run out of doors / or even / jump out of the window./ This is not / a very good idea, / and more people / are injured / in this way./ A good idea / is to open the door / when you feel an earthquake / but stay in the house.

Extra activity 2

- Ss work with a partner to roleplay a conversation between Anna Maria (the person speaking on the radio programme) and someone who has never lived in a country with earthquakes.

1d Writing

Aim: further practice of *should* and *shouldn't*.
Summary: Ss write an advice leaflet using *should* and *shouldn't*.

Main activity

- Ss work with a partner or in a small group. Ask Ss to share their ideas but they should each write the leaflet. Go around the class and help if necessary.

Extra activity

- Ask Ss to write some advice for someone who is going on a camping holiday.

Lesson 2 Your letters answered

2a New language

Aim: to present *I think/I don't think ... should* to give advice.
Summary: Ss choose the best reply for a problem page letter and then give their own advice.

Lead in

- Write the word *problems* on the board. Tell Ss to imagine that they are going to write to a teenagers' magazine about a problem. Ask for some typical teenage problems.

Main activity

- Ask Ss to read Nick's letter and the three replies silently and decide which ideas are best. They can choose good and bad ideas from all three replies. Ask individual Ss to give their opinions using:
I think Nick should ...
I don't think Nick should ...
Ss can then add some of their own advice.

Extra activity

- Books closed. Ss roleplay a conversation between Nick and a friend. The friend is giving him useful advice about what to do and what not to do before his exams.

1b Practice

What should you have in your emergency bag? Choose some of the things in the list. Not all of them are useful. Explain your choices.

a torch   a map   a whistle   a radio   some glue
some water   some batteries   a blanket
an umbrella   a pencil   a knife   some food

▶ You should have a torch in your emergency bag so you can see in the dark.
A map isn't very useful.

Can you think of any other things you should have in your bag?

1c Listening

Before you listen, read the list. Decide what you should not do with these things.

    heavy things on shelves
    plants in heavy pots
    windows
    doors

Now listen to part of a radio programme about earthquakes. What does the programme tell you?

1d Writing

Use information from this lesson and complete the advice leaflet in **1a**. Your leaflet should have two sections:

Good things to do

Bad things to do

You can add other points of your own.

Your letters answered

2a New language

Read this letter to a magazine, and the three replies. Which ideas do you think are best? What do you think Nick should do? What shouldn't he do?

Dear Carol

My problem is exams. I worry about them all the time. Sometimes I can't sleep and I can never remember anything. I study for hours and sometimes I read the same page ten times! But in the morning I can't remember anything. What can I do? Do your readers have any ideas?

Nick, London

1 Make some notes and read them often. Relax some of the time – it's wrong to study for hours. Have a warm drink before you go to bed. Don't worry about exams – they don't really matter!

2 Drink lots of tea and coffee and study all night. Write the most important facts on your hand. You won't forget them this way! Learn all your books by heart.

3 Underline important points in your school books. Go to bed early before an exam. Study the important points before you go to sleep. Watch television then you will feel tired! Read your books again in the morning.

▶ *I think Nick should … . I don't think Nick should …*

14

> **Helpline** – I don't think
>
> We put *not* with *I think* to make it negative:
>
> *I don't think this is a good idea.* (= This is not a good idea.)
>
> → GC p10

2b Practice

A friend wants to know how to learn a foreign language. Give him or her some advice. Use ideas from the list and add ideas of your own.

listen to songs   read interesting books
learn lists of words   study grammar every day
read magazines   listen to the news on
the radio   talk to tourists   watch foreign
television programmes   write to a penfriend
learn the dictionary by heart

▶ *I think you should ... . It's a good way to learn. I don't think you should ... . It's not a very easy thing to do.*

Give some advice. What should these people do?

- a student taking an important examination tomorrow
- a tourist visiting your country

2c Writing

Here are two more letters. Read them and write a reply to each one. Say what you think each person should do.

Dear Carol

I always feel bored in the school holidays. I usually watch television all day. I can't think of anything interesting to do and I feel bored. What do you think I should do?

Newton, São Paulo

Dear Carol

My little brother is driving me mad! He takes things from my room and makes a lot of noise. I can't do my homework! My parents don't do anything because they think he is wonderful. What should I do?

Yasemin, Ankara

Dear Newton/Yasemin

This is a difficult problem. First of all I think you should ... and you should also ... . I don't think you should ... . It's not a good idea. And you really shouldn't ...

Word check

advice	panic
battery	relax
bored	straight
earthquake	suggestion
emergency	the news
glue	try
it doesn't matter	whistle (n)
make notes	worry

60

Good advice 14

Helpline – I don't think

- Explain that we put *not* with *I think* to make the whole sentence negative, eg:
  I don't think you should learn everything by heart.
  NOT
  I think you shouldn't learn everything by heart.

2b Practice

Aim: further practice of *I think/I don't think ... should* to give advice.
Summary: Ss use cues to give advice about learning a foreign language.

Lead in

- Books closed. Ask Ss to suggest some good ways of learning a foreign language. Write some ideas on the board.

Main activity

- Ss read the list in the book and compare the ideas with their own. Ss work with a partner to practise giving advice about learning a foreign language.
- Ss work in small groups and think about advice for *a student taking an important examination tomorrow* and *a tourist visiting their country*. Each group should write at least four ideas for each situation. Go around the class and help if necessary. Ask different groups for their ideas and write the best on the board.

2c Writing

Aim: further practice of *I think/I don't think ... should* to give advice.
Summary: Ss read problem letters and write letters of reply giving advice.

Lead in

- Ask Ss to read the two letters silently and find the problem that each person has. Check answers.

Answers
Newton doesn't know what to do during the holidays – he's always bored.
Yasemin's younger brother annoys her a lot.

Main activity

- Ss work with a partner and think of some advice to give Newton and Yasemin. Ask individual Ss for their advice and write some ideas on the board in note form, eg:
  Newton: telephone a friend, meet a friend at a park
  Yasemin: spend a little time playing with your brother, don't shout at him
- Ss work individually to write the two replies. Early finishers exchange letters. Go around the class and help if necessary.

Extra activity

- Ss write a whole problem page using both the problems from the lesson and their own ideas. They can try to find suitable magazine pictures to make the page more colourful. Display the problem page(s) in class.

Word check

- Write these questions on the board:
  a What is good advice in an earthquake?
  b Where do you find a battery?
  c What telephone number should you ring in an emergency?
  d What do you do when you panic?
  e When do you listen to or watch the news?
  f When should you make notes?
  g What do you do when you relax?
- Divide the class into two teams. Tell Ss that you are going to ask them some questions using words from the Word check box. The first team to give all the correct answers wins.

14 Good advice

Check up Units 12–14

1

Aim: further practice of the past simple passive.
Summary: Ss complete a paragraph with the past simple passive form of verbs.

Lead in

- Write this sentence on the board:
  I broke my arm and a doctor <u>put</u> it in plaster.
- Ask Ss to change the underlined verb into the passive.
  I broke my arm and it was put in plaster.

Main activity

- Ask Ss to read the paragraph about Mrs Normal once quickly and answer this focus question:
  What happened to Mrs Normal?
  (She was in an accident and hurt her leg.)
- Ask Ss to read the passage again more slowly to complete the gaps with one of the answers in the past simple passive. Ss check verbs with a partner. Ask individual Ss to read out a sentence each.

Answers:

1 was involved	5 was taken	9 was allowed
2 was hit	6 was examined	10 was not visited
3 was thrown	7 was put	
4 was called	8 was told	

Extra activity

- Ask Ss to imagine that the Odds visited Mrs Normal in hospital. Ss work with a partner to think of three things that happened during the Odds' visit.

2

Aim: further practice of the past simple passive.
Summary: Ss rewrite sentences using the past simple passive.

Lead in

- Books closed. Tell Ss that the Odds visited Mrs Normal at home and it was disastrous. Ask Ss to predict why.

Main activity

- Ss work individually and rewrite each sentence. Ask individual Ss to come to the board and write sentences.

Answers:

a) Funny faces were drawn on Mrs Normal's plaster.
b) The dog was given most of the food from the fridge.
c) Four cups and three plates were broken.
d) Two of the best chairs were taken into the garden.
e) All Mrs Normal's chocolates were eaten.

Extra activity

- Ask Ss to write a short paragraph describing the Odds' visit and to give the paragraph a title.

3

Aim: further practice of word order in questions.
Summary: Ss reorder words and make questions.

Main activity

- Ss work individually and reorder the words to form questions. They then check with a partner. Ask individual Ss to write their questions on the board.

Answers:

a) Do you have to get up early every morning?
b) What should we do to make this town a better place?
c) What do you have to do at home this evening?
d) What should a good student do?

- Ss work with a partner and ask each other these questions. Ask individual Ss for their answers and write some of the ideas for questions b) and d) on the board.

Extra activity

- Ss work with a partner and write two or three more jumbled questions on a slip of paper. Collect the slips of paper and distribute them to other pairs. Ss reorder the words in the jumbled questions they receive and discuss the answers.

4

Aim: further practice of *didn't have to*.
Summary: Ss make sentences about Nick for three different situations.

Main activity

- Ss write two sentences for each situation. Ask individual Ss for their answers.

Extra activity

- Ask Ss to find out two things their partner didn't have to do last year but has to do this year.

5

Aim: further focus on the relation between spelling and pronunciation.
Summary: Ss compare the pronunciation of words with similar spelling.

Main activity

- Ask Ss to look at the examples in the SB. Read the examples aloud:
  cup /kʌp/   cupboard /kʌbəd/   (No)
  win /wɪn/   Winter /wɪntə/   (Yes)
- Ss decide if the pronunciation of the first word is repeated in the second word in each pair.
- Play the cassette twice for Ss to check their answers.

Answers:

a) yes	c) no	e) yes	g) no	i) yes
b) no	d) no	f) no	h) yes	j) no

Optional activity

- Ask Ss to think of similar examples and test their partners. (They may need to check their pronunciation with you first.)

UNITS 12–14

CHECK UP

1 Put one of the verbs into each space. Use the past simple passive.

> tell   allow   call   examine   hit   involve
> put   take   throw   not visit

Last week Mrs Normal ..1.. in an accident. She was going to work on the bus and the bus ..2.. by a lorry. Mrs Normal ..3.. out of her seat and hurt her leg. An ambulance ..4.. and she ..5.. to hospital. She ..6.. and her leg ..7.. in plaster. She ..8.. to stay in hospital for two days, but then she ..9.. to go home. Luckily she ..10.. by the Odds while she was in hospital, but when she came home they insisted on going round to see her.

2 The whole Odd family came to see Mrs Normal one morning. Lots of strange things happened that morning. Rewrite each sentence so that it begins with the word or words underlined.

a) Someone drew <u>funny</u> faces on Mrs Normal's plaster.
b) Someone gave <u>the dog</u> most of the food from the fridge.
c) Someone broke <u>four cups and three plates</u>.
d) Someone took <u>two of the best chairs</u> into the garden.
e) Someone ate <u>all</u> Mrs Normal's chocolates.

3 Make a question from each group of words.

a) up morning you do early every get have to?
b) make place we should town what a to better do this?
c) at have this home you what evening do do to?
d) student a should what do good?

Ask a partner the questions. Discuss the answers.

4 Write three things that Nick didn't have to do in each situation.

a) last week when there was a national holiday
b) last summer when the weather was very good
c) when he lived in a small village and not in a large city

5 Is the pronunciation of the first word repeated in the same way in the second word?

   1 <u>cu</u>p   2 <u>cu</u>pboard   *No*
   1 <u>wi</u>n   2 <u>wi</u>nter   *Yes*

a) 1 won   2 wonderful
b) 1 hear   2 heart
c) 1 get   2 vegetable
d) 1 age   2 damage
e) 1 ill   2 village
f) 1 over   2 discover
g) 1 table 2 suitable
h) 1 man   2 manage
i) 1 fact   2 factory
j) 1 miss 2 permission

Listen and check your answers.

15 Changes

used to; didn't use to

Old and new

1a New language

While they were on a Greek island, Vicky and George went to the cinema and saw a cowboy film. They remembered their visit to a Wild West museum in Texas. Look at the pictures. Compare life in the west of the USA now with life in the Wild West in the past.

▶ *Most people used to live in small wooden cabins, but nowadays they live in modern houses and flats.*

> **Helpline** – used to
>
> We use *used to* for habits/everyday actions in the past:
>
> *I used to live in a small town but now I live in a big city.*
> Pronunciation /juːs tə/
>
> → GC p11

Changes 15

Unit 15		Functions	Grammar
Lesson 1	Old and new	Contrasting past habits/everyday actions with habits/everyday actions in the present	Used to
Lesson 2	Turn over a new leaf	Contrasting past states with present states	Used to, didn't use to
Lesson 3	Words in action		

Word check

block of flats	phone (v)	slim
dark (n)	play with	topic
modern	protected	traffic
nails	recently	turn over a new leaf
nobody	shy	

Helpline – used to

- Explain that we use *used to* for habits and everyday actions in the past. If we say that someone used to do something, we mean that this person did it in the past but does not do it now, eg:
  She used to drive a car to work but now she rides a bike.
- Point out that the form *used to* + infinitive exists only in the past.

Lesson 1 Old and new

1a New language

Aim: to present *used to* to describe habits and everyday actions in the past.
Summary: Ss compare life in the old Wild West with life in the present West of the USA.

Lead in

- Write the words *cowboy film* on the board. Ask Ss if they have seen any cowboy films. Ask them to say what they can about cowboys and their way of life.

Main activity

- Read or play the introduction to the activity. Ask Ss to look at the example sentence:
  Most people used to live in small wooden cabins, but nowadays they live in modern houses and flats.
- Ss work with a partner and make similar sentences using the pictures. Go around the class and help if necessary. Ask individual Ss for the answers.

Answers:
They used to ride horses, but nowadays they drive cars.
They used to sing and play their guitars, but nowadays they watch television.
They used to travel by stagecoach, but nowadays they travel by plane.
They used to eat around campfires, but nowadays they eat at fast food restaurants.

- Ask Ss to think of some more differences between life in the Wild West in the past and life in the West of the USA nowadays, eg:
  They used to kill buffalo, but nowadays they protect them.

Teacher's Book Unit 15

15 Changes

1b Practice

Aim: further practice of *used to*.
Summary: Ss talk about the differences between the past and today.

Lead in

- Books closed. Ask Ss to say what the biggest changes have been in the last hundred years. Suggestions include:
  buildings   transport   free time activities   technology

Main activity

- Read the example. Ask Ss to look at the list of things people do nowadays. Ss work with a partner to make sentences about nowadays and what people used to do a hundred years ago. Go around the class and help if necessary. Ask individual Ss for their sentences.

Extra activity

- Ss write a complete paragraph using the information in activity 1b.

1c Practice

Aim: further practice of *used to* to talk about past habits.
Summary: Ss use pictures to compare Vicky and George's past life with their present one.

Lead in

- Books closed. Ask Ss to say how Vicky and George's lives have changed since they started their trip around the world.

Main activity

- Ss look at the pictures and make sentences about the changes in Vicky and George's lives. Ask individual Ss for their answers.

Answers:
1 They used to get up very early and then go to school but now they get up at about eight o'clock and have a swim before breakfast.
2 They used to have lessons in a classroom with a teacher but now they have lessons on the boat with their parents.

- Ask Ss to suggest other changes, eg:
  They used to wash their clothes in a washing machine but now they wash them by hand.
  They used to spend their free time watching television but now they go sightseeing.
  They used to have lots of space for their things but now they have only a few drawers.
  They used to phone their friends almost every day but now they can only write letters to them.

1d Listening

Aim: listening for gist and specific information; further practice of *used to*.
Summary: Ss identify topics, and then describe what each speaker says about the topics.

Lead in

- Ask Ss to guess what the people will say about each topic, eg:
  I think the speaker will say that the sea is more polluted now than it used to be.

Main activity

- Play the cassette once. Ss tick the topics that the people talk about. Ask individual Ss for the answers.

Answers:
pollution   traffic   people   jobs

- Ask Ss to listen again for detailed information about each topic. Ss should make some notes as they listen and then compare their notes with a partner. Go around the class and see how much information Ss have noted down. If necessary, play the cassette for a third time. Ask individual Ss for their answers.

Suggested answers:
The city used to be dirtier. There used to be more pollution but now it's cleaner.
The traffic used to move more quickly but now it's worse.
The people used to be more friendly but now they are too busy to smile.
Most people used to be fishermen but now they do different jobs.

Lesson 2 Turn over a new leaf

2a New language

Aim: to present *didn't use to*.
Summary: Ss compare the Odds five years ago with the Odds now and describe the differences.

Main activity

- Ask Ss to look at the pictures. Read the first example:
  Mrs Odd used to be slimmer.
  Ask:
  What is Mrs Odd like now?   (fatter)
  Say: *Mrs Odd used to be slimmer. She didn't use to be fat.*
  Read the second example.
- Ss work in pairs and think of differences. Ask individual Ss for sentences and write them on the board.

Answers:
Mrs Odd used to have long hair.
Mr Odd used to have a moustache. He didn't use to have short hair.
Ozzy used to suck his thumb. He didn't use to be so tall.
Olive used to bite her nails.

- Ask Ss to work with a partner and make True/False sentences about the Odds.

Helpline – didn't use to

- Explain that the negative form of *used to* is *didn't use to*.

1b Practice

Look at the list of things that people do nowadays. What happened a hundred years ago in your country, before these things were possible?

Nowadays lots of people …

live in blocks of flats in big cities   go everywhere by car   watch television in the evening   use computers   listen to radios   travel by plane   ride bicycles   cook frozen food   phone their friends

A hundred years ago …

most people used to …
only a few people used to …
nobody used to …
they used to … instead.

▶ *Nowadays lots of people live in blocks of flats. A hundred years ago most people used to live in small houses with gardens. Most people lived in small villages.*

1c Practice

Describe what Vicky and George used to do every day and what they now do.

▶ *They used to … but now …*

Can you think of any other changes for Vicky and George?

1d Listening

Listen to people talking about how their cities have changed. Tick ✓ the topics you hear them talking about.

pollution ☐   weather ☐   food ☐   traffic ☐   people ☐   jobs ☐

Listen again. What do they say about the topics you have ticked?

Turn over a new leaf

2a New language

Look at the pictures of the Odd family. One was taken yesterday and the other was taken ten years ago. What differences can you see?

▶ *Mrs Odd used to be slimmer.*
Olive didn't use to have glasses.

> **Helpline** – didn't use to
>
> The negative form of *used to* is *didn't use to*:
> I didn't use to be tall.
>
> → GC p11

15

2b Practice

Look at **2a**. Can you say similar things about yourself?

▶ *I used to bite my nails.
I didn't use to have long hair.*

2c Practice

Make a list of things you used to do/have/be when you were younger, but you don't do/have/be now. Use ideas from the list and add ideas of your own.

cry all the time   play with dolls
sleep in the afternoon
walk to school with my mother
be afraid of dogs/spiders/the dark
be very shy   have long hair
have glasses

Tell a partner about other things you used to do/have/be when you were younger.

▶ *When I was five I used to …*

2d Writing

Continue the paragraphs.

When I was younger, life was different. I used to … . I didn't use to … .

Now my life has changed. I … and I don't …

2e Writing

Write an advertisement to go with these illustrations.

CLOGGIE BOOTS
– make everyone your friend

Before I discovered Cloggie Boots I used to … . Other kids used to … . Nobody used to …

Now I wear **CLOGGIE BOOTS**

Word check

block of flats	phone (v)	slim
dark (n)	play with	topic
modern	protected	traffic
nails	recently	turn over a new leaf
nobody	shy	

Changes 15

2b Practice

Aim: personalized practice of *used to* and *didn't use to*.
Summary: Ss use the language in activity 2a to make true sentences about themselves.

Lead in

- Write the sentences from activity 2a on the board again if necessary.

Main activity

- Invite Ss to read out the sentences from the board which are true for them. Encourage them to read out sentences only if things are different now. For example, only Ss with short hair now should say *I used to have long hair*.

2c Practice

Aim: further practice of *used to* and *didn't use to*.
Summary: Ss make comments about themselves.

Lead in

- Books closed. Ask Ss to think of things they *used to do/have/be* when they were younger. Ask individual Ss for ideas and write them on the board.

Main activity

- Ask Ss to use their own ideas and the ideas from the list in the SB to make sentences with *used to* and *didn't use to*. Go around the class and help if necessary.

2d Writing

Aim: to compare past and present habits and everyday actions.
Summary: Ss write one paragraph about when they were younger and another paragraph about how their life has changed.

Main activity

- Ask Ss to use the information from activity 2c to write two paragraphs about themselves. Go around the class and help if necessary.

Extra activity

- Read out some of the paragraphs and ask Ss to guess who wrote them.

2e Writing

Aim: further written practice of *used to*.
Summary: Ss complete an advertisement.

Lead in

- Ask Ss what kind of shoes are popular these days. Write a list, eg *trainers, boots* on the board.
- They look at the top picture and say what used to happen. Ask them what happens in the bottom picture now that the boy wears Cloggie Boots.

Main activity

- Ss work in pairs and think of ideas for the advertisement about Cloggie Boots. They then write individually. Circulate the advertisements around the class or display them on the walls. Ss can vote for the best advertisement.

Word check

- Choose some words from the Word check box and write them on the board with some letters missing, eg:
  bl_ _ _ of fl_ts   (block of flats)
  m_d_rn   (modern)
  _ _body   (nobody)
  re_en_l_   (recently)
  raffi   (traffic)
- Ask Ss to fill the gaps (in notebooks, on the board or orally).
- Now ask Ss to think of an example sentence using each word. This can be set as a team game.

15 Changes

Lesson 3 Words in action

1

Aim: further focus on *shouldn't*.
Summary: Ss guess the missing words before listening, and then listen and confirm.

Lead in

- Ss read the song and try to guess the missing words.

Main activity

- Play the song twice and and ask Ss to complete the missing words. Ask how many they were able to guess.

Answers:

1 tell	2 writing	3 advice	4 think
5 answer	6 do	7 change	8 friends
9 think	10 try		

Extra activity

- Write the following words on the board:
  a) immediately (right away)
  b) two times (twice)
  c) opinion (point of view)
  d) come to a decision about (make up your mind)
     something
  e) answer (reply)
- Ask Ss to find a word or phrase in the song which has the same meaning.

2

Aim: focus on sentence stress.
Summary: Ss chant phrases from the song.

Lead in

- Books closed. Play the first three lines of the chorus of the song twice. Ask Ss to say which words are stressed.

Main activity

- Books open. Ask Ss to check if they correctly identified the stressed word. They then practise saying the lines of the chorus with a partner.

3

Aim: to focus on adjectives and adverbs ending with -*y*; giving advice.
Summary: Ss decide if words are adjectives or adverbs and then use the adjectives to give advice.

Main activity

- Ss decide which words in the list are adjectives and which are adverbs. Tell them to write two lists.

Answers:

Adjectives	Adverbs
friendly	gently
healthy	luckily
hungry	easily
dirty	loudly

- Ask Ss to make the adverbs into adjectives – *gentle, lucky, easy, loud*. Explain that words ending in -*ly* are usually adverbs. The adjective *friendly* is, of course, an exception and has no adverb form – we say *in a friendly way*.
- Ask Ss to make a sentence with each word. Go around the class and check. Then write some of the Ss' examples on the board.
- Ss work with a partner and give advice if they want (or don't want) to be like the adjectives in their list. Ask for some of their suggestions.

Suggested answers:
to be healthy
You should eat the right kind of food.
You should take lots of exercise.
You shouldn't stay inside all the time.
(not) to be hungry
You shouldn't talk too much at mealtimes!
You should always eat a good breakfast.
(not) to be dirty
You should have a shower every day.
You should always wash your hands before a meal.

4

Aim: further practice of the past simple passive.
Summary: Ss write sentences in groups and score points if no other group has the same sentence.

Lead in

- Write these sentences on the board:
  They <u>painted</u> our school last week. (Our school was painted last week.)
  They <u>repaired</u> our washing machine yesterday. (Our washing machine was repaired yesterday.)
  Ask Ss to make each sentence passive starting with the underlined words.
- Remind Ss that we use the passive when we are more interested in what happened than who did it.

Main activity

- Ss work in small groups and write one or more sentences with each verb. Tell Ss that they may write about historical events, eg:
  The printing press was invented by Gutenberg in the 1400s.
  The Colosseum was built between AD 69 and 81.
  Tutankhamun's tomb was found in 1922.
  'La Divina Commedia' was written by Dante.
- Group members take turns to read out their sentences. Groups score one point for a sentence which no other group has written.

Optional activity

- Ss work with a partner to make a story about their stolen bike. Tell them to use as many passive verbs as they can.

WORDS in ACTION

1 Before you listen to the song, guess the missing words.

You shouldn't do that
Too much advice, too much advice,
My friends always ..1.. me what to do!
So I'm ..2.. this letter to your magazine,
And I'd like some ..3.. from you.
Tell me what to ..4.., tell me what to do
I need an ..5.. right away.
For every time I ask my friends
This is what they say:

Chorus
Take my advice – you shouldn't do that.
It's not very nice – you shouldn't do that.
Think about it twice – you shouldn't do
that.
    No, you shouldn't do that!
    No, you shouldn't do that!

What can we ..6.., what can we say,
You really have to ..7.. your point of view.
You shouldn't always ask your ..8..
To tell you what to do.
Make up your mind, ..9.. for yourself,
It's easy when you start to ..10..
And when they give you their advice
Then you can reply:

Listen to the song and write the missing words.

2 Practise saying these lines from the song. Stress the syllables underlined.

<u>Take</u> my ad<u>vice</u> – you <u>should</u>n't do <u>that</u>.
It's <u>not</u> very <u>nice</u> – you <u>should</u>n't do <u>that</u>.
<u>Think</u> about it <u>twice</u> – you <u>should</u>n't do <u>that</u>.

3 Decide whether these words are adjectives or adverbs. Then use each word in a sentence.

    friendly gently luckily healthy
    easily hungry dirty loudly

▶ *adjective*   *There are lots of friendly people here.*

Use the adjectives and give some advice to a person who wants to be (or not to be) like that.

▶ *to be friendly*   *You should talk to people and help them.*

4 **The passive game** – Make a sentence in the past simple passive using each verb.

    steal invent build find write

▶ *My bike <u>was stolen</u> last week.*

16 Be careful!

could, might; gerund and infinitive: warnings

Safety first

1a New language

Nick and Helen interviewed a safety expert about everyday accidents. Read the article they wrote for *Brilliant*. Which pictures go with the article?

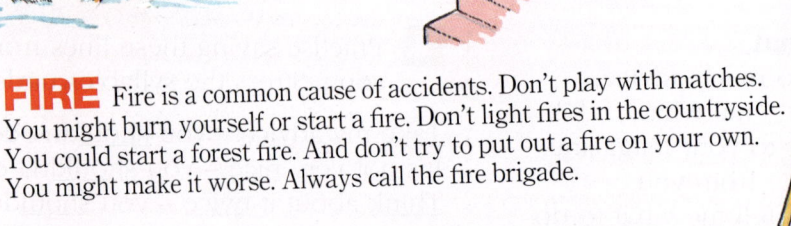

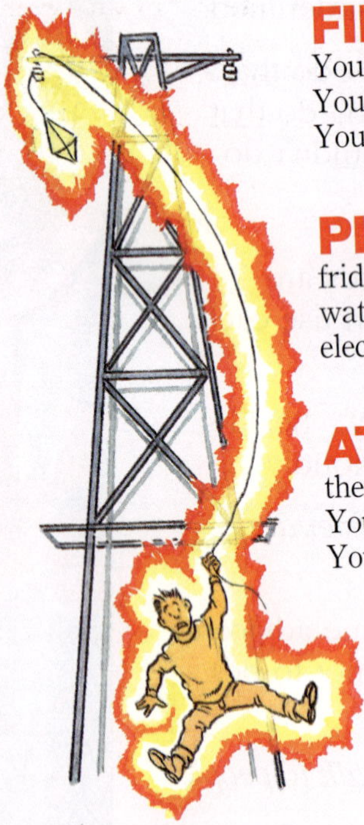

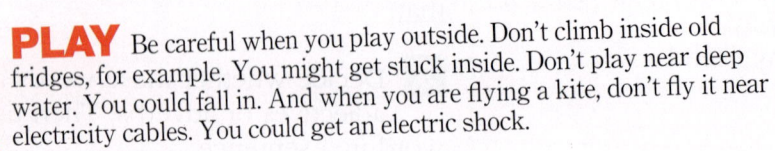

FIRE Fire is a common cause of accidents. Don't play with matches. You might burn yourself or start a fire. Don't light fires in the countryside. You could start a forest fire. And don't try to put out a fire on your own. You might make it worse. Always call the fire brigade.

PLAY Be careful when you play outside. Don't climb inside old fridges, for example. You might get stuck inside. Don't play near deep water. You could fall in. And when you are flying a kite, don't fly it near electricity cables. You could get an electric shock.

AT HOME Don't leave toys on the stairs. Someone might fall over them. Never play with electrical appliances, such as televisions or videos. You could start a fire or get a shock. And don't run around in the house. You might hurt yourself - or you might break the furniture.

Two pictures do not go with the article. Which pictures are they? What accidents might or could happen?

Helpline – could/might

Could and *might* do not change. Do not add *s* for he/she/it.

Don't play with matches. You might/could burn yourself.

Could and *might* mean the same in this sentence.

→ GC p11

Be careful! 16

Unit 16		Functions	Grammar
Lesson 1	Safety First	Describing possible events	Could, might
Lesson 2	Round the World problems	Describing possible events Giving warnings	Could, might Gerund or infinitive after certain verbs
Lesson 3	CHRIS 6		

Word check

abroad	everyday	lose
action	fall over something	monster
attack (v)	fire brigade	put out
avoid	headache	rob
careful	hurt (v)	warning
deep		

Lesson 1 Safety first

1a New language

Aim: to present *could* and *might* to express possibility.
Summary: Ss match pictures with an article and talk about accidents.

Lead in

- Books closed. Write *Everyday Accidents* and the three headings: *FIRE, PLAY* and *HOME* on the board.
- Ask Ss to suggest accidents that can happen in each situation. Put some of their ideas on the board in note form, eg:
  FIRE   oil in frying-pan catches fire
  PLAY   fall off your bike
  HOME   glass breaks

Main activity

- Read the introduction to the activity. Ask Ss to look at the pictures and decide which ones go with the article. Ask individual Ss for the answers.

Answers:
There is a picture for each of the following sentences:
a) Don't play near deep water.
b) Don't leave toys on the stairs.
c) Don't light fires in the countryside.
d) Don't fly kites near electricity cables.

- Ask Ss to say what could or might happen if you do the above things. Ask individual Ss for the answers.

Answers:
a) You could fall in.
b) Someone might fall over them.
c) You could start a forest fire.
d) You could get an electric shock.

- Ask Ss to say which pictures do not go with the article. Then ask what accidents could or might happen in these pictures. Individual Ss give answers.

Answers:
e) The dog might bite you.
f) You could fall off the ladder.

Extra activity

- Books closed. Ss work with a partner to roleplay a conversation with a younger brother or sister about doing dangerous things inside or outside the home. Tell Ss to give a reason for their advice, eg:
  S1: *Don't leave your lorry there.*
  S2: *Why can't I leave it here?*
  S1: *Because someone might fall over it.*

Helpline – could/might

- Explain that *could* and *might* are modal verbs. Modal verbs do not change form so they do not add *s* for *he/she/it*.
- Explain that *could* and *might* express the idea of possibility, eg:
  The child could/might fall. = It is possible that the child will fall.
- Point out that modal verbs have different meanings in different contexts. (For example, *could* can also be the past tense form of *can*.) It is, therefore, important to know the use and not just the form of modal verbs.

16 Be careful!

1b Practice

Aim: to practise *could* and *might* to express possibility.
Summary: Ss describe possible problems in given situations.

Lead in

- Books closed. Write the following headings on the board:
  an outing in a small boat   a camping holiday
  a visit to a large city   a trip abroad
- Ask Ss to suggest what might go wrong in each situation. Write some of their ideas in note form under the headings.

Main activity

- Books open. Ss work with a partner to talk about the things that might and could go wrong in each situation. They can use the ideas from the list in the SB and their own ideas. Go around the class and help if necessary. Ask individual Ss for their ideas.

1c Practice

Aim: to practise *could* and *might* to express possibility.
Summary: Ss speculate about the situation in the picture.

Lead in

- Ask Ss to look at the picture in the SB and to tell a partner what they can see. Ask individual Ss for their description of the scene.

Main activity

- Ss work with a partner and say what could or might happen in this picture, using some of the verbs from the list in the SB. Go around the class and help if necessary.
- Ask some pairs for their sentences and write them on the board.

Possible answers:
The kangaroo might attack the cat.
It could break its lead.
The kangaroo might bite the old lady.
She might drop the cat into the river.
Ozzy might jump in to save the cat.
He could hurt his arm on a rock.
The old lady might scream.

Optional activity

- Read out the following situation:
  You have heard that a tiger has escaped from your local zoo. You are walking to the park when a wild animal (it seems to be a tiger) comes out of someone's garden!
- Ss work with a partner and say what they might/could do and what might/could happen.

1d Writing

Aim: further practice with *could* and *might*.
Summary: Ss complete a leaflet warning about the dangers at school.

Lead in

- Ask Ss if there have been any accidents at their school. Find out how they happened.

Main activity

- Ss work individually to complete the leaflet about safety at school. They must include five dangers and what might/could happen, eg:
  Don't throw stones in the playground because you might hit someone.
- Early finishers read each other's leaflets and make suggestions for changes or additions. Go around the class and check.

Lesson 2 Round the World problems

2a New language

Aim: further practice of *could* and *might* to express possibility; practice of verbs with the gerund or infinitive.
Summary: Ss match warnings with things that could or might happen.

Lead in

- Ss look at the map in the SB and say where the Robinson family are now. They then predict some of the things they might or could do and see in Italy, eg:
  They might ride in a gondola in Venice.
  They could visit an ancient Greek temple in southern Italy.
  They could eat about 50 different kinds of pasta.

Main activity

- Read or play the introduction to the activity. Ask Ss to read the warnings (things you should and should not do) and match them with the explanations (reasons why you should or should not do them). Ss compare answers with a partner. Ask individual Ss for the answers.

Answers:
1 c)   2 a)   3 f)   4 d)   5 e)   6 b)

Extra activity

- Books closed. Read out the explanations from activity 2a and ask Ss to say the warnings.

Helpline – gerund and infinitive after certain verbs

- Ask Ss to cover the helpline and look at the warnings in activity 2a. Ask Ss to find:
  a) the verbs which are followed by the gerund (*-ing*)
     (*avoid, practise*)
  b) the verbs which are followed by the infinitive with to (*try, remember, forget*)
  (N.B. Some verbs like *try, remember* and *forget* have a different meaning when they are used with the gerund. They are not used with the gerund in this unit.)

1b Practice

Which problems could you have in these situations? What might go wrong? Use ideas from the list and add ideas of your own.

Situations
   an outing in a small boat   a camping holiday
   a visit to a large city   a trip abroad

Possible problems
   you fall in the water   you get lost
   wild animals attack you   you miss the
   plane/boat/train   you lose your money/tickets
   the weather changes   someone robs you

▶ *An outing in a small boat: You might fall in the water.   The weather could change suddenly.*

1c Practice

What could or might happen in these situat
Use some of these ve
and add other words:

   attack bite brea
   drop fall in hurt
   jump scream

▶ *The kangaroo could/might ...
Olive/Ozzy could/might ...
The old lady could/might ...*

1d Writing

Complete the leaflet about safety at school for teenagers. Include information about five dangers and what might/could happen. Use ideas from the list or use ideas of your own. Words from **1a** and **1b** might help you.

   running down the stairs   throwing things in the
   classroom   playing outside in the street
   leaving bags on the floor   leaning out of the
   window   pushing desks or chairs

School Safety

Schools are sometimes dangerous places, so always be careful.
Don't ... because ... . And don't ... because ... .
Remember, don't ... because ... . And don't ... because ... . And finally don't ... because ...

Round the World problems

2a New language

Last week Vicky and George were in Italy. They met a family who were travelling to India. They decided to give the family some advice about the problems of travelling. Here are some warnings they wrote. Match the warnings with the explanations of what could or might happen.

Warnings
1 Remember to drink only bottled water.
2 Try to stay out of the sun in hot weather.
3 Don't forget to keep your money in a safe place.
4 Practise saying a few useful phrases in the language before you arrive.
5 Try not to upset local people.
6 Avoid eating in cheap restaurants.

Explanations
a) It could give you headaches or make you feel ill.
b) The food might make you ill at first.
c) Tap water could give you problems with your stomach.
d) You might want to ask people the way, or ask for information.
e) They might not like your strange clothes.
f) A thief or pickpocket could easily rob you in the street.

16

> **Helpline**
>
> – gerund or infinitive after certain verbs
>
> Some verbs in this lesson are followed by:
>
> gerund (-ing): avoid, practise
>
> infinitive with to: try, remember, forget
>
> infinitive or gerund: start
>
> → GC p11

2b Practice

Make some warnings for tourists in your country about:

the beach   food and drink   travel   the weather

Use the warning verbs and tell the tourists what could or might happen. Use problems from the list.

Warning verbs   avoid, don't forget, remember, try to/try not to

Problems   get sunburned   get lost   get wet   get into trouble   feel cold/hot/ill   it could/might be dangerous/uncomfortable/expensive/crowded

2c Listening

Listen to Vicky and George talking to the family which is going to India. Choose the advice they give.

1 Remember not to …
  a) … feed animals in the street.
  b) … touch the monkeys.
2 Don't forget to …
  a) … take a raincoat.
  b) … take clothes for hot weather.
3 Avoid …
  a) … taking a lot of stomach pills.
  b) … eating things sold in the street.
4 Start …
  a) … reading your guidebook.
  b) … thinking about your trip.

2d Writing

Write a short leaflet for aliens who are visiting the earth as tourists. Use ideas from the lists and add ideas of your own.

Problem
  land your spacecraft in the sea
  talk to wild animals   visit big cities
  talk to humans

Possible result
  problems with fish?   they will eat you?
  people will call the police?   they will think you are a monster?

> *First of all, try not to land your spacecraft in the sea. It is full of fish and they might eat you and the spacecraft might …*

Word check

abroad	everyday	lose
action	fall over something	monster
attack	fire brigade	put out
avoid	headache	rob
careful	hurt [v]	warning
deep		

Be careful! 16

2b Practice

Aim: to practise using verbs (from activity 2a) to give warnings; further practice of *could* and *might*.
Summary: Ss use warning verbs to tell others what could or might happen in certain situations.

Lead in

- Books closed. Write these words on the board:
  Warning for tourists.
  Explain that this is the title of a leaflet. Ask Ss to predict what the leaflet might say, eg:
  Remember to change your money at a bank.
  Avoid buying things from people on the street.
  Write some of the Ss' ideas on the board.

Main activity

- Ss work with a partner and give warnings and explanations to tourists, eg:
  S1: *Avoid staying in the sun too long.*
  S2: *Oh, why? I want to get a good suntan!*
  S1: *It could be dangerous because you might get a headache or get sunburnt.*

Extra activity

- Ss use the information from activity 2b to write a leaflet giving advice to people visiting their country. They should find or draw some pictures to go with the leaflet. Display the leaflets in the classroom.

2c Listening

Aim: focus on warning verbs.
Summary: Ss listen and decide which warnings Vicky and George give.

Lead in

- Ask Ss to read the sentences and predict what advice Vicky and George give. Do not confirm.

Main activity

- Ask Ss to listen to the conversation twice. Ss compare their answers with a partner. Ask individual Ss for the answers and for reasons for them.

Answers:
1 a) Vicky does not say anything about touching monkeys.
2 a) George says that there are weeks when it rains all the time in India.
3 b) Vicky says that the food they sell in the street could make you feel ill. (She tells the family to take some stomach pills with them.)
4 b) George says that they should start planning their trip now. (The girl has already started reading the guidebook and George suggests that she should read it all, not start to read it.)

- Play the conversation again. Ask Ss to listen for the reasons that Vicky and George give for the first three pieces of advice they give in the conversation with the family:
  1 *The monkeys might jump on you or bite you.* (Monkey bites can be very dangerous – King Alexander of Greece died in 1920 from blood poisoning after a monkey bit him in the Royal Gardens in Athens.)
  2 *You could get very wet during the monsoons.*
  3 *You could get ill at first if you eat food from street-sellers.*

Extra activity

- Ask Ss to roleplay the conversation between Vicky or George and a member of the other family. They can also use ideas from activity 2a.

2d Writing

Aim: further practice of warning verbs.
Summary: Ss write a leaflet for aliens who are visiting the Earth as tourists.

Lead in

- Tell Ss that some friendly aliens from another planet are planning to visit the Earth. Ask Ss to predict their problems. Write some of Ss' ideas on the board.

Main activity

- Ask Ss to read the list of problems in the SB and suggest what could or might happen.
- Ss work individually to write the leaflet. Early finishers read each other's paragraphs. Go around the class and help if necessary.

Optional activity

- Ss write another leaflet for astronauts from Earth who are going to visit another planet. Display the leaflets in class.

Word check

- Divide the class into two teams. Read out these sentences:
a *My head hurts if I have one of these. I sometimes take an aspirin.* (headache)
b *If a building catches fire this will come.* (fire brigade)
c *This end of the swimming pool is dangerous if you can't swim.* (deep)
d *It had two heads, four eyes and it was green. What was it?* (monster)
e *If you don't keep your money in a safe place, this might happen.* (rob)
f *You shouldn't do this on your own if there is a fire.* (put out)
- The first team to say the right word from the Word check box gets a point. Ss get an extra point for spelling the word correctly.

Teacher's Book Unit 16

16 Be careful!

Lesson 3 CHRIS Episode 6

Aim: to read for specific information; to listen for specific information; to guess missing words from context.

The story so far:

Main activity

- Ss work with a partner to answer the questions about the story so far. Ask individual Ss for the answers.

Answers:
1 It's a famous monument in London etc.
2 The twins met a woman called Inspector Wendy Harman when they went there.
3 He has stolen some computer plans and he wants to sell them to a foreign company.

1

Lead in

- Ask Ss to guess what is going to happen next.

Main activity

- Ask Ss to read the next part of the story and answer the question. Ask individual Ss for ways of finishing Sandy's last sentence.

Extra activity

- Books closed. Ask:
  Why don't the twins think Harman is a real police inspector?
  Why must they act normally?

2

Main activity

- Ss work with a partner to find the clue in the notice. Ask individual Ss for suggestions but do not confirm the answer yet.

3

Main activity

- Play the cassette. Ss identify the clue and tick what the twins decide to do. Play the cassette more than once. Then ask Ss for the answer.

Answer:
take a trip on the river

Extra activity

- Ask Ss to listen again and answer these questions:
  1 What nearly happened to the ship which brought Cleopatra's Needle to Britain?
  2 Where is the Bay of Biscay?
  3 Have the twins been to Greenwich before?

Answers:
1 It nearly sank.
2 Near Spain.
3 Yes, they have. They used to go to Greenwich when they were little.

4

Main activity

- Ask Ss to read this part of the story again to fill in the missing words. Ss check with a partner. Ask individual Ss for their answers.

Answers:
1 them   4 next   7 idea
2 a   5 all   8 few
3 that   6 carefully 9 show
                       10 called

Extra activity 1

- Books closed. Write these sentences on the board:
  a) They looked at the notice and found a clue.
  b) Inspector Harman watched them.
  c) They found Greenwich in the A – Z.
  d) They were suspicious of the police inspector.
  e) They asked CHRIS some questions.
  f) The twins examined Cleopatra's Needle.
- Ask Ss to put them into the correct order according to what happened in this episode. Ask individual Ss for the answers.

Answers:
1 f)   2 b)   3 d)   4 a)   5 e)   6 c)

- Ask Ss to write Sandy's diary entry for this episode. They should begin:
  We looked at Cleopatra's Needle but ....

Extra activity 2

- Ask Ss to read the paragraph once quickly and answer the question:
  What is the A – Z?   (It is a book with all the streets of London.)

Extra activity 3

- Write these anagrams on the board:
  UTYSMOSIER (mysterious)
  LEENED (needle)
  TRISNCEPO (inspector)
  ARTOICAN (raincoat)
  MOLLYRAN (normally)
- Explain that these words are all in this episode but the letters are in the wrong order. Ask Ss to find the words.

Episode 6

CHRIS

The story so far:

1. What can you remember about Cleopatra's Needle?
2. Who did the twins meet when they went there?
3. What did they hear about Chris?

1 Read the next part of the story and answer the question.

▶ a

Sandy and Peter went and looked at Cleopatra's Needle. Inspector Harman was sitting on a bench nearby and talking to a man in a raincoat.

'I don't believe her story about Chris,' Sandy whispered.

'Neither do I,' said Peter. 'And how do we know that she is really a police inspector? She didn't show us her identity card.'

'You're right,' said Sandy. 'And I think I've found a clue.'

'A clue? What do you mean?' Peter replied.

'Just act normally, she's still watching. Look at the notice over there. Do you remember what CHRIS told us about the Needle? There's something wrong with the notice. It could be a message from Chris. Read it quickly and then we'll look for a phone box. I think we should …'

What do you think the twins should do? Finish Sandy's last sentence.

2 This is the notice that Sandy saw. Can you see the clue?

▶ b

CLEOPATRA'S NEEDLE IS AN EGYPTIAN OBELISK AND WAS BROUGHT TO LONDON IN 1878 IN A SPECIAL SHIP. IT WAS NEARLY LOST IN A STORM IN THE THAMES NEAR GREENWICH BUT WAS PLACED HERE IN 1878 AS A MEMORIAL TO THE NAPOLEONIC WAR

3 Listen to Sandy and Peter talking about the clue. Were you right? Tick ✓ what they decide to do.

    look at the map   take a trip on the river
    talk to CHRIS

4 Read the next part of the story. Some words are missing. Guess what they are.

▶ c

First Sandy and Peter found Greenwich on the map and then they asked CHRIS some questions. He gave ..^{1}.. this mysterious answer: 'A–Z'. The twins thought about this for ..^{2}.. long time but they couldn't understand what it meant. Then Peter remembered ..^{3}.. Chris used to look at a book when he walked around London. It was on the shelf ..^{4}.. to his desk and it was called *The A–Z of London*. It showed ..^{5}.. the streets. They found the pages for Greenwich and looked at them very ..^{6}.. They couldn't find anything. They spent an hour looking at the pages again and again. Then Sandy had an ..^{7}.. She started writing down the names of all the streets. After a ..^{8}.. minutes they knew what Chris was trying to ..^{9}.. them. Near the river there was a small street ..^{10}.. Cleopatra Road. They decided to go to Greenwich that afternoon.

CONSOLIDATION 2

1 Complete each sentence with *have to*, *don't have to*, *should* or *shouldn't*.

a) Cars ... stop when they come to a red traffic light.
b) You ... read without a good lamp, or you will hurt your eyes.
c) Tomorrow is a holiday and we ... go to school!
d) I'm sorry I can't come but I ... go to the dentist's.
e) Don't you feel cold? You ... wear a pullover in this weather!
f) Don't worry, you ... do the washing up. We'll put it in the dishwasher.
g) I think people ... be more careful when they cross the road.
h) You ... sit in the sun for hours. It's not good for you.

2 Make sentences like the example using two ideas from the list. Use each idea only once.

  find my umbrella/wear my raincoat

▶ *I couldn't find my umbrella so I had to wear my raincoat.*

find my umbrella   wear my raincoat
answer the question   take a taxi
find the bus station   stand on a chair   reach the top shelf   do the next one   understand the word
ask for directions   carry my suitcase
look it up in a dictionary

3 Use the information in the tables to make five statements about Nick and five statements about Helen.

Nick	Age 8	Now
sport	football	swimming
favourite subject	history	science
home	Brighton	London
free time	watch television	work for school magazine

Helen	Age 9	Now
hobby	stamp collecting	photography
pet	cat	dog
travel to school	on foot	on bike
spend money on	sweets	clothes and cassettes

▶ *When Nick was eight, he used to play football, but now he goes swimming. When Nick was eight he didn't use to go swimming. He used to play football then.*

4 Write two things that could or might go wrong for each situation.

a) camping
b) riding a bike
c) playing in the house
d) visiting a strange city

5 Read the letter from Helen to her penfriend, Annie. Rewrite each sentence so that it contains the word given.

Dear Annie
You asked me about your visit to England this summer.
a) I advise you to bring a raincoat and some pullovers. **(should)**
b) Last year I needed to wear a heavy coat in July! **(had)**
c) It's possible that the weather will be bad this year too. **(might)**
d) It's not necessary to bring a tennis racket. **(have)**
e) I've got three so I'll lend you one. **(can)**
f) And don't worry about speaking English. **(should)** I'll help you.

That's all for now.
Helen

70

Consolidation 2 Units 9–16

1

Aim: further practice of *have to, don't have to, should* and *shouldn't*.
Summary: Ss complete sentences.

Main activity

- Ask Ss to read each sentence carefully and then complete the space with one of the verb forms from the SB. Go around the class and help if necessary. Ask individual Ss for the answers.

Answers:
a) have to   d) have to   g) should
b) shouldn't   e) should   h) shouldn't
c) don't have to   f) don't have to

2

Aim: further practice of *couldn't* and *had to*.
Summary: Ss combine ideas and write sentences.

Main activity

- Read the example aloud:
  I couldn't find my umbrella so I had to wear my raincoat.
- Ask Ss to write five sentences as in the example. Explain that they can use each idea only once. Ss check their sentences with a partner.

Answers:
I couldn't answer the question so I had to do the next one.
I couldn't find the bus station so I had to ask for directions.
I couldn't reach the top shelf so I had to stand on a chair.
I couldn't understand the word so I had to look it up in a dictionary.
I couldn't carry my suitcase so I had to take a taxi.

3

Aim: further practice of *used to* and *didn't use to* to talk about past habits.
Summary: Ss write sentences based on information about Nick and Helen.

Main activity

- Read the example sentences in the SB:
  When Nick was eight, he used to play football, but now he goes swimming.
  When Nick was eight, he didn't use to go swimming. He used to play football then.
- Ss write five similar statements about Nick and Helen.

Answers:
When Nick was eight, his favourite subject used to be history, but now his favourite subject is science.
When Nick was eight, his favourite subject didn't use to be science. His favourite subject used to be history then.
When Nick was eight, he used to live in Brighton, but now he lives in London.
When Nick was eight, he didn't use to live in London. He used to live in Brighton then.
When Nick was eight, he used to watch television in his free time, but now he works for the school magazine.
When Nick was eight, he didn't use to work for the school magazine in his free time. He used to watch television then.
When Helen was nine, she used to collect stamps, but now she does photography.
When Helen was nine, she didn't use to do photography. She used to collect stamps then.
When Helen was nine, she used to have a cat, but now she has a dog.
When Helen was nine, she didn't use to have a dog. She used to have a cat then.
When Helen was nine, she used to travel to school on foot, but now she goes on her bike.
When Helen was nine, she didn't use to travel to school on her bike. She used to go on foot then.
When Helen was nine, she used to spend her money on sweets, but now she spends it on clothes and cassettes.
When Helen was nine, she didn't use to spend her money on clothes and cassettes. She used to spend it on sweets then.

- Ask Ss to find out similar information from a partner and write two or three sentences using *used to* and *didn't use to*.

4

Aim: further practice of *could* and *might*.
Summary: Ss write sentences saying what could go wrong in certain situations.

Main activity

- Ss work with a partner and write two (or more) things that could or might go wrong in the four situations in the SB. Ask individual Ss to read out one of their sentences and then ask the class to guess what the situation is. Write some of the sentences on the board.

5

Aim: further practice of modal verbs.
Summary: Ss rewrite a letter from Helen.

Lead in

- Write this example on the board:
  Perhaps it will rain tomorrow. (might)
- Ask Ss to rephrase the sentence using *might*:
  It might rain tomorrow.

Main activity

- Ask Ss to read Helen's letter and then rewrite each sentence using the word given.

Answers:
a) You should bring a raincoat and some pullovers.
b) Last year I had to wear a heavy coat in July.
c) The weather might be bad this year too.
d) You don't have to bring a tennis racket.
e) I can lend you one.
f) You shouldn't worry about speaking English.

Extra activity

- Ask Ss to write a similar letter to a penfriend who is going to visit them this summer.

Consolidation 2 Units 9–16

6

Aim: further practice of *going to*, *will* and the present continuous.
Summary: Ss complete a letter with the appropriate future form.

Main activity

- Ask Ss to read the letter once quickly to answer these focus questions:
  What does Annie ask Helen to do for her? (She asks her to lend material for a project on London.)
  What has Annie arranged for the end of the month? (She's arranged a party.)
- Ask Ss to read the letter again more slowly and put the verbs in brackets in the correct future form. Explain that in some sentences more than one answer is possible.

Answers:
a) *I'll arrive* or *I'm arriving*
b) *we'll have* or *we're going to have*
c) *we're going to write* or *we're writing*
d) *I'm going to look*
e) *I'll send*
f) *I'm going to have* or *I'm having*
g) *I'm going to relax*
h) *I'll see*

Extra activity

- Books closed. Read the letter aloud but pause before each preposition. Ask Ss to say the missing preposition, eg:
  I'm arriving ... Heathrow Airport ... 20th July ... 4.00.

7

Aim: further practice of the present simple passive.
Summary: Ss rewrite a paragraph using the passive form of verbs.

Lead in

- Write this sentence on the board:
  Workers make nice leather bags in Italy.
- Ask Ss to change the underlined verb into the present simple passive:
  Nice leather bags are made in Italy.
- Remind Ss that in passive sentences, it is not always necessary to say who does the action. Ask Ss to explain why. Make sure that everyone agrees that this is because we are interested in what is done and not who did it.

Main activity

- Ask Ss to rewrite the paragraph in the present simple passive and to make any other necessary changes. Ask individual Ss to read out parts of the paragraph.

Answers:
First of all, letters are posted in post boxes. After that, the boxes are emptied and the letters are sorted at the post office. The letters are taken to other towns in vans, or sent by train. In each town, the letters are sorted again and then delivered.

Extra activity

- Books closed. Write the following key words on the board:
  post boxes   post office   vans   train   letters
- Ss work with a partner and use the passive form to retell what happens to letters after they are posted.

8

Aim: further practice of the past simple passive and present simple passive.
Summary: Ss rewrite a paragraph using the passive form of verbs.

Lead in

- Ask Ss to name some famous bridges in their country and in other countries. Ask:
  What are they made of? How long are they?

Main activity

- Ask Ss to read the information leaflet about London Bridge and rewrite the paragraph using the past simple passive where possible. Ask Ss to check their paragraph with a partner. Then ask individual Ss to read out parts of the paragraph.

Answers:
The first bridge was made of wood and it was replaced by a stone bridge. This was begun in 1176 and finished in 1209. Shops and houses were built on the bridge. This old bridge was repaired many times and then it was knocked down finally in 1831 and a new bridge was put in its place. This bridge was sold in the 1960s when the present bridge was made and it was taken to Lake Havasu in the USA. It is used as an attraction for sightseers.

Extra activity

- Books closed. Write these key dates on the board:
  1176   1209   1831   1960s
  Ask Ss to recall the information.

9

Aim: further practice of quantity words *much*, *many*, *little*, *few*, *enough*.
Summary: Ss complete a letter from Helen.

Main activity

- Ask Ss to read Helen's letter once quickly to answer this question:
  Has she sent Annie any books? (No, but she's written to the Tourist Information Office for more information.)
- Ask Ss to read the letter again and complete the spaces with one of the words in the SB. Ask individual Ss for the answers.

Answers:
much time	few shops	enough money
many bookshops	enough things	few books
enough time	many maps	much
		enough space

6 Read Annie's reply and write each verb in brackets with *going to, will* or the present continuous. More than one answer might be possible.

Dear Helen
Thanks for your letter.
a) I've bought my ticket. I ... **(arrive)** at Heathrow Airport on 20th July at 4.00.
b) I'm sure we ... **(have)** a good time together.
c) Can you do me a favour? Next month we ... **(write)** a project about London.
d) I ... **(look)** for information in my local library next week, but there might not be enough.
e) Can you find some information for me? I ... **(send)** you some money if necessary.
f) I'm very busy at school, but at the end of the month I ... **(have)** a party.
g) After that I ... **(relax)** on holiday with you!
h) I ... **(see)** you soon.
Annie

7 Rewrite the paragraph so that each verb underlined is in a present passive form. Make any other necessary changes.

First of all people <u>post</u> letters in post boxes. After that, a postal worker <u>empties</u> the boxes, and workers <u>sort</u> the letters at the post office. The workers <u>take</u> the letters to other towns in vans, or the post office <u>sends</u> the letters by train. In each town, people <u>sort</u> the letters again and then postal workers <u>deliver</u> the letters.

8 Helen found this information in a leaflet. Rewrite the paragraph so that the verbs are in the past simple passive form where this is possible. Leave out any unnecessary words.

London Bridge has a long history. People made the first bridge of wood and they replaced it with a stone bridge. They began this in 1176 and they finished it in 1209. They built shops and houses on the bridge. They repaired this old bridge many times and then they knocked it down finally in 1831 and they put a new bridge in its place. They sold this bridge in the 1960s when they made the present bridge and people took it to Lake Havasu in the USA. They use it as an attraction for sightseers.

9 Read Helen's next letter to Annie. Put one of these words in each space.

much   many   little   few   enough

Dear Annie
I hope you received the leaflet about London. I haven't had ... time to find any other books, I'm afraid. There aren't ... bookshops near my house and I haven't got ... time to travel into the city centre because I'm very busy. I looked in a ... shops, but I couldn't find ... things and there weren't ... maps, only street guides. I found an expensive book, but I didn't have ... money for that. I went to the library too, but there were only a ... books on that kind of thing. They had some interesting information, but not very ... . So I'm going to write to the Tourist Information Office. Thanks for the photos. There isn't ... space for them in the magazine this month, but we'll put them in soon.
Love from your friend
Helen

17 Don't worry so much!

conditional 1: real situations: if sentences with imperative, if sentences with will

Not a care in the world

1a New language

The Odd children stayed at home on Saturday, but Mr and Mrs Odd went out. Here are some things Mr and Mrs Odd told the children before they left. Choose the best ending for each one.

1 If you play in the garden …
2 If the police come to the house …
3 If you feel hungry …
4 If it rains …
5 If you go out on your bikes …
6 If the television doesn't work …
7 If you do any housework …
8 If the kangaroo wants to go for a walk …

… don't dig too many holes this time.
… put the dirty clothes in the washing machine and the plates in the dishwasher.
… don't let it jump in front of people on bicycles.
… tell them you are not at home.
… don't eat the worms in the fridge. They're for fishing.
… remember to take the goldfish outside for a bath.
… don't try to wash it in the washing-machine this time. It makes the picture worse.
… lock the door, then open the window and put the key on the kitchen table.

Helpline

– if in real situations + imperative

When we talk about real situations, we use *if* + present simple + imperative.

If you play in the garden, don't dig too many holes!

If you play in the garden, lock the door.

→ GC p13

Don't worry so much! 17

Unit 17		Functions	Grammar
Lesson 1	Not a care in the world	Giving instructions about possible events	Real condition: if + present simple, + imperative
Lesson 2	Worry, worry, worry!	Making predictions about possible events	Real condition: if + present simple, + will
Lesson 3	Words in action		

Word check

alarm clock	during	look for
annoy	feel sick	miss (v)
bucket	hurry up	ready
catch a cold	in time	rude
close (v)	indoors	shout
coach		

Lesson 1 Not a care in the world

1a New language

Aim: to present sentences with *if* + imperative to talk about real situations.
Summary: Ss match sentence beginnings and endings.

Lead in

- Ask Ss to guess what instructions Mr and Mrs Normal give their children if they are going out for a few hours, eg:
Don't watch too much television.
Eat the sandwiches in the kitchen for lunch. Don't eat popcorn for lunch.
Don't fight.
Do some of your homework.
- Then ask what instructions Mr and Mrs Odd give their children.

Main activity

- Read or play the introduction. Ask Ss to find the best ending for the first sentence. Write the complete sentence on the board, making sure that you include a comma (,) before adding the second part.
- Ss match the beginnings and endings of the sentences and make Mr and Mrs Odd's instructions. Ss compare the endings they have chosen. Ask individual Ss for the answers.

Answers:
1 If you play in the garden, don't dig too many holes this time.
2 If the police come to the house, tell them you are not at home.
3 If you feel hungry, don't eat the worms in the fridge.
4 If it rains, remember to take the goldfish outside for a bath.
5 If you go out on your bikes, lock the door then open the window and put the key on the kitchen table.
6 If the television doesn't work, don't try to wash it in the washing machine this time.
7 If you do any housework, put the dirty clothes in the washing machine and the plates in the dishwasher.
8 If the kangaroo wants to go out for a walk, don't let it jump in front of people on bicycles.

Extra activity 1

- Ss work in pairs and roleplay the conversation between Olive or Ozzy and Mr or Mrs Odd. Tell them to add their own ideas:
S1: *What should we do if we feel hungry?*
S2: *Well, if you feel hungry, don't eat the worms in the fridge. They're for fishing. Eat the snail sandwiches.*

Extra activity 2

- Ss work with a partner and think of ways in which Mr and Mrs Normal might end the sentences if they were speaking to their children, eg:
If you play in the garden don't kick your ball into the flowers.

Helpline – if in real situations + imperative

- Explain that when we talk about real situations with events which we think may happen we use *if* + present simple + imperative, eg:
If you feel hungry, don't eat the worms in the fridge.
It it rains, take an umbrella.

17 Don't worry so much!

1b Practice

Aim: to practise *if* + imperative to talk about real situations.
Summary: Ss take the part of Mr or Mrs Odd and give instructions to their children.

Lead in

- Books closed. Tell Ss that they are Mr and Mrs Odd. They must give an instruction for some problems using *if* + imperative. Read out the example and then some of the problems from the list in the SB. Ask Ss to guess what instructions the Odds give their children, eg:
  T: *The electricity might go off.*
  S: *If the electricity goes off, sit on the roof.*

Main activity

- Ask Ss to read the problems in the SB silently and match them with appropriate actions. They then write sentences as in the example. Ss compare their sentences with a partner. Ask individual Ss for the answers.

Answers:
2 *If the electricity goes off, (don't) use the candles in the cupboard.*
3 *If the Normals ask you for lunch, (don't) stay at their house for the rest of the day.*
4 *If you feel hungry, (don't) eat the kangaroo's food in the fridge.*
5 *If you go out, (don't) leave your keys in the door.*
6 *If the kangaroo runs away, (don't) try to follow it on your bikes.*

1c Listening

Aim: further practice of *if* + imperative to talk about real situations.
Summary: Ss listen and complete Mrs Odd's instructions.

Lead in

- Ask Ss to read the sentences and guess Mrs Odd's instructions. Do not confirm answers yet.

Main activity

- Ask Ss to listen to the conversation between Mrs Odd and her children twice and complete Mrs Odd's instructions. Ask individual Ss for the answers.

Answers:
1 *If you go on a bus, don't throw things out of the window.*
2 *If you see a policeman, don't shout rude words.*
3 *If the Normal kids give you any food, don't eat it.*
4 *If they give you any chocolate, bring it home to me.*
5 *If you catch any fish, throw them back in the river.*

- Ask Ss what instructions their parents give them if they walk home from school by themselves, eg:
  Use the pedestrian/zebra crossings.
  Don't go to the park.
  Don't talk to strangers.
  Don't buy sweets.
  Don't run across the road.

- Ss work with a partner and write at least two instructions for a friend who is going home from school. Write some of Ss' sentences on the board.

Extra activity

- Books closed. Write the following key words on the board:
  bus   policeman   food   chocolate   fish
  Ss work with a partner and roleplay the conversation between Mrs Odd and Olive or Ozzy.

1d Writing

Aim: further practice of *if* + imperative to talk about real situations.
Summary: Ss write a guided paragraph giving instructions.

Lead in

- Put Ss into small groups. Ss discuss how they will complete the sentences and what other instructions they will add to the paragraph. Go around the class and help if necessary.

Main activity

- Ss write the paragraph individually. Offer help if necessary. Early finishers read each other's work.

Lesson 2 Worry, worry, worry!

2a New language

Aim: to present *if* + *will* in real situations.
Summary: Ss match Nigel's worries with Natalie's comments.

Lead in

- Ask Ss to think of two things they like and two things they dislike about going on a class trip by coach, eg:
  I like having fun with friends.
  I like looking at the countryside.
  I don't like feeling sick on the coach.
  I don't like getting tired.

- Ask Ss to guess if Nigel and Natalie Normal like school trips.

Main activity

- Read the introduction to the activity. Ss match Nigel and Natalie's comments. Then ask individual Ss for the answers:

Answers:
1 a   2 e   3 d   4 b   5 c

Extra activity

- Ss work with a partner. One of them reads Nigel Normal's comments. The other closes his or her book and tries to remember what Natalie tells her brother to stop him worrying.

1b Practice

You are Mr or Mrs Odd. Give instructions to the Odd children. Tell them to do something, or not to do something if something happens.

Problems
1 It might rain.
2 The electricity might go off.
3 The Normals might ask you for lunch.
4 You might feel hungry.
5 You might go out.
6 The kangaroo might run away.

Action
Close all the windows.
Leave your keys in the door.
Eat the kangaroo's food in the fridge.
Stay at their house for the rest of the day.
Use the candles in the cupboard.
Try to follow it on your bikes.

▶ *If it rains, close all the windows./If it rains, don't close all the windows.*

1c Listening

The Odd children are going fishing. Before you listen, guess Mrs Odd's instructions.

1 If … bus, don't throw things out of the window.
2 If … policeman, don't shout rude words.
3 If … food, don't eat it.
4 If … chocolate, bring it home to me.
5 If … fish, throw them back in the river.

Listen and complete each instruction.

Give two instructions to a friend who is going home from school.

1d Writing

Complete the paragraph of instructions for your class.

> Here are some instructions for everyone in the class. First of all, if the teacher is not here or is late … . Secondly, if you forget your homework … . Thirdly, if you want to leave the room during the lesson … . Finally, a very important instruction. If the lights go out or if there is an emergency …

Worry, worry, worry

2a New language

Tomorrow Natalie and Nigel Normal are going on a school trip. Nigel always worries, but Natalie doesn't. Match each of Nigel's comments with a comment from Natalie.

Nigel's comments
1 I know I won't be ready in time in the morning.
2 I don't want to be in the same seat as Ozzy Odd. He annoys me!
3 I don't like travelling by coach. I always feel sick.
4 It'll be late when we come back. I don't want to walk home from school in the dark.
5 The coach might leave without us. What'll we do then?

Natalie's comments
a) Don't worry! If you set the alarm clock, you'll wake up in time.
b) Don't be silly. If we ask Dad, he'll come and pick us up in the car.
c) If we're late for the coach, it'll wait for us.
d) If you take a travel sickness pill, you'll be fine.
e) If you sit next to me, you'll be all right. Don't worry.

I know I won't be ready in time in the morning.

Don't worry. If you set the alarm clock, you'll wake up in time.

17

2b New language

The Normals are on the school trip. Nigel is having some problems, but Natalie is helping him. Make an *if* sentence for Natalie to say in each situation, beginning *If you …* or *If you don't …* .

▶ *If you do that, I'll tell the teacher!*

1. Close the window. I don't want Nigel to catch a cold!
2. Don't drink that. You know you always feel sick on a coach.
3. Take this umbrella. You don't want to get wet!
4. Don't stand up. It's very easy to fall in the water!
5. Hurry up, the coach is leaving without us!

> **Helpline** – *if* in real situations + *will*
>
> When we talk about real situations, we use *if* + present simple + *will*:
> *If we stay awake all night, we'll be ready in the morning.*
> *If we don't get up early, we'll miss the coach.*
>
> → GC p13

2c Practice

You are going on a school trip. Your friend is worried. What do you say? Use ideas from the lists.

Your friend says:
I might run out of money!
I might miss the bus!
I might get lost in a strange town.
I might lose my bag!
I might forget my sandwiches!
It might be cold and rainy!

You say:
come back to look for you
lend you some
help you look for it
give you some
do something indoors
look after you

▶ *Don't worry! If …, I'll/we'll …*

2d Writing

You are going out for the day with a friend. Write a note and explain what you will do if there are any problems. Use ideas from **2b** and **2c**.

> I'm sure we'll have a great time on Saturday. You worry too much. If we get lost … . So that won't be a problem. And if it rains … . We aren't going very far, but if we get tired … . And don't worry about … *[add more ideas]* …

Word check

alarm clock	in time
annoy	indoors
catch a cold	look for
close (v)	miss (v)
coach	ready
during	rude
feel sick	shout
hurry up	

74

Don't worry so much! 17

2b New language

Aim: further practice of *if* + *will* in real situations.
Summary: Ss use comments and pictures to make sentences.

Lead in
- Books closed. Ask Ss to guess what problems Nigel has on the school trip.

Main activity
- Ask Ss to write Natalie's sentences in their exercise books. They then check their answers with a partner. Ask individual Ss for the answers.

Answers:
1 If you don't close the window, Nigel will catch a cold.
2 If you drink that, you'll be sick on the coach.
3 If you take this umbrella, you won't get wet.
4 If you stand up, you'll fall in the water.
5 If you don't hurry up, the coach will leave without us.

Extra activity
- Write these key words on the board:
  window   drink   umbrella   stand up   late for coach
  Ask Ss to use *if* + *will* and make Natalie's sentences.

Helpline – if in real situations + will

- Explain that when we talk about real situations, when we are sure about what we are saying, we can also use *if* + present simple, + *will* in the main clause, eg:
  If we're late for the coach, it'll wait for us.
  If Ozzy Odd annoys you, I'll talk to him.
  If you take a travel sickness pill, you won't be sick.
- Remind Ss that *won't* is the short form of *will not*.

2c Practice

Aim: further practice of *if* + *will* to talk about real situations.
Summary: Ss make comments on possible problems on a school trip.

Lead in
- Books closed. Ask Ss to describe the worst thing that has happened to them on a school trip or holiday.

Main activity
- Ask Ss to work with a partner. One of them is very worried about what might happen on the school trip. The other offers solutions for the friend's worries, eg:
  S1: *I might feel sick on the coach.*
  S2: *Don't worry! We'll give you a travel sickness pill before the journey.*
- Ss exchange roles. Go around the class and help if necessary.

2d Writing

Aim: further practice of *if* + *will* to talk about real situations.
Summary: Ss write a guided paragraph describing problems and solutions.

Lead in
- Ss work with a partner and decide where they might go and what they might do on a day out with a friend. They must then think about the possible problems and solutions to these problems, eg:
  S1: *We might get tired if we walk a long way.*
  S2: *If we get tired of walking, we'll have a rest under a tree.*
  S1: *We might walk into a field with bulls.*
  S2: *If we do that, we'll get out very quickly!*

Main activity
- Ss work with their partners to write the paragraph. Go around the class and help if necessary.

Word check
- In teams, Ss take it in turns to make sentences using one word from the Word check box and *if* + *will*. Ss score one point for each correct answer.

Teacher's Book Unit 17

17 Don't worry so much!

Lesson 3 Words in action

1

Aims: to read for gist and specific and detailed information.
Summary: Ss match jobs with sentences which describe the jobs; they find the names of two jobs in the text.

Lead in

- Books closed. Ask Ss to think of some dangerous jobs. Write their ideas on the board.

Main activity

- Make sure that Ss understand what the jobs are. Ask them to match the jobs with the statements about the jobs. Ask individual Ss for the answers.

Answers:
a) police officer   c) lifeguard on a beach
b) skyscraper builder   d) fire-fighter

- Ask Ss to read the texts silently and decide which jobs are described. Check answers:

Answers:
skyscraper builder   stunt double

- Ask Ss to guess what *stunt double* means from the context.

2

Aim: to look for specific vocabulary items in the text.
Summary: Ss answer questions about vocabulary items in the text.

Main activity

- Ask Ss to answer the questions about words and phrases from the text. They check their answers with a partner. Ask individual Ss for the answers.

Answers:
a) metal girders   c) tribe   e) a double
b) dizzy   d) a good head for heights

Extra activity

- Ask Ss:
Have you ever felt dizzy? When?
Who thinks they have a good head for heights? How do you know?
Can you name another Indian tribe?
Can you describe a scene from a film where you think they might use a double?

3

Aim: to focus on words with opposite meanings.
summary: Ss find words and phrases in the text with the opposite meanings of those given.

Main activity

- Ask Ss to find the words or phrases with the opposite meaning in the text. Ask individual Ss for the answers.

Answers:
a) make a mistake   c) dangerous   e) soft
b) high above the ground   d) hide

Optional activity

- Ss work with a partner and make a list of words with opposite meanings. They then use their list of words to test another partner.

4

Aim: to talk about the topic of the text, *dangerous jobs*.
Summary: Ss discuss the answers to two questions.

Main activity

- Ask Ss to read the text once more to find the answers to the two questions. Ask individual Ss for the answers.

Answers:
a) They have to walk on narrow metal girders.
   They are high above the ground.
   They might feel dizzy or fall.
b) A double is dressed like the actor and tries to hide his or her face.

Extra activity

- Ask Ss to find two differences between the jobs of:
a) a fire-fighter and a skyscraper builder
b) a police officer and a lifeguard

WORDS in ACTION

1 🎦 Vicky and George met some people with dangerous jobs when they were in the USA. Before you read, match the statements with the jobs.

lifeguard on a beach   fire-fighter   police officer   skyscraper builder

Which jobs are they talking about?
a) If you drive too fast, you might crash.
b) If you feel afraid, don't look down. You could fall!
c) If you see someone in trouble, you have to dive into the sea and help them.
d) You have to rescue people from burning buildings.

Which two jobs are described in the texts?

A Head for Heights

Some workers have to make the metal skeleton of a skyscraper. They work 250 metres above the ground! They have to walk on metal girders 15cms wide, and they try not to feel dizzy when they look down. If they make a mistake, perhaps it will be their last one. In the USA many of these skilled workers come from the same Indian tribe, the Mohawks. This tribe has developed a very good head for heights, and the Mohawks are not afraid of working high above the ground.

A stunt double takes the place of a film star when something dangerous is done. The double is dressed like the actor, and tries to hide his or her face. When we see an actor jump from a building, we really see the stunt double. Usually he or she falls onto something soft, but this part of the film is cut. In this way, the actor avoids getting hurt because all the dangerous things are done by the double.

2 Answer the questions about words and phrases from the text.

a) What is the *skeleton of* the building made from? Use another phrase from the text.
b) How do you feel if you look down when you are in a high place?
c) American Indians live in large groups. Which word describes this kind of group? Find a name in the text for one of these groups.
d) Some people do not feel afraid when they are in high places. Which phrase describes what they have?
e) Find a word that means *a person who looks the same as another person*.

3 Find words or phrases which have the opposite meaning to these words or phrases:

a) do everything right
b) a long way under
c) safe
d) show
e) hard

4 Answer these questions about the text.

a) What is difficult about the job of the workers on the skyscrapers? Find two things.
b) When we watch a film, why don't we know that a double is in the actor's place?

18 In the rainforest

*making suggestions: let's, how about … ?, why don't … ?, could;
expressing preferences: I'd rather*

The Programme for Belize

1a New language

Nick and Helen saw this article in a magazine. Read the article and answer the questions.

The Programme for Belize is an organization that is saving the rainforests of Belize, a small country in Central America. If you collect £25 you can buy an acre of rainforest and save it. In our schools competition, the group with the most interesting idea for collecting £25 will win a week's trip for four to Belize. You will visit Camp Rio Bravo, where scientists study the rainforest.

1 What does the Programme for Belize work to do?
2 What can you buy for £25?
3 What is the first prize?

1b New language

Helen and Nick's class decide to enter the competition. What should they do? Do you have any ideas?

Here are some suggestions made by the class. Choose a reply for each suggestion. You can use a reply more than once.

Suggestions
– Let's have a special football match. The people who watch can pay 10p each.
– Why don't we bring old things from home and have a sale?
– How about having a talent show?
– We could ask people to give us their small change.

Replies
– I don't think everyone likes sport.
– That's not a very interesting idea!
– It's an unusual idea, but will people be interested?
– Perhaps nobody will want to buy them!
– That's a good idea! Everyone will come!

Make some more suggestions from students in Helen and Nick's class. Use these ideas:

have a pet show   make things and sell them
organize a quiz evening
have bike races

In the rainforest   18

Unit 18		Functions	Grammar
Lesson 1	The Programme for Belize	Making suggestions	Let's, why don't we? how about?
Lesson 2	A visit to Rio Bravo	Expressing preferences	I'd rather
Lesson 3	CHRIS 7		

Word check

canoe	medicine	save
competition	organization	scientist
dress up	prize	soon
glad	rainforest	take a trip
make plans	sale	temple
		unusual

Lesson 1 The Programme for Belize

1a New language

Aim: to read for background information.
Summary: Ss read and answer direct questions.

Lead in

- Books closed. Ask Ss if they know where the country Belize is and if they know or can guess anything about it.
  Belize is in Central America, south of Mexico and north east of Guatemala; the country takes its name from the river which runs through the country. Part of the country is covered in rainforests. The capital, Belmopan, was destroyed by a hurricane in 1961 and rebuilt in 1965 eighty kilometres from its old position.
  Ask: *What do you know about the rainforests of South America?*

Main activity

- Ask Ss to read the short article about Belize silently and answer the questions. Ask individual Ss for the answers.

Answers:
1 It works to save the rainforests of Belize.
2 You can buy an acre of rainforest.
3 The first prize is a week's trip for four people to Belize (and to visit the camp where scientists study the rainforest).

Extra activity 1

- Ask Ss to complete these sentences:
  If we collect £25, we ...
  If we win the competition, ...
  If we visit camp Rio Bravo, ...

Extra activity 2

- Discuss with the class why it is important to save the rainforests. Ask:
  How can we help?

1b New language

Aim: to present ways of making and replying to suggestions.
Summary: Ss match suggestions with replies and then make more suggestions.

Lead in

- Books closed. Ask Ss to suggest some ideas for the competition and write them on the board.

Main activity

- Ask Ss to read the suggestions and replies silently. Ask two Ss to demonstrate the activity for the whole class, eg:
  S1: *How about having a talent show?*
  S2: *That's an unusual idea, but will people be interested?*
- Ss work with a partner and talk about what Helen and Nick's class could do to win the competition.
  Go around the class and help with the new language if necessary.

Extra activity

- Books closed. Write these key words on the board:
  football match   sale   talent show   change
  Ss make suggestions and replies.

18 In the rainforest

Helpline – making suggestions

- Read through the examples with the class. Ask Ss to make other suggestions with *Let's ...*, *Why don't we ...?*, *We could ...*, and *How about ...ing?*

1c Practice

Aim: to practise making and replying to suggestions.
Summary: Ss make suggestions and comment on them.

Lead in

- Ask Ss to describe the pictures.

Main activity

- Ask Ss to read the ideas for the pet show silently. They then discuss them with a partner using the language for suggestions and replies from activity 1b.

Extra activity

- Ss work in small groups. Ask them to think of different ideas for raising money. Set a time limit of three minutes for Ss to make more suggestions about what they could do. Ask groups to report back to the whole class and write the best ideas on the board. Ask other Ss to comment on the suggestions.

1d Listening

Aim: to listen for specific information.
Summary: Ss tick the points they hear on tape.

Lead in

- Ask Ss to read the sentences about the rainforests and predict which they are going to hear. Do not confirm yet.

Main activity

- Ss listen to the description of the rainforest twice and tick the points they hear. They then compare their answers with a partner.

Answers:
1 ✓
2 ✗ *They are very hot.*
3 ✓
4 ✗ *They live in the tops of the trees.*
5 ✓

Extra activity

- Write these questions on the board:
  a) Where are the rainforests?   (near the equator)
  b) How much rain falls in these forests?   (2 metres a year)
  c) What large animals live there?   (monkeys and snakes)
  d) Why are people cutting the trees down?   (to sell the wood and to make land for farms)
  e) Why do we need the rainforests?   (to make the air clean and because of the useful plants that grow there)
- Ss listen again and answer the questions.

- Ask Ss for the opposites of these adjectives which they hear in the listening:
  hot   wet   large   top   light   clean

Lesson 2 A visit to Rio Bravo

Aim: to present a series of activities in a reading text.
Summary: Ss read and choose the most interesting activities from a programme.

2a New language

Aim: to practise indicating preference.
Summary: Ss look at the activity programme and say which activities they think are the most interesting.

Lead in

- Books closed. Tell Ss that Helen and Nick's class won the competition and four students and one of their teachers are in Belize now. Write these activities on the board:
  collect flowers and plants in the rainforest   (no)
  have lessons about the trees of the rainforest   (yes)
  learn local dances   (yes)
  visit an ancient Roman temple   (no)
- Ask Ss to guess which two they can do in Belize.

Main activity

- Ask Ss to read the programme for part of the trip and see if they guessed correctly.

Main activity

- Ss read the programme and decide which activities are the most interesting. Ask them to choose three activities and tell a partner which ones they have chosen and why.

> **Helpline** – making suggestions
>
> There are many ways of making suggestions:
>   *Let's* bring old things from home. *Let's* = let us
>   *Why don't we* bring old things from home?
>   *We could* bring old things from home.
>   *How about* bringing old things from home?
>
>   → GC p13

1c Practice

The class decided to have a pet show at the school and made plans. You are students in the class. Look at these ideas and discuss them with a partner. Use the language from **1b**.

bring pets from home   organize rides on a camel
ask the local zoo for help   have a 'Best Pet' competition
have dog-training classes   take dogs for walks – for money
dress up as animals   sing animal songs

▶ *How about bringing pets from home?*
  – That's not a very interesting idea. Everyone will bring a dog or a cat!

1d Listening

Listen to the description of the rainforest. Tick ✓ the points you hear.

1 Rainforests are the home of many different plants and animals. ☐
2 The forests are cold most of the time and very wet. ☐
3 Rainforests are thousands of years old. ☐
4 The larger animals live on the ground under the tall trees. ☐
5 Man has cut down half of all rainforests in the world in the last 20 years. ☐

A visit to Rio Bravo

2a New language

Helen and Nick's class won the competition with their idea for a pet show. Four students went on the trip. One of their teachers went too. Read the programme for part of their trip and decide which activities are the most interesting.

Wednesday
morning: a trip into the rainforest
          go swimming OR go on the river in a canoe
afternoon: a visit to a Maya temple (1500 years old!)
          play volleyball OR learn local dances

Thursday
morning: lesson about medicines from trees
          take photos OR draw plants and flowers
afternoon: river project: collect fish OR make maps of rivers

Friday
morning: visit to the coral reef
          swim underwater OR take a trip in a glass-bottomed boat
afternoon: relaxation: play beach games OR go sightseeing

2b 🔊 New language

You are at Camp Rio Bravo. Work with a partner. Choose a part, A or B. Use the information in the programme in **2a** to have conversations like this:

A: What are we doing this morning?
B: There's a trip into the rainforest.
A: What do we do after that?
B: You can go swimming or go on the river in a canoe.
A: I'd rather go on the river in a canoe. It sounds more interesting.

2c Practice

Some British teenagers have won a competition and are on a visit to your country. Complete the dialogue with information about your country.

You: *What would you like to do today?*
Visitor: *I don't know. What do you think?*
You: *Let's go to … . It's … . Or we could …*
Visitor: *What's … like?*
You: *[give some details]*
Visitor: *I think I'd rather … . It's sounds more interesting.*

Make more dialogues with your visitors about other places in your country.

Do the same with this dialogue about food.

You: *What would you like to eat?*
Visitor: *I don't know. What do you think?*
You: *Why don't we have some … and some … ?*
Visitor: *What's … like?*
You: *[give some details] It's very tasty.*
Visitor: *I think I'd rather have …*

2d Writing

A friend is coming to stay with you. Write a letter and suggest some things to do.

Dear …
*I'm really glad that you are coming to stay at my house for a few days. I'm sure you will like it here. I've got lots of ideas for things to do. First of all why don't we … **[explain why this is interesting]** Then we could … . And how about …? Or perhaps you'd … . Anyway, we can decide all this later. I'll be at the bus station at 11.30 to meet you.*

See you soon
[your name]

Helpline – I'd rather

We use this to say what we prefer:
 Do you want to go swimming?
 – No thanks. I'd rather play volleyball.
(I'd = I would)
→ GC p13

Word check

canoe	organization	scientist
competition	prize	soon
dress up	rainforest	take a trip
glad	sale	temple
make plans	save	unusual
medicine		

In the rainforest 18

2b Practice

Aim: to present and practise *I'd rather*.
Summary: Ss roleplay dialogues based on the programme in activity 2a.

Main activity

- Ask two Ss to read out the model dialogue to demonstrate the activity for the rest of the class. Ss then work with a partner.
- They use the information about the programme in activity 2a to roleplay a conversation about the activities. They say what they'd rather do and give a reason. Go around the class and help if necessary. Ask individual Ss to say what they'd rather do and why.

Helpline – I'd rather

- Explain that we use *I'd rather* to express a preference, eg:
  Would you like to collect fish?
  No, I'd rather make maps of rivers.

2c Practice

Aim: further practice of making suggestions and *I'd rather*.
Summary: Ss roleplay dialogues between themselves and British visitors to their own country.

Lead in

- Ask Ss if any of them have had visitors from abroad. Ask:
  What did you show them in your city/area? Where did they go to eat?
  Write some ideas on the board.

Main activity

- Ask Ss to imagine that they have to plan the programme for the British teenagers who have won a competition to visit their country. Ss work with a partner (or in small groups) to write a plan for a 3-day programme. It should contain information about activities for mornings and afternoons and different kinds of food.
- Ss use their plan to complete and practise dialogues similar to those in the SB. Go around the class and help if necessary.

Extra activity

- Ask Ss to write one of the dialogues they practised.

2d Writing

Aim: further practice of making suggestions.
Summary: Ss write a letter to a friend who is coming to stay and suggest a programme of things to do.

Lead in

- Books closed. Ask Ss to suggest four things they could do at the weekend with a friend that they haven't seen for a long time. They should use different ways of making suggestions, eg:
  Let's visit the old harbour in the evening and eat a meal there.
  How about going to the new sports shop?
  Why don't we have a pizza?
  We could go to the cinema one evening.

Main activity

- Ss work individually and complete the letter in the SB. Go around the class and help if necessary.

Word check

- Ask Ss to find the nouns in the Word check box.
  (*canoe, competition, medicine, organization, prize, rainforest, sale, scientist, temple*)
- Tell Ss to think of an adjective to describe each of the nouns, eg:
  an exciting competition
- Then ask Ss to write four sentences using their pairs of adjective + noun, eg:
  The Programme for Belize organized an exciting competition.

18 In the rainforest

Lesson 3 CHRIS Episode 7

Aim: to read for specific and detailed information; to listen for specific information.

The story for far:

Main activity

- Ss work with a partner to answer the questions.

Answers:
1. The twins thought that she was probably not a real police inspector. They were suspicious of her.
2. A–Z was a book with all the streets of London in it.
3. The twins are going by boat to Greenwich.

1

Lead in

- Ask Ss what they think will happen next.

Main activity

- Ask Ss to read the story silently and decide if the statements are true or false. They can check with a partner. Ask individual Ss for their answers.

Answers:
a) False   b) True   c) True   d) False   e) False

2

Main activity

- Play the cassette twice. Ss listen to the conversation between the twins and tick the correct picture. Ask individual Ss for the answer.

Answer:
House called Sandy Rock. (Peter = rock)

Extra activity 1

- Ask Ss what the name Peter means. Ask them if any of their names mean something, eg:
  Lucia/Luke means light.

Extra activity 2

- Write these key words on the board:
  clue   Chris   shop   houses   name
- Play the cassette again. Then ask Ss to work with a partner and roleplay the conversation between the twins.

3

Main activity

- Ask Ss to read the next part of the story silently and decide the correct words or phrases. They can check with a partner. Then ask individual Ss for their answers.

Answers:
looked   opened   locked   top
street   followed her   stairs   in front of them

The last choice could be either *Chris* or *the man in the raincoat* – it depends on what Ss think is going to happen next.

4

- Ask Ss for their predictions for the next part of the story.

Extra activity 1

- Books closed. Write these sentences from the episode on the board or read them aloud as a dictation:
  Sandy and Peter decided to go ... Greenwich ... boat.
  Mrs Jackson made them some sandwiches ... lunch.
  The boat went ... Tower Bridge.
  He was sitting behind us ... the bus.
  Chris will be ... danger.
  It's the man ... the raincoat.
- Ss complete the sentences with the missing prepositions.

Extra activity 2

- Ask Ss to imagine they followed Sandy and Peter to Greenwich. They work with a partner and say what they saw.

Teacher's Book Unit 18

CHRIS

Episode 7

The story so far:

1. What did the twins think about Inspector Harman?
2. What was A-Z?
3. Where are the twins going next?

▶ a

Sandy and Peter decided to go to Greenwich by boat. There was a tourist boat that left from Westminster Bridge and they took the bus there. Mrs Jackson made them some sandwiches for lunch and they ate them on the way. The boat went under Tower Bridge and past Docklands with its new office blocks. It was a good way to see London. Suddenly Peter noticed something.

'Sandy, look at that man over there. I'm sure he was sitting behind us on the bus this morning.'

There was a tall man in a raincoat at the front of the boat, next to some foreign tourists.

'I don't think so, Peter. I'm more worried about Inspector Harman. If she follows us, then Chris will be in danger.'

1 Are these statements about the story true or false?

a) The twins took a boat from their house to Greenwich.   True/False
b) They didn't buy lunch on the boat.   True/False
c) Peter was worried about a man he saw on the boat.   True/False
d) The man in the raincoat was a foreign tourist.   True/False
e) Sandy saw Inspector Harman on the boat.   True/False

2 Listen to the next part of the story. What do the twins find in Cleopatra Road? Tick ✓ the picture.

3 Read the next part of the story. Choose one of the words or phrases underlined.

▶ b

Sandy and Peter stood outside the door and looked/walked up and down the street. The street/house was empty. Sandy knocked twice and they waited. The front door slowly closed/opened, but there was nobody there.

'Come on, Peter. I'm going in,' said Sandy and she stepped inside.

Peter followed her/went first and closed the door. There was a door on the right, but it was locked/open. In front of them were the stairs/kitchen. They walked up, trying not to make any noise. There was a door at the bottom/top. Before they could decide what to do, the door opened. And there standing behind them/in front of them was a tall man.

'It's Chris/Inspector Harman/the man in the raincoat!' said Sandy. 'What are we going to do now!'

4 What do you think happens next? Make a guess.

19 What have you been doing?

present perfect continuous

Life style

1a New language

Helen interviewed three people about their interests. Read the interviews and match the people with the pictures.

1

This is a very unusual sport! I started it just for a joke. I've been doing it for five years and I've collected 3 010 different ones from all over the world. That's a record! It's actually a very old game too. People have been playing with them for centuries. When you play you put 49 of them into a two-metre circle.

2

I think this is a really great sport! I saw some boys doing it and I decided to try it. I've been doing it for two years and I've just won my first competition. It's an old sport. People have been doing it for hundreds of years. It's not difficult if you practise. There was an Italian, Enrico Rastelli, who could throw ten balls at the same time!

3

This is really interesting, but you have to have the right equipment. I started when I was 10, so I've been doing it for four years. It's a good hobby for young people, because you learn a lot. It's not very popular, I suppose. I think that more grown up people than young people do it. People have been doing it for thousands of years.

These are some questions that Helen asked. Find the answers in the interviews. You won't find answers to all the questions in every interview.

1. When did you start doing this activity?
2. Why did you start?
3. How long have you been doing it?
4. Is it difficult?
5. Have people been doing this for a long time?

Work with a partner and practise the interviews.

Ask your partner about another activity.

Helpline

– present perfect continuous

present perfect of *be* + *-ing* form:

I/you/we/they
have ('ve) been   learning
she/he/it
has ('s)   been   learning

→ GC p13

What have you been doing? 19

Unit 19		Functions	Grammar
Lesson 1	Life style	Describing extended actions	Present perfect continuous For, since
Lesson 2	The bank robbery	Narrating past events	Present perfect continuous
Lesson 3	Check up Units 17–19		

Word check

actually	grown up	notebook
at once	hobby	outline
bank	important	popular
century	interest (n)	strangely
circle	joke	
equipment		

Helpline – present perfect continuous

- Explain that we form the present perfect continuous with *have/has been* + past participle, eg:
  People have been playing marbles for centuries.
  How long has he been collecting them?

- Explain that we use the present perfect continuous to express the idea of continuity, eg:
  People have been juggling for hundreds of years (and they still juggle these days).
  I've been learning English for two years (and I'm still learning).

- Point out that the present perfect continuous contrasts with the present perfect simple which can often express the idea of completion, eg:
  I've been reading that book all morning. (= I haven't finished it.)
  I've read that book. (= I've finished it.)

Lesson 1 Life style

1a New language

Aim: to present the present perfect continuous.
Summary: Ss match texts with pictures and then find answers to questions in the texts.

Lead in

- Ask Ss if they have any unusual interests (or know anyone who has). Write some of the interests on the board.
- Ask Ss to look at the photos and say what the boys are doing. You may need to teach the expressions *playing marbles, looking through a telescope* and *juggling*.

Main activity

- Ask Ss to read the three paragraphs silently and match them with the pictures. Ask individual Ss for the answers.

Answers:
1 playing marbles
2 juggling
3 looking through a telescope

- Ss read the paragraphs again and try to find answers to the questions in them. Point out that they won't find answers to all the questions in every interview.

- Ss work with a partner and interview each person using the questions. Tell them to invent answers if they do not find them in the texts. Go around the class and help if necessary. Ask Ss to use the questions and interview each other about another activity or sport.

Extra activity

- Books closed. Ask Ss to say what they can remember about each text. Encourage Ss to use the present perfect continuous for the appropriate information.

Teacher's Book Unit 19

19 What have you been doing?

1b Practice

Aim: to practise the present perfect continuous with *how long?*

Summary: Ss ask and answer questions in pairs.

Lead in

- Read the example. Then ask individual Ss to ask you a question with *How long*, eg:
  How long have you been working in this school?
  How long have you been teaching English?
  How long have you been living here?
  Answer the questions with both *since* and *for*, eg:
  S: How long have you been working in this school?
  T: For three years. Since 1992.

Main activity

- Ss work with a partner and ask each other questions using the ideas in the book and their own ideas, eg:
  playing basketball (or another sport)
  playing the piano (or another musical instrument)
  living in your present house
  Go around the class and help if necessary.

Helpline – for and since

- Explain that we use *for* to talk about a period of time, eg:
  We've been using this book for six months.

- Explain that we use *since* to talk about when the period of time started, eg:
  We've been using this book since September.

1c Listening

Aim: further practice of the present perfect continuous.
Summary: Ss match people, pictures and dates and then make statements.

Main activity

- Ask Ss to listen to the four people twice. Pause the cassette after each person during the first listening. Ss must match the people with the correct pictures and dates. They then check their information with a partner. Ask individual Ss for the answers.

Answers:
Jim – cooking, 1993
Anna – acting, 1990
Maria – roller-skating, 1994
Tony – taking photographs, 1992

- Ask Ss to write a sentence about each person using the present perfect continuous with *for*. Write one sentence on the board as an example, eg:
  Jim has been entering cooking competitions for ... years.
  (The number of years depends upon when you are using this book.)

- Ask individual Ss for the answers and write them on the board:
  Anna has been acting for ... years.
  Maria has been roller-skating for ... year.
  Tony has been taking photos for ... years.

Extra activity

- Play the cassette one or two more times. Ask Ss to listen for some more information about each person. Ask individual Ss what they heard and put notes on the board. Ss then work with a partner and roleplay an interview with one of the children using the notes on the board.

Lesson 2 The bank robbery

2a New language

Aim: practice of the simple past and the past continuous.
Summary: Ss complete a story based on pictures, questions and a text.

- Ask Ss to look at the pictures on page 81 of the SB and say what is happening. Write some useful vocabulary on the board as Ss use the words, eg:
  car, man, camera, shop window, bank
- Ss think about the questions below the second picture and answer them orally.
- Ss look at the pictures on page 82, and complete the text. Ask Ss to work with a partner to write the whole story. Go around the class and help if necessary. Ask Ss to read out sentences from their story.

Possible answers:
The man was outside a bank. He was taking photos of the bank and writing in a notebook. So Ozzy decided to phone the police. He went to a phone box and told them what was happening. 'I think the man's a bank robber,' he said. A police officer came and spoke to the strange man. The man showed her an identity card. Then the police officer said to Ozzy and Olive, 'Don't worry. I can explain everything.'

1b Practice

Ask a partner *How long ...?* questions:

learn English   write with this pen   come to this school   use this book   sit in this desk   live in this town/city/village

▶ *How long have you been learning English?*
– For more than twenty years. Since 1975.

Helpline – for and since

We use *for* to talk about a period of time:
   I've been learning English for eight months.

We use *since* to talk about when the period of time started:
   I've been learning English since October.
→ GC p14

1c Listening

Draw a line between the person and the activity. Draw another line between the person and the date when they started the activity.

Jim   Anna   Maria   Tony

1990   1991   1992   1993   1994   1995

Then make a sentence like this about each person:
▶ *[Name] has been [activity] for [number of years].*

The bank robbery

2a New language

Tell the story in the pictures. Look at Part 1 and Part 2 (on the next page). Use the story outline below the pictures and add ideas of your own. Make a guess about the end of the story. Then tell the whole story.

Part 1

Last week while the Odds were walking past the bank they saw a man who was acting strangely. [Where was he? What was he doing?]

19

Part 2

So Ozzy … and told them what was happening. 'I think the man is …,' he said. [Who did he phone? What did he say?]

A police officer came … . The man … [What did she do? What did he do?]

Then the police officer said to Ozzy and Olive, 'Don't worry … '

2b Practice

Complete the telephone call between Ozzy and the police sergeant at the police station. Use these verbs:

do   sit   stand   take photos   watch   write

Ozzy: We think there's a bank robber in a car outside the National Bank in Green Street.
Sergeant: How do you know he's a bank robber?
Ozzy: He … in his car for a very long time.
Sergeant: And how long … him?
Ozzy: For half an hour. We … outside a shop at the end of the street.
Sergeant: And what … for all that time?
Ozzy: He … of the bank and … in a notebook.
Sergeant: All right. Wait there. I'll send a police officer there at once.

Why was the man outside the bank? What was his job? What was he planning to do? Make some guesses!

Man: I've been taking photos of the bank for my job. I work as a … and my company is going to … the bank.

2c Practice

Look at the pictures and decide what these people have been doing all morning.

1   2

3   4

2d Writing

Write a letter to a penfriend. Use these verbs:

haven't written   have been busy   have been playing   have been studying   have you been doing?

Word check

actually
at once
bank
century
circle
equipment
grown up
hobby

important
interest (n)
joke
notebook
outline
popular
strangely

82

What have you been doing? 19

2b Practice

Aim: further practice of the present perfect continuous.
Summary: Ss complete a dialogue and the story about the man outside the bank.

- Ask Ss to complete the conversation between the police sergeant and Ozzy. They then check their answers with a partner. Ask individual Ss for the answers.

Answers:
Ozzy: He's been sitting in his car for a very long time.
Sergeant: And how long have you been watching him?
Ozzy: For half an hour. We've been standing outside a shop at the end of the street.
Sergeant: And what's he been doing all that time?
Ozzy: He's been taking photos of the bank and writing in a notebook.

- Ask Ss to answer the questions at the end of the story.

Possible answers:
Man: I work as an architect and my company is going to do some work at the bank.

2c Practice

Aim: further practice of the present perfect continuous.
Summary: Ss use pictures to say what people have been doing.

Main activity

- Ss work with a partner and say what the four people have been doing. They then write a sentence for each picture. Ask individual Ss for the answers.

Answers:
1 Ozzy's been playing football.
2 Olive's been sleeping.
3 Natalie's been studying.
4 Nigel's been shopping.

Extra activity

- Ask Ss to make up a short conversation for each of the pictures, eg:
  S1: What have you been doing?
  S2: I've been playing football.
  S1: Did your team win?
  S2: No, but we all enjoyed the match.

2d Writing

Aim: practice of the present perfect continuous and present perfect simple.
Summary: Ss use verb cues to write a short letter.

Main activity

- Ss work in pairs. They read the verb cues and think of possible sentences for the letter.

Possible answers:
I'm sorry I haven't written for a long time, but I have been busy. I have been playing basketball in the school team, and I have been studying a lot for my end of term examinations. What have you been doing lately? Write and tell me! That's all for now.

- Ask Ss to use their completed paragraph as a model for another letter to a penfriend. Go around the class and help if necessary.

Word check

- Choose some words from the Word check box and write them on the board with some letters missing, eg:
  c_ _t_ry   (century)
  ac_t_all_   (actually)
  _ok_   (joke)
  p_ _ul_r   (popular)
  in_ _re_t   (interest)
  c_r_le   (circle)
  Tell Ss that the words are from the Word check box and ask them to fill the gaps (in notebooks, on the board or orally).
- Now ask Ss to think of an example sentence using **each** word. This can be set as a team game.

19 What have you been doing?

Check up Units 17-19

1

Aim: further practice of real conditionals (*if* + present simple, main clause + *will*).
Summary: Ss complete sentences based on a picture.

Lead in

- Place a book on the edge of a desk where all Ss can see it. Say the beginning of this sentence:
  If I push this book, …
  Ss complete the sentence.
- Ask Ss to look at the picture in the SB and ask what George is doing. Make sure that everyone agrees that *he's painting/trying to paint the boat*.

Main activity

- Ss work with a partner and complete the sentences.

Possible answers:
If George slips, he will fall in the water.
If the pot of paint falls, it will ruin his clothes.
If the rope breaks, George will fall in the water.
If his parents see him, they will be very angry.

2

Aim: further practice of real conditionals.
Summary: Ss complete sentences.

- Ss work individually and complete the sentences. Ss then compare their answers with a partner.

Possible answers:
a) *If you help me paint the boat, I will do the cooking this evening.*
b) *If Mum sees you, she will be very angry.*
c) *If I fall in the water, I won't drown.*
d) *If you fall in, it will ruin your clothes.*
e) *If I don't finish today, I will continue tomorrow.*

3

Aim: further practice of real conditionals.
Summary: Ss make predictions about things that will happen to George.

- Ask Ss to imagine what George's parents say to him when they return.
- Ss work with a partner and write sentences beginning with *If …* Write Ss' sentences on the board.

4

Aim: making and replying to suggestions and expressing preferences.
Summary: Ss complete sentences.

Lead in

- Make a suggestion and then elicit some of the other ways of making suggestions and expressing preferences, eg:
  T: *Let's spend ten minutes on irregular verbs.*
  S1: *I'd rather not. Why don't we work on our projects?*
  S2: *Or how about reading our library books?*

Main activity

- Ss complete the sentences in their exercise books.

5

Aim: making and replying to suggestions and expressing preferences.
Summary: Ss practise dialogues in pairs.

Main activity

- Ask Ss to name some of the things they do at weekends or in the evenings. Ss then work with a partner and practise dialogues using the model in the SB.

6

Aim: further practice of the present perfect continuous.
Summary: Ss make comments for people in certain situations.

Lead in

- Say: *George is very tired. He started painting at seven o'clock this morning and he's still painting.* Ask a pair of Ss to ask and answer a question about George.
  S1: *How long has he been painting?*
  S2: *He's been painting for … hours/since …*

Main activity

- Ss write a comment for each situation using one of the verbs in the SB. Write answers on the board.

Answers:
a) *I've been waiting inside the post office all morning!*
b) *I've been looking for his wallet all morning!*
c) *I've been playing the guitar all morning!*
d) *I've been driving all morning!*
e) *I've been cleaning the house all morning!*
f) *I've been studying all morning!*
g) *I've been watching television all morning!*
h) *I've been walking in the rain all morning!*

7

Aim: focus on sentence stress and rhythm.
Summary: Ss say sentences with the correct stress.

Main activity

- Ask Ss to read the sentences aloud to a partner. Then play the cassette for them to listen and repeat.

Extra activity

- Ask Ss to work with a partner and change the endings of the sentences, eg:
  If you sit at the front, the teacher will ask you more questions!

UNITS 17-19

CHECK UP

1 Look at the picture and complete the sentences.

If George slips ...
If the pot of paint falls ...
If the rope breaks ...
If his parents see him ...

2 Complete each sentence about the situation in **1**.

a) **George:** If you help me paint the boat, I ...
b) **Vicky:** If ..., she will be vey angry!
c) **George:** If I fall in the water, I ...
d) **Vicky:** If ..., it will ruin your clothes!
e) **George:** If I don't finish today, I ...

3 You are one of George's parents. Say some things to him, beginning *If ...* .

4 Complete each sentence.

a) I don't want to stay here. Come on, let's ...
b) I don't want to go swimming. I'd rather ...
c) It's very hot today. How about ... ?
d) It's a very long walk to the station. Why don't ... ?

5 Make some dialogues like this:

▶ *Would you like to ... ?*
  – *No thanks, I don't really like ...*
  – *Why don't we ... ?*
  – *I don't think that's a very good idea. I'd rather ...*
  – *All right, let's do that then.*

6 Make a comment for each person, beginning *I've been ... all morning*! Use one of these verbs for each comment:

clean   drive   look for   play   study
wait   walk   watch

a) someone in a queue inside the post office
b) someone who has just found his or her lost wallet
c) someone with a guitar
d) someone in a car
e) someone in their living-room, with a vacuum cleaner
f) someone at a desk with lots of books
g) someone in front of a television
h) someone who has just arrived home with very wet clothes

7 📼 Say these sentences. Stress the syllables underlined.

a) If I <u>go</u> to the <u>shops</u>, I'll <u>buy</u> you some <u>cho</u>colate.
b) If you <u>sit</u> at the <u>front</u>, you'll <u>see</u> more <u>clear</u>ly.
c) If we <u>leave now</u>, we'll <u>get</u> there in <u>time</u>.
d) If he <u>comes</u> back <u>later</u>, <u>ask</u> him to <u>wait</u>.

Listen and repeat.

20 Are you sure?

can't be; must be

Spot the mistakes

1a New language

Nick wrote this puzzle for *Brilliant*. Read the puzzle and label the objects in the room. Then complete the answers.

Jack and Jean are hiding somewhere in this room, but where are they? In the room there is a large chest (1), but it is locked. There is a cupboard (2), but the doors are open and it is empty. There is also a filing cabinet (3) with three drawers (4). There is a large window, but there aren't any curtains. Next to the filing cabinet is a desk (5). We can see under the desk and there is no one there. There is a small cardboard box (6) on the desk. There is an armchair (7) and there is a sofa (8) against the wall.

▶ This is impossible! They can't be in the chest, because it's locked.
They can't be under the desk, because we can see that there is nobody there.
They can't be in the filing cabinet …
They can't be behind the curtains …
They can't be in the cupboard …
They can't be behind the armchair …
They can't be behind the sofa …
Where are they?

84

Are you sure? 20

Unit 20		Functions	Grammar
Lesson 1	Spot the mistakes	Describing certainty and uncertainty	Can't be
Lesson 2	Round the World album	Describing certainty and uncertainty	Can't be, must be
Lesson 3	Words in action		

Word check

against	hijacker	sausage
airline pilot	horse riding	sofa
armchair	label (v)	spaghetti
cardboard box	locked	
cool	painting	
filing cabinet		

- Ss read the puzzle again and with a partner say where Jack and Jean can't be, using the ideas in the SB. Encourage them to give reasons with their answers eg: *They can't be in the filing cabinet because the drawers are too small.*
- Ask Ss for their answers. Write some of the best ones on the board.

Answer:
It's a trick! Jack and Jean are not people, they are two white mice. They are in the cardboard box on the desk.

Lesson 1 Spot the mistakes

1a New language

Aim: to present *can't be* for expressing a logical deduction.
Summary: Ss study the puzzle and complete answers.

Lead in

- Ask Ss to describe what they can see in the picture. Make sure that they know the name for every object in the room that has a white box on it.

Main activity

- Explain to the Ss that every object with a white box on it is mentioned in the Puzzle in the SB, eg:
  a large chest = 1
- Ask Ss to read the Puzzle silently and label the objects. Ask individual Ss for the answers.

Answers:
From top left to bottom left: 4 window, 2 cupboard, 6 cardboard box, 5 desk, 3 filing cabinet, 7 armchair, 8 sofa, 1 chest.

Teacher's Book Unit 20

20 Are you sure?

1b Practice

Aim: practice of *can't be*.
Summary: Ss comment on pictures.

Main activity

- Read out the example. Ss then work with a partner and find mistakes in each picture. Go around the class and help if necessary. Ask individual Ss for the answers.

Answers:

2 This can't be an ancient Roman coin. The man's wearing a collar and tie. They didn't wear clothes like that in ancient Rome. Perhaps it's a fake coin.
3 The painting can't be by Leonardo da Vinci. He painted the Mona Lisa (La Gioconda) but the woman here is wearing a watch. They didn't have watches then.
4 The astronauts can't be on the moon because they aren't wearing helmets. There isn't any air on the moon!

1c Listening

Aim: further practice of *can't be*.
Summary: Ss listen to conversations and decide where the people are.

Main activity

- Play the cassette twice. Ask Ss to decide where the people are in each situation. Pause the cassette after each conversation during the first listening. Ss compare their answers with a partner. Ask individual Ss for the answers and their reasons. Remind them to use *can't be* in their answers.

Answers:

1 They are lost in a strange town. (They talk about a map, they mention a road name etc.) It can't be at a football match because there is no noise etc.
 Encourage similar comments for other answers.
2 They are in a classroom. (They talk about a question and an answer to a mathematical problem.)
3 They are in the street. (They talk about someone called Bill who is over there.)
4 They are in front of the TV. (They are talking loudly so they are probably at home. They say they'll find out next week so it must be a TV serial.)

Lesson 2 Round the World album

2a New language

Aim: to present *must be* for expressing a logical deduction.
Summary: Ss make deductions about places in the pictures.

Lead in

- Ask Ss to say which countries the Round the World Kids have visited. Give Ss time to look back at the Round the World units to remind themselves of the places Vicky and George have been to. Ask: *What did Vicky and George do and see in these countries?*

Main activity

- Read the introduction to the activity and ask Ss to look at the first picture and the example. Ss then make sentences about the other three pictures using *must be*. Encourage them to give a reason for their answers. Ask individual Ss for the answers.

Possible answers:

The second picture must be in Australia because I'm sure the city is Sydney. It can't be any other country.
I think the third picture must be in Texas because the driver's wearing a cowboy hat.
The fourth picture must be in Egypt because they have pyramids there.

Optional activity

- Ask Ss to say what monument or scene they would show for a picture of their country or city.

1b Practice

Here are some more puzzle pictures. What is wrong in each picture?

1 Is he really an airline pilot?

▶ *No, he can't be an airline pilot! He's wearing glasses. You have to have very good eyes to be a pilot. Perhaps he's a hijacker!*

2 Is this really an ancient Roman coin?

3 Is this painting really by Leonardo da Vinci?

4 Are they really on the moon?

1c Listening

Where are the people in each conversation? Tick ✓ your answer.

1 at a football match ☐   lost in a strange town ☐
  in a running race ☐
2 in a shop ☐   at the railway station ☐
  in a classroom ☐
3 in the street ☐   in Australia ☐   at Bill's house ☐
4 at the theatre ☐   in front of the TV ☐
  in a library ☐

Round the World album

2a New language

Vicky and George have visited lots of different countries on their round the world trip. Here are some photos from their album. Can you guess the country in each photo? There are some clues to help you.

▶ *I think the first picture must be in Italy. She's carrying some spaghetti and a long sausage.*

2b Practice

Read these extracts from Vicky's diary. Work with a partner and guess where she must be. All the countries are on the map.

1 This is a very small island but there are lots of tourists. It's really hot here and we've been swimming all morning, but it's cooler than it was in Egypt. Tomorrow we are leaving and sailing west to Italy …

▶ A: *They must be in Egypt.*
  B: *No, they can't be in Egypt, because it says, 'It's cooler than it was in Egypt'. They must be …*

2 We like it here and we can talk to people easily because they all speak English, of course. George keeps saying silly things, like 'Will we fall off the world here?' It's the middle of December but it's summer here …

3 Yesterday we went horse riding and George thought he was a real cowboy. He fell off the horse about ten times too. We met some real cowboys but they have got motorbikes, not horses!

4 There is so much to see here! It's a very large country. We've seen elephants and monkeys and some beautiful temples. Yesterday we had a lovely meal. George thought all the food here was very hot but it isn't true.

5 This is a very busy city and the people are very friendly. We've been to a wonderful museum and to the desert. Next week we're going on a trip down the river to see another ancient city. I haven't been on a camel yet, but I want to try …

Helpline – must and can't

When we are certain about something we can use *must*:
  It must be in Italy. I'm sure it is.
Can't is the opposite.
  It can't be in Italy. I'm sure it isn't.

→ GC p14

2c Writing

You are on a trip round the world. Write a paragraph in your diary with a description of a place, like the paragraphs in **2b**. Do not give all the details, because you want your readers to make some guesses about it. When you have finished, show your paragraph to others in the class. Ask them to decide where the place must be.

Word check

against
airline pilot
armchair
cardboard box
cool
filing cabinet
hijacker

horse riding
label (v)
locked
painting
sausage
sofa
spaghetti

Are you sure? 20

2b Practice

Aim: to practise *must be* and *can't be*.
Summary: Ss make deductions about the places described in Vicky's diary.

Main activity

- Read the introduction to the activity, the first extract and the example. Ss complete the example:
  They must be in Greece.
  Ask Ss to read the texts silently and decide which countries they describe. They then work with a partner and make dialogues about the pictures using *must be* and *can't be*. Go around the class and help if necessary. Ask individual Ss for the answers.

Answers:
They must be in Australia.
They must be in the USA.
They must be in India.
They must be in Egypt.

Extra activity

- Ss write a short description of an everyday object. They then read their description to their partner who must guess what the object is, eg:
  S1: It's a large electrical appliance. You put food and drink in it to keep them cold.
  S2: It must be a fridge.

Helpline – must and can't

- Read the rules and examples with the class.
- Make sentences with *I'm sure it is* and *I'm sure it isn't*, eg:
  I'm sure it isn't in Mexico.
- Ss rephrase your sentences using *must be* or *can't be*, eg:
  It can't be in Mexico.

2c Writing

Aim: to practise *must be* and *can't be*; to write a short description of a place.
Summary: Ss write a short description and then ask a partner to make guesses about the place.

Main activity

- Ask Ss to think of a place, either a country or a city, that they know something about and then to write a paragraph giving some details. They can use the texts in activity 2b as models. Ss show their paragraph to one or more Ss who must guess where it is, eg:
  This is a famous city which is built on a river. A lot of tourists go there every year to visit the monuments and churches like St Peter's.
  S1: It must be Rome.

Extra activity

- Ask Ss to bring or draw pictures for the places in their descriptions. Stick the descriptions and pictures to a large piece of cardboard in random order so that Ss can read and match them.

Word check

- Ask Ss to choose pairs of words from the Word check box which might be found together, eg:
  airline pilot + hijacker
  filing cabinet + locked
  armchair + sofa
  sausage + spaghetti
  cardboard box + label
- Ss must be prepared to explain their choice, eg:
  An airline pilot might meet a hijacker on the plane.

20 Are you sure?

Lesson 3 Words in action

1

Aim: further practice of the language of making suggestions.
Summary: Ss guess the missing words in the song and then listen to confirm.

Lead in

- Ask Ss to read the song and guess the missing words. Do not confirm yet.

Main activity

- Ask Ss to listen to the song twice and write the missing words. Ask individual Ss for the answers:

Answers:

1 go	5 come	9 watch	13 come
2 take	6 making	10 meet	14 remember
3 sit	7 read	11 walk	
4 fight	8 play	12 waiting	

- Ss sing the song.
- Ask Ss to listen to the song again and write down all the suggestions that are made in the song. Ask Ss how to make the suggestions in different ways, eg:
  Why don't we go for a walk outside?
  How about taking our bikes and going for a ride?
- Ask Ss which programmes they watch on television. Write the different types of programmes on the board, eg:
  films   documentaries   cartoons   news programmes
- Ask Ss to make a list of other activities they could do instead of watching television. Write some of their ideas on the board.

2

Aim: focus on the formation of nouns, verbs and adjectives.
Summary: Ss make words from other words.

Lead in

- Write the following headings and examples on the board:

verb	noun	adjective
write	....	X
X	stranger	....

- Ask Ss to tell you the missing words. (writer, strange)

Main activity

- Ask Ss to complete the table in the SB and then check their words with a partner. Ask individual Ss for the answers.

Answers:
a) description
b) dangerous
c) friendly
d) painter   paint
e) robber   robbery
f) scientist
g) suggest
h) organize

Extra activity 1

- Ask Ss to write sentences with some of the new words.

Extra activity 2

- Ss work in small groups and write a short story using all the words.

3

Aim: practice of the gerund as a noun.
Summary: Ss use adjectives to describe six activities.

Main activity

- Read the example. Ss work with a partner and use the adjectives to describe activities. Go around the class and check Ss' sentences. Write the most imaginative sentences on the board.

Extra activity

- Ask Ss to look through their Word check lists and find more adjectives. They then write three or four more sentences with these adjectives.

4

Aim: focus on verb/noun collocation.
Summary: Ss match verbs and nouns and make sentences.

Main activity

- Give Ss two minutes to match the verbs with the nouns. Ask individual Ss for the answers and write them on the board.

Answers:
enter a room, enter a competition
break a leg, break a window
rob a bank, rob a person
take a photo, take an examination
cook vegetables, cook a meal

- Ss make a sentence for each expression using a variety of tenses.

WORDS in ACTION

1 🔊 Before you listen to the song, guess the missing verbs.

I'd rather watch TV

Let's ..1.. for a walk outside.
— I'd rather watch TV.
Let's ..2.. our bikes and go for a ride.
— I'd rather watch TV.
You ..3.. every evening and it's just not right,
Watching the police and the cowboys ..4..,
Why don't you ..5.. out with me tonight?
— I'd rather watch TV.

You can't be serious, you must be crazy,
It's driving you mad and it's ..6.. you lazy.
You don't ..7.. books and you don't run and ..8..,
You just ..9.. a little black box all day.

Let's ..10.. some friends in the square.
— I'd rather watch TV.
Let's ..11.. along the street in the evening air.
— I'd rather watch TV.
I've been ..12.. for a month or more
And every night I ..13.. round and knock on your door.
Don't you ..14.. what your legs are for?
— I'd rather watch TV.

Listen to the song and write the missing words.
Which programmes on television do you usually watch? Have you ever thought of doing other things instead?

2 Make words that belong to the same family as the words given.

a) **verb**: describe   **noun**: …
b) **noun**: danger   **adjective**: …
c) **noun**: friend   **adjective**: …
d) **verb**: paint   **nouns**: a person: … a thing: …
e) **verb**: rob   **nouns**: a person: … a thing: …
f) **noun**: science   **noun**: a person: …
g) **noun**: suggestion   **verb**: …
h) **noun**: organization   **verb**: …

Use each new word in a sentence.

3 Describe six activities. Use each of these adjectives.

    dangerous
    exciting
    unusual
    popular
    impossible
    tiring

▶ *Riding a motorbike is dangerous.*

4 Make two expressions with each verb, using nouns from the list. Then use the expressions in sentences.

Verbs
    enter   break   rob   take   cook

Nouns
    bank   person   vegetables   photo
    meal   leg   room   examination
    window   competition

21 Just imagine!

would: imaginary situations; conditional 2: unreal situations

What would you do?

1a New language

Read Helen's interviews about survival. Do you agree with the answers?

Helen: Imagine that you are alone on a small island. How would you survive? What would you do first?

Anna: I'd build a shelter first. I'd use branches from trees. I'd build it near the stream.
Jim: I'd look for food first! I'd eat fruit but I wouldn't eat strange plants!
Maria: I'd make a fire first. Then people would see the smoke and they would rescue me.
Tony: I'd make a boat first. I'd use pieces of wood from the beach. I'd leave the island as soon as possible. It would be dangerous to stay there.

Which of these things would you do? How would you do them?

go fishing   catch animals   send messages   make a tree house

Describe two things you wouldn't do.

▶ *I wouldn't sleep on the beach. It would be dangerous.*

Helpline

– would in imaginary situations

When we talk about imaginary situations we use *would*:
  I'd build a shelter first.
  I wouldn't eat strange plants.
  (I'd = I would)

→ GC p14

88

Just imagine! 21

Unit 21		Functions	Grammar
Lesson 1	What would you do?	Describing imaginary situations	Would, wouldn't
Lesson 2	Changing places	Describing imaginary situations	Unreal conditional: if + past tense + would
Lesson 3	CHRIS 8		

Word check

branch	imaginary	signal
castaway	invisible	spend money on
change places	journalist	survive
ghost	nearby	wood
gold	present (n)	
head teacher	rule	

Helpline – would in imaginary situations

- Explain that we use *would* to talk about imaginary situations, eg:
  He'd make a boat.
  I wouldn't go into the forest.

Lesson 1 What would you do?

1a New language

Aim: to present *would* to talk about imaginary situations.
Summary: Ss comment on suggestions about survival.

Lead in

- Ask Ss to look at the picture in the SB and to describe what they can see. Write the word *Survival* on the board. Tell the class that the people are doing these things in order to stay alive, or to survive.

Main activity

- Read Helen's introduction. Tell Ss that Helen is describing an imaginary situation. Explain that the situation is not real but that the teenagers in Helen's interview are imagining what they would do in this situation.
- Ss read what the four teenagers say. Ask them to identify Anna, Jim, Maria and Tony in the picture. Ask them which one of the activities they would do first in the same situation.
- Ask Ss to suggest other things that they would do on the island. Write some of their ideas on the board, eg:
  climb to the highest point on the island
  look for friendly islanders
  make a weapon
  go into the forest
- Ss work with a partner and use their own ideas and those in the SB to talk about the things they would and wouldn't do. Go around the class and check that Ss are using *would* and *wouldn't* correctly.

21 Just imagine!

1b Practice

Aim: to practise *would* to talk about imaginary situations.
Summary: Ss say what they would do in other difficult situations.

Lead in

- Write the three situations on the board. Ask Ss to suggest what they would do in each situation.

Main activity

- Ask individual Ss what they would and wouldn't do in the first situation. Ss then work with a partner and talk about the other two situations.

Extra activity

- Ask Ss to write two sentences about each situation, eg: *I wouldn't take my shoes off.   I'd walk at night.*

1c The castaway game

Aim: further practice of *would* to talk about imaginary situations.
Summary: Ss decide what to buy as part of a game.

Lead in

- Books closed. Write the name *Robinson Crusoe* on the board and find out who has read the book or seen a film. Ask Ss to explain what happened to Crusoe: *His ship was wrecked and he spent many years as a castaway on a desert island.*
- Books open. Ss name the objects in the picture.

Main activity

- Read the introduction to the activity. Ask Ss what they would buy. Then ask Ss to work with a partner and decide what they would and wouldn't buy.
- This activity can be played as a game in groups. Each person has to say something they would buy. Anyone who repeats an item is out of the game. The winners are either the last Ss left after a time limit or the game can be played until only one person is left.

1d Listening

Aim: to listen for specific information; to practise *would* to talk about imaginary situations.
Summary: Ss listen and choose the situation each speaker is talking about. They then say what they would do in each situation.

Lead in

- Ask Ss to look at the different situations and imagine what they would do in each. Do not ask for answers – this can be done after the listening.

Main activity

- Ss listen twice and decide which situation each speaker is talking about. Pause after each speaker and ask Ss to note the words which helped them to guess the answer. Ss check their answers with a partner.

Answers:

1	seeing a wild animal	(dangerous one/lion or tiger)
2	finding some money	(how much)
3	being ill	(tell mother/for something serious, the doctor would come)
4	breaking your watch	(at school we have a bell/kids look at theirs all through the lesson)

- Ss work in small groups and say what they would do in the four situations. Groups report to the whole class.

Possible answers:

1 I wouldn't say anything.
   I would stand still. (I wouldn't move.)
2 I would ask people near me if it belonged to them.
   I'd give it to my teacher.
   I'd take it to the police station.
3 I'd drink something hot.
   I'd go to bed.
   I'd stay at home.
   I wouldn't go to school.
   I'd read my favourite book or watch television.
   The doctor would come.
4 I'd look in the street.
   I'd ask someone.   I'd take it to a shop.
   I'd ask my parents to buy a new one.

Lesson 2 Changing places

2a New language

Aim: to present the unreal conditional 2.
Summary: Ss read an interview and then roleplay interviews.

Lead in

- Ask Ss what the head teacher of a school does.

Main activity

- Read aloud or play the conversation between Nick, Anna and Jim. Ask Ss to cover the words and repeat Nick's questions:
  Which person would you like to be for one day?
  What would do you do if you were that person?
- Ask individual Ss for Anna and Jim's replies. Ss use the ideas in the SB and then answer the same questions. Ask individual Ss to say something about their partner's answers, eg: *If Penny were a very rich person she'd build a sports centre in her town.*

| Helpline | – if in unreal conditions + would

- Explain that when we talk about unreal situations we use *if* + past tense, + *would*, eg:
  If I saw a wild animal, I'd stand still.
- Point out to Ss that *were* is used after *I/he/she/it* in more formal English but *was* can be used in less formal situations, eg:
  T to S: *If I were you, I'd look for that encyclopedia in the school library.*
  S to S: *If I was you, I'd tell the teacher.*

1b Practice

Imagine that you are in these difficult situations. What would you do? What wouldn't you do? Use the ideas in the lists and add ideas of your own.

1 Lost in the desert
take your shoes off   walk at night   take your shirt off and put it on your head   write a message in the sand

2 Forest fire
run into the forest   call the fire brigade   find help   look for water

3 Shipwrecked and in the water
swim to the shore   look for other boats   make a signal   shout

1c The castaway game

You are Robinson Crusoe, castaway on a desert island. Luckily you have a large chest of pirate's gold and there is a Castaway Superstore on a nearby island. However, you can only put a few things in your canoe. What would you buy? Why? Don't forget – the store sells everything!

1d Listening

Listen to these people talking about what they would do in different situations. Tick ✓ the situation each speaker is talking about.

1 seeing: a ghost ☐   a burglar ☐   a wild animal ☐
2 finding: some money ☐   an animal ☐   a lost child ☐
3 being: lost ☐   cold ☐   ill ☐
4 breaking: your pen ☐   your watch ☐
            your electronic calculator ☐

What would you do in these situations?

Changing places

2a New language

Would you like to change places with someone? Nick talked to some friends at school.

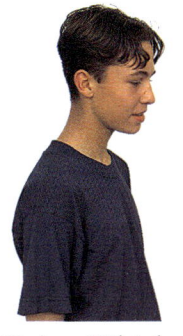

Nick: Which person would you like to be for one day? What would you do if you were that person?
Anna: The head teacher of the school! If I were the head teacher I'd change some of the school rules. I'd give the students more holidays! I wouldn't give any homework!
Jim: A famous journalist! If I were a journalist I'd interview my favourite singers. I'd visit them at home.

Ask a partner the same questions. Use some of the ideas in the list.

a famous person from your country
a very rich person
a Superhero   an invisible person

Helpline

– if in unreal conditions
+ would

When we talk about unreal situations, we use *if* + past tense.
We can use *were* instead of *was* after I/he/she/it:
If I were the head teacher, I'd change some of the school rules.

→ GC p14

21

2b New language

Nick asked Jim about things that would change his life.

Nick: What would really change your life?
Jim: If I had a helicopter my life would be different! I'd fly to the beach every day and I'd visit all my friends in different countries. I wouldn't be late for school.

Ask a partner the same question. Use ideas from the pictures.

2c Practice

What would you do every day if you lived in these places? Use the ideas with the pictures and ideas of your own.

1 swim/catch fish

2 go dancing/ go shopping

3 go skiing/ stay at home

▶ If I lived on a tropical island, I'd get up in the morning and swim for an hour. After that I'd …

2d Writing

Complete the paragraphs.

If I were a rich and famous person I would do lots of things. First of all I'd buy … and … I'd live … and I wouldn't … . Every day I'd … and I wouldn't … .

I would also give my family lots of presents. I'd give my parents … and I'd give my … a … . If I were rich I'd have lots of free time. I'd … and I'd … . I wouldn't … I'd have long holidays …
[say where]

Word check

branch	imaginary	signal
castaway	invisible	spend money on
change places	journalist	survive
ghost	nearby	wood
gold	present (n)	
head teacher	rule	

90

Just imagine! 21

2b New language

Aim: to practise the unreal conditional.
Summary: Ss speculate about changes in their lives.

Lead in
- Books closed. Ask Ss to imagine things that would really change their lives. Write a few of their ideas on the board.

Main activity
- Read aloud the conversation between Nick and Jim. Ask Ss to add to Jim's ideas, eg:
  If I had a helicopter, I'd visit all the famous places in my country.
- Ask Ss to look at the pictures and make a question for each picture. Ask individual Ss for the questions:
  What would you do if you had a motorbike?
  What would you do if you had a lot of brothers and sisters?
  What would you do if you had a video camera?
  What would you do if you found a chest full of money?
  What would you do if you had a time machine?
- Ss work with a partner and ask each other these questions. Go around the class and help if necessary. Ask individual Ss to say what their partner would do in some of the situations, eg:
  If Harry had a video camera, he'd video his younger sister.
  If Teresa had a time machine, she'd travel back in time and she'd meet some famous people.

Optional activity
- Dictate these beginnings of conditional sentences or write them on the board:
  a) *If I lived in Paris, ...*
  b) *If I had a mountain bike, ...*
  c) *If my brother broke my personal stereo, ...*
  d) *If I were very hungry, ...*
  e) *If I were late for school, ...*
  f) *If our teacher gave us a lot of homework, ...*
- Ask Ss to complete them using their own ideas. Ask individual Ss for answers.

2c Practice

Aim: further practice of the unreal conditional.
Summary: Ss use pictures to talk about what they would do if they lived in certain places.

Lead in
- Ask Ss to look at the three pictures in the SB and briefly describe the places, eg:
  In picture 1 you can see a tropical island with a beautiful beach.
  In picture 2 you can see skyscrapers in New York.
  In picture 3 you can see a wooden house in the mountains.

Main activity
- Ss suggest things they would do in each of the places using the ideas given for each picture. Then ask them to work with a partner and imagine how they would spend a whole day in each of the places. Go around the class and help if necessary. Ask individual Ss to talk about their imaginary day in one of the places.

Extra activity
- Ask Ss to talk about places where they would not live and give reasons why not, eg:
  I wouldn't live in the jungle because I hate snakes.

2d Writing

Aim: further practice of the unreal conditional.
Summary: Ss complete two paragraphs with what they would do if they were rich and famous.

Lead in
- Ask Ss to say some of the things they would do if they had lots of money. Write some of their ideas on the board.

Main activity
- Ss work individually to complete the paragraphs in their exercise books. Go around the class and help if necessary. Early finishers exchange paragraphs.

Word check
- Put the following anagrams on the board:
  SACTWAAY   (castaway)
  SBLEINVII   (invisible)
  NJUOSTRAIL (journalist)
  GASLNI   (signal)
  HBANCR   (branch)
  DOWO   (wood)
  Explain that the letters of each word are in the wrong order and ask Ss to find the words.
- Now ask Ss to use each word once to make up six sentences.

21 Just imagine!

Lesson 3 CHRIS Episode 8

Aim: to read for specific information; to listen for specific information; to narrate a story.

The story so far:

- Ask Ss to work with a partner to answer the questions.

Answers:
1 They went to Greenwich by boat.
2 They went into the house called Sandy Rock.

The answers to questions 3 and 4 depend on the predictions that Ss made during Episode 7.

1

Lead in

- Books closed. Write the headline *Computer crooks caught – Police thank twin detectives* on the board. Ask Ss to say what they think happened.

Main activity

- Ask Ss to read the newspaper article silently and answer the questions.

Answers:
a) Brian Wilson is a police officer.
b) Wendy Harman is a criminal. She is a member of a gang which has been stealing computer game programs in England, France and Germany.
c) They phoned the police and checked if Wendy Harman was a real police inspector.

Extra activity

- Ask Ss to read the newspaper article again and find at least five words connected with the police and criminals. Ask Ss for their answers.

Answers:
crooks   detectives   arrested   gang   stealing   steal   thieves

2

Lead in

- Ask Ss to read the questions and guess what the answers are. Do not confirm yet.

Main activity

- Play the conversation twice. Ss listen and answer the questions. Ask individual Ss for their answers.

Answers:
a) Yes. Brian Wilson, the detective, told him about the gang's plans to steal his program.
b) They needed proof that they wanted to steal the plans.
c) It was one of the crooks, Paul Dennis.
d) No.
e) Ss guess where the games program was.

Extra activity

- Play the cassette again but pause it at different points in the story for Ss to narrate what happened.

3

Extra activity

- Ss read CHRIS's message and find out where the games program was. (It was in the computer all the time.)

Main activity

- Ask Ss to read the message again and work out the meaning of the last part with a partner. Ask Ss for their answer.

Answer:
Perhaps computers are very clever
But only people can have adventures
And enjoy themselves

4

Extra activity

- Use the recorded version of the episodes to help Ss remember the story. You can play extracts and ask Ss to give ideas. They then prepare the whole story by writing down some key words or phrases first. Go around the class and help if necessary.

Main activity

- Ss work with a partner and retell the story.

Extra activity 1

- Write these words on the board:
  arrest   look for   steal   pretend   set a trap
- Ss write a sentence about the episode for each word.

Extra activity 2

- Ss write True/False statements about either Episode 8 or the whole story.

Extra activity 3

- Ask Ss to imagine that they are going to rewrite the story so that it happens in their capital city. Ask them what important places and monuments they would use.

Episode 8

CHRIS

The story so far:

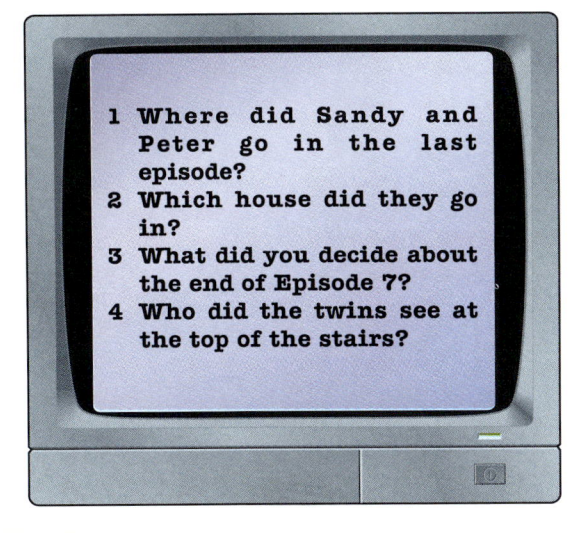

1. Where did Sandy and Peter go in the last episode?
2. Which house did they go in?
3. What did you decide about the end of Episode 7?
4. Who did the twins see at the top of the stairs?

▶ **a**

Computer crooks caught – Police thank twin detectives

Police in Greenwich have arrested two members of a gang which has been stealing computer games programs in England, France and Germany. Wendy Harman and Paul Dennis were arrested by Detective-Sergeant Brian Wilson at a house in Cleopatra Road, Greenwich.

'We have been looking for these two for six months,' said Detective-Sergeant Wilson. 'We knew that they were trying to steal Chris Talbot's new games program, but then Chris disappeared. Luckily Chris's brother and sister phoned us and told us about Harman. She was pretending to be a policeman, and was trying to find Chris. So we set a trap for the thieves, and luckily they fell right into it. Thanks to Peter and Sandy - and a computer called CHRIS!'

1 Answer these questions.

a) Which of these people is a police officer?
   Paul Dennis   Brian Wilson   Chris Talbot
b) Who exactly is Wendy Harman?
c) Do you know now what Peter and Sandy did after they left Cleopatra's Needle?

2 Listen to Sandy and Peter talking to their brother Chris and explain these points about the story.

a) Did Chris know that some thieves were trying to steal his computer game program?
b) Why didn't the police arrest the thieves before they arrived at the house?
c) Who was the person at the top of the stairs?
d) Was the computer disk at the house?
e) Can you guess where the games program was?

3 Read the message from CHRIS. Can you understand the last part?

▶ **b**

```
Hello, my name is CHRIS. Did I help
you? Did you follow the clues in the
story? I expect you have guessed where
the program was. I had it safe inside me
all the time! We computers are very good
at keeping secrets. And we are very
helpful - if you tell us exactly what to
do. But I have one last puzzle for you.

Pex rhq apx scq omx puq tex rsq arx
evq erx ycq lex veq rqx
Bux toq nlx ypq eox plq ecx anq hax veq
adx veq ntx urq esx
Anq dex njq oyx thq emx seq lvx esq

Think about it!
```

4 Explain the whole story to a partner!

22 Difficult moments

revision: tenses, articles; verbs followed by infinitive or gerund

How embarrassing!

1a Practice

Helen asked people to describe an embarrassing moment. Tell the story of each of the pictures. Use these notes:

Where was it/where were you?   What was happening?
What happened?   What did you do? What did other people do?

1b New language

The pictures in **1a** go with these stories, but there are some mistakes in them. What is wrong with the pictures?

1 **My worst moment** was in a concert at school a few years ago. I was playing the violin and I was sitting at the front. Everyone could see me. Suddenly two of the strings broke and there was a horrible noise. I didn't know what to do, so I just stopped playing and sat there.

2 **Two years ago** we went to France. We were travelling by train from Paris to Lyons. We couldn't understand French very well and when the train stopped we thought the station was Lyons, so we got off. It was the wrong station and we had to wait three hours for the next train.

3 **My friend**, Lee, is a waiter in an expensive restaurant. Once we had dinner there on my birthday. While Lee was serving me, I moved my chair and he dropped a plate of soup on my mother's head. We all laughed but my mother was very upset!

Difficult moments 22

Unit 22		Functions	Grammar
Lesson 1	How embarrassing!	Narrating past events	Definite/ indefinite/zero article
Lesson 2	The Round the World Kids	Describing events in a narrative	Verbs followed by infinitive or gerund
Lesson 3	Check up Units 20–22		

Word check

at last	horrible	soup
carry on	have dinner	stupid
completely	have lunch	waiter
embarrassing	serious	windsurfing
get off	serve	

Lesson 1 How embarrassing!

1a Practice

Aim: revision of tenses.
Summary: Ss use pictures to tell the stories.

Lead in

- Write the words *embarrassing situations* on the board. Ask Ss to describe embarrassing situations, eg:
  You forget your words in a play.
  Your teacher discovers you have told a lie.
  You arrive too early for a party.

Main activity

- Ask Ss to look at the pictures in the SB and describe the embarrassing moments as if they had happened to them. Give Ss a few moments to prepare what they are going to say about the first picture. Ask individual Ss to tell the story, eg:
  I was marching in the street with my band and I was at the back. I was playing my drum when suddenly it broke. Everyone looked at me and laughed.
- Ss work with a partner and tell the other stories. Go around the class and check that they are using the correct tenses. Ask individual Ss to tell the stories for the whole class.

1b New language

Aim: further practice of tenses; focus on the definite, indefinite and zero article.
Summary: Ss compare texts with the pictures and look for mistakes in the pictures.

Lead in

- Books open, texts covered. Make some true/false statements for each picture, eg:
  Picture 1: I was playing the piano. I was sitting.
- Ss decide if the statements are true or false and correct the false ones, eg:
  I was playing the drum. I was standing.

Main activity

- Ask Ss to read the texts silently. They then work with a partner and discuss the differences between the texts and the pictures. Ask individual Ss to suggest mistakes in the pictures.

Extra activity

- Dictate one of the texts to the class. Ss can then read the text in the SB and check their dictation.

Teacher's Book Unit 22

22 Difficult moments

Helpline – articles

- There are many rules about the use of articles. This section focuses on some of the most common uses. Explain the following rules:

a) Without an article
The article is not used with:
- certain common expressions, eg:
*at school/university   by train/car/bike   in class
at home   to have breakfast/lunch/dinner*
- the names of countries (with a few exceptions), cities or languages, eg:
I live in Brazil where we speak Portuguese. The capital city is Rio de Janeiro.
Exceptions are:
the United States of America, the Netherlands

b) With *the* (definite article)
The definite article is used:
- when we describe the playing of musical instruments, eg:
to play the piano/guitar/flute

c) With *a* or *an* (indefinite article)
The indefinite article is used with:
- the expressions *few* and *little*, eg:
*Only a little soup fell on the floor.
Luckily, only a few people heard the horrible noise.*
Without the articles these expressions usually have a negative meaning and suggest *not as much/many as one would like*, eg:
Few schools have computers.
- jobs, eg:
She's an architect. He wants to be a teacher.

- Ask Ss to read the texts in activity 1b again and find examples of no article, the definite article and the indefinite article.

1c Practice

Aim: to practise articles (*a/an, the* or zero article).
Summary: Ss make and then use questions which include articles.

Main activity

- Give Ss about two minutes to prepare the questions. Check answers.

Answers:
1 Can you speak French/German/Italian?
2 Have you ever been to the USA/France/England?
3 What time do you usually have lunch/dinner/breakfast?
4 Can you play the piano/the guitar?
5 Do you usually come to school by train/on foot/by bus?
6 Do you want to be a singer/a teacher/a doctor?

- Practise a few questions with the whole class. Ss work with a partner to ask each other the questions or ask Ss to get up, walk around the classroom and ask any student a question.
- Ask Ss to report back about the Ss they have worked with, eg: *Peter can play the piano but he's never been to England.*

Lesson 2 The Round the World Kids

2a New language

Aim: to present more verbs followed by the infinitive or the gerund.
Summary: Ss complete the text with the verbs, all of which are followed by the infinitive or the gerund.

Lead in

- Ask Ss to look at the picture in the SB but to cover the text. Read out the first sentence of the story:
Something silly happened to us in Italy.
Ask Ss to guess what happened to George and Vicky.

Main activity

- Ask Ss to read the story once silently to get the general meaning. They then read the story again more slowly in order to fill in the missing verbs in the correct tense.

Answers:
1 forgot   5 decided   9 pretended
2 refused   6 wanted   10 stopped
3 managed   7 tried
4 carried on 8 kept

- Ss divide the verbs into two groups, those followed by the infinitive and those followed by the gerund.

Helpline – verbs followed by infinitive or by gerund

- Ask Ss to make sentences with some of the verbs.
- Verbs such as *forget, try, stop, like* can be followed by either the infinitive or the gerund but the meaning is slightly different. Do not introduce both forms here.

2b Listening

Aim: further practice of verbs followed by the infinitive or the gerund.
Summary: Ss listen and complete sentences.

Lead in

- Ask Ss to suggest ways of completing the sentences about Vicky and George. Do not confirm yet.

Main activity

- Ask Ss to listen twice and complete the sentences. Pause between each extract to give Ss time to write.

Answers:
1 Vicky has decided to (go back and) visit all the countries again.
2 George didn't like being on the boat all the time. He didn't like sleeping on the boat after a few months.
3 Vicky didn't mind cleaning the kitchen and doing the shopping and cooking (or doing dirty jobs like ...).
4 George would like to become a member of the windsurfing team at his watersports club.
5 Vicky hasn't managed to put all her photos into albums.
6 George keeps thinking he is still on the boat.

Helpline – articles

Without an article:
  at school   France   Paris
  by train   French
  We had dinner.
With *the*:
  I was playing *the* violin.
With *a*:
  a few years ago   he is *a* waiter

→ GC p15

1c Practice

Complete the questions by choosing a word or words from the list. Use *a/the* or no article. Ask a partner the questions.

train school French singer USA piano home lunch France dinner foot work German teacher bus Italian doctor England breakfast guitar

1 Can you speak ...?
2 Have you ever been to ...?
3 What time do you usually have ...?
4 Can you play ...?
5 Do you usually come to school by/on ...?
6 Do you want to be ...?

The Round the World Kids

2a New language

Read the extract from Vicky's diary and decide which words are missing. Use each verb only once. Put each verb in a suitable tense.

carry on   decide   forget   keep   manage
pretend   refuse   stop   try   want

Something silly happened to us in Italy. We always enjoy sightseeing but on this day we ..1.. to take a map with us.
  George ..2.. to ask for directions and we ..3.. to get lost. We ..4.. walking along the same road for ages and then we ..5.. to take a taxi.
  When we ..6.. to get out we had some language problems! We ..7.. to talk to the taxi-driver but he just ..8.. laughing. To make the taxi stop we ..9.. to be ill.
  Then the driver ..10.. laughing and became very serious. He took us to the hospital and we felt really stupid!
  We had to walk all the way back to the harbour from there, because we didn't have any more money.

Helpline – verbs followed by infinitive or by gerund

Verbs followed by infinitive with *to*:

forget manage try would like refuse pretend decide want plan

Verbs followed by gerund *-ing*:

carry on keep like enjoy practise not mind stop

→ GC p15

2b Listening

Listen to Vicky and George and complete these sentences.

1 Vicky has decided to ...
2 George didn't like ...
3 Vicky didn't mind ...
4 George would like to ...
5 Vicky hasn't managed to ...
6 George keeps ...

2c Practice

Look at what Vicky and George say. Then talk to a partner about something that:

1 … you often forget to do.
2 … you'd like to do this summer.
3 … you want to do, but never manage to do because you don't have enough time.
4 … you like doing after school.
5 … you are planning to do soon.
6 … you have decided to do recently.

1 You always forget to take the map.

2 I'd like to spend all day at the beach today.

3 I never manage to write any letters.

4 I like sailing at the weekend.

5 We're planning to go home next month.

6 George has decided to have windsurfing lessons.

2d Writing

You are Vicky or George. Write a letter to a friend and tell him or her about your plans for next year. Choose from the suggestions given.

Dear …
At last I have finally managed to write to you! I've been making some plans for next year. I am making lots of plans for the future. As you know, … [say what you like/enjoy doing, what you never manage to do, what you always forget to do]. Next year I am going to change completely! … [say what you have decided to do, what you are going to try to do, what you want to do, what you would like to do, what you are planning to do and what you are going to stop doing]. What do you think?
Best wishes
[your name]

Word check

at last	have lunch
carry on	serious
completely	serve
embarrassing	soup
get off	stupid
horrible	waiter
have dinner	windsurfing

Difficult moments   22

2c Practice

Aim: further practice of verbs followed by the infinitive or the gerund.
Summary: Ss read what Vicky and George say and then use the same verbs to tell a partner about themselves.

Lead in

- Ask Ss to look at the pictures in the SB and read what Vicky and George say. Ask Ss to cover the speech bubbles and repeat the sentences.

Main activity

- Ask individual Ss to make questions about the six things in the list, eg:
  1 What do you often forget to do?
  2 What would you like to do this summer?
- Ss work with a partner and ask each other these questions. Go around the class and help if necessary.

Extra activity

- Ss write sentences about their partner.

2d Writing

Aim: further practice of verbs followed by the infinitive or the gerund.
Summary: Ss complete a letter using verb cues.

Lead in

- Books closed. Prepare Ss orally for the written task by asking them to say what George or Vicky:
  - likes or enjoys doing
  - never manages to do
  - always forgets to do
  - has decided to do
  - is going to try to do
  - wants to do
  - would like to do
  - is planning to do
  - is going to stop doing

Main activity

- Ss work individually to write the letter. Go around the class and help if necessary.

Extra activity

- Ask Ss to write a similar letter about themselves.

Word check

- Ask Ss to find the verbs in the Word Check box: (carry on, get off, have dinner, have lunch, serve)
- Write the following sentences on the board:
  a We usually _____ at about eight o'clock. (have dinner)
  b I want to _____ my guitar lessons. (carry on)
  c The driver stopped the bus because I wanted to _____ (get off)
  d While the waiter was _____, he dropped the soup. (serve)
- Ask Ss to complete the sentences with the correct forms of the verbs from the Word check box..

22 Difficult moments

Check up Units 20-22

1

Aim: further practice of *must be* and *can't be*.
Summary: Ss match comments with situations.

Lead in

- Write the following incomplete sentences on the board:
  This month usually has 28 days so it ... February.
  It ... any other month.

  This month has the fewest letters and begins with M so it ... May. It .... March.
  Ss complete the sentences with *must be* and *can't be*.

Main activity

- Ask Ss to read the comments carefully and match each one with a situation. Ask individual Ss for the answers.

Answers:
a) You must be Tom's sister!   d) You must be tired!
b) She must be the thief!   e) It must be three o'clock!
c) This can't be the place!   f) This can't be the answer!

- Ss work with a partner and make a short dialogue based around each situation, eg:
  S1: *You must be Tom's sister!*
  S2: *Yes, I am. Who are you? Are you a friend of his?*
  S1: *Yes, I'm in his class at school.*
- Ask Ss to be ready to act out at least one of their dialogues in front of the class. Go around the class and help if necessary.

2

Aim: further practice of the unreal conditional.
Summary: Ss ask each other what they, the Odds and the Normals would do in certain situations.

Lead in

- Say:
  What would you do if you found some ancient coins?
  Listen to a few answers and write one of them on the board, eg:
  If I found some ancient coins, I'd take them to our local museum.

Main activity

- Ask Ss to write a question for each situation. Ask individual Ss for the questions and write them on the board:
  a) *What would you do if there was/were a metre of snow outside your house?*
  b) *What would you do if you saw a lion in your garden?*
  c) *What would you do if you were lost in a strange foreign city?*
  d) *What would you do if you caught a burglar in your house in the middle of the night?*
  e) *What would you do if an alien landed its spaceship outside your house?*

- Ss work with a partner and decide what the Odds and Normals would do.

3

Aim: further practice of verbs followed by the infinitive or the gerund.
Summary: Ss complete a text with verbs, all of which are followed by the infinitive or the gerund.

Lead in

- Books closed. Ask:
  What would your parents do if you bought a crocodile as a pet?
  Do you have any other pets? What would happen to them if you bought a crocodile?

Main activity

- Ss read the paragraph quickly to understand the general meaning. They then read it more slowly and put the verbs into the spaces. Ss read out a sentence each from the story. Write the verbs on the board.

Answers:
1 wanted   5 started   9 carried on
2 would like   6 tried   10 forgot
3 managed   7 didn't mind
4 enjoyed   8 decided

4

Aim: to revise the definite, indefinite and zero article.
Summary: Ss complete a text with articles or leave the spaces blank.

Main activity

- Ask Ss to read the paragraph silently and quickly to understand the general meaning. Then ask them to read it more slowly and complete it.

Answers:
1 A   5 -   9 -   13 the   16 the
2 a   6 -   10 -   14 -   17 the
3 the   7 the   11 the 15 the   18 the
4 -   8 a   12 -

5

Aim: focus on unstressed words.
Summary: Ss say sentences and phrases.

Main activity

- Ss work with a partner and say the sentences. Check that they are not stressing the words in italics.
- Ask Ss to listen to the sentences on the cassette once. Listen again and repeat each sentence after the cassette.
- Point out that the words *four* and *for* and *two* and *to* almost never have the same pronunciation in normal conversation because the number is usually stressed but the preposition is not.

UNITS 20-22

CHECK UP

1 Choose a comment from the list to say in each situation.

> You must be tired!
> This can't be the answer!
> This can't be the place!
> She must be the thief!
> It must be three o'clock!
> You must be Tom's sister.

a) You meet someone for the first time.
b) You are reading a detective story.
c) You look at your street map, and then look at the name of the street.
d) You meet a friend who has been running in a marathon race.
e) You haven't got a watch and guess the time.
f) You are having problems with your homework.

Make a short dialogue for each situation.

2 Make *What would you do, if … ?* questions for these situations.

a) There is a metre of snow outside your house.
b) You see a lion in your garden.
c) You are lost in a strange foreign city.
d) You catch a burglar in your house in the middle of the night.
e) An alien lands its spaceship outside your house.

What would the Odds and the Normals do in these situations?

3 Put one of these verbs into each space. Use each verb only once.

carried on   decided   enjoyed   forgot   liked   managed
started   tried   wanted   would like

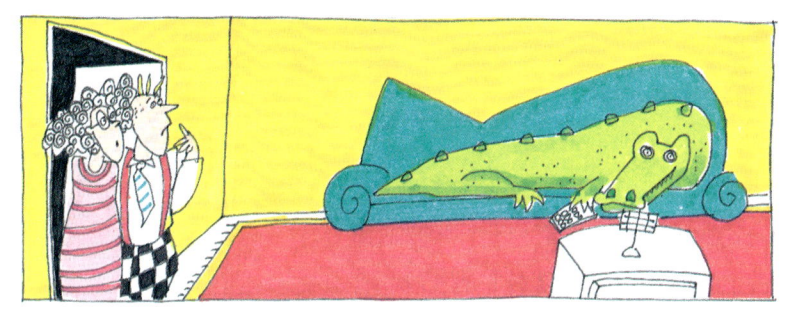

Last week Mr Odd bought a new pet. He ..1.. to make life more interesting for the kangaroo. 'I'm sure it ..2.. to have a friend,' he thought. He ..3.. to find a crocodile for sale in a pet shop and he brought it home. Unfortunately the kangaroo ..4.. being the only pet in the house. When it saw the crocodile it ..5.. jumping up and down. Mr Odd ..6.. to catch it, but it ran round and round the kitchen. The crocodile ..7.. being with the kangaroo, because it was very friendly. But Mr Odd ..8.. to put the kangaroo upstairs, where it ..9.. jumping up and down – on the roof. He ..10.. to tell Ozzy and Olive about the crocodile and when they came home it was sitting in the living room watching television.

4 Put *a/an* or *the* in each space, or leave the space blank.

..1.. few months ago the Normal family bought ..2.. pet dog. It was a large Alsatian dog and it slept in a special dog-house in ..3.. garden. One day when ..4.. Mr and Mrs Normal were at ..5.. work and the children were at ..6.. school, Mr Odd was practising playing ..7.. violin in his garden. At that time he was ..8.. drummer in a band. The band played in a hotel in ..9.. Bristol and Mr Odd travelled there by ..10.. train twice a week.

Unfortunately ..11.. Normals' dog didn't like ..12.. violin music and it jumped into ..13.. Odds' garden and ate ..14.. Mr Odd's violin. Luckily ..15.. kangaroo came outside and frightened ..16.. dog, so it ran away. But Mr Odd lost ..17.. job in ..18.. band.

5 🔊 Say these sentences/phrases.

1 I used *to* be *as* tall *as* you.
2 *A* lot *of* noise.
3 *A* trip *for* two *to* London.
4 Hats *and* coats *and* trousers.

Listen and repeat.

23 What did you see?

revision of tenses: past simple, past continuous; time expressions

At the Supermarket

1a New language

Last week Nick was in a real newspaper. Read the headline from the news story. What do you think happened?

the supermarket robbery goes wrong

The police questioned these three people. Here are the beginnings of their reports.

WITNESS REPORT 1

Nick Porter

I was waiting in a queue at the check-out inside the supermarket. While I was standing there I noticed a man in a plastic raincoat. ...

WITNESS REPORT 2

Kelly Andrews, Supermarket manager

I was putting the money into the safe when the phone rang. My assistant, Mike Briggs, answered it. ...

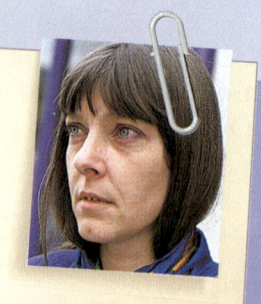

WITNESS REPORT 3

Jane Barrett

I was sitting in my car outside the supermarket. I was waiting for my daughter, Jill, who was doing some shopping. ...

Here are the ends of their reports. Put the parts together and complete the three reports. Put four sentences in each report.

1 While Mike was on the phone, someone knocked at the door, and Mike opened it.
2 He was tall and thin, he was holding a bag and he was talking to the cashier.
3 A man with a mask over his face pushed past Mike and came into the room.
4 While I was looking for the change she seemed very nervous.
5 Then the cashier stood up and they went to the manager's office together.
6 I gave her the change and she went to the phone box opposite the supermarket.
7 I pressed the alarm bell and the two men got frightened and ran away.
8 When she finished her call, she got into a car, a red Ford Escort.
9 A few minutes later a bell started ringing and two men pushed through the queue.
10 Then a tall thin man came to the door, with one of the cashiers.
11 They ran outside, got into a car and a girl drove them away.
12 While I was sitting there, a girl in jeans and a coat came to the car and asked for some change for the phone.

What did you see? 23

Unit 23		Functions	Grammar
Lesson 1	At the supermarket	Describing past events in a narrative	Tense contrasts: past simple, past continuous, present perfect simple
Lesson 2	All in the past	Describing events in a narrative. Talking about when things happen	Tense contrasts: past simple, past continuous, present perfect simple
Lesson 3	Words in action		

Word check

ankle	knock (v)	ring (v)
alarm bell	mask	robber
cashier	nervous	thin
drive away	prepare	witness
headline	press	
jeans		

Ask individual Ss for the answers.

Answers:
Report 1: 2, 5, 9, 11
Report 2: 1, 3, 10, 7
Report 3: 12, 4, 6, 8

Lesson 1 At the supermarket

1a New language

Aim: further practice of past tenses.
Summary: Ss complete witness reports, using given sentences.

Lead in

- Books closed. Write the headline from the SB on the board:
  Supermarket robbery goes wrong
- Ask Ss if they have ever seen a robbery. Ask what happened.

Main activity

- Books closed. Tell Ss that Nick was a witness at this robbery. Ask them to close their eyes for a minute and imagine what happened. Ask for ideas.
- Books open. Read the introduction to the activity. Then read out the beginning sentence of each witness's report. Ask questions about each witness to check that Ss understand where they were, eg:
  Where was Nick? What did he see?
- Ss work with a partner and match the sentences to each witness's report. Each report has four sentences which match. Go around the class and help if necessary. Tell Ss to look for clues in the sentences that may help them recognize which report the sentence belongs with, eg: names, pronouns, places, people, times.
  Ss must make a written note of which sentence belongs with which report. When Ss have matched all of the sentences, tell them to look at the first report and the four sentences that go with it. They then put the sentences into the correct order to complete the report. They follow the same procedure for the other two.

Teacher's Book Unit 23

23 What did you see?

- Ss read the reports silently again and then cover the words. They then work with a partner to answer the questions about the robbery. Ask individual Ss for the answers.

Answers:
1. There were two robbers (or three, if you include the girl). One robber was wearing a mask and the other was wearing a plastic raincoat. The girl was wearing jeans and a coat.
2. She was making a phone call.
3. The bag was to put the money in.
4. They went to the manager's office.
5. She was putting money into the safe.
6. Mike, the assistant manager, answered the phone.
7. The robber with the mask came into the office.
8. The girl outside was probably talking to Kelly's assistant.
9. She pressed the alarm bell.
10. The men got frightened and ran away.

Extra activity

- Books closed. Read out the beginnings of two or three sentences from the reports and ask Ss to complete them, eg:
  I was waiting for my daughter who …
  While Mike was on the phone …
  Ss then begin sentences for their partner to complete.

1b Practice

Aim: further practice of past tenses.
Summary: Ss look at pictures of a robbery and then roleplay an interview between a witness and a newspaper reporter.

Lead in

- Ask:
  What things can a witness tell the police?
  What information is most useful?

Main activity

- Ask Ss to work with a partner. One of them is a witness to the robbery in the pictures and the other is a newspaper reporter. Ask Ss to spend a few minutes preparing their story or thinking of questions. Go around the class and help if necessary. When pairs finish the interview, Ss should change roles.

Extra activity

- Let Ss record and listen to their own interviews. They can then comment on and correct their own or their partner's mistakes.

1c Listening

Aim: to listen for specific information.
Summary: Ss listen and use the pictures in activity 1b to correct the witnesses' stories.

Lead in

- Ask Ss to describe in detail what you were wearing in a lesson which took place more than one or two days before. Ss will probably not all remember very accurately – they may confuse what you wore one day with the clothes that you wore another day. Point out that witnesses don't always remember things very well.

Main activity

- Ask Ss to listen to the three witnesses twice and note down any mistakes they make. Pause the cassette after each speaker to give Ss time to make notes. Ask Ss to compare their notes with a partner.

Answers:
Jill is the most accurate witness.
Brian gets it all wrong! The woman was only talking to one man. This man wasn't wearing jeans but a long raincoat. The woman didn't drop her bag. It was snatched by the man in jeans. The two men didn't start to fight. The man on the motorbike wasn't a policeman – he was driving the getaway vehicle. The men didn't run away – they were stopped by the kids.
David is also a rather bad witness! The man and the woman were not looking at a newspaper but at a map. The woman did not hit the man with her bag. The man in jeans and the man on the motorbike were also robbers.

Extra activity

- Ask Ss to write a witness report of another robbery. (It can either be imaginary or they can describe one which they have heard of or read about in the news.) Ask them to draw or find a picture to accompany the report and display the reports in class.

Lesson 2 All in the past

2a New language

Aim: further practice of past tenses; to present time expressions.
Summary: Ss decide on explanations for extracts.

Lead in

- Ask Ss to look at the explanations and give their own examples of each.

Main activity

- Ask Ss to read the extracts and match them with the explanations. Ask individual Ss for the answers.

Answers:
a story from history: Finally, on October 12th 1492 … 1 e)
an explanation: a very simple reason for this. … 2 a)
an event in the news: to open the new hospital and … 3 b)
an apology: I'm really awfully sorry but … 4 d)
a joke: Two American tourists were on … 5 f)
a description of a holiday: While we were driving through … 6 c)

Extra activity

- Ask Ss to choose one of the extracts and add one or two more sentences.

Teacher's Book Unit 23

Now answer these questions about the robbery that went wrong.
1. How many robbers were there? What were they wearing?
2. What was the girl doing while the men were inside the supermarket?
3. Why do you think the man was holding the bag?
4. What did the man and the cashier do?
5. What was the manager doing when the phone rang?
6. Who answered the phone?
7. What happened while Kelly's assistant was talking on the phone?
8. Who do you think was talking to Kelly's assistant on the phone?
9. What did Kelly do when the door opened?
10. What happened after that?

1b Practice

With a partner, choose a part, Student A or Student B. Look at the pictures and use the information in your conversation.

Student A
You were a witness to a robbery. Look at the pictures. Think about what happened and prepare to tell your story to Student B.

Student B
You are a newspaper reporter. Prepare some questions about the robbery. Use the questions in **1a** for ideas. Then interview Student A.

1c Listening

Listen to these witnesses of the robbery in **1b**. The witnesses make mistakes. Can you correct their stories?

Jill   Brian   David

23

All in the past

2a New language

Where do these extracts come from? Match each one with an explanation.

Explanations:
1 a story from history
2 an explanation
3 an event in the news
4 an apology   5 a joke
6 a description of a holiday

Extracts

a) … a very simple reason for this. You see, I've been in bed for a week. Last Friday, while I was playing tennis, I slipped and hurt my ankle and that's why I couldn't …

b) … to open the new hospital and when he arrived at the railway station, a group of schoolchildren danced and gave him flowers. Later he told reporters that …

c) … While we were driving through Winchester a terrible storm started and so in the end we decided to stay there for the night. We had a great time the next day, because it is a very interesting place and so …

d) … I'm really awfully sorry, but while I was carrying it into the kitchen I dropped it and it broke. Of course I'll buy you a new one …

e) … Finally, on October 12th 1492, the ship arrived at an island in the Caribbean after a long and difficult voyage. When they saw land, they thought they were in India but later …

f) … Two American tourists were on a week's tour of nine countries in Europe. One morning they were having breakfast when one asked the other, 'Do you know which country this is?'
The other one replied, 'Well, it's Tuesday today so this must be …',

23

Helpline – time expressions

Points in the past: last Friday   when ...
on October 12th   one morning   then
at six o'clock   in 1492   a year ago

Periods of time: for a week   all day

A series of events: after that   later
finally/in the end

→ GC p15

2c Writing

Use the questions in **2b** and make another story about four friends. Show your story to other students and decide which story is the most interesting.

2b Practice

Look at each of these pictures. Then tell the story to a partner.

Your story should answer these questions:

When did it happen?   Where did it happen?   Who was there?
What were they doing?   Why did two leave the room?   What did the others do while they were gone?   What did people say?
[Use direct speech].   What exactly happened in the end?

Word check

ankle	nervous
alarm bell	prepare
cashier	press
drive away	ring [v]
headline	robber
jeans	thin
knock [v]	witness
mask	

98

What did you see? 23

Helpline – time expressions

- Read through the examples with the class.
- Ask Ss to find the expressions in the extracts in activity 2a. Then ask them to think of other time expressions to add to the lists, eg:
  Points in the past: on Monday, in October
  Periods of time: of a few days, all morning
  A series of events: first, next

2b Practice

Aim: further practice of past tenses; practice of time expressions.
Summary: Ss tell a story based on pictures, using questions given as a guide.

Main activity

- Ss work with a partner. Ask them to look at each picture and to tell you waht they can see in each one.
- Explain that they are going to tell a story about the Odds and the Normals using the pictures in the SB. Tell them to look at the questions at the bottom of the page and explain that their stories should answer these questions. Remind Ss to use time expressions in their stories. Go around the class and help if necessary. Ask individual Ss to narrate their story.

2c Writing

Aim: further practice of past tenses; further practice of time expressions.
Summary: Ss tell a story based on the story in activity 2b.

Main activity

- Ask Ss to write a story about four friends, using the questions in activity 2b to help them. Go around the class and help if necessary. Ask Ss to read as many of the other Ss' stories as they can and then vote on the best. These could be put on the wall for other Ss to read.

Word check

- Divide Ss into groups of three or four. Ask them to write a short story using as many words from the Word check box as possible. Give the groups about ten minutes to prepare their story. One person from each group reads out the story.

23 What did you see?

Lesson 3 Words in Action

1

Aim: to introduce the topic of the text.
Summary: Ss answer questions before reading and then compare information in the text with their answers.

Lead in

- Books closed. Show Ss the pictures in the SB and ask them to guess what the text is about.

Main activity

- Ask Ss to read the two pre-reading questions in 1 and discuss the answers with a partner.

Possible answers:
a) You could find mainly things which people have left behind, eg money, jewellery, or possibly ancient coins.
b) Gold coins might come from a wreck.

- Ask Ss to read the text quickly and answer this question:
Who was Kip Wagner? (He was a man from Florida who managed to find a lot of gold and silver from some old Spanish shipwrecks.)

2

Aim: to look for specific vocabulary items in the text.
Summary: Ss find words or phrases with the same meaning as those in a list.

Main activity

- Ask Ss to read the text again to find words or phrases with the same meaning as the words and phrases in the list. Ss check their answers with a partner.
Ask individual Ss for the answers.

Answers:
a) worth   c) shipwrecks   e) looked for
b) hurricane   d) remained   f) treasure

3

Aim: to read and infer information from a text.
Summary: Ss answer questions about the text.

Main activity

- Ask Ss to read the text carefully to find the answers to the questions about the text.

Answers:
a) Because the water was very deep and the Spanish divers didn't manage to bring up all the coins.
b) The maps and descriptions helped Kip find all the wrecks.
c) Because Kip's company had eight divers and they were looking for 'pieces of eight'.

4

Aim: to involve Ss in thinking about the topic of treasure hunting.
Summary: Ss guess answers to questions about the text.

Main activity

- Ask Ss to use their general knowledge to guess the answers to the two questions.

Possible answers:
a) The ships were carrying gold and silver back to Spain. They had taken it from the local people of Cuba.
b) He used a metal detector.

5

Aim: to practise talking about an unreal situation.
Summary: Ss say what they would do if they found a fortune.

Main activity

- Ask Ss to write two answers to the question. Go around the class and help if necessary. Write some of the Ss' sentences on the board.

Extra activity

- Ss write five questions that they would ask Kip Wagner about how he found the coins. They then work with a partner to roleplay the interview.

WORDS in ACTION

1 When Vicky and George were in Florida, they read about Kip Wagner. Before you read, give some answers to these questions.

a) What valuable things could you find on a beach?
b) If you find some gold coins in the sea, where might they come from?

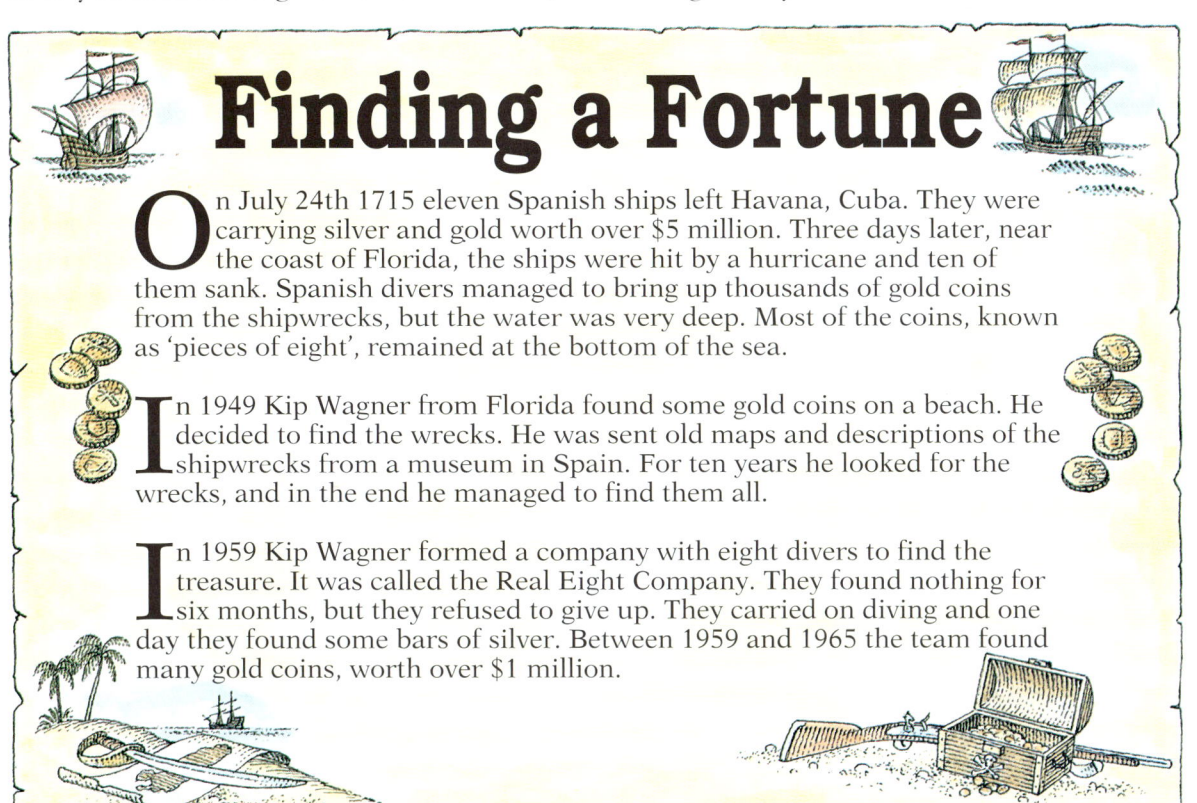

Finding a Fortune

On July 24th 1715 eleven Spanish ships left Havana, Cuba. They were carrying silver and gold worth over $5 million. Three days later, near the coast of Florida, the ships were hit by a hurricane and ten of them sank. Spanish divers managed to bring up thousands of gold coins from the shipwrecks, but the water was very deep. Most of the coins, known as 'pieces of eight', remained at the bottom of the sea.

In 1949 Kip Wagner from Florida found some gold coins on a beach. He decided to find the wrecks. He was sent old maps and descriptions of the shipwrecks from a museum in Spain. For ten years he looked for the wrecks, and in the end he managed to find them all.

In 1959 Kip Wagner formed a company with eight divers to find the treasure. It was called the Real Eight Company. They found nothing for six months, but they refused to give up. They carried on diving and one day they found some bars of silver. Between 1959 and 1965 the team found many gold coins, worth over $1 million.

2 Find words or phrases in the text which are used with the same meaning as these words or phrases.

a) with a value of
b) a very strong wind
c) ships that have sunk
d) stayed
e) tried to find
f) a lot of money, sometimes found by good luck

3 Answer these questions about the text.

a) Why didn't Kip find all $5 million?
b) How did the information from Spain help Kip?
c) Why was Kip's company called the Real Eight Company? There are two reasons!

4 Guess the answers to these questions about the text.

a) Why were the Spanish ships carrying gold and silver? Where did it come from? Where were the ships going?
b) How did Kip find the coins on the beach?

5 What would you do if you found a fortune?

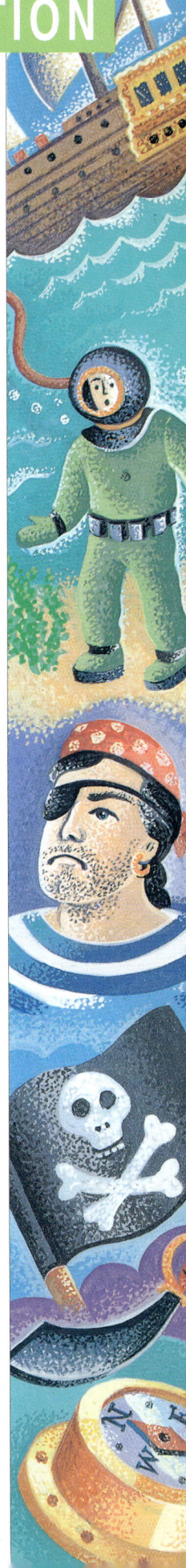

24 FINAL CONSOLIDATION

1 Read the last page of Vicky's diary. Put each verb into a suitable tense.

July 21st

It's lovely summer's day and I ..1.. (**sit**) on the boat on the last day of our trip. I ..2.. (**write**) the last page in my diary of our trip round the world! Tomorrow morning our boat ..3.. (**be**) in Plymouth. Our adventure ..4.. (**nearly finish**). We ..5.. (**travel**) now for two years and we ..6.. (**visit**) lots of different countries. We ..7.. (**have**) a great time on the boat and we ..8.. (**see**) lots of interesting things in many different countries. I ..9.. (**always remember**) this trip. It ..10.. (**be**) the most exciting time of my life so far! But all good things ..11.. (**come**) to an end. Soon we ..12.. (**be**) at home and in September we ..13.. (**go back**) to school. I ..14.. (**look forward**) to seeing all my friends again. I ..15.. (**not see**) them for two years.

2 Vicky and George are now back in England. Ask them some questions about their trip to go with these answers.

a) ...?
Yes, we did. We studied maths and geography and learned Spanish.
b) ...?
Most days we used to help with the boat, or sunbathe in the warm weather.
c) ...?
We usually slept on the boat, but when we were in Australia we stayed with friends.
d) ...?
We've bought small presents for some of our friends, but it's impossible to buy presents for everyone.
e) ...?
We didn't really have any dangerous moments! Crossing the Atlantic was dangerous, I suppose.
f) ...?
Of course, we have learned lots of things!
g) ...?
Most evenings we went to sleep early, because we had to get up early the next morning.
h) ...?
We'd like to go again, but for a shorter trip next time.

3 Put each verb into either the past simple or the past continuous.

Last Tuesday was the big day! Vicky and George finally ..1.. (arrive) at school after their round the world trip. There was a special school assembly and the two travellers ..2.. (give) a short talk about their adventure. George ..3.. (describe) the trip and explained about each country. While he ..4.. (talk), Vicky ..5.. (show) some slides. There were some good pictures of the boat and the family. In one picture, Vicky and George ..6.. (dance) at a Mexican fiesta. Then they ..7.. (play) cassettes of music from all the different countries on the trip. While we ..8.. (listen) to the music, they ..9.. (answer) our questions. Everyone ..10.. (think) that this was a really interesting way to start the school year.

# Final consolidation 24

1

Aim: further practice of tenses.
Summary: Ss complete a letter with verbs in an appropriate tense.

Lead in

- Ss say what the Robinson family did and saw in the countries they visited on their trip around the world.

Main activity

- Ask Ss to read the extract from Vicky's diary silently once and say briefly what it is about. Then ask them to read the diary extract more slowly in order to put the verbs in the correct tense. Ask individual Ss for the answers.

Answers:

1	I'm sitting	9	will always remember
2	I'm writing	10	It has been
3	will be	11	come
4	has nearly finished	12	will be
5	have been travelling	13	are going back
6	have visited	14	am looking forward
7	have had	15	haven't seen
8	have seen		

Extra activity

- Tell Ss to imagine that Vicky did not enjoy the trip. They write some sentences from the last page of her diary about what she disliked.

2

Aim: further practice in making questions.
Summary: Ss read answers and write questions for them.

Main activity

- Ask Ss to read Vicky and George's answers carefully and then write the questions. Ask individual Ss for the answers.

Possible answers:

a) Did you have lessons during your trip?
b) What did you do the rest of the time?
c) Where did you sleep?
d) Have you bought any presents?
e) Did you have any dangerous moments?
f) Have you learnt anything?
g) What time did you go to bed?
h) Would you like to do it again?

- Ask Ss to practise the questions and answers with a partner. Encourage them to make some more questions. Go around the class and help if necessary.

3

Aim: further practice with the past simple and the past continuous tenses.

Lead in

- Books closed. Tell Ss that Vicky and George talked to everyone at their school about their trip around the world. Read aloud the following sentences or write them on the board:
  They showed a video.
  They played cassettes of music from different countries.
  Vicky played her guitar with music from different countries.
  They held up photos.
  They played interviews with people they met.
  They showed slides.
- Ask Ss to predict which of these things Vicky and George did or used to make their talk more interesting.

Main activity

- Ask Ss to read the paragraph once to confirm their predictions. They then read the paragraph again more slowly and put the verbs in the correct tense. Ask individual Ss for the answers.

Answers:

1	arrived	4	was talking	7	played
2	gave	5	showed	8	were listening
3	described	6	were dancing	9	answered
				10	thought

24 Final consolidation

4

Aim: further practice with *going to* and present continuous.
Summary: Ss write questions for certain situations.

Lead in

- Ask Ss to ask you about your plans for this weekend. Make sure that Ss use either the present continuous or the future with *going to*.

Main activity

- Ask Ss to work with a partner. One of them is Vicky or George and the other is a friend who asks questions using the information in the SB. Ss then change roles and practise the questions and answers again.

Possible answers:
a) What are you doing on Saturday?
b) Where are you going next summer?
   What are you going to do next summer?
c) Are you going to write a book about your trip around the world?
d) What are you doing tomorrow evening?
e) Are you going to go back to any of the countries you visited?

Optional activity

- Ss ask their partner similar questions about their own future plans.

5

Aim: further practice of the language of giving advice (*should, shouldn't, have to* and *don't have to*).
Summary: Ss complete a text with verbs.

Lead in

- Books closed. Ask Ss to predict what advice Vicky and George give in a talk about sailing and living on a boat. Write a few of Ss' suggestions on the board.

Main activity

- Ask Ss to read the text quickly once to confirm if their predictions were correct. They then read the text again more carefully to complete the spaces with *should, shouldn't, have to* and *don't have to*. Ask individual Ss for the answers.

Answers:
1 shouldn't   2 have to   3 have to
4 shouldn't   5 have to   6 don't have to
7 have to   8 should

Optional activity

- Ask Ss to write a similar text about another activity or sport.

6

Aim: further practice of *too* and *enough* and the comparative and superlative forms of adjectives.
Summary: Ss complete sentences.

Main activity

- Ask Ss to read each sentence from George's letter carefully and complete the space with one word. Ss check their answers with a partner. Ask individual Ss for the answers.

Suggested answers:
a) slowly   e) enough
b) big/large   f) more/harder
c) best   g) enough
d) too   h) happier, relaxed

Extra activity

- Ask Ss to use four or five of the missing words in their own sentences.

7

Aim: further practice of making arrangements, inviting, refusing, making requests.
Summary: Ss decide what they would say in certain situations.

Main activity

- Ask Ss to read each situation and think about what they would say. They then work with a partner and roleplay each situation. Ss exchange roles for extra practice. Go around the class and help if necessary.

8

Aim: further practice of real and unreal conditionals.
Summary: Ss complete sentences.

Main activity

- Ss work with a partner and complete the sentences in an interesting or a funny way. Go around the class and help if necessary. Ask individual Ss for their answers and write a variety of sentences on the board.

Extra activity

- Books closed. Ask Ss to think of different beginnings for the sentences on the board.

4 Ask Vicky and George some questions, using *going to* or the present continuous.

a) You want to invite Vicky and George to your party on Saturday. Ask them about their arrangements for that day.
b) Ask Vicky and George about their travel plans for next summer.
c) You want to know Vicky and George's plans for writing about their trip around the world.
d) You want to see their slides again. Ask them about their arrangements for tomorrow evening.
e) Ask them about their plans for going back to any of the countries they visited.

5 Vicky and George are giving another talk. This time it is about sailing and living on a boat. Complete each sentence with *should, shouldn't, have to* or *don't have to*.

First some advice. You ..1.. take lots of things with you, because there isn't much room on a boat. You ..2.. live in a very small space. And a boat can be a dangerous place. You ..3.. to wear a lifebelt. That's the rule on our boat. And it's a good idea to have someone with you who knows the sea well. You ..4.. go sailing alone. There are lots of rules that you ..5.. learn too.

On the other hand, living on a boat is lots of fun. You ..6.. look for something to do. You are always busy. You ..7.. work too, that's true, but most of the work is good fun, and you learn lots of interesting things.

If you think you are interested in sailing, you ..8.. write to your nearest sports centre. You can usually learn the basics there before you go to sea!

6 Complete each sentence from George's letter with one suitable word.

a) Time goes more ... on a boat. The days seem longer!
b) It's not as ... as a house, but comfort isn't everything!
c) It was the ... two years I have ever had!
d) Sometimes I think the trip was ... short.
e) There wasn't ... time to see everything in every country.
f) But I learned a lot and studied ... than at school!
g) Sometimes the days didn't seem long ...! There was always lots to do.
h) Now I'm back I feel ... and more ... than before!

7 What do you say in these situations?

a) Ask a friend about his/her arrangements for tomorrow evening and then invite him/her to the cinema.
b) A friend has invited you to his/her party. Make an excuse and say politely that you can't go.
c) You and your friends are trying to decide what to do this weekend. Make some suggestions.
d) A friend asks you to go to the cinema. You don't like this idea. Say what you would like to do.
e) It is cold in this room. Explain and ask someone to close the window.

8 Think of a good ending for each sentence.

a) If you see George tomorrow, ...
b) If you need some help, ...
c) If it's cold tomorrow morning, ...
d) If you drop that box, ...
e) If you feel hungry, ...
f) If I had a small boat, ...
g) If I lived in the country, ...
h) If I met [a famous person - say who], ...
i) If I had a racing bike, ...
j) If I were a film star, ...

9 What would you do if you …

a) … met a foreign tourist of your own age. He/She couldn't speak English and was lost?
b) … were on a school trip. You got lost, the bus left and you were left behind in a strange town with very little money?
c) … arrived home one day. There was nobody at home and you didn't have your keys?
d) … half way to school you realised that all your books were at home. You needed your books but you didn't want to be late?
e) … your plane crashed into the sea and you were alone on a desert island?
f) … looked out of your window one morning and saw an alien spaceship outside your house?

10 Chose an answer for each question in the quiz.

1. The first Mickey Mouse cartoon was …
2. The ball-point pen was …
3. *The Adventures of Sherlock Holmes* was …
4. The first plane was …
5. The Great Pyramid at Giza in Egypt was …
6. The telephone was …
7. The battle of Marathon was …
8. The first landing on the moon was …
9. The first radio message across the Atlantic was …
10. The tomb of the pharaoh Tutankhamun was …

… built for King Kufu.
… made in 1928.
… written by Sir Arthur Conan Doyle.
… fought by the ancient Greeks and Persians.
… invented by the Biro brothers.
… sent in 1901.
… found by Howard Carter in 1922.
… flown by the Wright brothers.
… invented by Alexander Graham Bell in 1876.
… made in 1969.

Final consolidation 24

9

Aim: further practice of unreal conditionals.
Summary: Ss decide what they would do in certain situations.

Main activity

- Ss work individually and write a sentence for each situation. Go around the class and help if necessary. Ask individual Ss to read out their sentences and write one sentence for each situation on the board.

Extra activity

- Ask Ss to think of other similar situations. Then ask other Ss to say what they would do in these situations.

10

Aim: further practice of the past simple passive.
Summary: Ss complete sentences about events in history.

Main activity

- Ss work with a partner and complete the sentences. Set a time limit of two minutes. Ask some pairs of Ss for the answers.

Answers:

1. *The first Mickey Mouse cartoon was made in 1928.*
2. *The ball-point pen was invented by the Biro brothers.*
3. *'The Adventures of Sherlock Holmes' was written by Sir Arthur Conan Doyle.*
4. *The first plane was flown by the Wright brothers.*
5. *The Great Pyramid at Giza in Egypt was built for King Kufu.*
6. *The telephone was invented by Graham Alexander Bell in 1876.*
7. *The battle of Marathon was fought by the ancient Greeks and Persians.*
8. *The first landing on the moon was made in 1969.*
9. *The first radio message across the Atlantic was sent in 1901.*
10. *The tomb of the pharaoh Tutankhamun was found by Howard Carter in 1922.*

Extra activity 1

- Books closed. Read out the beginning of each sentence and ask Ss to complete it, eg:
  The first Mickey Mouse cartoon was ...

Optional activity

- Ask Ss to write two or three sentences about historical facts using the past simple passive.

24 Final consolidation

11

Aim: further practice with *must be, might be* and *can't be*.
Summary: Ss complete short texts.

Main activity

- Ask Ss to read each text carefully and then complete it with one of the phrases in the SB. Ask individual Ss for the answers.

Answers:
a) This can't be   c) It must be   e) It can't be
b) It might be   d) This must be   f) This might be

Extra activity

- Ask Ss to write three or four similar texts using some of the phrases from the SB.

12

Aim: further practice of the definite, indefinite and zero article.
Summary: Ss complete a letter.

Main activity

- Ask Ss to read the letter silently but quickly and answer the question:
  How many questions does Annie ask? (Six)
- Ss read the letter again more slowly and complete the spaces. Ask individual Ss for the answers.

Answers:
1 -   3 -   5 -   7 -   9 -
2 -   4 the   6 -   8 the   10 a

13

Aim: further practice of verbs followed by the infinitive or the gerund.

Main activity

- Ask Ss to read the letter and complete the spaces with appropriate verbs in a suitable tense. Ss check their answers with a partner. Ask individual Ss for the answers.

Answers:
1 am trying   4 like   7 have decided
2 haven't forgotten 5 have stopped
3 have managed   6 would you like

14

Aim: further practice of questions in a variety of tenses.
Summary: Ss ask and answer questions in pairs.

Main activity

- Ss work with a partner and ask each other the questions in the SB. Ask Ss to try to find out more information from their partner, eg:
  What was the last book you read? Did you buy it or borrow it from a library?
  Go around the class and help if necessary.

Extra activity

- Ask Ss to write a short paragraph with some of the information that they learnt about their partner.

11 Complete what each person says with one of the phrases.

> It must be … This might be …
> It might be … This must be …
> It can't be … This can't be …

a) I'm sorry, but I think you're wrong. … your book, because yours has got a red cover and anyway, this one has got my name on it!
b) I don't know where the Hotel Splendide is, I'm afraid. … in Bridge Street, because there are lots of hotels there, but I'm not really sure.
c) I put my wallet in my bag, I'm sure I did. … here somewhere, I know it is.
d) Well, the address on the invitation says '36 Green Road' and this is number 36. … the house where the party is.
e) Are you sure your watch is right? We left at 6.00 and we've been walking for more than an hour. … only ten past six!
f) … Sally. I can't see very clearly from here, but this person is wearing a short red coat and Sally usually wears a short red coat. I could be wrong, of course!

12 Put *a/an* or *the* into each space, or leave the space blank.

> Dear Helen
>
> I have some questions about schools in England. Do you go to ..1.. school by ..2.. bus or do you walk? Do you have ..3.. lunch there? And do you learn to play ..4.. piano at school or at ..5.. home? Do you learn only ..6.. English, or do you learn ..7.. other languages too? What is ..8.. most interesting lesson you have at ..9.. school? Do you know what you want to be when you leave? I hope to become ..10.. doctor one day.
>
> Write soon
>
> Annie

13 Rewrite each sentence so that it contains one of the verbs given in a suitable form.

> decide   forget   like   manage   stop
> try   would like

> Dear Annie
>
> Thanks for your letter. At the moment I ..1.. to make a list of things we can do during your visit. I ..2.. (not) to look for information for your project. I'm still looking! I ..3.. to send you a few things. Have you received them yet? I hope you ..4.. writing projects in English. It's good practice, anyway. I'm afraid I ..5.. practising my French because I've been so busy, but perhaps we can talk in French sometimes when we meet. By the way, ..6.. (you) to go to Scotland? My parents ..7.. to go there this year for their holiday.
>
> Write soon
>
> Helen

14 Ask a partner these questions.

a) What are you doing tomorrow night?
b) What was the last book you read?
c) What are you going to do this summer?
d) Would you like to meet me this evening?
e) What do you usually do at the weekend?
f) What were you doing at eight o'clock last night?
g) What interesting things have you done so far this week?
h) What do you have to do tomorrow?
i) Where were you born?
j) What is your favourite place like?
k) How long have you been learning English?
l) If you could travel to any country in the world, which one would you visit?

Songs

Unit 1 Words in action

The Aliens
One day they took a trip, they climbed into their ship,
And waved their alien friends goodbye,
They passed a thousand stars, turned left at planet Mars,
And came down from the sky.

I saw them from below, and went to say hello
When they landed outside one day.
They came inside for tea, and now as you can see
They don't want to go away!

Chorus
They're running, they're jumping, they're climbing, they're falling
They're flying all over the place,
They're eating, they're drinking, they're singing, they're shouting
They're laughing in my face.

They come with me to school, they make me feel a fool,
They answer all the questions wrong,
They follow me down the street, and stamp upon my feet
And can't even sing this song.

They never sleep at night, they don't turn off the light,
They drop books on the floor.
They're very very small, you can't see them at all
And here they come once more.

Chorus
They're running, they're jumping, they're climbing, they're falling
They're flying all over the place,
They're eating, they're drinking, they're singing, they're shouting
They're laughing in my face!

Unit 7 Words in action

Oh, have you ever ...?
   Oh, have you ever ...?
   Oh, have you ever ...?
Have you ever walked home in the rain?
Have you travelled on an express train?
Have you ever climbed an apple tree?
Have you ever made a cup of tea?
Have you swum in a swimming-pool?
Have you ever been late for school?
Have you ever dropped your pen on the floor?
Have you ever sung this song before?
   Oh, have you ever ...?
   Oh, have you ever ...?

I've walked in the rain with my shoes all wet,
I haven't ever travelled on a train, not yet,
No, I've never climbed an apple tree,
Yes, of course I've made a cup of tea,
I've swum in a pool not far from here
I haven't been late for school this year,
No, I've never ever dropped my pen,
I've sung this song but I can't remember when ...

Unit 9 Words in action

Would you like to sail around the world?
Would you like to come with me
On a trip across the sea?
Would you like to sail away
For an ocean holiday?
Would you like to have some fun
On tropical islands in the sun?

Would you like to sail around the world?

Would you like to slowly float
On our little sailing boat?
Would you like to hear the cry
Of the sea-birds in the sky?
Would you like to swim below
Where the playful dolphins go?

Would you like to sail around the world?

Unit 15 Words in action

You shouldn't do that
Too much advice, too much advice,
My friends always tell me what to do!
So I'm writing this letter to your magazine,
And I'd like some advice from you.
Tell me what to think, tell me what to do
I need an answer right away.
For every time I ask my friends
This is what they say:

Take my advice – you shouldn't do that.
It's not very nice – you shouldn't do that.
Think about it twice – you shouldn't do that!
   No, you shouldn't do that!
   No, you shouldn't do that!

What can we do, what can we say,
You really have to change your point of view.
You shouldn't always ask your friends
To tell you what to do.
Make up your mind, think for yourself,
It's easy when you start to try.
And when they give you their advice
Then you can reply:

Take my advice – you shouldn't do that.
It's not very nice – you shouldn't do that.
Think about it twice – you shouldn't do that!
   No, you shouldn't do that!
   No, you shouldn't do that!

Unit 20 Words in action

I'd rather watch TV

Let's go for a walk outside.
– I'd rather watch TV.
Let's take our bikes and go for a ride.
– I'd rather watch TV.
You sit every evening and it's just not right,
Watching the police and the cowboys fight,
Why don't you come out with me tonight?
– I'd rather watch TV.

You can't be serious, you must be crazy,
It's driving you mad and it's making you lazy,
You don't read books and you don't run and play,
You just watch a little black box all day,

Let's meet some friends in the square.
– I'd rather watch TV.
Let's walk along the street in the evening air.
– I'd rather watch TV.
I've been waiting for a month or more
And every night I come around and knock on your door.
Don't you remember what your legs are for?
– I'd rather watch TV.

Wordlist

Unit 1
activity
answer (v)
article
aunt
back (=return)
beach
beginning
bottle
check (v)
country
cousin
dangerous
describe
detail
discuss
do training
drop
environment
event
everyday
fantastic
feeling
fill in
film
fire
follow
fool
forest area
go climbing
go running
go sailing
go sightseeing
go swimming
great (=very good)
guess (v)
holidays
information
inside
interview (v)
land (v)
lie (v)
magazine
make sure
match (v)
mean (v)
missing
mountain
north
note (n)
once more
outside
paragraph
part
partner
pass (v)
penfriend
people
piece
place (n)
plastic bag
police
postcard
really (adv)
remember
rubbish
rubbish bin
same
sand
sandwich
seaside
seat
similar
sometimes
stamp (v)
stay (v)
table
teenager
tourist
training ground
turn off (light)
uncle
use (v)
usually
wave (n)
weather
wrong

Unit 2
accident
ambulance
block (v)
boring
both
burglar
ceiling
change your mind
chat (v)
cheer (v)
clean (adj)
clean (v)
code
collect
compare
computer
computer program
cross (v)
decide
different
disappear
dramatic
elder
ending
episode
exact
fall down
fall in
finally
fish (v)
fridge
funny
get ready
go out (lights)
happen
harbour
have a bath
idea
interested
jump out
kitchen
leave
light
living-room
look after
look around
make a survey
meet
message
move (v)
museum
next door
nothing
pay for
period of time
power failure
refer
report (n)
round the world
sad
sail (v)
savings
screen
shell
special
star (n)
stare (v)
survey
turn something on
twin
wave (v)
wet

Unit 3
basket
blanket
bookshelf
brackets
brake (n)
broken
bucket
camel
camper van
carry
choice
choose
cinema
comfortable
comment (n)
cost
cut (v)
damage (v)
damaged
desert
dirty
each other
electric fire
expensive
family
fast
flippers
for example
furniture
garden
get on well with
glasses
heavy
horror film
hot air balloon
interviewer
jump up and down

Wordlist

kangaroo
kind (n)
large
light (adj)
manager
mountain bike
neighbours
noise
noisy
normal
odd
off road vehicle
other
paint (v)
pair (a pair of)
parent
powerful
puzzle
quiet
quiz
racing bike
rally
roller-skates
roof
saddle
safe (adj)
situation
size
spring cleaning
strange
strong
suitable
tall
team
thick
thousand
transport
tyre
useful
van
vehicle
wash
wear
wheel (n)

Unit 4

about
active
also
area
below
between
before
busy
carpet
continue
conversation
corner
cover (v)
crack (n)
curtain
decorate
degree
dormant
earth
easy
encyclopedia
erupt
explanation
fall off
feed
fix
form (v)
gas
get up
have a great time
healthy
hope (v)
imagine
intention
just
kilometre
ladder
learn
magma
necessary
only
opposite
paint (n)
piano
put on (clothes)
rock (n)
send
so far, so good
surface
take a photo
take down
tasty
technical
temperature
tidy (v)
travel (v)
visit (v)
volcano

Unit 5

album
ancient
archeologist
ask for permission
beautiful
become
birth
bone
building
burn (v)
carefully
clue
coin
column
come on
difficult
dig (n)
dinosaur
discover
discovery
drawing
envelope
exciting
famous
farmer
field
find (v)
find out
gangster
huge
interesting
investigate
kidnap
library
local
lose your memory
make a map
map
member
metal-detector
million
moment
mosaic floor
mysterious
next
object (n)
over (=more than)
owner
paper (= newspaper)
past
permission
person
pirate
plan (n)
poster
pot
problem
programme
records (n.pl)
routine
silent
spy
traveller
uncover
unfold
valuable
villa
work (n)
work out

Unit 6

accent
all over the world
always
at the moment
because
blouse
borrow
bowl
buy
casually
centre (n)
chicken
chilly
coast
cooking
cotton
crowded
delicious
diary
difference
dress (v)
early
either … or
extract (n)
fit (v)
floor
glass
impression
in fact
kid
late
leather
less (adv)
letter
lovely
material
mess
nearly
nicely
notice (v)
office block
often
opinion
oven
packet
plastic
plate
present (n)
recipe book
reply (n)
restaurant

Wordlist

river
salad
sea food
seem
shirt
shop (v)
shop for
shop window
short-sleeved
silk
skirt
smartly
so far
spend time
statement
stay with
study (v)
surprise
take something seriously
traditional
true
try on
type
underlined
unfortunately
washing up
windy

Unit 7

alien (n)
astronaut
at first
boss
cadet
camp (n)
capsule
checklist
direct (v)
easily
exercise
express train
Extra Terrestrial (n)
fail
flight (n)
for ever
giant
go wrong
have room for
hide
in emergencies
instead of
invite
keep
later on
link (n)
live (adj)
luckily

main
make a telephone call
mission
moon
no one
of course
party
plan (v)
possible
practise
project (n)
queue (n)
real
receive
repair (v)
rescue (v)
return (v)
rocket
room (=space)
safely
satellite
send a message
shuttle
space
space capsule
space flight
space station
spacecraft
spacesuit
success
successful
telescope
thanks to
together
TV screen
unsuccessful
wait (v)
whole (adj)

Unit 8

afraid
as usual
ask the way
bat (n)
bring
camera
catch a bus
dialogue
disaster
dustbin
excuse me
feather
giraffe
hummingbird
hump
invitation
key

km an hour
knowledge
lock (v)
look for
lost
loudly
name
negative
ostrich
play (n)
positive
rubbish bag
show
someone
sorry
swan
tag question
tap
tickets
turn off
umbrella
understand
whale

Consolidation 1

actor
address
CD
impossible
lend
lunchtime
manage
passport
pyramid
questionnaire
record (n)
shelf

Unit 9

accept
across
amazing
arrangement
bath
concert
connection
cooker
cry (n)
definite
dolphin
excuse (n)
explain
factory
favourite
float
future
give an interview

give up
go out (trip)
hairdresser's
hospital
in secret
island
keep trying
kit
make an excuse
National Youth Orchestra
ocean
photo session
playful
politely
refuse (v)
reply (v)
rest (v)
sailing boat
sea-bird
secret
slowly
sports day
sportswear
study for (v)
superstore
take a dog for a walk
test (n)
tight
train (v)
tropical

Unit 10

all the time
along with
average
awful
bean
boat
box
breathe
bump into
bunk bed
cabin
compared to
contain
cupboard
description
dig (v)
dish
dust (n)
earphones
eating habit
enjoy
eucalyptus tree
expect
fault
fit in

Wordlist

garlic
good luck!
habit
half
hole
home
human (n)
hungry
insect
kilo
leaf
loaf of bread
meat
metal
move around
olive oil
onion
overcrowded
password
plane
rain (n)
rice
salt
several
share (v)
smoke (n)
space (= room)
sunbathe
supermarket
terrible
tiny
trolley
vegetable
wait for
weigh

Unit 11

assistant
begin
best wishes
bit (a bit)
broadcast (n)
change (n)
channel
cheese
company
dentist
director
dive (v)
do press-ups
doubles
each
exactly
finish
help (n)
in the way
last (v)

list (n)
look forward to
margarine
need (v)
next to
omelette
on the air
order (n)
organize
pay someone back
phone box
playback
prediction
probably
promise (n)
promise (v)
race (v)
record (v)
repeat
request
serve (a tennis ball)
show (TV programme)
show (v)
sight
small screen (=television)
souvenir
sports field
take (time)
take part
tape (n)
thanks a lot
track
video
video camera
video camera operator
video playback
worried

Unit 12

adventure
age
air conditioning
another
appear
ask the way
autumn
canal
candle
castle
change money
cheap
come from
common
cook (n)
cook (v)
countryside
deck

do the washing up
explorer
extra
farming
free
frozen
give permission
heading
history
housework
hunt (v)
ice
instead of
invent
kill
lake
learn by heart
light (v)
lighthouse
mark (n)
meal
need (n)
nut
oil
pass through
pepper
phrasebook
preserve
reach
refrigerator
root
rule (n)
site
sleeping bag
spend time
still (adv)
subject
sugar
tinned
top
torch
travel (n)
uniform
village
wedding
winter

Unit 13

alive
believe
beside
bottle bank
bury
caused by
chemical
chest
city council

cleaner (n)
control (v)
cut down
destroy
dig up
divide
duck
elect
electricity
end (v)
exhaust fumes
fact
far away
front
hard
landfill
lift (n)
load (v)
mainly
memorial
metal
monkey
not exactly
nowadays
obelisk
organic
per cent
pharoah
place (v)
plant (n)
plant (n=factory)
play cards
poisonous
pollution
print (v)
produce (v)
project
recyclable (adj)
recycled
recycling
rhinoceros
section
sell
separate (v)
serve (v)
sink
smog
store (n)
storm
textile
war
waste (n)
well (adj)
wonder (n)

Unit 14

add

Wordlist

advice
battery
bored
dictionary
don't worry
doorway
drive someone mad
earthquake
emergency
exam
feel (v)
foreign language
give advice
glue
illustrate
it doesn't matter
knife
leaflet
little (= younger)
make notes
news (the news)
panic
pencil
point (n)
relax
rush (out)
shelter
space
straight (adv)
suggestion
take an examination
tired
try
underline (v)
warm
whistle (n)
wonderful
worry (v)

Unit 15

advertisement
be afraid of
bite your nails
block of flats
buffalo
cabin (=wooden house)
cowboy
cry (v)
dark (n)
doll
flat (n)
friendly
gently
hungry
illustration
instead
job

make up your mind
modern
nails
nature park
nobody
phone (v)
play (v)
point of view
protected
recently
right away
shy
slim
stagecoach
steal
take someone's advice
tick (v)
topic
traffic
turn over a new leaf
Wild West
wooden

Unit 16

abroad
act (v)
action
appliance
attack
avoid
bench
bottled water
break (v)
burn yourself
cable
careful
cause (n)
danger
deep
electric shock
electrical appliance
electricity cable
everyday
expert
fall over something
fire brigade
get a shock
get into trouble
get lost
get stuck
get sunburned
get wet
guidebook
headache
hurt yourself
identity card
ill

kite
lean (out of)
lose
match (n)
monster
normally
on your own
outing
phrase
pickpocket
pill
police inspector
push (v)
put out
raincoat
rob
run around
safety expert
scream (v)
stairs
stomach
such as
tap water
thief
throw (v)
touch (v)
uncomfortable
upset (v)
warning
whisper (v)
wild animal

Consolidation 2

advise
attraction
bridge
deliver
dishwasher
do someone a favour
knock something down
lamp
post (v)
post box
present (adj)
pullover
replace
sightseer
sort (v)
stone (adj)
street guide
suitcase
tennis racket
tourist information office
traffic light

Unit 17

above

alarm clock
annoy
builder
catch a cold
chocolate
close (v)
coach (n)
develop
dizzy
double (n)
during
feel sick
film star
fine (= not ill)
fire-fighter
fishing
get hurt
girder
go fishing
goldfish
ground
head for heights
hurry up
in time
indoors
instruction
lifeguard
look for
look on the bright side
make a mistake
miss (v)
perhaps
pick someone up
rainy
ready
rude
run away
run out of
set the alarm clock
shout (v)
skeleton
skilled
skyscraper
stunt double
travel sickness pill
tribe
washing machine
without
work (v=function)
worker
worm

Unit 18

acre
behind
bottom
bus station

Wordlist

canoe
competition
coral reef
dance (v)
dog-training
draw
dress up
empty
enter (a competition)
glad
glass-bottomed
in front of
last (adj)
later
locked
make plans
Maya
medicine
organization
pet
pet show
prize
rainforest
relaxation
sale
save
scientist
small change
soon
step (v)
suggest
take a trip
talent show
temple
think about
training
underwater
unusual
volleyball

Unit 19

actually
angry
at once
bank
bank robber
break
century
circle
clearly
desk
end (n)
equipment
grown up
guitar
hobby
interest (n)

joke
line (n)
notebook
outline
police officer
police station
popular
pot of paint
rope
ruin (v)
sergeant
slip
strangely
vauum cleaner
wallet

Unit 20

against
air
airline pilot
armchair
cardboard box
cool
crazy
expression
filing cabinet
hijacker
horse riding
hot (=spicy)
label (v)
lazy
locked
mad
middle
painting
popular
railway station
rob
sausage
serious
silly
sofa
spaghetti
square (n)
tiring

Unit 21

arrest (v)
branch
castaway (n)
catch
change places
computer disk
crook
detective
electronic calculator
fall into a trap

first of all
follow a clue
ghost
gold
head teacher
helicopter
helpful
imaginary
invisible
journalist
keep a secret
nearby
present (n)
pretend
rich
rule (n)
set a trap
shipwrecked
shore
signal
speaker
spend money on
stream
superhero
survival
survive
unreal
wood

Unit 22

at last
band
carry on
completely
crocodile
detective story
driver
drummer
embarrassing
forget
get off
have dinner
have lunch
horrible
marathon race
mistake
recently
serious
serve
soup
string
stupid
twice
upset (adj)
violin
waiter
windsurfing

Unit 23

alarm bell
ankle
apology
awfully
bars of silver
cashier
check-out
correct (v)
diver
diving
drive away
fortune
frightened
give up
gold
headline
hurricane
hurt (v)
in the end
jeans
knock (v)
land (n)
mask
nervous
plastic (adj)
prepare
press
push
push past
push through
reason
reporter
ring (v)
robber
robbery
safe (n)
schoolchildren
shipwreck
silver
simple
thin
tour
treasure
voyage
witness (n)
worth
wreck

Final consolidation

alone
by the way
cassette
comfort
cover (n)
crash (v)
doctor

Wordlist

fiesta
landing
lifebelt
on the other hand
realize
school assembly
slide (n)
sunbathe
the basics
tomb

Grammar checkpoint

Contents

Unit 1   Revision: past simple, present simple, present continuous; *go + -ing*
Unit 2   Past simple and past continuous; *when, while*
Unit 3   Revision: comparative and superlative adjectives; *not as ... as; too, not enough*
Unit 4   Present perfect simple; *ever* and *yet; just*
Unit 5   Present perfect simple and past simple; *since, for; ago*
Unit 6   *What's it like?;* comparisons with adverbs; order of adjectives
Unit 7   *Could, couldn't; be able to*
Unit 8   Tag questions for checking
Grammar check   Units 1–8
Unit 9   Present continuous: future use; invitations; *would like; I don't think so, I'm afraid I can't*
Unit 10   Revision: countable and uncountable nouns; *much, many, little, few, not enough*
Unit 11   *Will; going to;* making requests
Unit 12   *Have to, don't have to; had to; couldn't*
Unit 13   Present simple passive; past simple passive
Unit 14   *Should, shouldn't; I think, I don't think*
Unit 15   *Used to; didn't use to*
Unit 16   *Could, might;* gerund and infinitive
Grammar check   Units 9–16
Unit 17   Conditional 1: real situations: *if* sentences with imperative; *if* sentences with *will*
Unit 18   Making suggestions: *let's, how about ... ?, why don't ... ?, could;* expressing preferences: *I'd rather*
Unit 19   Present perfect continuous; *for, since*
Unit 20   *Can't be, must be*
Unit 21   *Would:* imaginary situations; conditional 2: unreal situations
Unit 22   Revision: articles; verbs followed by infinitive or gerund
Unit 23   Revision: past simple, past continuous; time expressions
Grammar check   Units 17–23

Unit 1

1 Revision: past simple

▶ We use the past simple for finished events in the past.
▶ Regular verbs are the verbs which make the past simple with -ed.

affirmative
full forms

| I stayed |
| you stayed |
| he/she/it stayed |
| we stayed |
| they stayed |

negative

full forms	contractions
I did not stay	I didn't stay
you did not stay	you didn't stay
he/she/it did not stay	he/she/it didn't stay
we did not stay	we didn't stay
they did not stay	they didn't stay

questions	short answers
did I stay?	Yes, I/you/he/she/it/we/they **did**.
did you stay?	No, I/you/he/she/it/we/they **didn't**.
did he/she/it stay?	
did we stay?	
did they stay?	

▶ In questions the subject comes **after** *did*.
▶ Irregular verbs do not make the past simple with -ed. You must learn the past simple form for these verbs. There is a list of verbs on page 15.
▶ We make questions and negatives in the same way as with regular verbs. Be careful! The question and negative use the stem of the verb, not the past simple.

affirmative	question	negative
I had	did I have?	I didn't have
I went	did I go?	I didn't go

▶ Remember to use *did* to make the past simple with *wh-* questions.
What did you see? *Why did you go?*
Where did you go? *When did you go?*

2 Revision: present simple, present continuous

▶ We use the present simple to describe an everyday action or a habit. We often use frequency adverbs (*always, usually, sometimes, never*) with the present simple.
*Where do you **usually go**?*
*We **usually stay** with my uncle and aunt.*
▶ We use the present continuous to describe what is happening now, at the moment we speak.
*At the moment we **are staying** in Sydney.*
Note: we can only use some verbs in the simple form, not the continuous. We use the present simple with verbs that describe feelings.
*Where do you **want** to go next year?*

3 Go + -ing

▶ We often use *go + -ing* to talk about sports activities.
go swimming   go climbing   go sailing
go skiing   go fishing
Note: we do not use *play* in this way.
play beach games
▶ We can also use *go + -ing* to describe free time activities.
go shopping   go dancing   go sightseeing

Unit 2

1 Past simple and past continuous

▶ We use the past continuous to talk about something which was happening at a past time.
*What **were** the children **doing** at that time?*
*They **were learning** to sail.*
▶ When we are telling a story, we can use the past continuous to give a background description.
*When we started the trip it **was raining**.*
▶ We sometimes use the past continuous and the past simple in one sentence. We use the past continuous to describe a longer action or situation. We use the past simple to describe a

shorter action which happened in the middle of the longer action.
*While we **were walking** around the town, we **met** some friends from England.*
▶ We can also use the past continuous to describe two actions which were happening at the same time in the past.
*At eight o'clock Vicky and George **were swimming**, but I **was getting** ready for school.*
▶ We make the past continuous like the present continuous, but with *was* and *were*.

affirmative
full forms

| I **was** waiting |
| you **were** waiting |
| he/she/it **was** waiting |
| we **were** waiting |
| they **were** waiting |

negative

full forms	contractions
I **was not** waiting	I **wasn't** waiting
you **were not** waiting	you **weren't** waiting
he/she/it **was not** waiting	he/she/it **wasn't** waiting
we **were not** waiting	we **weren't** waiting
they **were not** waiting	they **weren't** waiting

questions	short answers
was I **waiting?**	Yes, I/he/she/it **was**. (NO contraction)
were you **waiting?**	Yes, you/we/they **were**. (NO contraction)
was he/she/it **waiting?**	No, I/he/she/it **wasn't**.
were we **waiting?**	No, you/we/they **weren't**.
were they **waiting?**	

▶ In questions the subject comes **after** *was/were*.

❷ When, while

▶ We use *when* and *while* to describe things that happen at the same time.
▶ *When* refers to an exact time, and we usually use it with the past simple.
*Jim was having a bath when the lights **went out**.*
▶ *While* refers to an action happening in a period of time, and we usually use it with the past continuous.
***While** they **were having** lunch, some dolphins jumped out of the water.*

Unit 3

❶ Revision: comparative adjectives

▶ We use comparatives when we compare two things or people.
▶ We make the comparative form of most one syllable adjectives by adding *-er*.
*fast fast**er** light light**er***
▶ With one-syllable adjectives ending in one vowel and one consonant, we double the last consonant and add *-er*.
*big big**ger***
▶ With adjectives of two or more syllables, we put *more* in front of the adjective. Most adjectives with two or more syllables follow this rule.
*expensive   **more** expensive*
*comfortable **more** comfortable*
▶ With adjectives ending in a consonant + *y*, we change *y* to *i* and add *-er*.
*noisy nois**ier***
▶ Some adjectives have irregular forms.
*good **better** bad **worse***
▶ We use comparative + *than* when we compare things. We do not stress *than* /ðən/.
*A mountain bike is **stronger than** other bikes.*

❷ Revision: superlative adjectives

▶ We use superlatives when we compare one thing in a group with all the other things in the group. Phrases with the superlative often have *the* in front of the adjective.
*A hot air balloon is **the quietest** kind of transport.*
▶ We form superlatives by adding *-est*.
▶ The spelling rules for superlatives are the same as for comparatives.
▶ With adjectives of two or more syllables, we put *most* in front of the adjective. Most adjectives with two or more syllables follow this rule.
*expensive   **the most** expensive*
*comfortable **the most** comfortable*
▶ With adjectives ending in a consonant + *y*, we change *y* to *i* and add *-est*.
*noisy nois**iest***
▶ Some adjectives have irregular forms.
*good **best** bad **worst***

❸ Not as ... as ...

We use *not as* + adjective *as ...* to say that two things or people are different in some way.
*A racing bike is **not as fast as** a mountain bike.*

This means the same as:
A mountain bike is faster than a racing bike.

④ Too, not enough

▶ We use *too ...* and *not ... enough* to give the idea that we cannot do something.
*The water is **too cold**. (I can't go swimming.)*
▶ *Too* comes before the adjective.
We can give the same idea with *not ... enough*:
*The water is **not warm enough**.*
(I can't go swimming.)
Enough comes after the adjective.
Note: look at the difference between *too* and *very*:
*This is a **very** long film. It lasts more than two hours.*
*This film is **too** long. I can't sit here and watch any more!*

Unit 4

① Present perfect simple

▶ We use the present perfect to describe events in the recent past, when we do not say the exact time of the event.
We've sent you all postcards.
▶ We also use the present perfect to describe events in a person's life, when we do not say the exact time of the event.
I've visited that museum twice.
▶ We make the present perfect of regular verbs with *has/have* + the past participle. With regular verbs the past participle is the same as the past simple form.

affirmative

full forms	contractions
I **have started**	I**'ve started**
you **have started**	you**'ve started**
he/she/it **has started**	he/she/it**'s started**
we **have started**	we**'ve started**
they **have started**	they**'ve started**

negative

full forms	contractions
I **have not started**	I **haven't started**
you **have not started**	you **haven't started**
he/she/it **has not started**	he/she/it **hasn't started**
we **have not started**	we **haven't started**
they **have not started**	they **haven't started**

questions	short answers
have I **started**?	Yes, I/you/we/they **have**. (NO contraction)
have you **started**?	Yes, he/she/it **has**. (NO contraction)
has he/she/it **started**?	No, I/you/we/they **haven't**.
have we **started**?	No, he/she/it **hasn't**.
have they **started**?	

▶ In questions the subject comes **after** *have/has*.
▶ Irregular verbs have an irregular past participle. You must learn the past participles for these verbs. There is a list of verbs on page 15.

② Ever and yet

▶ We often use *ever* and *not ... yet* with the present perfect. *Ever* means 'at any time' and we can use it when we ask questions about a person's life.
*Have you **ever** visited Italy?*
▶ *Not ... yet* means 'not so far' or 'not at the moment of speaking'.
*They **haven't** visited Brazil **yet**.*

③ Just

▶ We often use *just* with the present perfect. *Just* means 'very recently'.
*Ozzy isn't here. He has **just** left the room.*

Unit 5

① Present perfect simple and past simple

▶ When we talk about an indefinite time in the past, we use the present perfect.
***Have** you ever **visited** the Parthenon?*
Yes, I have.
When did you go there?
I went there in August last year.
Once we know that someone has done something in their life, we use the past simple to talk about it.
▶ Compare past simple and present perfect simple events:

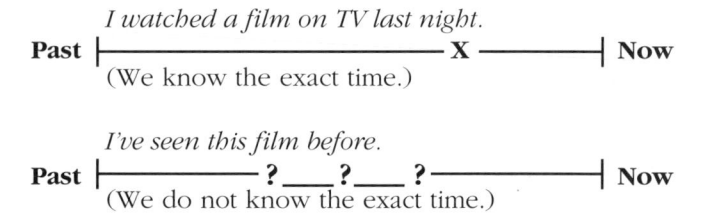

I watched a film on TV last night.
Past |————————————— X ———| Now
(We know the exact time.)

I've seen this film before.
Past |————— ? ___ ? ___ ? ————| Now
(We do not know the exact time.)

222

2 Since, for

▶ We use *since* with the present perfect to describe how long something has continued. *Since* refers to the beginning of a period of time.

Since 1990 I have visited the villa twice.

Past |————?——?——————————| Now
(1990) (We do not know exactly when.)

▶ We can use *for* with the present perfect or past simple. *For* refers to a period of time.
Jill has been an archeologist for ten years.
(= She is still an archeologist.)
She worked on that dig for two years.
(= She does not work on that dig now.)

▶ Sometimes it is possible to say the same idea with either *for* or *since*.
Now it's six o'clock. I've been here for three hours.
Now it's six o'clock. I've been here since three o'clock.

3 Ago

▶ We use *ago* to refer to points of time in the past. We use it with the past simple. *Ago* comes after the time word.
They discovered the villa twenty years ago.

Unit 6

1 What's it like?

▶ We use *What's ... like?* when we want to know someone's opinion about something. We only use it as a question. It does not mean the same as *Do you like ...?*
What's Melbourne like? It's one of the largest cities in the country.
What's the food like? It's tasty.

2 Comparisons with adverbs

▶ We can make comparisons with adverbs in the same way as we do with adjectives.
Australian kids dress more casually and take things less seriously.
The children here don't work as hard at school.

▶ We make most comparative adverbs with *more*.
casually ⟶ **more** casually

▶ With one-syllable adverbs, we add *-er*.
hard ⟶ hard**er**
late ⟶ lat**er**
fast ⟶ fast**er**

Note: With *early*, we change *y* to *i* and add *-er*.
early ⟶ earl**ier**

▶ Some adverbs have irregular comparative forms.
well ⟶ **better**
badly ⟶ **worse**

▶ We can also make comparisons with frequency adverbs.
They eat more often than we do.

3 Order of adjectives

▶ When we use two or more adjectives before a noun, they usually go in the following order:

	size	colour	type/nationality	material	+ NOUN
A	large	red			plate.
A			traditional	cotton	bag.

Unit 7

1 Could, couldn't

▶ We use *could* and *couldn't* as the past tense of *can* and *can't* when we talk about ability.
We could see pictures of the earth.
We couldn't stand up.

▶ We do not pronounce the *l* in *could*.
could = /kʊd/

affirmative
full forms

| I **could swim** |
| you **could swim** |
| he/she/it **could swim** |
| we **could swim** |
| they **could swim** |

negative

full forms	contractions
I **could not swim**	I **couldn't swim**
you **could not swim**	you **couldn't swim**
he/she/it **could not swim**	he/she/it **couldn't swim**
we **could not swim**	we **couldn't swim**
they **could not swim**	they **couldn't swim**

questions	short answers
could I **swim**?	Yes, I/you/he/she/it/we/they **could**.
could you **swim**?	No, I/you/he/she/it/we/they **couldn't**.
could he/she/it **swim**?	
could we **swim**?	
could they **swim**?	

▶ In questions the subject comes **after** *could*.

❷ Be able to

▶ We can use *be able to* instead of *can* and *could* to talk about ability.
*Astronauts **are able to** (= can) walk in space.*
*They **were able to** (= could) see the earth clearly.*

▶ When we want to describe something that someone could do and did do on a particular occasion, we can only use *was/were able to*, not *could*.
*Astronauts **were able to** repair the telescope.*

Unit 8

Tag questions

▶ Tag questions are expressions like *doesn't it?* or *haven't you?* which come at the end of a statement.

▶ We can use tags at the end of a statement to ask a question. In this case the intonation rises.
*You haven't read this book, **have you**?*
(= Have you read this book?)

▶ We can also use tags at the end of a statement to ask someone to agree with us. This is not a real question and the intonation falls.
*It lives in China, **doesn't it**?*
Note: the tag questions in this unit are this type of checking question.

▶ We usually put a positive tag after a negative statement and a negative tag after a positive statement.

     −   +   +   −
*It **isn't** white, **is** it?*   *You **are** ready, **aren't** you?*

▶ We make present simple tag questions with *do*, *does*, *doesn't* or *don't*.
*It lives in China, **doesn't** it?*
*They don't talk, **do** they?*

▶ We make past simple tag questions with *did* or *didn't*.
*You locked the door, **didn't** you?*
*You didn't leave the windows open, **did** you?*

▶ With some verbs we use the same verb in the tag as in the statement.
*It **isn't** white, **is** it?*
*It **can** run fast, **can't** it?*

▶ When the verb in the statement is *have got*, we use *have/haven't* in the tag question.
*It's **got** one hump, **hasn't** it?*
*They **haven't got** feathers, **have** they?*

Grammar check Units 1-8

❶ Choose the correct sentence in each pair.

a) 1) I am finished my homework.
    2) I have finished my homework.
b) 1) What were you doing at eight o'clock?
    2) What you were doing at eight o'clock?
c) 1) You are tall, aren't you?
    2) You are tall, isn't it?
d) 1) Argentina is not as large as Brazil.
    2) Argentina is not large as Brazil.
e) 1) There are lots of big red buses in London.
    2) There are lots of red big buses in London.

❷ Choose the best phrase in *italics* in each sentence.

a) Last summer *I stayed/I have stayed* in Scotland.
b) What *are you usually doing/do you usually do* in the holidays?
c) Last night *I was arriving home/I arrived home* at midnight.
d) *I came/I have come* to this class three months ago.
e) Please don't make any noise. *I try/I am trying* to study.
f) While *I painted the ceiling/I was painting the ceiling*, the phone rang.
g) *Have you finished yet?/Did you finish yet?*
h) *Did you go/Have you been* to Italy last year?

3 Make a sentence from each group of words.

a) new what your like school is
b) than car is plane a faster a
c) shorts like green your I new
d) goes Saturday always on Sue swimming
e) his smartly more Tom brother than dresses
f) enough of piece not this large is paper

4 Underline the error in each sentence.

a) I haven't finish my letter yet.
b) This soup is not enough hot.
c) What your town is like?
d) You like chewing gum, like you?
e) The astronauts couldn't be able to repair the telescope.
f) Thank you for this present. It is too beautiful.
g) This book is more longer than the other one.
h) What did you did yesterday evening?

5 Complete each question with a tag.

a) You are Naomi's sister, ... ?
b) Nigel has got a dog, ... ?
c) You live in that house, ... ?
d) Olive goes to your school, ... ?
e) We can leave our bikes here, ... ?
f) Olive and Ozzy made a mistake, ... ?
g) You know the answer, ... ?
h) George went swimming, ... ?

6 What do you say? Complete each sentence.

a) A: What .... ?
   B: It's got busy streets, and lots of cars and tall buildings.
b) A: Where .... ?
   B: I went to the cinema with my sister.
c) A: What .... ?
   B: I was having a bath. I couldn't see anything, and I was frightened!
d) A: .... to Rome?
   B: Yes, I have. I went there two years ago.
e) A: I can't put these books on the shelf.
   B: Why not?
   A: I'm ....
f) A: What did you think of these two books?
   B: The first one .... as the second one.

Unit 9

1 Present continuous: future use

▶ We use the present continuous to describe a definite arrangement in the future. For example, we use it when we talk about social activities, or appointments we have written in a diary. We usually give the time and/or day of the arrangement.
*What is Bryan **doing** on Monday morning?*
*He's **opening** the Sports Superstore in Bristol.*

2 Invitations: *would like; I don't think so, I'm afraid I can't*

▶ We often use *Would you like to …?* to make an invitation.
***Would you like to** see a play on Saturday?*
***Would you like to** come to our sports day on Saturday?*
▶ We do not pronounce the *l* in *would*.
would = /wʊd/
▶ We use *I'd love to* to accept an invitation (= say yes).
***Would you like to** see a play on Saturday?*
I'd love to.
Note: *I'd* means *I would*.
▶ We use *I'm afraid I can't* to refuse an invitation (= say no). This means *I'm sorry, but I can't*. When we refuse an invitation, we often tell the person about another appointment or arrangement to explain why we cannot do something.
Would you like to come to our sports day on Saturday?
***I'm afraid I can't**. I'm going out with my family.*
▶ Before we invite someone to do something, we often ask a question to find out if that person is free at a certain time.
***Are** you **doing** anything on Saturday evening?*
If we are not sure about our arrangements for that time, we can reply:
I don't think so. (= I don't think I'm doing anything, but I'm not sure.)
I think so. (= I think I am, but I'm not sure.)

Unit 10

1 Revision: countable and uncountable nouns

▶ Countable nouns are nouns that we can count. They have a singular and a plural form.
a bicycle   two bicycles
▶ Uncountable nouns are nouns that we cannot count. They do not have a plural form.
metal   rice   meat   fish
▶ We use a singular verb with uncountable nouns.
*The meat **is** on the table.*

2 Much, many, little, few, not enough

▶ We use *much, many, little, few* and *not enough* to talk about quantity.

Much, many
▶ We use *much* and *many* in questions and negative sentences. We use *much* with uncountable nouns and *many* with plural countable nouns.
questions
*How **much** metal does he eat?*
*How **many** bicycles has he eaten?*
negatives
*He doesn't eat **much** metal.*
*He hasn't eaten **many** bicycles.*

Little, few
▶ We use *very little* with uncountable nouns. It means the same as *not much*.
*There is **very little** food here.* (= There isn't much food here.)
▶ We use *very few* with plural countable nouns. It means the same as *not many*.
*There are **very few** fish here.* (= There aren't many fish here.)

Too much, too many; not enough
▶ We do not usually use *much* and *many* in *affirmative* sentences, but we use *too much* and *too many*.
▶ We use *too much* with uncountable nouns.
*There is **too much** meat.* (= I can't eat it all.)
▶ We use *too many* with plural countable nouns.
*There are **too many** potatoes.* (= I can't eat them all.)
▶ We use *not enough* with uncountable nouns and plural countable nouns.
*We can't sit here. There are**n't enough** chairs.*
*We can't sit here. There is**n't enough** room.*

Unit 11

1 Will

▶ We use *will* and *won't* when we make a prediction. This means when we say what we think will happen in the future.
*It **will be** cold tomorrow.*
*Your team **won't win** the game on Saturday.*
▶ We can use *probably* with *will* and *won't* to say that we think something will happen, but we are not very sure.
*The programme will **probably** take two hours.*
Note: *probably* comes before *won't*.
*It **probably** won't rain.*
▶ We can use *will* and *won't* when we make promises.
*I'**ll help** you tomorrow.*
*I **won't be** late.*

affirmative

full forms	contractions
I will arrive	I'll arrive
you will arrive	you'll arrive
he/she/it will arrive	he/she/it'll arrive
we will arrive	we'll arrive
they will arrive	they'll arrive

negative

full forms	contractions
I will not arrive	I won't arrive
you will not arrive	you won't arrive
he/she/it will not arrive	he/she/it won't arrive
we will not arrive	we won't arrive
they will not arrive	they won't arrive

questions	short answers
will I arrive?	Yes, I/you/he/she/it/we/they will.
will you arrive?	No, I/you/he/she/it/we/they won't.
will he/she/it arrive?	
will we arrive?	
will they arrive?	

▶ In questions the subject comes **after** *will*.

2 Going to

▶ We use *going to* to talk about plans for the future. We have already decided to do these things at the moment we speak.
*Nick **is going to talk** to the tennis players.*

3 Making requests

▶ We use *can* and *could* to ask someone to do something for us.
Can you **open** the door, please?
Could you **open** the window, please?
Note: *could* is more polite.

▶ We can answer either *Yes, of course* or *Sorry but* + an explanation.
Could you open the door, please?
Yes, of course.
Could you open the window, please?
Sorry but it's too high.

▶ We can also use *Would you mind* + *-ing* to make polite requests.
Would you mind opening the window?

▶ We can answer *No, of course not* (= Yes, I'll do it) or *Sorry but* + an explanation (= No).
Would you mind opening the door?
No, of course not. (= I'll open the door.)
Would you mind opening the window?
Sorry but it's too high.

Unit 12

1 Have to, don't have to

▶ We use *have to* to describe something that is necessary.
I **have to get** up early to go to school.

▶ We also use *have to* to talk about rules.
Sue **has to wear** a uniform.

▶ Note: we also use *must* when we talk about rules. There is a small difference between *must* and *have to*. Compare:
You **must** cross at the traffic lights.
(The speaker thinks it is necessary.)
You **have** to wear seat-belts in a car.
(It is the law.)

▶ We use *don't have to* to describe something that is not necessary.
David **doesn't have to wear** a uniform.

▶ Note: there is a big difference between *mustn't* and *don't have to*. Compare:
You **mustn't** eat it. (= Do not eat it.)
You **don't have to** eat it. (= It is not necessary to eat it, but you can if you want.)

affirmative
full forms

| I have to wear |
| you have to wear |
| he/she/it has to wear |
| we have to wear |
| they have to wear |

negative
full forms   **contractions**

full forms	contractions
I do not have to wear	I don't have to wear
you do not have to wear	you don't have to wear
he/she/it does not have to wear	
	he/she/it doesn't have to wear
we do not have to wear	we don't have to wear
they do not have to wear	they don't have to wear

questions   **short answers**

questions	short answers
do I have to wear?	Yes, I/you/we/they do.
do you have to wear?	Yes, he/she/it does.
does he/she/it have to wear?	No, I/you/we/they don't.
do we have to wear?	No, he/she/it doesn't.
do they have to wear?	

▶ In questions the subject comes **after** *do*.

2 Had to

▶ We use *had to* to talk about something that was necessary in the past.
They **had to sleep** on deck in their sleeping bags.

▶ We use *did* and *didn't* to make negatives, questions and short answers.
They **didn't have to do** any lessons on Wednesday.
Did they **have to get** up early on Thursday morning?
Yes, they **did**./No, they **didn't**.

3 Couldn't

▶ *Couldn't* is the negative of *could*. We use it to describe something we were unable to do on a particular occasion.
They **couldn't sleep** in their cabin.

Unit 13

1 Present simple passive

▶ We use the passive when we do not know who or what does something.
*Bicycles **are stolen** from the school every day.*
(We do not know who steals the bicycles.)

▶ We also use the passive when we are not interested in who or what does something.
*The front part **is used** for organic waste.*
(We are interested in what the front part is used for. We are not interested in who uses it.)
*Different types of rubbish **are put** into each bin.*
(We are interested in what is put into each bin. We are not interested in who puts the rubbish in.)

▶ We make the present simple passive with the present simple of *be* (*am/are/is*) + the past participle. There is a list of irregular past participles on page 15.

▶ The object of an active verb becomes the subject of a passive verb.
Active: *The people on the project use **two different dustbins**.*
Passive: ***Two different dustbins** are used.*

2 Past simple passive

▶ We make the past simple passive with the past simple of *be* (*was/were*) + the past participle.
*The chest **was buried** under the ground.*
*The numbers used in Europe today **were invented** 1500 years ago.*

▶ When it is important to say who or what does something we include the agent (the subject of an active sentence) in a passive sentence. We introduce the agent with *by*.
***The Earl of Sandwich** invented sandwiches.*
*Sandwiches were invented **by the Earl of Sandwich**.*

Unit 14

1 Should, shouldn't

▶ We use *should* and *shouldn't* when we give our opinion about what we think is right or wrong.

▶ We often use *should* and *shouldn't* when we give advice.
*You **should shelter** under a table.*
(It is a good thing to do.)
*You **shouldn't panic**.* (It is not a good thing to do.)

▶ We do not pronounce the *l* in *should*.
should = /ʃʊd/

affirmative
full forms

I should have
you should have
he/she/it should have
we should have
they should have

negative
full forms   **contractions**

I should not have	I shouldn't have
you should not have	you shouldn't have
he/she/it should not have	he/she/it shouldn't have
we should not have	we shouldn't have
they should not have	they shouldn't have

questions   **short answers**

should I have?	Yes, I/you/he/she/it/we/they **should**.
should you have?	No, I/you/he/she/it/we/they **shouldn't**.
should he/she/it have?	
should we have?	
should they have?	

▶ In questions the subject comes **after** *should*.

2 I think, I don't think

▶ We often use *I think/I don't think* with *should*.
***I think** Nick should relax some of the time.*
***I don't think** Nick should study for hours.*
Note: we do not say *I think you shouldn't ...*

Unit 15

Used to; didn't use to

▶ We use *used to* to talk about habits/everyday actions in the past.
I used to play tennis but I stopped 3 years ago. (= I often played tennis in the past but I do not play now.)

▶ We also use *used to* to talk about past states/situations which are no longer true.
*I **used to live** in a small town but now I live in a big city.*

Note: the pronunciation of *used to* is /juːs tə/.

▶ The negative form of *used to* is *didn't use to*.
*I **didn't use to be** tall.*

affirmative
full forms

I **used to live**
you **used to live**
he/she/it **used to live**
we **used to live**
they **used to live**

negative
full forms   **contractions**

I **did not use to live**	I **didn't use to live**
you **did not use to live**	you **didn't use to live**
he/she/it **did not use to live**	he/she/it **didn't use to live**
we **did not use to live**	we **didn't use to live**
they **did not use to live**	they **didn't use to live**

questions   **short answers**

did I **use to live**?	Yes, I/you/he/she/it/we/they **did**.
did you **use to live**?	No, I/you/he/she/it/we/they **didn't**.
did he/she/it **use to live**?	
did we **use to live**?	
did they **use to live**?	

▶ In questions the subject comes **after** *did*.

Unit 16

❶ Could, might

▶ We use *could* and *might* when we talk about things that are possible in the present or future.
*Don't play with matches. You **might** burn yourself.* (= Perhaps you will burn yourself.)
*Don't light fires in the countryside. You **could** start a forest fire.* (= Perhaps you will start a forest fire.)

▶ There is not much difference in meaning between *might* and *could*. *Might* is more sure than *could*.
Note: the negative *might not* (contraction: *mightn't*) has the same meaning. We cannot use *could not* like this.
*It **might not** rain.* (= Perhaps it won't rain.)

❷ Gerund and infinitive

▶ We use the gerund after:
  avoid   ***Avoid eating** in cheap restaurants.*
  practise   ***Practise saying** a few useful phrases.*

▶ We use the infinitive with *to* after:
  try   ***Try to stay** out of the sun in hot weather.*
  remember   ***Remember to drink** only bottled water.*
  forget   ***Don't forget to keep** your money in a safe place.*

Note: we can use the gerund after *try*, *remember* and *forget* but with a different meaning. These meanings are not used in this unit.

▶ We can use the gerund or the infinitive with *to* after:
  start   ***Start reading/to read** your guidebook.*

Note: there is not much difference in meaning between these two forms.

Grammar check Units 9-16

1 Underline the error in each sentence.

a) Would you mind to open the window?
b) There are very little milk in the bottle.
c) Mr Odd's car was stealing yesterday.
d) I hadn't to go to school yesterday.
e) What do you going to do in the summer?
f) This food is not enough hot.
g) Please avoid to make too much noise in the hospital.
h) Do you use to play basketball?

2 Put one word in each space.

a) There is very .... sugar in this packet. We need some more.
b) How .... meat do you usually eat?
c) The traffic in this city is terrible. There are too .... cars.
d) There is .... much noise here. I can't sleep.
e) There .... not much information in this book.
f) Very .... people like my dog, Bonzo.
g) I can't eat this food. You have put .... much salt in it.
h) There aren't .... books for everyone in the class.

3 Choose the best phrase in *italics* in each sentence.

a) *Could you mind closing/Would you mind closing* the door?
b) *You shouldn't eat/You don't have to eat* too much chocolate.
c) Be careful! You *should fall/might fall*.
d) At our school we *have to wear/should wear* school uniform.
e) Take your umbrella. It *would/could* rain.
f) I can't come out now. I *have done/have to do* some homework.
g) Could you *helping/help* me with this bag?
h) *I don't think you should go/I think you shouldn't go*.

4 Put each verb in brackets ( ) in the passive.

a) Yesterday my lunch .... (eat) by the cat.
b) That castle .... (build) in 1391.
c) Our rubbish bins .... (collect) every Thursday.
d) Football .... (play) all over the world.
e) This picture .... (paint) by Leonardo da Vinci.
f) Every year a prize .... (give) to the best student.
g) Thousand of books .... (borrow) from this library every day.
h) My bike .... (steal) last week.

5 Choose the correct sentence in each pair.

a) 1) George will have a party on Saturday.
   2) George is having a party on Saturday.
b) 1) I'll see you tomorrow.
   2) I see you tomorrow.
c) 1) What you are going to do in the summer?
   2) What are you going to do in the summer?
d) 1) Don't worry. I won't be late.
   2) Don't worry. I'm not being late.
e) 1) I can't come to your party. I'm going to the doctor's.
   2) I can't come to your party. I'll go to the doctor's.
f) 1) It's raining tomorrow.
   2) It's going to rain tomorrow.
g) 1) Will you do anything on Saturday afternoon?
   2) Are you doing anything on Saturday afternoon?
h) 1) I think our team is going to win tomorrow.
   2) I think our team is winning tomorrow.

6 Complete each sentence. Write one word in each space.

a) When I was young I .... to bite my nails.
b) Yesterday I .... to get up early to catch a train.
c) Please .... to take your bags with you when you go.
d) I think you .... take more exercise.
e) I'd like to come to your party, but I'm .... I can't.
f) Could you .... Helen to phone me, please?
g) There aren't .... knives and forks for everyone.
h) Always wear a seat-belt in a car. You .... have an accident.

230

Unit 17

❶ Conditional 1: real situations: *if* sentences with imperative

▶ We use the first conditional (or conditional 1) to talk about real situations. We call these real situations because there is a possibility that they will happen in the future.

▶ We can make conditional 1 with *if* + present simple + imperative.

if clause	main clause
If you **play** in the garden,	**don't dig** too many holes!
If you **play** in the garden,	**lock** the door.

(Perhaps you will play in the garden, perhaps you won't.)

❷ Conditional 1: real situations: *if* sentences with *will*

▶ We also make the first conditional (or conditional 1) with *if* + present simple + *will* + infinitive without *to*.

if clause	*main* clause
If we **stay** awake all night,	we**'ll be** ready in the morning.
If we **don't get** up early,	we**'ll miss** the coach.

Unit 18

❶ Making suggestions: *let's, how about … ?, why don't … ?, could*

▶ A suggestion is when we give ideas about ways of doing something to other people. There are many ways of making suggestions.
Let's + infinitive without *to*
Let's bring old things from home.
Note: *Let's = let us*
▶ *How about* + *-ing?*
How about bringing old things from home?
Why don't we + infinitive without *to?*
Why don't we bring old things from home?
▶ *Could* + infinitive without *to*
We **could bring** old things from home.

❷ Expressing preferences: *I'd rather*

▶ We use *I'd rather* + infinitive without *to* to say what we prefer.
Do you want to go swimming?
No thanks. **I'd rather play** *volleyball.*
Note: *I'd = I would*

Unit 19

❶ Present perfect continuous

▶ We use the present perfect continuous to describe something which started in the past and has continued up to the present.
I've been learning English for five years.
▶ We also use the present perfect continuous to describe something which has continued up to the recent past, and we can see the results of the action in the present.
Your clothes are dirty. What **have** *you* **been doing***?*
I've been fixing my bike.
▶ We make the present perfect continuous with the present perfect of *be* + *-ing*.

affirmative

full forms	contractions
I **have been learning**	I**'ve been learning**
you **have been learning**	you**'ve been learning**
he/she/it **has been learning**	he/she/it**'s been learning**
we **have been learning**	we**'ve been learning**
they **have been learning**	they**'ve been learning**

negative

full forms	contractions
I **have not been learning**	I **haven't been learning**
you **have not been learning**	you **haven't been learning**
he/she/it **has not been learning**	he/she/it **hasn't been learning**
we **have not been learning**	we **haven't been learning**
they **have not been learning**	they **haven't been learning**

questions	short answers
have I **been learning**?	Yes, I/you/we/they **have**.
have you **been learning**?	Yes, he/she/it **has**.
has he/she/it **been learning**?	No, I/you/we/they **haven't**.
have we **been learning**?	No, he/she/it **hasn't**.
have they **been learning**?	

▶ In questions the subject comes **after** *have/has*.

2 For, since

▶ We use *for* and *since* with the present perfect continuous to describe how long something has continued.
For refers to a period of time.
I've been learning English *for eight months*.
Since refers to the beginning of a period of time.
I've been learning English *since October*.

Unit 20

Can't be, must be

▶ A <u>deduction</u> is when we decide what we think because of something we know or can see. We use *can't be* and *must be* when we make deductions.
▶ We use *can't be* when we are certain that something is not true.
They **can't be** in the chest because it's locked.
▶ (= I am sure that they are not in the chest.)
We use *must be* when we are certain that something is true.
The first picture **must be** in Italy because she's carrying some spaghetti.
(= I am sure that it is in Italy.)

Unit 21

1 Would: imaginary situations

▶ We use *would* when we talk about imaginary present or future situations.
What **would** you **do** first on a desert island? (You do not live on a desert island.)
I'd build a shelter.
▶ We do not pronounce the *l* in *would*.
would = /wʊd/

affirmative
full forms

I **would swim**
you **would swim**
he/she/it **would swim**
we **would swim**
they **would swim**

negative

full forms	contractions
I **would not swim**	I **wouldn't swim**
you **would not swim**	you **wouldn't swim**
he/she/it **would not swim**	he/she/it **wouldn't swim**
we **would not swim**	we **wouldn't swim**
they **would not swim**	they **wouldn't swim**

questions — **short answers**

questions	short answers
would I **swim**?	Yes, I/you/he/she/it/we/they **would**.
would you **swim**?	No, I/you/he/she/it/we/they **wouldn't**.
would he/she/it **swim**?	
would we **swim**?	
would they **swim**?	

▶ In questions the subject comes after *would*.

2 Conditional 2: unreal situations

▶ We use the second conditional (or conditional 2) to talk about unreal present or future situations. We call these unreal because there is not much possibility that they will happen.
If I were the head teacher, I'd change some of the school rules. (I am not the head teacher and there is not much possibility that I will be.)
▶ We make conditional 2 with *if* + past simple + *would* + infinitive without *to*.

if clause	main clause
If I had a helicopter,	my life **would be** different.
If I had a helicopter,	I **wouldn't be** late for school.

▶ We often use *were* instead of *was* for I/he/she/it.
If I were a journalist, I'd interview my favourite singers.
Note: we often use *If I were you* to give advice.
If I were you*, I'd go to the doctor.*

Unit 22

1 Revision: articles

▶ We do not usually use an article before the names of:

places for activities	*I was in a concert at* **school**.
countries	*Two years ago we went to* **France**. (Note: we say **the USA**.)
towns and cities	*We were travelling from* **Paris** *to* **Lyons**.
kinds of transport	*We were travelling by* **train**.
languages	*I couldn't understand* **French** *very well*.
meals	*We had* **dinner** *in an expensive restaurant*.

▶ We use *the* when we talk about playing a musical instrument.
I was playing **the violin**.
▶ We use *a/an* when we say a person's job.
My friend is **a waiter**.
▶ We use *a* before *few* to mean *some*.
I went there **a few** *years ago*.

2 Verbs followed by infinitive or gerund

▶ We use the infinitive with *to* after:
*forget   manage   try   would like   refuse
pretend   decide   want   plan*
Note: we can use the gerund after *try* and *forget* but with a different meaning. These meanings are not used in this unit.
▶ We use the gerund after:
*carry on   keep   like   enjoy
practise   not mind   stop*

Unit 23

Time expressions

▶ We use the following time expressions with periods of time:
for *a week*   **all** *day*
▶ We use the following time expressions to describe a series of events:
after that   later   finally/in the end

▶ We use the following time expressions with points in the past:
last *Friday*   **when ...**   **on** *October 12th*
one *morning*   *a year* **ago**   **at** *six o'clock*
in *1492*   **then**

Irregular verbs

infinitive	past simple	past participle
begin	began	begun
bite	bit	bitten
break	broke	broken
bring	brought	brought
build	built	built
catch	caught	caught
choose	chose	chosen
cost	cost	cost
cut	cut	cut
dig	dug	dug
do	did	done
drive	drove	driven
fall	fell	fallen
feed	fed	fed
feel	felt	felt
find	found	found
fly	flew	flown
forget	forgot	forgotten
get	got	got
give	gave	given
go	went	been/gone
have	had	had
hide	hid	hidden
hold	held	held
hurt	hurt	hurt
keep	kept	kept
know	knew	known
make	made	made
meet	met	met
put	put	put
ride	rode	ridden
run	ran	run
send	sent	sent
set	set	set
show	showed	shown
spend	spent	spent
stand	stood	stood
take	took	taken
tell	told	told
wear	wore	worn

Grammar check Units 17-23

1. Underline the error in each sentence.

a) How long are you learning English?
b) My father is doctor.
c) This mustn't be the street we want.
d) If you will want any help, I will help you.
e) I'd rather going to the cinema.
f) How about we have a party on Saturday?
g) If I would be you, I wouldn't do that.
h) I have been studying since three hours.

2. Put one word in each space.

a) Vicky and George left England .... July.
b) They have been in Mexico .... the beginning of October.
c) They get up every morning .... seven o'clock.
d) Have you had a postcard from them .... ?
e) The family stayed in Bermuda .... a week.
f) They left Bermuda .... Saturday.
g) Their parents had the idea for the trip two years ....
h) They've been having lessons on the boat .... day.

3. Complete each sentence, using the verbs in brackets ( ).

a) If it .... (rain), ... (stand) under a tree.
b) If I .... (be) you, I .... (buy) a new bike.
c) If I .... (have) any problems with my homework, I .... (phone) you.
d) If you .... (see) Helen, ... (tell) her to meet us at six o'clock.
e) If I .... (have) a helicopter, I .... (fly) to school.
f) If Ozzy .... (not buy) food for the kangaroo, it .... (be) hungry.
g) If there .... (be) a good programme on television tonight, I .... (watch) it.
h) If at first you .... (not succeed), ... (try) again.

4. Choose the best phrase in *italics* in each sentence.

a) *Do you rather/Would you rather* watch television or listen to music?
b) *Let's go/Let's going* to the beach tomorrow.
c) *What would you doing/What would you do* first on a desert island?
d) *How about going fishing/How about we go fishing?*
e) *It can't be /It mustn't* be seven o'clock yet!
f) *Why don't we play/Why don't we playing* basketball?
g) Do you want tea or coffee? – *I'd rather tea/I'd rather have tea.*
h) *You can be/You must be* Vicky's brother, George.

5. Put *a/an* or *the* into each space, or leave the space blank.

a) What did you eat today for .... breakfast?
b) My mother is .... dentist.
c) How long have you been learning .... French?
d) Can you play .... piano?
e) I go to school by .... bus.
f) Have you ever been to .... United States?
g) Is Helen at .... home?
h) Our plane landed in .... Ankara late at night.

6. Complete each sentence. Write one word in each space.

a) I really enjoy .... in the summer.
b) We .... to visit Paris next year.
c) I feel very hungry, and I can't stop ....
d) Did you manage .... your homework?
e) I wanted to leave early, but my teacher .... to let me go.
f) My neighbours .... making a lot of noise at night.
g) Are you going to .... learning English next year?
h) I .... to lift Ozzy's suitcase, but it was too heavy.

Tapescripts

Unit 1 Happy holidays

Unit 1 Back again

Unit 1 1a Practice

Helen: Hi, I'm Helen.
Nick: And I'm Nick. Do you remember us?
Nick: It's the beginning of a new school year, so we interviewed people for our school magazine, *Brilliant*. We asked them about their summer holidays. Read their answers and make their questions.
Tina: I stayed for three weeks. It was great.
Un-named boy: Yes, I did. I had a fantastic time.
Girl: I went swimming every day and played beach tennis.
Jim: We usually stay with my uncle and aunt in Wales.
Maria: To the same place again. It was really good.
Tony: I went to Scotland and stayed with my penfriend.

Unit 1 Holiday stories

Unit 1 2b Listening

Colin: I went on a football holiday this year in Manchester. That's in the north of England. I stayed with my aunt. I went for a week in September before school started. There were about twenty boys and a few girls, not many, and we went every day to Manchester United football club, to their training ground. All the other boys and girls were my age. I'm thirteen. It was really good. We did a lot of different things. We watched films and learned how to play well, like real footballers. We did training too. Sometimes we ran, sometimes we had short games, about fifteen minutes. We had lunch at the club. Some of the Manchester United players were there and they talked to us. It was a good holiday and I enjoyed it. It was better than going to the seaside, for me anyway.

Maria: I went to Crete this summer. Crete is a very large island in the Mediterranean, and it's part of Greece. We went in August for a fortnight, that's two weeks. There was me, my mum and dad and my little brother, Sammy. He's only four and he's a bit difficult sometimes …you know, he cries a lot. Anyway, we stayed in a chalet, that's a small house near the beach. You don't have meals there, only breakfast, so we bought fruit and bread and things for lunch and in the evening we ate out. What did I do? Well, I went swimming every day. The water was really warm, and the beach was all sand. We went sightseeing, and we went for walks sometimes and I read three books.

Tina: This year I went to a summer camp in the USA, that was my holiday. The camp was near a place called Greenville which is in the state of Maine. That part of the USA is near Canada. I went with my two brothers for two weeks in July. There were a hundred teenagers there, all from different countries. And there were six camp leaders. They were really nice. It wasn't really camping because we stayed in little wooden bungalows. There were six girls in my bungalow. We cooked all our own food. I enjoyed that bit, it was fun. Some of the food was awful, mainly the bits that I cooked actually! We went for walks and we played games and sang and danced in the evening. The camp was near a lake and some of us went in a little boat. We had very good weather too. I got really brown.

Unit 1 2e Listening

Eleni: Everyone enjoys a summer holiday, but when some people go home, their rubbish stays behind. You know the people I mean. When they spend a day at the beach, they leave their rubbish on the sand. When they travel by boat, they throw things into the sea. Plastic bags and bottles are often dangerous for birds and fish, so please put them in a rubbish bin.
Some people light fires in forest areas. This is very dangerous in summer. Others break bottles and don't clear up the pieces. So, tourists, please make sure that your rubbish goes home with you. We live here, and when you go home, we are still here!

Unit 1 Words in action 1

The Aliens

One day they took a trip, they climbed into their ship
And waved their alien friends goodbye,
They passed a thousand stars, turned left at planet Mars,
And came down from the sky.

I saw them from below, and went to say hello
When they landed outside one day.
They came inside for tea, and now as you can see
They don't want to go away!

Chorus
They're running, they're jumping, they're climbing, they're falling
They're flying all over the place,
They're eating, they're drinking, they're singing, they're shouting
They're laughing in my face.

Tapescripts

They come with me to school, they make me feel a fool,
They answer all the questions wrong,
They follow me down the street, and stamp upon my feet
And can't even sing this song.

They never sleep at night, they don't turn off the light,
They drop books on the floor.
They're very very small, you can't see them at all
And here they come once more.

They're running, they're jumping, they're climbing, they're falling
They're flying all over the place,
They're eating, they're drinking, they're singing, they're shouting
They're laughing in my face!

Unit 2 What happened?

Unit 2 Round the World

Unit 2 1a New language

Alan and Jean Robinson: We had the idea for the trip while we were cleaning our house! We found an old book about a family that sailed round the world. At the time the children were learning to sail and they liked the idea of the trip. So we decided to use our savings and go! We are both teachers, so the children are doing their lessons with us.

Vicky: The first two days of the trip were difficult. When we started the trip it was raining. All our friends were waving goodbye and cheering as the boat left the harbour. I felt happy and sad at the same time!

George: Strange things happen too! We crossed the Atlantic and stopped on the island of Bermuda. We stayed there for a week and looked around. While we were walking around the town we met some friends from England. They were staying there on holiday!

Unit 2 When the lights went out

Unit 2 2a Listening

Jim: Help, turn the lights on. I can't see!

Luke: What's next, oh no, maths. Now, what have I got tonight, page 16, … exercise four, oh well, now … Oh bother, there's no light …

Sally: I'm sure it's on now, it says 8 o'clock in the paper, I don't want to miss it, ah here it is … Oh no, what happened, there's a power failure …

Man: Hm, this is nice.
Woman: Is there any salt?
Boy: Pass the potatoes, please.
Paula: Oh I can't see.

Mike: Now let me see, chop the onion and fry until golden, yes, then add the meat … Oh no, not again … The power's off!

Unit 2 CHRIS Episode 1

(a)
There was nothing special about Friday. Sandy got home from school, went into the kitchen, opened the fridge as usual, drank some milk, and went to see her elder brother, Chris. Chris worked with computers. He wrote computer games programs, and his office is on the ground floor of the house. She knocked at the door, but he wasn't there. Her twin brother, Peter, was sitting at Chris's desk, staring at a computer. There was a piece of paper on it that said, 'For Sandy and Peter'.
Sandy wasn't very interested in computers then. She did not like computer games, and she thought computers were boring. This is the story of how she changed her mind.

(b)
Sandy sat down at the desk next to Peter. 'Where's Chris?' she asked.
'I don't know. I asked Mrs Jackson. She was cleaning the windows when I came home. But she didn't know.'
Mrs Jackson lived next door to the twins and looked after them when Chris was not there.
'He doesn't usually disappear without leaving a note,' said Sandy.
'And there is something else' said Peter. 'I found this computer when I came home. It wasn't here this morning. I turned it on. Look at the screen.'
Hello, my name is CHRIS. My name means Computer Help: Reporting Information Service. You can talk to me, and I understand. Your brother asked me to answer your questions.

3
Sandy: Have you got any ideas, Peter? What do we do now?
Peter: We ask it a question, of course, like it says.
Sandy: But how? I don't know anything about computers.
Peter: I know! Chris wanted you to learn but …
Sandy: All right, all right. Tell me what to do.
Peter: We can talk to this computer. It says so on the screen, see?
Sandy: Right then, first question. Where is Chris?
Computer voice: Hello, my name is CHRIS. Can I help you? What's your name?
Sandy: My name's Sandy. Where is Chris?
CHRIS: I am here.
Peter: We want to know about our brother Chris, not you. What did he tell you?
CHRIS: Hello, my name is CHRIS. Can I help you? Who are you? You aren't Sandy.
Peter: No, I'm Peter.
CHRIS: Hello, Peter, hello Sandy. Ask your questions please.
Sandy: Where did our brother Chris go?
Peter: And why did he leave?
Sandy: And when will he be back?
CHRIS: Read this message. It's in code.

Tapescripts

Unit 3 Make your choice

Unit 3 Choosing a bike

Unit 3 1b Listening

Helen: Ok, first one. I put 'false'.
Nick: I put 'true'. It depends how fast you want to go.
Helen: No, you're wrong. Mountain bikes are strong but not as fast as racing bikes. How about 2?
Nick: That's easy. 'False'. Mountain bikes are really light.
Helen: Right, I agree. And 3 is 'true' too.
Nick: But it depends how much you want to pay!
Helen: Don't be difficult! All good mountains bikes cost a fortune! And 4 is true, right?
Nick: Well, that one's a bit difficult. It's not always true. But I suppose it is usually true. And 5 is false, because you need very thin tyres on a racing bike.
Helen: Right. I think 6 is true because a racing bike usually has a very thin saddle because you sit with your arms like this, down at the front, so you can go fast. But when you ride a mountain bike you need a comfortable saddle.
Nick: That's right, it's true. And 7 is true . Do you agree?
Helen: Of course. They are always very strong. But what about 8?
Nick: It's true. You need very good brakes on a mountain bike.
Helen: Well, that's that! Aren't I clever!

Unit 4 So far, so good

Unit 4 The Round the World Kids

Unit 4 1a New Language

Vicky: Sorry we haven't talked to you before. We've been very busy!
George: We've sent you all postcards. Have they arrived?
Vicky: We've had a great time and we've visited lots of places.
George: It really has been an interesting trip! We can tell you about some of the things we've done so far. We've …

Unit 4 1b Listening

Interviewer: Vicky, and George, you're now in Mexico. Can you tell us about the trip so far? Which countries have you visited?
Vicky: We've visited the USA and Mexico so far, and the West Indies. We're going to Brazil at the end of the month, I think.
Interviewer: And what kind of things have you done? For example, what about food? Have you eaten the local food?
George: Well, usually we eat on the boat, but we have eaten in restaurants too. We've eaten Mexican food, hot food with lots of pepper! And we've eaten West Indian food too. It's fantastic …
Interviewer: And what about languages? Have you spoken Spanish in Mexico?
Vicky: No, we haven't tried. We can't understand people very easily …
George: We only arrived here a few days ago, so we haven't had any time to practise.
Interviewer: But have you had Spanish lessons?
Vicky: Oh yes, we have had lots of lessons on the boat. And we've got some cassettes.
Interviewer: And what other things have you done?
George: We've taken lots of photos, and we've written postcards to our friends in England.
Interviewer: And have you met any other teenagers?
Vicky: We haven't met any Mexican teenagers. I think that when we make some friends, then we can start practising our Spanish.
Interviewer: And is there anything else you'd like to tell us about?
George: We'll, we've done two or three silly things. I've fallen in the sea twice...
Vicky: … and I've fallen in the sea three times!

Unit 4 What has he done?

Unit 4 2b Listening

A

Cat yowling, breaking glass

B

door opening, sharp intake of breath, scream, sound of body falling in a faint

C

long 'Aaah' as of someone about to fall, then sound of falling ladder

D

sound of 'Whoops!', then splat and dripping sound as of tin of paint falling on someone's head

E

kangaroo noises, growling followed by sharp 'Ouch' as of person being bitten by savage kangaroo that has not been fed

Unit 4 Words in action 1

What is a volcano? About 50 kilometres below the surface of the earth the temperature is hotter than 1000 degrees centigrade. The rock here has melted and it moves like water. It is called magma. Sometimes the magma comes up to the surface through cracks in the rock. Then the rock forms a small hill, a volcano.

There are more than 600 active volcanoes on earth. About half of these are in the area of the Pacific Ocean and there are two hundred in Iceland. 'Active' means that the volcano is actually erupting and hot rocks and gases are coming out of it. Only about thirty volcanoes are active all the time and most volcanoes are dormant. Many volcanoes stay dormant for hundreds of years. The largest active volcano on earth is Mauna Loa in Hawaii, which is 4168 metres high. Mount Etna in Sicily has erupted about 150 times in the last 3500 years.

Tapescripts

Unit 5 Time travellers

Unit 5 A visit to the past

Unit 5 1a New Language

Sheila: I started helping some archeologists when I was thirteen. When I was younger, I didn't like history at school. Then two years ago I read about this Roman villa in the local paper. I came here one Saturday afternoon, and they gave me some easy jobs to do.

I've learnt a lot about the Romans on this dig. I haven't found any thing exciting yet. Most of the work is routine. I've helped with the records - we make drawings of things we find, and write about them. So far we've found coins, broken pots and the walls of the villa. I've taken photos and made cups of tea! The most exciting moment was in 1993 when two of the team found a beautiful mosaic floor.

Unit 5 Discoveries

Unit 5 2a New language

Maria: I have discovered some interesting information about the year of my birth. I have investigated the year 1982. Last summer I went to the local library one Saturday and looked at old newspapers. And since then I have made an album with pictures of people, cars, singers, and other things.

Colin: We live in an old house and last year I started to find out about its history. Every Friday for a month I went to the library and I looked at old maps and plans, I found the names of all the people who have lived there. Now I know the names of all the owners of the house since 1861.

Tina: When I was six, my dad said, 'Come on, let's go and find a dinosaur.' And I did. I saw a huge bone in the rock. It was a bone from a stegosaurus, which was 175 million years old. That was eight years ago. Since then I've found other small things called ammonites and trilobites.

Unit 5 2c Listening

Two boys with a metal detector have discovered thousands of Roman coins in a field in Essex, north of London. The boys, David Farley and his friend, Paul James, found ten coins at the end of last month in a field near Colchester. They took them to the local museum, and since then archeologists have discovered more than five thousand coins. The police have refused to give an exact description of the place, and the boys have kept the secret too. 'People have found lots of old coins in this area before,' said museum director, Diana Longley, 'but most of the coins have disappeared.' Yesterday the museum showed some of the coins to journalists, and the two boys described how they found the treasure - worth two million pounds.

Unit 5 CHRIS Episode 2

(a)
Sandy and Peter looked at the computer screen.
'What on earth does it mean? We want an easier clue please, CHRIS!' said Peter.
Some different words appeared and CHRIS said, ' This is my second message.
'It's another code,' said Sandy. 'Where has our brother gone? Just tell us that.'
But the computer was silent.
'I know this message,' said Peter. 'It's easy.'

(b)
They took the envelope back to Chris's room and Sandy opened it.
What's inside?' asked Peter.
In the envelope was a map of London. Sandy unfolded the map and put it on the desk.
'Chris has sent us this map, I'm sure of it,' said Sandy. 'He's trying to help us. Where is the NT? That's the problem.'
The twins started looking at the map very carefully.

4
Suddenly they heard a noise.
Sandy: What's that?
Peter: There's someone at the door.
Sandy: Who is it?
Peter: There's nobody there. That's funny! Wait a minute …
Sandy: What are you doing?
Peter: I'm looking in the box. Perhaps it was the postman. But, no, this isn't the right time … Sandy!
Sandy: Well, there's a letter. What does it say on the envelope?
Peter: It's got our names on it. But there isn't a stamp. Perhaps Chris has been here!

c
Sandy: I've found it, Peter, NT – it's the National Theatre. Chris went there last week I think. Come on, we can go there on the bus.
Peter: What for?
Sandy: We can look for this person, Ann or Alan. The mysterious A.
Peter: It doesn't say that his or her name is A, Sandy. It says "the person with A". It's a difficult puzzle!

Unit 6 What's it like?

Unit 6 The Round the World Kids

Unit 6 1a New language

a) It's tasty. Some is the same as English food, but there is lots of seafood, and Chinese and Vietnamese food. There are lots of Greek restaurants too.

b) It's one of the largest cities in the country, with over three million people. Most people live in houses with gardens, but there are some big office blocks in the centre. The river is really lovely.

c) They're friendly, but we can't always understand their accents! They seem to come from all over the world too.

d) It's cold in July and warm in January. The weather changes very quickly. Yesterday it was sunny and today it's windy and chilly. In fact, it's nearly the same as in England.

e) The cities are crowded and busy, and there are lots of big cars. We've sailed along the coast and we went to Brisbane and Sydney before we came here. The trees and flowers everywhere are really beautiful.

Unit 6 1b New language

Vicky: We are staying with some friends of my dad's and the children are nearly the same age as George and me. I think that we work much harder at school in England! Australian kids dress more casually and take things less seriously. They spend most of the time swimming and playing tennis ! They go to bed later than us too.

George: We're staying with a family and there are two kids nearly the same age as us. They get up earlier than we do and they work harder at school. They spend more hours at school than us, for a start. I think that the kids at our school dress more smartly.

Unit 6 Born to shop

Unit 6 2a Listening

Vicky: Yesterday I did some shopping, and bought some souvenirs, and a few presents. It's Mum's birthday next week, so I bought her a small traditional bag. I went to a really interesting shop called Aboriginal Handicrafts. They sell all kinds of things made by aborigines, the people of Australia. Then I went to a street market and looked at some clothes. There were some lovely silk things, they are Chinese, I think, and I bought a very nice shirt, a green one. I'm thinking of giving it to George on his birthday. And finally I wanted a souvenir of Melbourne, so I bought this small glass bowl with flowers painted on it. I just hope I don't break it on the way home.

Unit 6 2b Practice

Vicky's mum: It looks really great.
Assistant: It's $95
Vicky: Yes, I'd like to try on that long blue coat in the window.
Vicky: It fits me nicely. Do you like it, Mum?
Assistant: Can I help you?
Vicky: How much is it?
Assistant: Does it fit you? Or is it too big?

Unit 6 Check up 6

| done | boat | meet | on | give |
| bit | eat | wrote | gone | fun |

Unit 7 Watch this space !

Unit 7 Space cadets

Unit 7 1a New language

LIFE IN SPACE - ON THE GROUND!
Teenagers in the USA, in Japan, and in Belgium have discovered a new kind of holiday - space camp. I asked two space cadets to tell us about 'Space on Earth'.

Carol: It was a really interesting week! We lived in a building just like a space station. It was called Space Habitat. I lived with five other girls in a 'sleep station'. We could use computers there and we could do special exercises too. So it was the same as living in space. One day three of us stayed for an hour inside an Apollo space capsule. It was really small . We couldn't stand up!

Tom: We wore spacesuits too. I couldn't walk at first, but later on it was easier. We also directed a space shuttle mission - not a real one of course! We could see pictures of the Earth on the TV screens and we could talk to the astronauts in our shuttle.

Unit 7 1c Listening

Helen: Carol, can you tell us about some of the things you could do when you were at the space camp?
Carol: We could do most things that real astronauts do, but of course we couldn't go into space! That's too dangerous, and anyway, this wasn't an expensive holiday! We could do things like eat the same sort of food that astronauts eat. The food is all in plastic bags on a little tray. It was tasty, actually! As I said, we couldn't go into space, but we used computers to make it real - it's called simulation. In fact real astronauts learn how to fly with computers before they go into space. You sit in the spacecraft and the computer gives you information, so you think you are really flying. The spacecraft moves too!
Helen: How about you ,Tom? What can you tell us?
Tom: Well, there were lots of interesting things we could do. For example, we could make a small rocket and fire it. My rocket crashed, I'm afraid. It wasn't very successful. We could put on spacesuits and practise walking about. That was interesting. Of course, in space you don't have any weight and you sort of float about, like in the water. We didn't do that exactly, but there was a machine with wires, like in the circus, so you could practise being in space. There was a real shuttle in our space camp … this was in Alabama in the USA. The space shuttle was called *Pathfinder*, and we could sit in it and do all the things that real astronauts do. I would really like to walk in space, but of course we couldn't do that!
Helen: And did you see any aliens, or any space ships?
Carol: Only when we watched television in the evening!

Tapescripts

Unit 7 Space for peace

Unit 7 2a New language

Landing on the Moon

Seven Apollo spacecraft visited the moon between 1969 and 1972. One, *Apollo 13*, went wrong and it was not possible for the astronauts to land. Luckily it was possible for them to return to earth safely.

Satellites

Thanks to space satellites we receive information about the weather and it is possible to make telephone calls more easily. In 1990 the space shuttle put the giant Hubble telescope into space. It did not work well at first and in 1993 the shuttle returned to the telescope and astronauts repaired it.

Space Stations

The Russian *Mir* space station went into space in 1986. Between 1986 and 1992 it was possible for many astronauts, men and women, to visit it. They came from countries such as Japan, Hungary, Syria, India, France and Britain. Two astronauts stayed there for a whole year.

Unit 7 2d Listening

ET is a film that tells the story of an alien, or extra-terrestrial, who visited the earth in a spacecraft. Unfortunately for ET, his friends in the spacecraft took off while he was having a walk in the woods, and he wasn't able to leave. He met some children in a house nearby, and made friends with them. He was able to hide in their bedroom. Then ET was able to make a radio which sent a message to his friends in the spacecraft. Scientists on earth were looking for him but the children were able to take him to his spacecraft in the end on their bicycles.

Unit 7 Words in action 1

Oh, have you ever …?
Oh, have you ever …?
Oh, have you ever …?
Have you ever walked home in the rain?
Have you travelled on an express train?
Have you ever climbed a tree?
Have you ever made a cup of tea?
Have you swum in a swimming-pool?
Have you ever been late for school?
Have you ever dropped your pen on the floor?
Have you ever sung this song before?
Oh, have you ever …?
Oh, have you ever …?

I've walked in the rain with my shoes all wet,
I haven't ever travelled on a train, not yet,
No, I've never climbed an apple tree,
Yes, of course I've made a cup of tea,
I've swum in a pool not far from here
I haven't been late for school this year,
No, I've never ever dropped my pen,
I've sung this song but I can't remember when …

Unit 8 Home and away

Unit 8 Animal time

Unit 8 1a New language

Helen: It lives in China, doesn't it?
Nick: Yes, that's right.
Helen: It runs very, fast, doesn't it?
Nick: Yes, it does. At 90 kilometres an hour.
Helen: They don't live at the North Pole, do they?
Nick: No, they don't.
Helen: They don't talk, do they?
Nick: No, they don't.

Unit 8 1d Listening

(a)
A: Excuse me, this one goes to the Zoo, doesn't it?
B: Yes, it does, I'm going there myself. You aren't from here, are you?
A: No, I'm from Scotland.
B: I thought you were.

(b)
A: You haven't seen mine, have you?
B: No, I haven't. Is it this one?
A: No, mine's the blue one. I thought that one was yours.
B: No, mine's a leather jacket.

(c)
A: Hello, you're Diana, aren't you?
B: That's right. How do you do?
A: Pleased to meet you. I'm Philip. You don't know Liz, do you?
B: No, I don't. Hi, Liz, I'm Diana.

(d)
A: Excuse me, this is the way to the town centre, isn't it?
B: No, you're going the wrong way. Go down that street and then go straight on.
A: You don't know Sycamore Street, do you?
B: Yes, it's along here on the left.

(e)
A: Karen! That is you, isn't it? You don't remember me, do you?
B: Charlie! Hi! How nice to see you!
A: It's been a long time, hasn't it? How are you?
B: Oh I'm fine. I've got a job. I'm in the police. And you can't park your car here!
A: Sorry! I'm just going …

Unit 8 What happened?

Unit 8 2a New language

Mr Odd: Right, let's go. We're going to have a really good time.
Mrs Odd: You locked the door, didn't you dear?
Mr Odd: Yes.
Mrs Odd: And you didn't leave the windows open, did you?
Mr Odd: No, of course I didn't. Don't worry about the house. Let's enjoy our day at Funworld.

Unit 8 CHRIS Episode 3

1
a) Do you know this man? He's our brother, Chris. And he's disappeared.
b) My name's Anna. But why do you want to know?
c) Sorry, I've never seen him before.
d) What's on at the theatre this week?
e) Excuse me, but what's your name?
f) There are two plays on this week - *Arms and the Man* and *Antony and Cleopatra.*

2
Sandy: Oh dear, I feel tired after all that. And we still don't know the answer.
Peter: Well, there are three possibilities, aren't there? Maybe it's that girl at the theatre - Anna. That's A, isn't it. But perhaps I'm wrong.
Sandy: What about the names of the plays? *Arms and the Man* - Arms begins with A. Perhaps that means that we are looking for a man!
Peter: We are looking for a man, aren't we? We're looking for Chris.
Sandy: What about the other play, *Antony and Cleopatra?* The message said, 'Find the person with A', didn't it? So A is Antony and the answer is Cleopatra.
Peter: That's it! Brilliant! You're right. But what does it mean?
Sandy: I know! You remember that restaurant we went to with Chris on his birthday, don't you? It was called 'Cleopatra's'.
Peter: No, it was called 'Patricia's'. I remember it well - I ate too much.
Sandy: Wait a minute, we've forgotten about CHRIS. Ask him.
Peter: CHRIS, is 'Cleopatra' the answer?
CHRIS: Yes, Cleopatra is the answer. Look at the map.
Sandy: This is it, look, on the map. Here on the other side of the river, it says 'Cleopatra's Needle'. It's a stone from ancient Egypt.
Peter: Right, tomorrow we'll go back on the bus and look at it. And there is another thing, Sandy. Did you see that woman in the queue at the theatre? She was on the bus too. Do you think she is following us …?

Unit 9 Arranging the future

Unit 9 What's he doing on Monday?

Unit 9 1a New language

Helen: Can we interview him on Monday morning?
Manager: I'm sorry, but he's opening the new Sports Superstore in Bristol on Monday morning.
Nick: And what's he doing on Monday afternoon?

Unit 9 1d Listening

Nick
Woman's voice: Are you ready for Saturday, Nick? Have you got everything?
Nick: I think so. I've got my ticket, and I phoned Aunt Brenda and Uncle Harry last night. They're meeting me at the station.
Woman: Well, have a nice time. And don't forget to invite Linda and Paul for your birthday. They are your favourite cousins …

Helen
Helen: We've got two tests on Monday, and three on Tuesday. So I've got lots of work to do, but it's history first, and I like that, so that's not too bad. I've made a plan for each day: Saturday morning is history, then Saturday afternoon is Maths. On Sunday I'm having a rest in the morning. Sunday afternoon is chemistry, and I'm doing all the rest on Monday evening. Anyway, see you on Monday morning, and good luck …

Vicky and George
Vicky: Have you got the invitation?
George: Yes, here it is. It says 'Golden Bay Beach' and we can go there on the bus. Look, there's a map on the back.
Vicky: Great. I'm really looking forward to it. I haven't been to a party for ages.
George: Yes, I'm sure it's going to be good. The invitation says 'Come and meet all our friends and enjoy an Australian beach party. Saturday 7.30. See you then, Maria and Carlos.'

Unit 9 Words in action 1

Would you like to sail around the world?
Would you like to come with me
On a trip across the sea?
Would you like to sail away
For an ocean holiday?
Would you like to have some fun
On tropical islands in the sun?

Would you like to sail around the world?

Would you like to slowly float
On our little sailing boat?
Would you like to hear the cry
Of the sea-birds in the sky?
Would you like to swim below
Where the playful dolphins go?

Would you like to sail around the world?

Tapescripts

Unit 10 Habits and home

Unit 10 Eating habits

Unit 10 1a New language

Michel 'Mangetout' Lotito, a Frenchman, eats metal things! Since he was 16 he has eaten seven bicycles, seven televisions, a supermarket trolley and a small plane. He eats about a kilo of metal every day. He cuts the metal into tiny pieces first!

In Spain in 1987 Josep Gruges made a giant paella, a Spanish dish. It contained 3700 kilos of rice, 3000 kilos of meat and fish, 1400 kilos of beans and onions, along with 200 kilos of garlic and 400 litres of olive oil. Forty thousand people ate it for lunch!

In seventy years of life the average British person eats 420 chickens, 3500 loaves of bread, 4000 kilos of potatoes, and 2000 kilos of vegetables. He or she also drinks 93 000 cups of tea.

Unit 10 1b New language

1
This animal eats only leaves from eucalyptus trees. There are 350 kinds of leaves, but it eats very few of them - only five kinds! It also drinks very little water because the leaves contain all the water it needs.

2
There is little to eat and drink in deserts and so very few animals live there. However, this animal digs a hole and waits for rain. It can stay in its hole for eleven months of the year.

3
Compared to this animal, humans eat very little! In one day it can eat the same as a person eats in one year.

Unit 10 The Round the World Kids

Unit 10 2a New language

Vicky: One problem of living on a boat is space. You bump into things all the time! I keep a lot of my things in a box under my bunk bed. It's my fault because I brought lots of clothes and books and they won't fit in my cupboard.
George and I share a cabin. I have half and he has the other half. He is impossible. He has a radio and plays it loudly all the time. He hasn't got any earphones and I can't sleep.

Unit 10 2c Listening

(a)
Mum: George, have you put the things on the table?
George: Yes, everything's ready.
Mum: Come on George, you can't count. There are four of us, remember? There …

(b)
Vicky: Dad, it's time for lunch.
Dad: Sorry, love, I've got to fix the engine. It'll be dark soon.
Vicky: But don't you want to eat anything?
Dad: I'll eat it later. There …

(c)
George: You've cooked a lot of food. We can't eat all this.
Vicky: Why not? Aren't you hungry.
George: Yes, I am. But this is enough food for ten people! There …

(d)
George: Here is the fish. Ouch, the dish is hot.
Vicky: Well, put it on the table, then, silly.
George: No, I'll put it on this chair, so don't sit on it. I can't put it on the table, there …

(e)
Mum: Do you like it George?
George: Not really, no. Sorry.
Vicky: But what's wrong with my lovely cooking?
George: I don't like the taste. There …

Unit 10 CHRIS Episode 4

(a)
Sandy: CHRIS, this is Sandy. We're going to Cleopatra's Needle tomorrow. Are we doing the right thing? Can the police help us?
CHRIS: Hello, Sandy. This is CHRIS, the Computer Help Reporting Information Service. Can I help you?
Peter: We need some help, CHRIS. What will we find at Cleopatra's Needle?
CHRIS: I am not able to answer your questions this time. Please give me the password first.
Sandy: Password? What password? Oh dear, another puzzle!
CHRIS: Your brother Chris gave you the password …

2
Sandy: CHRIS, we don't know the password. Can you help us?
CHRIS: I'm sorry. I am not able to help you.
Peter: I'm going to try some words. CHRIS, listen. This is the password: Cleopatra's Needle.
CHRIS: I'm sorry, that isn't the password!
Sandy: What on earth is it?
Peter: CHRIS said something about it. He said, 'Your brother, Chris, gave you the password.' But what did Chris give us?
Sandy: The password is 'letter'.
CHRIS: I'm sorry, that isn't the answer.
Peter: 'Map', the password is 'map'.
CHRIS: I'm sorry, that isn't the answer.
Sandy: Wait a minute, Peter. Think about it again. What did Chris give us?
Voice: Can you guess the password?
Sandy: Chris gave us a letter with a map in it. We've tried both those words and they don't work. It was a map

242

of London. And we found NT on it, the National Theatre.
Peter: CHRIS, the password is NT.
CHRIS: I'm sorry, that isn't the answer.
Sandy: One last try! CHRIS, the password is 'London'.
CHRIS: Thank you, Sandy. You are right. The password is 'London'. I have some information for you. Please turn on my printer. I am going to print it now.

(b)
Chris
Dear Sandy and Peter,
Well done! You've understood my messages so far, so I expect you are going to 'the person with A' next. I am not going to say much in this letter because I want you to work hard before you find me!
I have disappeared for a few days. I hope that Mrs Jackson is looking after you well. I needed a holiday, and I want you to have some fun with CHRIS, and do some sightseeing in London. I've left lots of clues for you, so good luck! Please think about the information very carefully. CHRIS will help you, but he doesn't know all the answers. Enjoy the puzzle! I hope it teaches you that computers are fun!
Chris
PS Before you go to visit 'the person with A', ask CHRIS for some more information.

Unit 11 On the air

Unit 11 Stars of the small screen

Unit 11 1b Listening

Nina: OK everyone, this is what we're going to do. Don't worry if things go a bit wrong, because we can always do some parts again. We're going to do ten interviews altogether. Nick, you're going to talk to the tennis players, and Helen, you're going to talk to people on the sports field. Mike is going to organize the order of this, you know, who you talk to first. We're going to do a rehearsal first, just to practise a bit. So Helen, at the beginning of the interview just say the number of the interview and the name of the person, so we know who is who. OK? Don't worry, I'm going to help you when we do the real thing! Sue is going to stand next to you, and she is going to film the people you interview only, not you. She's going to film you at the beginning. So don't move, OK? And Sue is going to tell you when to start. Mike's going to give you a list of possible questions at the beginning and we can talk about those first. Perhaps you've got some better questions. I'm going to watch the video playback and check that everything was OK. Right, any questions, then?

Unit 11 Outside broadcast

Unit 11 2a New Language

Nick: Would you mind repeating your answer?
Helen: Could you tell me your name, please?

Unit 11 Check up 5

should   would   could   listen   science   castle
thought   high   weigh   front   brother   love

Unit 12 Follow the rules

Unit 12 School rules

Unit 12 1a New language

Nick: Sue goes to school in a village.
Sue: The school is next door to my house, so there isn't any travelling. We can't wear just any clothes - we wear a blue top, and black trousers or skirt. School starts at 9.00. We have a lot of lessons and some of them are difficult. There are tests every week, and we do extra work at lunchtime when our marks are bad. And we have lots of homework! On Wednesday afternoon there aren't any lessons and we go for trips or do sports. And we can choose some extra subjects. I'm learning the guitar and I do painting.

Nick: David Aitken learns at home with his parents. Some school children in Britain do this.
David: I left my school two years ago and now I don't have any school rules. I can start my lessons and finish them when I want. I don't wear a uniform, and I can work on one subject for a day or a week! I have some lessons with teachers, but they visit the house. I can do projects in the countryside or in the town library, or I can work on my computer. I still do sports with other kids, but at weekends.

Unit 12 The Round the World Kids

Unit 12 2b Listening

Vicky: On Wednesday morning we started walking into the town. We wanted to find the town centre.
George: We thought we were going in the right direction, but we got lost and we couldn't find the way.
Vicky: We had to ask someone the way. I spoke in English but he couldn't understand.
George: And then he spoke in Arabic to us and we couldn't understand him!
Vicky: Then we wanted to buy some souvenirs in the market, but we didn't know the prices of anything. And we couldn't explain, so we had to show the man the words in the phrasebook.
George: Then when we got to the restaurant we had another problem.
Vicky: The waiter said lots of things to us in Arabic but we couldn't understand him.
George: Then we tried to understand the menu but it was impossible. We couldn't understand a single word!
Vicky: So we had to go into the kitchen and look at all the food and point at the things we wanted. George was really embarrassed.
George: That's enough, Vicky, they don't want to know everything!

Tapescripts

Unit 12 2c Practice

On Wednesday we had a free day – no lessons! We walked around the city in the morning. We now have a map so it wasn't necessary to ask people the way all the time!

George and I visited the old castle, which was the site of the ancient lighthouse, the Pharos. It wasn't very far away, so we walked instead of taking a bus. While we were there, we met some students. There was no need to use the phrasebook because they spoke English. One of them invited us to his brother's wedding party that evening.

Mum and Dad gave us permission to stay out late and we had a great time. There was dancing and singing, and it was really interesting. We stayed here on Thursday too, so there was no need to get up early in the morning.

Unit 12 Words in action 1

Food through the ages

The earliest people, before the age of farming, spent nearly all their time looking for food. The men hunted and the women and children collected nuts, leaves, roots and insects. There wasn't enough in one place, and people had to move around.

Thousands of years later, food was still a problem. In the middle ages (1000 - 1500), farmers had to kill all their animals in the autumn because there wasn't enough food for them in the winter. They had to put salt with the meat to preserve it, and the cooks had to make lots of tasty sauces when they cooked the meat.

In 1810 a Frenchman invented tinned food , and after the 1850s it became more common. Also, special ships carried cheap frozen meat from Australia and South America to Europe. Then people did not have to buy fresh food every day.

Unit 13 Did you know?

Unit 13 Green corner

Unit 13 1a Practice

The people on the project use two different dustbins, a brown one and a green one.
They put different types of rubbish into each bin.
The brown bin has two sections.
They use the front part for organic waste, like fruit and vegetables.
They use the other section for things which are not suitable for recycling.
They fill the green bin with recyclable things.
They take glass bottles to the bottle bank.
People collect the rubbish as usual.
At the SORT plant people separate the types of rubbish from the green bin.
They divide the rubbish into eighteen different types of paper, plastics, metals and textiles.

Unit 13 1c Listening

This week on *Green Corner* we are looking at recycling, and at some everyday objects which are made from – rubbish! Yes, you did hear correctly. All the things we're going to talk about today are made from things we throw away in the dustbin. And we're going to start with rubbish too. This is a rubbish container, it's the kind that stands in the street and is collected by the rubbish van. This one is made from old cans. So the next time you drink your favourite soft drink, don't throw the can away. Now the next things we've got here are two badges, very nice ones. They were both made by Sue Sherman, who comes from London. They're made from metal foil cartons, the kind you get from takeaway food shops. So whenever you buy your favourite takeaway food, you can make yourself a badge. They make great presents. Next is a carrier bag, the kind they give you in the supermarket. Well, this one is made from old plastic bottles. The plastic is collected and recycled, so nothing is wasted. And finally – sorry about that – yes, I've got a cold so I need some paper tissues. Believe it or not, these tissues are made from old newspapers. But they haven't got any words on them, they are clean and white and – very soft. That's all for today!

Unit 13 It's hard to believe

Unit 13 2c Listening

Welcome to the Empire State Building. Before you begin your visit, stand here in the magnificent lobby, and listen to these interesting facts about the building. As you listen, you can admire the paintings of the Seven Wonders of the World.

First of all, the building was begun in 1929 and finished in 1931. From top to bottom it is 381 metres high - and it was the tallest building in the world until 1973. It was built by three thousand workers, who took only fifteen months to complete the job. They could do this because many of the parts of the building were made in factories in other parts of New York State.

Fifteen thousand people work in the building and about two million tourists come to see the building every year. There are more than one hundred floors- one hundred and two to be exact - and if you want to go up the stairs to the top floor, there are 1860 steps! Most people find it 's easier to take one of the seventy three lifts! Every day an army of cleaners cleans the offices – one hundred and fifty people are employed to do this.

The building also has an interesting history. For example, one summer's day in 1945 a plane – a B25 bomber – crashed into the 79th floor. The building is so strong that there was very little damage. Now walk across the lobby to the lifts ...

Unit 13 CHRIS Episode 5

(a)
Cleopatra's Needle. This is an Egyptian obelisk, and is over 3500 years old. It was made for the Pharaoh, Thotmes III. It was brought to London in 1878. £15,000 was collected from people in Britain to pay for it. A special ship, called 'Cleopatra', was built. The obelisk was loaded onto the ship in Alexandria and the 'Cleopatra' was pulled by another ship. The 'Cleopatra' nearly sank in a storm in the Bay of Biscay, but finally arrived in London in January 1878. The obelisk was placed beside the Thames in London as a memorial to the war with Napoleon which ended in 1815. A similar obelisk was given to France and still stands in the Place de la Concorde in Paris.

(b)
Sandy: Well, this is it, Peter. What do we do now?
Peter: We look for the next clue, I suppose.
Woman: Hello, are your names Peter and Sandy?
Sandy: Yes, they are! But how did you know? Are you a friend of Chris's?
Woman: Not exactly. My name is Wendy Harman, Inspector Wendy Harman. I'm from the police. We are trying to find your brother. Do you know where he is?
Peter: No, we don't. We're looking for him too. But why do you want him?
Woman: Come over here and sit down, and I'll tell you.

3
Inspector: Now, first of all, tell me what you know about Chris.
Sandy: Well, he disappeared on Friday. And he left some messages for us in his computer.
Peter: He has gone on holiday for a few days. And he has given us a puzzle to help us find him.
Inspector: I'm afraid that your brother has stolen the program for a new computer game. We think he is going to sell it to a foreign company. It is on a computer disk. We want to get the disk back. And we think he has it with him.
Sandy: Are you sure about this? I don't think that our brother is a thief.
Inspector: I'm quite sure. And I think that he is going to meet you here, and he is going to give you the disk.
Peter: Well, actually we're just going to look at the Needle, and then we're going home. Goodbye.
Sandy: You weren't very polite to her, Peter.
Peter: Shh, she's listening. Don't you remember her? She was at the National Theatre. She's following us. And I don't think she is a police inspector.

Unit 14 Good advice

Unit 14 Emergency

Unit 14 **1c** Listening

Interviewer: We know that most earthquakes are quite small, so is there anything we can do to make our homes safer and protect ourselves? Well, people who live in countries where they have a lot of earthquakes are beginning to learn how to live with them. I talked to Anna-Maria, who comes from Southern Italy.
Anna-Maria: There are some simple things you can do if you live in an earthquake country. First of all you should think about the dangerous things inside your house. Shelves, for example. Don't put heavy things on shelves, because they will fall off the shelf, and perhaps onto your head. Bookshelves, for example. I had a friend with bookshelves above her bed, and every time there was just a small earthquake the books fell off the shelf. That's very dangerous.
Interviewer: What about other things that fall down inside the house?
Anna-Maria: Well, many people have plants in heavy pots on the window - what do you call it...
Interviewer: The window-sill? The little shelf outside the window?
Anna-Maria: Yes, the window sill. Or on the balcony. When there is an earthquake, these pots fall down, and they are very dangerous for the people in the street.
Interviewer: And when we were talking earlier, you mentioned something about doors and windows.
Anna-Maria: Yes. Sometimes we know that an earthquake is coming or we can feel it beginning. Some people run out of the door or even jump out of the window. This is not a very good idea, and more people are injured this way. A good idea is to open the door when you feel an earthquake but stay in the house. This is because the walls often move and after the earthquake it is difficult to open the door and go out. Don't forget, after one earthquake there is usually another one.

Unit 14 Your letters answered

Unit 14 **2a** New language

Nick: Dear Carol,
My problem is exams. I worry about them all the time. Sometimes I can't sleep, and I can never remember anything. I study for hours and sometimes I read the same page ten times! But in the morning I can't remember anything. What can I do? Do your readers have any ideas?
Nick, London

Carol: 1 Make some notes and read them often. Relax some of the time - it's wrong to study for hours. Have a warm drink before you go to bed. Don't worry about exams - they don't really matter!
2 Drink lots of tea and coffee and study all night. Write the most important facts on your hand. You won't forget

Tapescripts

them this way! Learn all your books by heart.
3 Underline important points in your school books. Go to bed early before an exam. Study the important points before you go to sleep. Watch television then you will feel tired! Read your books again in the morning.

Unit 14 Check up 5

Examples: 1 cup   2 cupboard
              1 win   2 winter

a) 1 won   2 wonderful
b) 1 hear   2 heart
c) 1 get   2 vegetable
d) 1 age   2 damage
e) 1 ill   2 village
f) 1 over   2 discover
g) 1 table   2 suitable
h) 1 man   2 manage
i) 1 fact   2 factory
j) 1 miss   2 permission

Unit 15 Changes

Unit 15 Old and new

Unit 15 1d Listening

(a)
I remember this city ten years ago and it's a better place to live in now. It used to be a very dirty place, you know, there was lots of pollution, lots of smoke. But now it's much cleaner, the air is better. So that has been a change for the good.

(b)
A few years ago it was easy to take your car into the city centre, the traffic used to move quickly. But now there are too many cars, it's impossible, and it's difficult to park your car too. It's getting worse all the time.

(c)
This city has changed a lot. The people here used to be more friendly, they used to help you, they used to laugh and talk a lot. But now people are always busy, they don't smile any more. That's what I think, anyway.

(d)
When I was younger, most people in this town used to be fishermen, used to go to sea, you know. It used to be an important place for fish. But now there aren't many people doing that, they don't catch many fish, they say. So people have different jobs, they sell cars, they work in offices. There aren't many fishermen now.

Unit 15 Words in action 1

You shouldn't do that

Too much advice, too much advice,
My friends always tell me what to do!
So I'm writing this letter to your magazine,
And I'd like some advice from you.
Tell me what to think, tell me what to do
I need an answer right away.
For every time I ask my friends
This is what they say:

Take my advice - you shouldn't do that.
It's not very nice - you shouldn't do that.
Think about it twice - you shouldn't do that!
No, you shouldn't do that!
No, you shouldn't do that!

What can we do, what can we say,
You really have to change your point of view.
You shouldn't always ask your friends
To tell you what to do.
Make up your mind, think for yourself,
It's easy when you start to try.
And when they give you their advice
Then you can reply:

Take my advice - you shouldn't do that.
It's not very nice - you shouldn't do that.
Think about it twice - you shouldn't do that!
No, you shouldn't do that!
No, you shouldn't do that!

Unit 16 Be careful!

Unit 16 Safety first

Unit 16 1a New language

FIRE Fire is a common cause of accidents. Don't play with matches. You might burn yourself or start a fire. Don't light fires in the countryside. You could start a forest fire. And don't try to put out a fire on your own. You might make it worse. Always call the fire brigade.
PLAY Be careful when you play outside. Don't climb inside old fridges, for example. You might get stuck inside. Don't play near deep water. You could fall in. And when you are flying a kite, don't fly it near electricity cables. You could get an electric shock.
AT HOME Don't leave toys on the stairs. Someone might fall over them. Never play with electrical appliances, such as televisions or videos. You could start a fire or get a shock. And don't run around in the house. You might hurt yourself - or you might break the furniture.

Unit 16 Round the World problems

Unit 16 2c Listening

Girl: We've got a guidebook, and there is some advice in it too. But it doesn't always explain things very clearly. For example, here it says 'Remember not to give food to the monkeys in the street.' What's wrong with that?
Vicky: Well, there are lots of monkeys in some cities, and they are a big problem. They might jump all over you or bite you. It could be dangerous.

Boy: And what about this. It says 'Don't forget to take a raincoat and umbrella with you.' That can't be right. India is a hot country, isn't it?
George: It is a hot country, but you might get wet all the same! There are rainy weeks called 'monsoons' when it rains all the time.
Girl: What about food? I haven't read anything about that yet.
Vicky: You have to be careful. For example, avoid eating the food they sell in the street, at first anyway. It's delicious, but it could make you feel ill. Take some stomach pills with you!
Boy: And what's your advice about sightseeing. What are the best things to see?
George: There are so many good things! It's a very big country. I think you should read all of your guidebook, and start planning your trip now. Talk to your parents about it too.
Girl: Well, thanks a lot, I'm sure your advice will be useful. We're really looking forward to it.
Vicky: We had a great time there, and I'm sure that you will too!

Unit 16 CHRIS Episode 6

(a)

Sandy and Peter went and looked at Cleopatra's Needle. Inspector Harman was sitting on a bench nearby, and talking to a man in a raincoat.
'I don't believe her story about Chris,' Sandy whispered.
'Neither do I,' said Peter. 'And how do we know that she is really a police inspector? She didn't show us her identity card.'
'You're right,' said Sandy. 'And I think I've found a clue.'
'A clue? What do you mean?' Peter replied.
'Just act normally. Be careful, she's still watching. Look at the notice over there. Do you remember what CHRIS told us about the Needle? There's something wrong with the notice. It could be a message from Chris. Read it quickly, and then we'll look for a phone box.
I think we should …!'

3
Peter: Now we're home we can talk, Sandy.
Sandy: Yes, did you spot the clue, Peter?
Peter: I think so. Do you remember what CHRIS said? The special ship which was carrying the Needle nearly sank.
Sandy: Yes, that's right.
Peter: But the place where it nearly sank was different on the notice. It wasn't near Greenwich. It was in the Bay of Biscay, which is near Spain.
Sandy: That's it, so Greenwich is a clue. But what does it mean?
Peter: Well, Greenwich a place on the river in London. We used to go there when we were little, don't you remember? We could go there now. We can go on a boat. It's a very interesting trip.
Sandy: Or we could ask CHRIS about it. He might know something.

Peter: That's a good idea. And there's that map that came in the letter. Perhaps we should look at that too.
Sandy: Well, what do you think?
Peter: I think we should ask CHRIS first.
Sandy: But we've got the map right here.
Peter: Oh all right, but can you find Greenwich on it?

Unit 17 Don't worry so much!

Unit 17 Not a care in the world

Unit 17 1c Listening

Mrs Odd: Where are you two going?
Ozzy: Out, mum.
Mum: Where do you mean, out?
Olive: We're going fishing with the Normal kids from next door.
Mum: Well, don't get into trouble, or I'll tell your father.
Ozzy: Yes, mum.
Mum: If you go on the bus, don't throw things out the window like last time.
Olive: We're not taking the bus, mum. We're walking.
Mum: And if you see a policeman, don't shout rude words.
Ozzy: No, mum, I promise I won't.
Mum: And another thing. What about lunch?
Olive: We're taking sandwiches. See, I've made them.
Mum: All right, but be careful of those Normal kids. They're very strange. If they give you any food, don't eat it. It might be poisoned.
Ozzy: What about chocolate, mum?
Mum: If they give you any chocolate, bring it home to me. I'll taste it first.
Olive: Yes, mum.
Mum: And if you catch any fish, throw them back in the river. Your father's going fishing tomorrow, and if you catch all the fish he'll be very upset!

Unit 17 Words in action 1

A Head for Heights
Some workers have to make the metal skeleton of a skyscraper. They work 250 metres above the ground! They have to walk on metal girders 15cms wide, and they try not to feel dizzy when they look down. If they make a mistake, perhaps it will be their last one. In the USA many of these skilled workers come from the same Indian tribe, the Mohawks. This tribe has developed a very good head for heights, and the Mohawks are not afraid of working high above the ground.

A stunt double takes the place of a film star when something dangerous is done. The double is dressed like the actor, and tries to hide his or her face. When we see an actor jump from a building, we really see the stunt double. Usually he or she falls onto something soft, but this part of the film is cut. In this way, the actor avoids getting hurt because all the dangerous things are done by the double.

Tapescripts

Unit 18 In the rainforest

Unit 18 The Programme for Belize

Unit 18 1a New language

The Programme for Belize is an organization that is saving the rainforests of Belize, a small country in Central America. If you collect £25 you can buy an acre of rainforest and save it. In our schools competition, the group with the most interesting idea for collecting £25 will win a week's trip for four to Belize. You will visit Camp Rio Bravo, where scientists study the rainforest.

Unit 18 1d Listening

Thank you for coming today everyone, and we hope you have enjoyed our Animal Day. As you know, we are collecting money to help the rainforest in Belize. But how much do you know about rainforests? Here is some information. We hope you find it interesting.

Rainforests grow in very hot countries, near the equator. In them there are tall trees and many kinds of plants and hundreds of animals and insects. They are very wet places. More than two metres of rain can fall there in a year - that's forty times the rain we have here in England! And they are very hot too. Very few people live in the rainforests, and the forests have been there for thousand of years. The trees are very tall, and most large animals, like monkeys and snakes, live in the tops of the trees. We call this top part of the forest the canopy. On the ground there isn't a lot of light. At the moment the rainforests are in danger because people are cutting down the trees, sometimes to sell the wood, and sometimes to make land for farm animals. In the last twenty years, we have lost half of all the rainforests in the world. And we need them because they help to make the air clean all over the world. And because many useful plants grow in them.

Unit 18 A visit to Rio Bravo

Unit 18 2b New language

A: What are we doing this morning?
B: There's a trip into the rainforest.
A: What do we do after that?
B: You can go swimming or go on the river in a canoe.
A: I'd rather go on the river in a canoe. It sounds more interesting.

Unit 18 CHRIS Episode 7

(a)
Sandy and Peter decided to go to Greenwich by boat. There was a tourist boat that left from Westminster Bridge, and they took the bus there. Mrs Jackson made them some sandwiches for lunch, and they ate them on the way. The boat went under Tower Bridge and past Docklands with its new office blocks. It was a good way to see London. Suddenly Peter noticed something.

'Sandy, look at that man over there. I'm sure he was sitting behind us on the bus this morning.'
There was a tall man in a raincoat at the front of the boat, next to some foreign tourists.
'I don't think so, Peter. I'm more worried about Inspector Harman. If she follows us, then Chris will be in danger'

2
Narrator: Sandy and Peter soon found Cleopatra Road. It was a short road and they walked up and down it twice and looked at all the houses.
Sandy: The problem is, which house are we looking for? If Chris is here, I'm sure there will be a clue for us.
Peter: Perhaps the clue is a number. Let's think. Look, why don't we go home first and ask CHRIS?
Sandy: I'd rather look around here. We have to find the clue, that's all.
Peter: There's that shop. Perhaps it sells computers.
Sandy: No, I don't think so. There are some radios in the window, but there aren't any computers.
Peter: If we look carefully at all the houses, perhaps we'll see a clue.
Sandy: Yes, that might be the answer. Maybe Chris has put his name in the window.
Peter: Wait a minute, Sandy. Look at the name of that house. There on the gate. Can you see?
Sandy: It's my name.
Peter: And mine too. 'Peter' means rock.
Sandy: Well, this is the house, then ...

Unit 19 What have you been doing?

Unit 19 Life style

Unit 19 1a New language

Jim: This is a very unusual sport! I started it just for a joke. I've been doing it for five years and I've collected 3010 different ones from all over the world. That's a record! It's actually a very old game too. People have been playing with them for centuries.
When you play you put 49 of them into a two-metre circle.

Boy: I think this is a really great sport! I saw some other boys doing it and I decided to try it. I've been doing it for two years and I've just won my first competition. It's an old sport. People have been doing it for hundreds of years. It's not difficult if you practise. There was an Italian, Enrico Rastelli, who could throw ten balls at the same time!

Girl: This is really interesting, but you have to have the right equipment. I started when I was 10, so I've been doing it for four years. It's a good hobby for young people, because you learn a lot. It's not very popular, I suppose. I think that more grown up people than young people do it. People have been doing it for thousands of years.

Tapescripts

Unit 19 · 1c Listening

Tony: My name's Tony, and I've been doing this since 1992. I like this kind of activity, because it's technical but it's also good fun, and I can meet my friends here and have a good talk. You have to understand how your camera works and about light and things like that. I've been having lessons for the past year, and my photos have improved a lot. Recently I've learned about taking close-ups and doing portraits, pictures of people. It's really interesting.

Maria: I'm Maria. I started doing this when I was a kid, in the street usually. That's a bit dangerous. I used to fall over a lot as well. Since I moved to this town in 1994 I've been coming to this club. I've learned how to dance, and I've also been in some races. That is really exciting! It's not difficult to learn, but you have to buy the right kind of skates. I like dancing best, I think.

Jim: My name's Jim, and I've been coming to this club since 1993. I started this when I was at school, but not very seriously just because I felt hungry sometimes. But at this club I've been entering competitions. It's not really difficult, but you have to be organized and have a few basic skills. You also have to learn how to make healthy dishes. And of course, you mustn't eat too much!

Anna: Hello, I'm Anna, and I've been doing this since 1990. My parents started taking me with them when I was about fourteen, and so I learned a lot when I was young. This is really good fun, but you have problems with your voice, so you have to have lessons, and also you must know something about the stage and things like that. I've been in ten different productions, and so far I haven't forgotten my lines. The best moment I suppose is at the end of the play when everyone applauds!

Unit 19 Check up 7

a) If I go to the shops, I'll buy you some chocolate.
b) If you sit at the front, you'll see more clearly.
c) If we leave now, we'll get there in time.
d) If he comes back later, ask him to wait.

Unit 20 Are you sure?

Unit 20 Spot the mistakes

Unit 20 · 1a New language

Jack and Jean are hiding somewhere in this room, but where are they? In the room there is a large chest, but it is locked. There is a cupboard, but the doors are open and it is empty. There is also a filing cabinet with three drawers. There is a large window, but there aren't any curtains. Next to the filing cabinet is a desk. We can see under the desk, and there is no one there. There is a small cardboard box on the desk. There is an armchair, and there is a sofa against the wall.

Unit 20 · 1c Listening

1
A: This is the place, look, it says 'Norwich Road'.
B: It can't be Norwich Road. Look at the map. Norwich Road is here. And we are here, I think.
A: We can't be here. That's the cinema, over there. So we're here.
B: We can't be. It's a different cinema …

2
A: Well, I think this is the answer.
B: It can't be. You've put this 'six' in the wrong place.
A: Are you sure?
B: Look at the question, it says 'How many days does it take?' The answer can't be forty-nine thousand four hundred and six.
A: Perhaps you're right. Let's try again …

3
A: I'm sure that's Bill over there, you know, Sue's brother.
B: It can't be. He's in Australia.
A: Are you sure? Perhaps he's back.
B: No, he can't be. He only left last week. It can't be him.
A: Well, it looks just like him, doesn't it …

4
A: I think the girl in the hotel is the murderer.
B: No, she can't be. She's in love with Tom.
A: I don't think she is. I think she's in love with that other man, you know, the detective.
B: No, she can't be in love with him. Anyway, we'll find out next week. We must remember to watch …

Unit 20 Round the World album

Unit 20 · 2b Practice

1 This is a very small island but there are lots of tourists. It's really hot here, and we've been swimming all morning, but it's cooler than it was in Egypt. Tomorrow we are leaving and sailing west to Italy …

2 We like it here, and we can talk to people easily because they all speak English, of course. George keeps saying silly things, like 'Will we fall off the world here?' It's the middle of December but it's summer here …

3 Yesterday we went horse riding and George thought he was a real cowboy. He fell off the horse about ten times too. We met some real cowboys but they have got motorbikes, not horses! …

4 There is so much to see here! It's a very large country. We've seen elephants and monkeys and some beautiful temples. Yesterday we had a lovely meal. George thought all the food here was very hot but it isn't true.

5 This is a very busy city and the people are very friendly. We've been to a wonderful museum and to the desert. Next week we're going on a trip down the river to see another ancient city. I haven't been on a camel yet, but I want to try …

Tapescripts

Unit 20 Words in action 1

I'd rather watch TV

Let's go for a walk outside.
- I'd rather watch TV.
Let's take our bikes and go for a ride.
- I'd rather watch TV.
You sit every evening and it's just not right,
Watching the police and the cowboys fight,
Why don't you come out with me tonight?
- I'd rather watch TV.

You can't be serious, you must be crazy,
It's driving you mad and it's making you lazy,
You don't read books and you don't run and play,
You just watch a little black box all day,

Let's meet some friends in the square.
- I'd rather watch TV.
Let's walk along the street in the evening air.
- I'd rather watch TV.
I've been waiting for a month or more
And every night I come around and knock on your door.
Don't you remember what your legs are for?
- I'd rather watch TV.

Unit 21 Just imagine!

Unit 21 What would you do?

Unit 21 **1a** New language

Helen: Imagine that you are alone on a small island. How would you survive? What would you do first?
Anna: I'd build a shelter first. I'd use branches from trees. I'd build it near the stream.
Jim: I'd look for food first! I'd eat fruit but I wouldn't eat strange plants!
Maria: I'd make a fire first. Then people would see the smoke and they would rescue me.
Tony: I'd make a boat first. I'd use pieces of wood from the beach. I'd leave the island as soon as possible. It would be dangerous to stay there.

Unit 21 **1d** Listening

1 First I think I'd be frightened. I wouldn't say anything, I'd just stand very still and I'd think about what I could do. Sometimes when they see you they are frightened too. So I'd just stand very still. It really depends what kind it is, a really dangerous one, like a lion or a tiger, or not. But still, there aren't any of those in my country!

2 First I'd ask the people near there about it, to see if it belonged to anybody. And it depends on the place - at school I think I'd give it to my teacher. Sometimes other kids leave things in the classroom. In the street - I don't really know. It depends on how much. I'd take it to the police station I think.

3 First I'd drink something hot, and I'd go to bed. I'd tell my mother too. Then perhaps I'd stay at home, I wouldn't go to school. I'd read my favourite books or watch television all day. For something serious, the doctor would come I suppose.

4 I'd look in the street, or I'd ask someone. At school it's better not to have one, I think, because we have a bell, so we always know. Some kids look at theirs all through the lesson. I'd take it to a shop, a place where they fix them. Or I'd ask my parents to buy me a new one.

Unit 21 Changing places

Unit 21 **2a** New language

Nick: Which person would you like to be for one day? What would you do if you were that person?
Anna: The head teacher of the school! If I were the head teacher I'd change some of the school rules. I'd give the students more holidays! I wouldn't give any homework!
Jim: A famous journalist! If I were a journalist I'd interview my favourite singers. I'd visit them at home.

Unit 21 CHRIS Episode 8

(a)
COMPUTER CROOKS CAUGHT – POLICE THANK TWIN DETECTIVES
Police in Greenwich have arrested two members of a gang which has been stealing computer games programs in England, France and Germany. Wendy Harman and Paul Dennis were arrested by Detective-Sergeant Brian Wilson at a house in Cleopatra Road, Greenwich.
'We have been looking for these two for six months,' said Detective-Sergeant Wilson. 'We knew that they were trying to steal Chris Talbot's new games program, but then Chris disappeared. Luckily Chris's brother and sister phoned us and told us about Harman. She was pretending to be a policewoman, and was trying to find Chris. So we set a trap for the thieves, and luckily they fell right into it. Thanks to Peter and Sandy - and a computer called CHRIS!'

2
Sandy: Well, Chris, we have found you at last!
Chris: Yes, it's good to see both of you. But I don't understand something …
Peter: You don't understand! You are the one who has been leaving us all those difficult clues and puzzles.
Chris: And I hope you enjoyed finding me. But why were the police here? And who was that woman and the man they arrested?
Sandy: It's quite simple really. While we were looking for you, we had another adventure at the same time, you see.
Peter: First we met that woman, Wendy Harman.
Sandy: She pretended to be a policewoman, but we knew she wasn't. She was trying to find you because she wanted to steal your new game program. She and her

partner, Paul Dennis, started following us. He was the man on the boat, Peter. You were right.

Peter: I told you he was following us! Anyway, after we met Wendy Harman we phoned the police and told them the whole story. The police were watching us too! You see, they couldn't find the thieves. They had to wait for us to find you first. They knew the thieves were waiting for us to find you - and the program.

Chris: I was certainly surprised when we met at the top of the stairs and you both started talking at the same time about the police and computer thieves.

Sandy: And then Wendy Harman and Paul Dennis arrived, and the police came and arrested them. Clever, wasn't it?

Chris: Yes, very clever. Well done, both of you!

Peter: If we told our friends at school, they would never believe us!

Sandy: And the program is safe too. Can we see the disk, Chris?

Chris: See it? I haven't got it here. I came for a holiday, remember? This is a friend's house. And I've been relaxing and sailing on the river for three lovely days!

Peter: Not all the time. You came back and gave us that envelope, didn't you?

Chris: No, I asked Mrs Jackson to do that for me. In fact, she's meeting us all at Patricia's restaurant tomorrow night for dinner. That's your prize for finding me! Oh and by the way, you'll like the name of the new game. It's called 'Looking for Chris!'

Sandy: Very funny! But where is the new game program? Don't tell me Mrs Jackson has got that too?

Chris: No, it has been near you all the time, in a very safe place. Can't you guess where it is?

Unit 22 Difficult moments

Unit 22 How embarrassing!

Unit 22 1a Practice

Girl: My worst moment was in a concert at school a few years ago. I was playing the violin, and I was sitting at the front. Everyone could see me. Suddenly two of the strings broke and there was a horrible noise. I didn't know what to do, so I just stopped playing and sat there.

Boy: Two years ago we went to France. We were travelling by train from Paris to Lyons. We couldn't understand French very well, and when the train stopped we thought the station was Lyons, so we got off. It was the wrong station and we had to wait three hours for the next train.

Girl: My friend, Lee, is a waiter in an expensive restaurant. Once we had dinner there on my birthday. While Lee was serving me, I moved my chair and he dropped a plate of soup on my mother's head. We all laughed but my mother was very upset!

Unit 22 The Round the World Kids

Unit 22 2b Listening

Vicky: I really enjoyed the trip, it was the most wonderful thing I've ever done. We missed some work at school I suppose, but we learned a lot of other things. One day I'm going to go back and visit all the countries again, I'm sure ...

George: There were lots of good things about the trip. I liked meeting young people from all over the world and seeing so many famous places. The food was good too, well usually. The only problem was being on the boat all the time, as it was very small and after a few months I wanted to sleep in a real house for a change!

Vicky: I didn't have any problems really. At first I felt seasick but after a few days I felt all right. There were some difficult and some dirty jobs on the boat too: cleaning the deck, for example, and using ropes and things like that. I didn't know what to do at first, but after a few weeks I found all the dirty jobs really interesting and enjoyable, and I looked forward to them!

George: The best part of the trip for me was learning about water sports. I wasn't a very good swimmer before we left, but I learned to swim really well, and I learned sailing of course, and windsurfing which is really fantastic. I've joined a watersports club near home and I want to try to become a member of the windsurfing team.

Vicky: I learned a lot too and I have decided that I want to be a photographer when I leave school. My parents say that I'll change my mind but I don't think I will. I really enjoy taking photos and we have a darkroom at home so I can develop and print my own pictures. I took lots of photos on the trip, and I am still working on the films. I've got about three hundred photos and I'm still putting them into albums, but I haven't finished yet ...

George: It's hard to believe that the trip has finished, really. It became a part of our lives. In fact I often wake up in the middle of the night and I think that I'm still on the boat. It's silly really. I can hear the water and the birds, but then I remember that I'm at home, and it's just noises outside. I'll never forget our trip, it was a wonderful way to see the world.

Unit 22 Check up 5

a) I used to be as tall as you.
b) A lot of noise.
c) A trip for two to London.
d) Hats and coats and trousers.

Tapescripts

Unit 23 What did you see?

Unit 23 At the supermarket

Unit 23 1c Listening

Jill: I was buying a magazine and while I was coming out of the shop I saw a woman standing just outside. She was talking to a man, they were looking at a map. He was tall and he was wearing a long raincoat, I think. Anyway, a second man ran past and took the woman's handbag. The first man tried to stop him, and chased him down the street, but I don't think he caught him.

Brian: I was doing my shopping and as I was coming out of the bread shop I saw everything. A woman was talking to two men. They were both wearing jeans and t-shirts. Then one of the men took the woman's bag and both men ran away. Then a man on a motorbike came, I think he was a policeman. The men ran away and the policemen followed them.

David: While I was walking along Downs Road I saw a man outside the newspaper shop. He was talking to a woman and they were looking at a newspaper, I think. He was wearing a long raincoat. Then he took the woman's handbag and he ran away. Some other people ran after him and tried to catch him - a man in jeans, and a man on a motorbike. They caught him I think.

Unit 23 Words in action 1

Finding a fortune

On July 24th 1715 eleven Spanish ships left Havana, Cuba. They were carrying silver and gold worth over $5 million. Three days later, near the coast of Florida, the ships were hit by a hurricane and ten of them sank. Spanish divers managed to bring up thousands of gold coins from the shipwrecks, but the water was very deep. Most of the coins, known as 'pieces of eight', remained at the bottom of the sea.

In 1949 Kip Wagner from Florida found some gold coins on a beach. He decided to find the wrecks. He was sent old maps and descriptions of the shipwrecks from a museum in Spain. For ten years he looked for the wrecks, and in the end he managed to find them all.

In 1959 Kip Wagner formed a company with eight divers to find the treasure. It was called the Real Eight Company. They found nothing for six months, but they refused to give up. They carried on diving and one day they found some bars of silver. Between 1959 and 1965 the team found many gold coins, worth over $1 million.

Progress tests

Progress test 1 Units 1–8

Part 1: Grammar and vocabulary
[50 Marks]

1 Circle the best answer a, b, c or d.

1 We usually .... with my grandparents in the summer.
   a are staying
   b will
   c stay
   d were staying

2 The burglar broke into our house .... we were out.
   a and
   b while
   c before
   d so

3 The Robinsons .... round the world in a boat.
   a waved
   b drove
   c rode
   d sailed

4 I can't ride this bike. It's .... big.
   a much
   b too
   c enough
   d quite

5 This comic is more expensive if you .... the prices.
   a look
   b complete
   c buy
   d compare

6 .... you ever seen a volcano?
   a have
   b do
   c are
   d did

7 She has a lot of homework so she's too .... to help you.
   a safe
   b working
   c busy
   d active

8 Archeologists .... the Greek Temple last year.
   a find out
   b dug
   c learned
   d discovered

9 What's the weather .... in your country?
   a for
   b like
   c making
   d as

10 The tourist office can give you the .... you need.
   a informations
   b knowledge
   c surprise
   d information

   ...../10 marks

Progress tests

2 Complete the sentences using *could* or *couldn't* and a verb from the box.

> learn   ride   speak   swim   watch

1 The Mexican children didn't understand English so we .... to them.
2 She .... about computers at the computer summer camp.
3 .... you really .... a camel when you were there?
4 A hundred years ago people .... television.
5 I .... when I was five, but I can now.
...../5 marks

3 Complete the sentences using the past simple or past continuous forms of the verbs in brackets.

1 I had the idea for the interview while I .... (look) at the video.
2 She .... (break) her glasses while she was playing basketball.
3 While Alex was studying for a test his brother .... (watch) television.
4 George .... (clean) the boat quickly while everyone was sleeping.
5 When we were fishing a dolphin .... (jump) out of the water once and then disappeared.
6 While my friends were doing a Maths test I .... (be) at the dentist.
...../6 marks

4 Circle the best answer.

1 English people seem to speak *quickly/more quickly quickest* than my teacher.
2 I think my class works much *hard/more hard/harder* than their class.
3 The weather isn't *as good/as well/more good* this summer, is it?
4 That Disney film is *so exciting/less exciting/very exciting* than the first one.
5 Do you go to bed *later/more later/lately* than her?
6 I'm going to get up *earliest/most early/earlier* tomorrow.
...../ 6marks

5 Complete the sentences using the correct question tag.

1 *Brilliant* is a fantastic magazine, ... ?
2 You've met before, ... ?
3 Tigers can run very fast, ... ?
4 He did well in his last test, ... ?
5 Vicky's been to Greece, ... ?
6 You're coming to the party, ... ?
7 The Robinson's are travelling round the world, ... ?
8 Olive couldn't find her key, ... ?
9 We were at school when it happened, ... ?
10 They sent letters to their friends by computer, ... ?
...../10 marks

6 Complete the sentences by putting the adjectives in brackets into the correct order.

1 My father's wearing a .... pullover. (red/woollen/long)
2 I bought two .... belts. (leather/expensive)
3 Nick likes wearing .... T-shirts. (cotton/white/large)
4 My parents bought a .... vase. (small/blue)
5 That's a .... toy. Don't buy it. (plastic/cheap)
...../5 marks

7 Complete the sentences with the past simple or present perfect simple form of the verbs in brackets.

1 Our teacher .... (live) in Brazil for a long time.
2 The archeologists .... (give) the ancient coins to the museum a few months ago.
3 The Robinsons .... (not/finish) their trip yet.
4 My father .... just .... (stop) smoking.
5 Vicky and George .... (not/go) sightseeing yesterday.
6 .... you ever .... (find) anything interesting?

7 The policeman .... (catch) the burglars last night.

8 I .... (not/eat) octopus since last summer.

...../8 marks

Part 2: Reading [10 marks]

Read the text. Then read the statements below and say whether they are true or false.

Last summer my parents agreed to let me go to a basketball summer camp by the sea. My cousin, Steven, and a couple of friends came too. We were all very excited because it was our first time away from home. The advertisement for the camp said:

'Practise basketball with trainers from well-known teams.
Wonderful food.
Learn lots of new sports.
Never be bored.'

Well, we didn't see any professional trainers. The children usually organized their own basketball matches and sometimes there was an older person who gave us a few ideas. We went to the beach every day and some of the younger boys and girls learnt how to swim but we all knew how to swim already. The best thing was playing ball games in the sea. The only other sport was table tennis but there were always other children using the table.

I took a lot of comics with me and read them all three times because I didn't know what else to do. The food was quite good but there wasn't enough of it so we bought a lot of extra snacks and ice creams. Steven also spent quite a lot of money phoning home in the first week because he felt homesick and his parents took him home before the end of the camp. Never again!

1 The writer went to the camp with a lot of friends. T/F? ....

2 He didn't want to got to the camp. T/F? ....

3 The advertisement said that the children could play in teams with famous trainers. T/F? ....

4 The children expected to do a lot of interesting things at the camp. T/F? ....

5 There was always an adult to give advice during basketball games. T/F? ....

6 Some children learnt to swim at the camp. T/F? ....

7 The writer bought some comics and read them a lot of times. T/F? ....

8 The food was awful. T/F? ....

9 the writer's parents were very angry with the camp. T/F? ....

10 The writer's cousin left before the end of the camp. T/F? ....

...../10 marks

Part 3: Writing [10 marks]

Write a short article for your school magazine about a discovery that archeologists made in your country. Imagine you were helping with the dig. You may use some or all of the ideas in the box to help you. Write 50–80 words.

> Why were you there?   What were you doing?
> Where were they digging?   What did they find?
> What did they do next?   Did the newspapers or TV report it? What future plans are there?

....
....
....
....
....
....
....
....
....
....
....
....
....
....
....
....

...../10 marks

Test total ...../70 marks = ...%

Progress test 2 Units 9–16

Part 1: Grammar and vocabulary
[50 marks]

1 Circle the best answer a, b, c or d.

1 We can't sit down. There aren't .... chairs.
  a much
  b lot
  c some
  d enough

2 Can you .... me a pen, please?
  a borrow
  b write
  c lend
  d gave

3 She .... a pop star this afternoon.
  a interviews
  b is interviewing
  c used to interview
  d interviewing

4 I .... my bedroom with my sister.
  a save
  b divide
  c manage
  d share

5 Would you .... helping me with this heavy suitcase?
  a like
  b want
  c try
  d mind

6 Don't throw things .... the window. It's dangerous.
  a out
  b through
  c near
  d to

7 Are you doing anything .... Saturday evening?
  a by
  b on
  c in
  d the

8 My parents .... to let me go to a summer camp.
  a wouldn't
  b said
  c avoided
  d promised

9 It wasn't far so we walked instead .... taking a bus.
  a of
  b to
  c for
  d from

10 Most kinds of plastic are suitable for ....
  a recycle
  b to recycle
  c recycling
  d recycled

11 Don't play with matches. You .... start a fire.
  a have
  b might
  c can
  d would

12 Could he .... me later?
  a phone
  b to phone
  c phoning
  d phones

...../12 marks

2 Complete the sentences with a word from the box. You can use the words more than once.

enough few little many much

1 It isn't healthy to eat too .... chocolate.
2 I'm afraid there are too .... words in this composition. Please write some more.
3 How .... questions have you answered?
4 I don't know .... people at my new school.
5 She did the project with very .... help from her teacher.
6 Help yourself to some more meat if you haven't had ....
7 The library has'nt got .... information on that writer.
8 There are very .... spelling mistakes this time

...../8 marks

3 Complete the sentences using will or going to and a verb from the box.

arrive do not/make show take visit

1 Fifteen students .... Britain this summer.
2 I promise I .... on time tomorrow.
3 The journey .... probably .... two hours.
4 If you come to my house I .... you my pet turtle.
5 What job .... she .... when she finishes college.
6 We promise we .... a noise.

...../6 marks

4 Complete the sentences with the correct form of have to or not have to.

1 There was no electricity so we .... light a candle.
2 Pilots .... wear uniforms.
3 .... she .... get up early to go to school?
4 Last year I .... do much homework. I have a lot more this year.
5 His home is near his school so he .... catch a bus.
6 .... we .... finish our projects before next month?

...../6 marks

5 Complete the paragraph with a word from the box. There is one extra word.

collect rubbish product glass environment recycle

In my town we are doing something to help the (1) .... We put our (2) .... into different bins. For example, we have a bin for plastic things, another for paper and a third for (3) .... bottles. People (4) .... the rubbish and take it to different factories and there they can (5) .... it into new things.

...../5 marks

6 Complete the paragraph with used to or didn't use to and a verb from the box.

be go live talk live travel listen

Fifty years ago more people (1) .... in the villages in my country.
They (2) .... to other places because very few families owned cars. Most of them (3) .... farmers or fishermen. In the evenings they (4) .... or perhaps they (5) .... to the radio (if they had one) and they (6) .... to bed early. The houses were not big but the grandparents always (7) .... together with their children and grandchildren.

...../7 marks

7 Complete these sentences with the correct form of the verb in brackets.

1 Remember .... (bring) your dictionaries to class tomorrow.
2 Try .... (not arrive) late.
3 Practise .... (say) those new English words.
4 Don't forget .... (buy) some milk.
5 Avoid .... (stay) in the sun too long.
6 Don't start .... (make) a noise again.

...../6 marks

Progress tests
Part 2: Reading [10 marks]

Read this letter to a magazine then answer the questions below.

Dear Penny,

My problem is my homework. I never seem to have time to finish it. When I come from school my father have something to eat together and then he goes and works on his computer in the study. I usually turn on my radio, lie on my bed, and I sometimes fall asleep for an hour. Then my brother comes home at about five. We chat for a while and usually make some sandwiches to eat before he goes out again. After this I start my homework but my school friends often phone me and we chat for ages. At seven I turn on the television as I don't like missing my favourite programme. I have supper with my parents at about eight and then try to finish my homework. By ten o'clock I feel quite tired so I go to bed. I set my alarm clock for six in the morning but I don't always hear it. Do you have any ideas?

Eric, Manchester

a) Read the statements about the text and say whether they are true or false.

1 Eric finds his homework too difficult. T/F? ....
2 He always sleeps in the afternoon. T/F? ....
3 Eric's brother comes home after him. T/F? ....
4 Eric eats sandwiches for lunch. T/F? ....
5 His friends telephone him about school problems. T/F? ....
6 There is one TV programme that he always watches in the evening. T/F? ....
7 His whole family was together in the evening. T/F? ....

...../7 marks

b) Give Eric some advice about his problem. Write three sentences, one using *should* and two using *shouldn't*.

1 ....
2 ....
3 ....

...../3 marks

Part 3: Writing [10 marks]

Write a letter to your penfriend telling him or her about what you have done to improve your English in the last 6 months. You may use some or all six of the ideas in the box to help you. Write about 60–80 words.

> read English comics and magazines
> listen to English songs
> revise new words
> record cassettes to send to each other
> watch English films
> learn irregular verbs

...../10 marks

Test total ...../70 marks = ...%

Progress test 3 Units 17–23

Part 1: Grammar and vocabulary
[60 marks]

1 Circle the best answer a, b, c or d.

1 He'd rather .... than do his homework.
   a playing
   b to play
   c plays
   d play

2 How about .... to the cinema tonight?
   a to go
   b going
   c for go
   d you go

3 My sister .... old coins.
   a picks
   b looks
   c collects
   d rescues

4 Put the dirty plates in the ....
   a fridge
   b dishwasher
   c washing-machine
   d computer

5 I've been waiting in this .... for hours.
   a row
   b list
   c queue
   d stop

6 My mother spent a lot of money .... her new computer.
   a for
   b on
   c in
   d from

7 It's easy to ride a bike .... you learn when you are young.
   a whether
   b while
   c for
   d if

8 Helen goes to school .... foot because she likes walking.
   a on
   b with
   c by
   d the

9 Can you remember your most .... moment?
   a embarrassed
   b embarrasses
   c embarrassing
   d embarrass

10 Did you see the .... in today's newspaper?
   a titles
   b headlines
   c heading
   d prints

11 There is a man at the circus .... can eat fire.
   a where
   b which
   c who
   d what

12 A .... got into their house and stole some money.
   a pickpocket
   b ghost
   c hijacker
   d burglar

...../12 marks

2 Complete these conditional sentences with the correct form of the verb in brackets.

1 If you .... (feel) thirsty, drink some water.

2 If you speak more slowly, I .... (understand).

Progress tests

3 What .... you .... (do) if you met an alien?

4 Don't kick your ball into the neighbour's garden if you .... (play) outside.

5 Mrs Robinson may write a book about their world trip if she .... (have) enough time.

6 If I .... (be) a pop singer I'd wear a silver shirt!

7 Which country .... you .... (visit) if you could choose?

8 If I .... (find) an ancient coin, I'd study it first and then I'd give it to a museum.

9 If you carry on walking down this road, you .... (get) to the post office in five minutes.

10 I .... (revise) vocabulary from our book if I had a word test. ...../10 marks

3 Complete the sentences with a preposition from the box.

| to   into   in   at   in   to   on   at |

1 Nick was waiting .... a queue in the supermarket.

2 When we arrived .... the airport we went to the check-in desk.

3 The first telephone call was made .... 10th March, 1876.

4 A tall girl came .... the bank.

5 Tell us what happened .... the end.

6 If you go .... Britain, don't just visit London.

7 We got off the bus .... the wrong bus-stop.

8 I can't remember how .... work your computer. ...../8 marks

4 Complete the sentences with can't be or must be.

1 She .... a basketball player. She's so tall.

2 That .... our teacher. He doesn't wear glasses.

3 Phone the number again. He .... at home.

4 That photo .... of Cairo. I can see the Eiffel Tower.

5 This answer .... wrong. I checked it three times.

6 You .... joking! I didn't borrow your pen. ...../6 marks

5 Complete the sentences with for or since.

1 I've known Penny .... we were children.

2 They've been building that new bridge .... last April.

3 I've been at the station .... two hours.

4 There hasn't been any news about the lost climbers .... last night.

5 That city has been recycling rubbish .... about three years.

6 She's wanted to learn the guitar .... a long time. ...../6 marks

6 Complete the mini dialogues with the present simple, past simple or present perfect continuous form of the verb in brackets.

1 **A:** How long .... you .... ? (wait)
  B: Since about ten o'clock.

2 **A:** What .... you .... ? (do)
  B: I'm an engineer.

3 **A:** When .... you .... (send) that letter?
  B: A month ago.

4 **A:** People .... (draw) since ancient times.
  B: How .... we .... ? (know)
  A: From the drawings they have found in caves.

5 **A:** I .... (read) this book for months but I still haven't finished it.
  B: Why not? Is it so boring?

6 **A:** .... she usually .... (cycle) to work?
  B: Only in summer.

7 **A:** What clothes .... they .... (take) when they visited Tunisia?
  B: Very light summer clothes.

8 **A:** I .... (try) to find the answer to this Maths problem for half an hour. Can you help me?
  B: Let me see. No, sorry. I .... (not know) how to do it. ...../8 marks

7 Complete the sentences with the gerund or infinitive with *to* form of the verb from the box.

be walk buy interview change visit travel
learn make speak

1. Helen managed .... two famous pop singers for her school magazine.
2. She enjoys .... how to play new games on her computer.
3. Ozzy pretended .... ill.
4. You can't learn a foreign language well if you don't practise it.
5. The teacher refused .... the date of the test.
6. Keep on .... ! We'll get there soon.
7. Please write me a letter if you decide to .... to Italy.
8. I'd really like .... a new bike.
9. You'll hear the music better if you stop .... a noise.
10. The Robinsons don't plan .... for more than a year.

...../10 marks

Part 2: Reading [10 marks]

Read the text. Then read the statements and say whether thay are true or false.

Tutankhamun was an Egyptian pharaoh, who died in 1352 BC. Not many people knew his name before the royal tomb was discovered by Howard Carter in 1922. Inside the tomb there were wonderful treasures such as jewels, vases, furniture and the body of Tutankamun, the boy king, who was wearing a gold mask. There were several rooms in the tomb and at the doorway of one room they found a statue of a god which looked like a dog. The ancient Egyptians believed that the dead went on living so they provided them with enough things to protect them in their continuing journey through the underworld. We have learnt a lot about life in Ancient Egypt from this discovery.

Tomb-robbers often got inside royal tombs and stole the valuable things they found but this did not happen to Tutankhamun. Perhaps this was because of the words written inside his tomb: 'Death will come to those who disturb the sleep of the Pharaohs ...' Many strange and unfortunate things have happened to people connected with the discovery. One of the people who found the tomb, Lord Carnarvon, lost an arm when his gun went off accidentally. He died two months later and by 1929, 12 more of the original team were also dead.

1. Tutankhamun has always been very famous. T/F? ....
2. His tomb contained very valuable things. T/F? ....
3. The pharaoh died when he was quite young. T/F? ....
4. There was just one large room in the tomb. T/F? ....
5. They found the body of a dog in the tomb. T/F? ....
6. The ancient Egyptians had special beliefs about their dead. T/F? ....
7. The discovery has taught us a lot about the way of life in those times. T/F? ....
8. Tomb-robbers has already taken many things from Tutankhamun's tomb. T/F? ....
9. The writer suggests a reason why this tomb was still full of treasures. T/F? ....
10. We know how Lord Carnarvon died. T/F? ....

...../7 marks

Progress tests
Part 3: Writing [10 marks]

You won the first prize of a competition. The prize was a holiday for two weeks in your favourite city with your family. Describe your holiday. You may use all or some of the ideas in the box. Write between 60–80 words.

> Where did you go?
> Why did you choose this city?
> What did you do there?
> What did you like best/least?
> Did anything unusual happen?

...../10 marks

Test total ...../80 marks = ...%

End of book test

Part 1: Grammar and vocabulary
[70 marks]

1 Circle the best answer a, b, c or d.

1 Would you .... answering a few questions?
   a like
   b know
   c mind
   d can

2 Pandas live in China, ... they?
   a live
   b don't
   c do
   d are

3 How .... milk do you drink for breakfast?
   a like
   b many
   c often
   d much

4 The pilot wasn't .... to land the plane in the fog.
   a couldn't
   b managed
   c able
   d knowing

5 I'd .... have a cool drink than an ice cream, please.
   a like
   b want
   c rather
   d prefer

6 When George woke up his sister was ....
   a sleeping
   b sleep
   c to sleep
   d sleeps

7 If I .... you I'd go to the dentist.
   a am
   b been
   c will be
   d were

8 I'm .... I can't catch that train. It's too early.
   a worried
   b afraid
   c unable
   d manage

9 You .... go to bed late before an exam.
   a can't
   b doesn't
   c must
   d shouldn't

10 Ozzie didn't .... to have a pet snake.
   a use
   b rather
   c keep
   d wanted

...../10 marks

2 Circle the odd word out.

1 environment	rubbish	recycle	map
2 organize	scientist	collect	decide
3 test	exam	find	quiz
4 ankle	leg	shirt	foot
5 robber	burglar	alarm bell	waiter
6 spaghetti	sausage	meal	invitation
7 accident	disaster	fire	holiday
8 hungry	chilly	noise	dirty
9 carpet	moon	cupboard	sofa
10 lorry	continent	country	city

...../10 marks

Progress tests

3 Complete the sentences using the past simple, past continuous, present perfect simple or present perfect continuous tense of the verbs in brackets.

1 Nick .... just .... (finish) an interview with his favourite singer.

2 Olive and Ozzy .... (wash) their parents' car when the kangaroo jumped on top of it.

3 Sandy and Peter .... (solve) all of the computer's puzzles and found their brother.

4 The Robinsons .... (travel) for a number of months and the trip isn't over yet.

5 Vicky .... (do) a project on South America last month.

6 Mrs Odd .... (be) in hospital since last Tuesday.

7 Which island .... Anna .... (like) best?

8 What .... Chris .... (do) when the police found him?

9 The Robinsons used to live in a house but they .... (live) on a boat since they left Britain.

10 *Brilliant* .... (win) a competition for the best school magazine last year.   ...../10 marks

4 Complete the mini dialogues using a word or phrase from the box.

| Would you mind |
| I don't think so |
| too much |
| how much |
| What's it like? |
| how embarrassing |
| why don't we |
| I'd rather |
| as dangerous as |
| doesn't it |

1 **A:** .... ?
   B: It's a crowded and busy place.

2 **A:** .... check our library for that information?
   B: That's a good idea.

3 **A:** Can you solve this puzzle?
   B: No, ...

4 **A:** Would you like some orange juice?
   B: No, ... have water, please.

5 **A:** .... not smoking in here?
   B: Oh, I'm sorry. I'll go outside.

6 **A:** The train arrives in five minutes, ...
   B: Yes, that's right.

7 **A:** Snakes aren't .... people think.
   B: I wouldn't be too sure!

8 **A:** My brother got into the wrong car yesterday.
   B: .... !

9 **A:** I've decided to buy this computer.
   B: .... is it?

10 **A:** Why aren't you eating your spaghetti?
   B: Because you put .... salt in the water.
   ...../10 marks

5 Complete the text using *a*, *an* or no article.

(1) .... United States of America is (2) .... huge country with many cities on both (3) .... east and west coast. One of (4) .... most important cities in (5) .... west is San Francisco. In (6) .... 1848 (7) .... gold was discovered in the hills near San Francisco. (8) .... year later (9) .... city's population increased from 2000 to 25000 but only (10) .... few of these people found enough gold to become rich.
Today lots of (11) .... tourists visit San Francisco. Its cable cars are very popular with both (12) .... tourists and (13) .... inhabitants of this beautiful city. The cable cars are pulled by (14) .... heavy wire rope (called a cable) under (15) .... street. If you ride them to (16) .... top you can enjoy (17) .... wonderful view of the city's famous Golden Bridge. It is also (18) .... international city because many people from (19) .... other countries have moved to live and work there. In fact, San Francisco has (20) .... largest number of Chinese people outside Asia.
...../20 marks

264

6 Complete the paragraph using a preposition from the box.

on at to in with on

The Moon

The first man-made object, a Russian spacecraft, landed (1) .... the moon. (2) .... 1959. Ten years later (3) .... September 13, 1969 two American astronauts reached the moon. They found that it was covered (4) .... holes or craters. The astronauts returned (5) .... earth with a lot of moon rocks and scientists now believe the moon must be (6) .... least 4,600 million years old.

...../6 marks

7 Put the words into the right order to make a correct sentence.

1 too/in/you/sugar/coffee/have/my/put/much

....

2 quiz/expected/easier/I/the/history/was/than

....

3 baseball hat/a/got/cotton/white/Isabel/has/

....

4 Robinsons/have/the/many/visited/how/places/?

....

...../4 marks

Part 2: Reading [10 marks]

Read the text. Then read the statements and say whether they are true or false.

Christopher Columbus was an Italian from Genoa. He wanted to find a new route to Asia. He thought he would reach India and China more quickly if he sailed west. At that time most people believed you would fall of the edge of the world if you sailed too far. Columbus and other sailors, however, believed that the world was round because a ship seemed to become lower and lower on the horizon as it sailed away.

Columbus needed money so he went to see the Spanish King and Queen. They were interested but took a long time to decide. Columbus demanded ten percent of all treasure that he found there and this shocked Queen Isabella and King Ferdinand but finally they agreed. They gave him two ships and money to make this journey. In 1492 Columbus set sail with the *Nina*, the *Pinta* and the *Santa Maria*. This last ship was a ship he had rented and as it was the largest, he was travelling on it. Each ship had an interpreter who knew some of the language that people spoke in Asia.

For three weeks he and his men saw no land. Columbus did not tell his crew about the distance they travelled each day. He did not want them to guess that he did not know exactly where they were going. Then, on October 12, they reached an island near America which Columbus called San Salvador. After leaving San Salvador Columbus discovered the islands of Cuba and Haiti where he left some men. When he returned to Spain he was given a hero's welcome.

1 Christopher Columbus wanted to see if he could find a new continent. T/F? ....

2 He sailed west to reach Asia. T/F? ....

3 Some people thought the world was round. T/F? ....

4 Many people believed that you would meet with disaster if you sailed too far. T/F? ....

5 The Spanish King and Queen agreed to help with the journey at once. T/F? ....

6 Isabella and Ferdinand gave him all his ships. T/F? ....

7 Columbus thought some of his men would be able to speak to the local people when he found land. T/F? ....

8 Columbus did not know how far they travelled each day. T/F? ....

9 They reached the American continent on October 12. T/F? ....

10 The Spanish people were very pleased with him when he returned from his journey. T/F? ....

...../10 marks

Progress tests
Part 3: Writing [10 marks]

Your class has won a competition. The prize is a lot of money for your school. Say what you would do with the money and give reasons why. You may use some or all of the ideas in the box to help you. Write 60–80 words.

> build a new library
> create a computer room
> buy new equipment for the gym
> give the teachers some presents
> paint the school

...../10 marks

Test total ... /80 marks = ...%

Progress tests: Answers

Progress test 1
Units 1–8

Part 1: Grammar and vocabulary
[50 marks]

1
1 c
2 b
3 d
4 b
5 d
6 a
7 c
8 d
9 b
10 d
...../10 marks

2
1 couldn't speak
2 could learn
3 could you really swim
4 couldn't watch
5 couldn't ride
...../5 marks

3
1 was looking
2 broke
3 was watching
4 cleaned
5 jumped
6 was
...../6 marks

4
1 more quickly
2 much harder
3 as good
4 less exciting
5 later
6 earlier
...../6 marks

5
1 isn't it?
2 haven't you?
3 can't they?
4 didn't he?
5 hasn't she?
6 aren't you?
7 aren't they?
8 could she?
9 weren't we?
10 don't they?
.../10 marks

6
1 long, red, woollen
2 expensive, leather
3 large, white, cotton
4 small, blue
5 cheap, plastic
...../5 marks

7
1 has lived
2 gave
3 haven't finished
4 has just stopped
5 did not (or didn't) go
6 have you ever found
7 caught
8 have not (or haven't) eaten
...../8 marks

Part 2: Reading
[10 marks]

1 F
2 F
3 F
4 T
5 F
6 T
7 T
8 F
9 F
10 T
...../10 marks

Part 3: Writing
[10 marks]

Student generated answer. Look for correct syntax, correct grammar, correct use of vocabulary, complete subject matter and correct length.
...../10 marks

Grammar and vocabulary ...../50 marks
Reading ...../10 marks
Writing ...../10 marks
Total: Progress test 1
...../70 marks = ...%

Progress test 2
Units 9–16

Part 1: Grammar and vocabulary
[50 marks]

1
1 d
2 c
3 b
4 d
5 d
6 a
7 b
8 d
9 a
10 c
11 b
12 a
...../12 marks

2
1 much
2 few
3 many
4 many
5 little
6 enough
7 much
8 few
...../8 marks

3
1 are going to visit
2 I'll arrive
3 will probably take
4 I'll show
5 is she going to do
6 won't make
...../6 marks

4
1 had to
2 have to
3 Does she have to
4 didn't have to
5 doesn't have to
6 Do we have to (or Will we have to)
...../6 marks

5
1 environment
2 rubbish
3 glass
4 collect
5 recycle
...../5 marks

6
1 used to live
2 didn't use to travel
3 used to be
4 used to talk
5 used to listen
6 used to go
7 used to live
...../7 marks

7
1 to bring
2 not to arrive
3 saying
4 to buy
5 staying
6 making
...../6 marks

Part 2: Reading
[10 marks]

a)
1 F
2 F
3 T
4 F
5 F
6 T
7 F
...../7 marks

b)
Some suggested answers:
He should start his homework quickly after lunch.
He shouldn't turn on his radio.
He shouldn't lie on his bed.
He shouldn't talk to his friends for so long on the phone.
He shouldn't watch television if he hasn't finished his homework
...../3marks

Progress tests: Answers

Part 3: Writing
[10 marks]

Student generated answer. Look for correct syntax, correct grammar, correct use of vocabulary, complete subject matter and correct length.
...../10 marks

Grammar and vocabulary ...../50 marks
Reading ...../10 marks
Writing ...../10 marks
Total: Progress test 2 ...../70 marks = ...%

Progress test 3
Units 17–23

Part 1: Grammar and vocabulary
[60 marks]

1
1 d
2 b
3 c
4 b
5 c
6 b
7 d
8 a
9 c
10 b
11 c
12 d
...../12 marks

2
1 feel
2 will understand
3 would you do
4 play
5 has
6 were (or was)
7 would you visit
8 found
9 will get
10 would revise
...../10 marks

3
1 in
2 at
3 on
4 into
5 in
6 to
7 at
8 to
...../8 marks

4
1 must be
2 can't be
3 must be
4 can't be
5 can't be
6 must be
...../6 marks

5
1 since   4 since
2 since   5 for
3 for   6 for
...../6 marks

6
1 have you been waiting
2 do you do
3 did you send
4 have been drawing, do we know
5 have been reading
6 does she usually cycle
7 did they take
8 have been trying, don't know
...../10 marks

7
1 to interview
2 learning
3 to be
4 speaking
5 to change
6 walking
7 visit
8 to buy
9 making
10 to travel
...../10 marks

Part 2: Reading
[10 marks]

1 F   6 T
2 T   7 F
3 F   8 T
4 F   9 T
5 T   10 F

Part 3: Writing
[10 marks]

Student generated answer. Look for correct syntax, correct grammar, correct use of vocabulary, complete subject matter and correct length.
...../10 marks

Grammar and vocabulary ...../60 marks
Reading ...../10 marks
Writing ...../10 marks
Total: Progress test 3 ...../80 marks = ...%

End of book test

Part 1: Grammar and Vocabulary
[70 marks]

1
1 c
2 b
3 d
4 c
5 c
6 a
7 d
8 b
9 d
10 a
...../10 marks

2
1 map
2 scientist
3 find
4 shirt
5 waiter
6 invitation
7 holiday
8 noise
9 moon
10 lorry
...../10 marks

3
1 has just finished
2 were washing
3 solved
4 have been travelling
5 did
6 has been
7 did Anna like
8 was Chris doing
9 have been living/have lived
10 won
...../10 marks

4
1 What's it like
2 Why don't we
3 I don't think so
4 I'd rather
5 Would you mind
6 doesn't it?
7 as dangerous as
8 How embarrassing!
9 How much
10 too much
...../10 marks

5
1 The
2 a
3 the
4 the
5 the
6 no article
7 no article
8 A
9 the
10 a
11 no article
12 the
13 the
14 a
15 the
16 the
17 a
18 an
19 no article
20 the
...../20 marks

6
1 on
2 in
3 on
4 with
5 to
6 at
...../6 marks

7
1 You have put too much sugar in my coffee.
2 The history quiz was easier than I expected.
3 Isabel has got a white cotton baseball hat.
4 How many places have the Robinsons visited?
...../4 marks

Part 2: Reading
[10 marks]

1 F   6 F
2 T   7 T
3 T   8 F
4 T   9 F
5 F   10 T
.…/10 marks

Part 3: Writing
[10 marks]

Student generated answer. Look for correct syntax. correct grammar, correct use of vocabulary, complete subject matter and correct length.
…/10 marks

Grammar and vocabulary ...../70 marks
Reading ...../10 marks
Writing ...../10 marks
Total: Progress test 3 ...../90 marks = ...%

Test book key

Test 1

Units 1–3

1 mark is given for each correct answer unless otherwise stated.

A Vocabulary and structure — 60 marks

1
1 b
2 b
3 c
4 c
5 a
6 d
7 c
8 a
9 d
10 d

10 marks

2
1 am writing
2 moved
3 needs
4 is painting
5 is doing
6 is resting
7 were moving
8 came
9 said
10 met
11 was going
12 were going
13 asked
14 Did you enjoy
15 didn't have

15 marks

3
1 When did you go to Spain?
2 How often does John go to the cinema?
3 Is the machine working?
4 What were you doing when I called?
5 What are you doing?
6 Where did she stay?
7 What were you watching at four o'clock yesterday afternoon?
8 What did you do last night?
9 Why are you running?
10 Where does Charles work?

2 marks for each correct answer = 20 marks

4
1 longer than
2 higher than
3 not as fast as/less fast than
4 newer
5 not as expensive as/less expensive than

5 marks

5
1 holidays
2 penfriend
3 information
4 sightseeing
5 comfortable
6 beaches
7 fantastic
8 compared
9 expensive
10 travel

10 marks

B Reading and writing — 40 marks

1 T   6 T
2 F   7 F
3 T   8 T
4 F   9 F
5 T   10 F

10 marks

2
1 Because the lift wasn't working and the stairs were full of smoke.
2 They opened a window and shouted for help.
3 Because the building was getting hotter and hotter.
4 They climbed down a/the fire-engine's ladder.
5 Because she wants to rest there for a week before she goes home.

2 marks for each correct answer = 10 marks

3 20 marks

Vocabulary and structure ...../60 marks
Reading and writing ...../40 marks
Total ...../100 marks

Test 2

Units 4–6

A Vocabulary and structure — 60 marks

1
1 b   6 b
2 c   7 a
3 a   8 c
4 b   9 b
5 d   10 d

10 marks

269

Test book key

2
1 went
2 Have you seen
3 have lived
4 worked
5 came
6 hasn't written
7 saw
8 Did you speak
9 gave
10 Have you read

10 marks

3
1 harder than
2 less seriously than
3 earlier than
4 more loudly than
5 not as friendly as/less friendly than

5 marks

4
1 long, red, woollen
2 small, traditional, wooden
3 large, black, German
4 short-sleeved, yellow, cotton
5 small, green, sports

5 marks

5
1 Have you visited the new museum yet?
2 What did you do yesterday?
3 How long has he lived here?
4 What are the Greeks like?
5 When did they see the film?
6 How many pages have you written so far?
7 How often do you go on holiday?
8 Why didn't Tom go to work?
9 Where did Richard and Ben go last week?
10 Have you (ever) lived in Australia?

2 marks for each correct answer = 20 marks

6
1 ancient
2 library
3 helpful
4 interesting/exciting
5 busy
6 exciting/interesting
7 find out
8 discoveries
9 bones
10 differences

10 marks

B Reading and writing 40 marks

1
1 They believe that they are animals which we don't know about and that live at the bottom of the loch.
2 They believe that Nessie has lived there since pre-historic times/for many years.
3 Because Loch Ness is deep, very cold and dark.
4 Because for most of the last million years, Loch Ness was under ice more than a kilometre deep.
5 It must have travelled across land (to reach the loch).

2 marks for each correct answer = 10 marks

2
1 F
2 T
3 F
4 T
5 F
6 F
7 F
8 F
9 T
10 F

10 marks

3 20 marks

Vocabulary and structure ...../60 marks
Reading and writing ...../40 marks
Total ...../100 marks

Test 3
Units 7–8

A Vocabulary and structure 60 marks

1
1 b   6 d
2 a   7 a
3 c   8 a
4 b   9 d
5 a   10 c

10 marks

2
1 could, has learnt
2 Did you see, came, were watching, missed
3 haven't you visited, am studying, don't have
4 wasn't working, was able, came
5 is staying, stays
6 haven't you

1 mark for each correct verb = 15 marks

3
1 g   6 e
2 j   7 f
3 b   8 c
4 h   9 d
5 a   10 i

10 marks

4
1 Could you understand him?
2 Where was he able to hide?
3 How often/When do you eat cornflakes?
4 What could Mozart do when he was four?
5 Which exercise are you doing?
6 Where have they gone?
7 How did she come to work?
8 How were you able to get out?
9 Who was making the noise?
10 How do you get on with Mary?

10 marks

5
1 haven't you
2 didn't he
3 can she
4 are they
5 aren't I

5 marks

Test book key

6
1 building
2 owner
3 boring
4 giraffe
5 get up
6 normal
7 destroy
8 future
9 raincoat
10 safe

10 marks

B Reading and writing
40 marks

1 Suggested answers
1 He was from Italy.
2 They were trying to find a way to reach China, Japan and India.
3 He believed this because the earth was round.
4 He asked them for money.
5 The King and Queen of Spain gave him money.
6 He had three ships.
7 They were afraid because they couldn't find land.
8 They have this name because Columbus believed they were Indians.
9 He made four journeys altogether.
10 He died in Spain.

2 marks for each correct answer
20 marks

2 20 marks

Vocabulary and structure ...../60 marks
Reading and writing ...../40 marks
Total ...../100 marks

Test 4
Units 9–11

A Vocabulary and structure   60 marks

1
1 b
2 c
3 c
4 a
5 c
6 d
7 a
8 b
9 b
10 d

10 marks

2
1 will rain
2 going to be
3 hasn't finished
4 am visiting
5 was sleeping
6 are you going
7 didn't come
8 goes
9 have finished
10 going to live

10 marks

3
1 Where are you going this weekend?
2 Do you think it will snow?
3 How many players are there in a team?
4 What's he going to watch tonight?
5 Who's Mary going to phone?
6 What is she doing on Saturday?
7 Is there enough tea?
8 What would you like to do today?
9 Will you take my/our photo?
10 Where would you like to go for your holiday?

2 marks for each correct answer = 20 marks

4
1 There isn't enough coffee for everyone.
2 There are too many people on this bus.
3 Would you like to come to our house this weekend?
4 Is there enough food for us all?
5 (Please) Could you turn off the radio, (please)?
6 (Next week) he's flying to Scotland (next week).
7 I'm afraid I can't come to work tomorrow.
8 There was too much noise in the classroom.
9 I'm going to tell Robert the good news tonight.
10 She had very little money in her purse.

10 marks

5
1 get up
2 metal
3 boring
4 weather
5 return
6 wool
7 leave
8 dig
9 full
10 contain

10 marks

B Reading and writing
40 marks

1
1 F
2 T
3 T
4 F
5 F
6 T
7 F
8 F
9 T
10 T

10 marks

2
1 He works for a travel agency.
2 He must go on the holiday first to make sure that nothing will go wrong and that people will be comfortable and enjoy themselves.
3 He travelled there on a sailing-boat.
4 He is going (to go) on a safari to take photos of wild animals.
5 He doesn't have difficulty communicating because he speaks eight languages.

2 marks for each correct answer = 10 marks

3 20 marks

Vocabulary and structure ...../60 marks
Reading and writing ...../40 marks
Total ...../100 marks

Test 5
Units 12–14

A Vocabulary and structure   60 marks

1
1 b
2 c
3 a
4 b
5 d
6 c
7 a
8 b
9 c
10 d

10 marks

Test book key

2
1. The first aeroplane was built by the Wright Brothers.
2. The school is opened at eight o'clock every morning.
3. They are taught history three times a week.
4. The pupils were taken round the museum by the guide.
5. The rubbish is collected from our street every morning.
6. The telephone was invented by Alexander Graham Bell.
7. The cat is fed twice a day.
8. The windows are washed every Saturday morning.
9. The painting was finished before lunch.
10. The letters were kept in a drawer.

10 marks

3
1. What should I do?
2. Do you/we have to do any homework?
3. Where are Fiat cars made?
4. What do we have to do?
5. Could they catch the thief?
6. How many poems did they have to learn?
7. How much has Roger spent?
8. Which one's the best?
9. How often/When are the roads cleaned?
10. Do you think he'll come?

10 marks

4
1. i
2. a
3. e
4. g
5. b
6. j
7. c
8. f
9. h
10. d

10 marks

5
1. earthquake
2. damage
3. village
4. destroyed
5. floor
6. Unfortunately
7. electricity
8. candles
9. adventure
10. brave

10 marks

6
1. Could you
2. shouldn't
3. has to
4. I don't think
5. couldn't
6. Would you like
7. I think
8. had to
9. don't have to
10. should

10 marks

B Reading and writing   40 marks

1
1. T
2. F
3. F
4. T
5. F
6. T
7. T*
8. F
9. T
10. F

10 marks

2
1. You have to speak French and German, and you have to travel a lot.
2. She speaks French very well, but she's forgotten most of her German.
3. She likes her house and she doesn't like staying in strange hotels all the time.
4. She'd rather get an ordinary job in an office here.
5. She thinks she'll apply for the job.

2 marks for each correct answer = 10 marks

3 20 marks

Vocabulary and structure
                ...../60 marks
Reading and writing
                ...../40 marks
Total ...../100 marks

Test 6
Units 15–16

A Vocabulary and structure   60 marks

1
1. shy
2. slim
3. avoid
4. traffic
5. run out of
6. deep
7. fall in
8. fell over
9. hurt
10. headache

10 marks

2
1. c
2. a
3. d
4. b
5. d

10 marks

3
1. staying
2. to post
3. to finish
4. writing
5. to buy

5 marks

4
1. Some money was stolen from my drawer.
2. I am driven to school every day.
3. We were told not to go out at night.
4. His letters are typed for him.
5. She is given a present every Christmas.

2 marks for each correct answer = 10 marks

5
1. You don't have to wear a uniform at this school.
2. It might rain tomorrow.
3. You should not phone me in the morning.
4. You could get lost without a map.
5. I didn't have a map, so I had to ask someone.

2 marks for each correct answer = 10 marks

Test book key

6
1. How did you use to go to school?
2. When did John paint the house?
3. What did John paint last week?
4. Who painted the house last week?
5. How many pieces of chocolate would you like?
6. How long have they known Richard?
7. Could you do the exercise?
8. Where does she go every weekend?
9. Did you use to work there?
10. What should he do?

10 marks

7
1. Nowadays/Now
2. leaf
3. dirty
4. abroad
5. brigade
6. look
7. bottled
8. advice
9. Avoid
10. cause

10 marks

B Reading and writing   40 marks

1
1	f	6	g
2	b	7	a
3	d	8	j
4	i	9	e
5	c	10	h

2 marks for each correct answer = 20 marks

2 20 marks

Vocabulary and structure
               ...../60 marks
Reading and writing
               ...../40 marks
Total ...../100 marks

Test 7
Units 17–19

A Vocabulary and structure   60 marks

1
1	c	6	d
2	a	7	b
3	c	8	a
4	b	9	b
5	b	10	c

10 marks

2
1. Have you seen
2. have been working
3. were you doing, saw
4. moved
5. has been writing, hasn't finished
6. wrote, hasn't replied, have been waiting

1 mark for each correct verb = 10 marks

3
1. If the weather is good, we'll go for a picnic.
2. He'll go to university if he gets good marks in his exams.
3. If you go out, put your hat and coat on.
4. If you visit Maggie, don't forget to give her this book.
5. I'll come and see you if I have time.

2 marks for each correct answer = 10 marks

4
1. How long have you been learning English?
2. What have you been doing all day?
3. Did you use to walk to school?
4. What will you do if he doesn't come?
5. Who's been using my camera?

2 marks for each correct answer = 10 marks

5
1. competition
2. prize
3. dishwasher
4. scientist
5. important
6. medicine
7. all over the world
8. popular
9. neighbours
10. looks after

10 marks

6
1	set	6	once
2	During	7	heights
3	prize	8	unusual
4	robbery	9	rainforest
5	equipment	10	scientist

10 marks

B Reading and writing   40 marks

1 Suggested answers
1. It was a monster with a human's body and a bull's head.
2. It belonged to King Minos and it was kept under the ground in a labyrinth.
3. He sent seven boys and seven girls from Athens into the tunnels to the Minotaur.
4. The people of Athens killed his son, Androgeos.
5. He designed the labyrinth where the Minotaur was kept.
6. He made some wings and flew away.
7. He flew too near the sun, his wings melted and he fell into the sea.
8. He was sure he could kill the Minotaur.
9. She gave him a ball of thread to find his way out of the labyrinth.
10. There was an earthquake, the King's palace fell down, the labyrinth was destroyed and the body of the Minotaur was buried for ever.

2 marks for each correct answer = 20 marks

Vocabulary and structure
               ...../60 marks
Reading and writing
               ...../40 marks
Total ...../100 marks

Test book key

Test 8

Units 20–22

A Vocabulary and structure 60 marks

1
1. d
2. a
3. d
4. c
5. b
6. b
7. d
8. a
9. b
10. d

10 marks

2
1. go/went, will catch/would catch
2. were, would buy
3. see, tell
4. will/would visit, have/had
5. would be able, were

1 mark for each correct verb = 10 marks

3
1. to give
2. driving
3. playing
4. making
5. to be

5 marks

4
1. -
2. the
3. a
4. a
5. an

5 marks

5
1. went
2. was already having
3. arrived
4. were even swimming
5. likes
6. has had
7. works
8. invites
9. am certainly going
10. has already invited

10 marks

6
1. What do you like doing at the weekends?
2. What would you do if you had a lot of money?
3. Have you spoken to John?
4. Where have they gone?
5. What will you do if there are no buses?
6. Did he manage to get a ticket?
7. How long has he been sleeping?
8. How often does she visit you?
9. Would you leave your job if you were rich?
10. When did you decide to go?

10 marks

7
1. stream
2. under
3. attack
4. hurt
5. popular
6. borrow
7. cabinets
8. wonderful
9. dive
10. save

10 marks

B Reading and writing 40 marks

1
1. If we didn't have its heat and light, there wouldn't be life here.
2. We get coal, gas and oil.
3. They have come from plants and animals that grew in sunlight millions of years ago.
4. They thought that the Sun was a god.
5. It has nine planets.
6. It is the galaxy that the Sun is in.
7. The nearest star is 4.3 light years away from us.
8. It is the distance that light travels in one year.
9. It would take 4.3 years.
10. It would take us 40,000 years.

2 marks for each correct answer = 20 marks

2 20 marks

Vocabulary and structure ...../60 marks
Reading and writing ...../40 marks
Total ...../100 marks

Test 9

Units 23–24

A Vocabulary and structure 60 marks

1
1. c
2. c
3. a
4. a
5. d
6. b
7. b
8. d
9. d
10. a

10 marks

2
1. have been standing
2. hasn't come
3. have you ever seen
4. met
5. was
6. have been talking
7. haven't been listening
8. was looking/have been looking
9. have gone
10. were you looking

10 marks

3
1. Where have you been for the last six months?
2. I've been studying very hard because I'm taking my final exams next month.
3. What will you do if you pass your exams?
4. I want to go to Britain for a few months to practise my English.
5. Have you ever been to Britain before?
6. No. It'll be my first time if I go.
7. I went to London last year and I enjoyed it very much.
8. Really? If you were offered a job there would you go?
9. No. The weather isn't warm enough for me.
10. Yes, and I was told by a friend last week that the people there aren't as friendly as the people here.

2 marks for each correct answer = 20 marks

Test book key

4
1. What were you doing when the bank was robbed?
2. What has he been doing all day?
3. When are you going to decide?
4. Why didn't they come?
5. Where are you going tonight?
6. Does she ever visit you?
7. How long did you did you stay there?
8. Will you tell Billy?
9. Why was she running?
10. How long have you lived here?

10 marks

5
1. witness
2. terrible
3. nervous
4. important
5. straight
6. opposite
7. bell
8. drove away
9. of course
10. headlines

10 marks

B Reading and writing 40 marks

1
1. e
2. c
3. j
4. g
5. b
6. a
7. h
8. f
9. i
10. d

2 marks for each correct answer = 20 marks

2 20 marks

Vocabulary and structure ...../60 marks
Reading and writing ...../40 marks
Total ...../100 marks

End of book test

A Vocabulary and structure 60 marks

1
1. c   6. a
2. b   7. d
3. b   8. a
4. d   9. c
5. c   10. b

10 marks

2
1. The bank robbers were arrested yesterday afternoon.
2. The dog is taken for a walk every morning and every evening.
3. These cars aren't made here any more.
4. We weren't told what to do.
5. Is English taught here?

5 marks

3
1. aren't, will fall
2. wouldn't do, were
3. were, would marry
4. see, tell
5. will/would visit, have/had

5 marks

4
1. was trying
2. caught
3. have been going
4. refuses
5. haven't learnt/don't learn/am not learning
6. to send
7. is taking
8. has happened
9. travels
10. will hear

10 marks

5
1. to take
2. not to go
3. playing
4. listening
5. to move

5 marks

6
1. d   2. a   3. e
4. b   5. c

5 marks

7
1. Where was he taken?
2. How long has she been waiting for me?
3. How did you have to go to town?
4. Who used to be your best friend at school?
5. Why can't it be Sid?
6. What is he going to talk about?
7. How many biscuits have you eaten today?
8. What are the village people like?
9. Which exam did you do yesterday?
10. How often/When do they come to see you?

10 marks

8
1. hide   6. plate
2. horrible   7. warm
3. brave   8. carry
4. imagine   9. attack
5. glue   10. look after

10 marks

B Reading and writing

1 Suggested answers
1. We don't expect them to work for us.
2. Because the person's hand was resting on the dog's shoulder.
3. The Pharoahs kept cats and dogs.
4. Because people lose interest in them.
5. You should get a goldfish.
6. Animals that live in cages usually don't live for a long time.
7. Because they need space.
8. Small animals are usually the cheapest to keep.
9. you should get a pet when you have your own home.
10. It will feel unhappy.

2 marks for each correct answer = 20 marks

2 20 marks

Vocabulary and structure ...../60 marks
Reading and writing ...../40 marks
Total ...../100 marks

Workbook answers

Unit 1

1a
1. live
2. stay
3. didn't stay
4. went
5. stay
6. stayed
7. was
8. had
9. went
10. played
11. is
12. want

1b
1. Where did you stay?
2. Who did you go with?
3. What did you do there?
4. How long did you stay?
5. Did you have a good time?

1c
1. Does he play beach tennis on holiday?
2. Did he play (beach tennis) yesterday?
3. Is he playing (beach tennis) now?

1d
1. is
2. are visiting
3. are staying
4. went
5. had
6. had
7. saw

1a
They sometimes lie on the beach. They usually go fishing. They sometimes go sailing. They usually play beach volleyball. They usually have a good time.

2a
1. Do you remember Nick and Helen?
2. Alexia and her brother usually stay in a hotel.
3. Nick didn't go skiiing this summer.
4. Is Helen having a good time?
5. Where do you want to go next year?
6. We arrived home last week?

2b
They stayed at the Paradise Hotel. They went swimming and sailing. They lay on the beach. They visited the town of Milos and they went sightseeing. They had a fantastic time!

2c
1. didn't go
2. didn't lie
3. wasn't
4. stayed
5. didn't stay

Words in action

3a
Things to do in the mountains: camping, skiing, climbing
Things to do on the beach: fishing, sailing, swimming
Things to do in town: sightseeing, dancing, shopping

3b
1. to
2. on
3. in
4. in
5. on
6. in
7. with
8. with
9. in
10. by
11. into

3c
1. They went with their parents. The weather was good. They stayed in a hotel. They went swimming and sightseeing.
2. She stayed there for two weeks in July. She went with her family The weather was bad. She stayed in a large hotel. She went dancing, sightseeing and to the cinema.

3d
Student generated answer

Unit 2

1a
I was walking   was I walking?
I was not/wasn't walking

you were walking   were you walking
you were not/weren't walking

he/she/it was walking
was he/she/it walking?
he/she/it was not/wasn't walking

we were walking   were we walking?
we were not/weren't walking

they were walking
were they walking?
they were not/weren't walking

1b
1. Were they watching TV? Yes, they were.
2. Was she lying on the beach? Yes, she was.
3. Was he swimming? No, he wasn't.
4. Were they having a picnic? Yes, they were.
5. Was she throwing rubbish into the sea? No, she wasn't.

1c
1. While she was sailing, she fell into the water.
2. They met some friends while they were walking.
3. While they were camping, they saw a forest fire.
4. He was visiting a museum when the vase broke.
5. While they were playing, a dolphin jumped out of the water.

1d
1. trip
2. cabin
3. harbour
4. sailing
5. waves
6. fishing

Workbook answers

2a
1. I was playing a computer game when the alien arrived.
2. I was reading a magazine when the alien arrived.
3. I was cooking when the alien arrived.
4. We were having lunch when the alien arrived.
5. I was watching TV when the alien arrived.

2b
1. We visited a museum while we were staying in London.
2. We were watching TV when there was a power failure.
3. We saw some nice shells while we were walking along the beach.
4. We were playing beach tennis when the ball went into the sea.

2c
1. was watching
2. looked
3. was
4. decided
5. was getting
6. heard
7. looked
8. was climbing
9. had

2d
Student generated answer

CHRIS Episode 1

3a
1. was
2. was working
3. had
4. decided
5. was using
6. had
7. decided
8. was going
9. was writing
10. took
11. finished
12. uses
13. is
14. is missing

3b
1. Yes, he liked computers when he was a student.
2. He was working every day after school.
3. He used his savings to pay for his first computer.
4. It took him months to write his first games programme.
5. He writes games programmes for Banana Computers.
6. He is missing at the moment.

3c
1. isn't
2. like
3. is talking
4. is giving
5. don't understand, is

Unit 3

1a
1. lighter
2. faster
3. more powerful
4. quieter
5. more comfortable
6. more dangerous

1b
1. as light as
2. as fast as
3. as powerful as
4. as quiet as
5. as comfortable as
6. as dangerous

1c
1. The sailing boat is the lightest.
2. The racing boat is the fastest.
3. The power boat is the most powerful.
4. The sailing boat is the quietest.
5. The power boat is the most comfortable.
6. The racing boat is the most dangerous.

1d
1. the fastest
2. longest
3. more comfortable
4. comfortable
5. faster
6. quiet
7. more dangerous
8. dangerous

1e
Student generated answer

2a
1. c
2. g
3. h
4. d
5. f
6. b
7. a

2b
1. big enough
2. too heavy
3. fast enough
4. too old
5. too dangerous

2c
1. Skateboarding isn't safe enough.
2. They aren't small enough.
3. Mountain bikes are too slow.
4. The students are too noisy.
5. The box isn't light enough.
6. Your hands are too dirty.

Check up: Units 1–3

3a
1. are having
2. isn't
3. rains
4. is raining
5. are staying
6. go

3b
She went shopping. She went to a disco and she wrote postcards.

3c
A man was sitting on a bench. He was reading a newspaper. Two people were talking. Oh, yes. Two children were climbing a tree. A girl was putting rubbish in a rubbish bin. And there was a boy. He was running.

Unit 4

1a
I have/'ve been   have I been?
I have not/haven't been

you have/'ve been   have you been?
you have not/haven't been

he/she/it has/'s been   has he/she/it been?
he/she/it has not/hasn't been

we have/'ve been   have we been?
we have not/haven't been

they have/'ve been   have they been?
they have not/haven't been

1b
1. have you ever fallen?
2. have you ever played?
3. have you ever collected?
4. have you ever eaten?
5. have you ever visited?
6. have you ever met?
7. have you ever written?
8. have you ever seen?

1c
1. We have cooked supper. We haven't eaten it yet.
2. She has had Spanish lessons. She hasn't visited Spain.
3. I haven't sent a letter to my penfriend. I haven't written one yet.
4. They haven't met him yet. They have spoken to him on the phone.
5. He hasn't done his homework yet. He hasn't had the time.

Workbook answers

2a
3 She has had breakfast.
4 She hasn't cleaned the carpet.
5 She has written a letter to her penfriend.
6 She hasn't eaten lunch.
7 She hasn't fed Woofa.

2b
Student generated answers

2c
1 He has just fallen off
2 They have just painted
3 They have just cleaned
4 Woofa has just bitten
5 She has just dropped

2d
1 I have done them all.
2 Have you tidied your room yet?
3 I have just done it.
4 Have you fed Woofa?
5 He hasn't eaten all day.
6 Have you seen him?
7 I have been very busy.
8 Have you done your homework yet?
9 Woofa has just eaten it!

2e
1 I have/haven't eaten
2 I have/haven't read
3 I have/haven't played
4 I have/haven't walked
5 I have haven't done
6 I have/haven't cleaned

Words in action

3a
2 c
3 a
4 b

3b
1 metres
2 times
3 years
4 degrees
5 kilometre

3c
1 Have you ever done an easy job? I have/haven't done an easy job.
2 Have you ever eaten tasty food? I have/haven't eaten tasty food.
3 Have you ever sent a postcard to a friend? I have/haven't sent a postcard to a friend.
4 Have you ever taken a photograph of a green elephant? I have/haven't taken a photograph of a green elephant.

Unit 5

1a
2 I live in London now.
3 I don't live in London now.
4 I live in London.
5 I don't live in London now.
6 haven't finished

1b
1 started
2 have had
3 started
4 have been
5 have been
6 haven't finished

1c
1 was
2 erupted
3 covered
4 discovered
5 found
6 began
7 have uncovered
8 have learnt/learned
9 have uncovered
10 have found
11 lived

1d
1 since
2 ago
3 for
4 yet
5 ago
6 since

2a
2 yes
3 yes
4 no
5 no

2b
1 Has she worked at the museum since she was ten? No, she hasn't.
2 Has she been an archeologist for ten years? Yes, she has.
3 Did she go on a dig last summer? Yes, she did.
4 Has she ever taken photographs of things from digs? Yes, she has.
5 Has all her work been routine? No, it hasn't.
6 Did workers find a Roman building under the museum in 1988? Yes, they did.

2c
1 dig
2 records
3 photos
4 drawings
5 history
6 coins
7 wall

2d
Student generated answer

CHRIS Episode 2

3a
1 b
2 b
3 b
4 a
5 a

3b
1 CHRIS is faster than the Wellington.
2 CHRIS isn't as old as the Wellington.
3 CHRIS is more useful than the Wellington.
4 The Wellington isn't as big as CHRIS.
5 The Wellington isn't as expensive as CHRIS.

Unit 6

1a
1 What's the food like?
2 What was the weather like on Saturday?
3 What's the weather like today?
4 What are the people like?

1b
1 tasty
2 interesting
3 expensive
4 busy
5 difficult
6 great

1c
2 adverb
3 adverb
4 adjective
5 adjective
6 adverb

1d
1 He goes running as often on the boat as he did in England.
2 He writes letters less often on the boat than he did in England.
3 He tidies his cabin/room as often on the boat as he did in England.
4 He does his homework as often on the boat as he did in England.
5 He watches TV less often on the boat than he did in England.
6 He reads books more often on the boat than he did in England.
7 He goes swimming more often on the boat than he did in England.

2a
size:	large, long, small
colour:	green, red, yellow
type:	short-sleeved, traditional, waterproof
material:	leather, plastic, wool

Workbook answers

2b
1. A long grey skirt.
2. (A pair of) white cotton shorts.
3. A small grey leather jacket.
4. A large wool pullover.
5. A long black waterproof raincoat.

2c
1. try on
2. fit
3. looks
4. is
5. costs

2d
Student generated answer

Check-up: Units 4–6

3a
1. have done
2. have visited
3. have stayed
4. has eaten
5. have climbed
6. have travelled
7. have seen
8. have had

3b
1. have just discovered
2. have not finished
3. has been
4. hasn't visited, visited
5. came, made, began
6. haven't found

3c
1. People in Bermuda take things less seriously than people in England.
2. I don't dress as casually as my sister.
3. That car goes faster than this car.
4. It doesn't rain as often in Bermuda as it does in London.
5. My brother works harder than I do/me.
6. My friend doesn't go to school as early as I do/me.

Unit 7

1a
I could walk   could I walk?
I could not/couldn't walk

you could walk   could you walk?
you could not/couldn't walk

he/she/it could walk
could he/she/it walk?
he/she/it could not/couldn't walk

we could walk   could we walk?
we could not/couldn't walk

they could walk   could they walk?
they could not/couldn't walk

1b
1. couldn't use
2. couldn't find
3. could see
4. couldn't understand
5. couldn't eat
6. couldn't visit
7. could go

1c
1. She couldn't use the computer yesterday but she can use it today.
2. They couldn't watch TV yesterday but they can watch it today.
3. He could wear the shirt yesterday but he can't wear it today.

1d
Student generated answers

2a
3. She wasn't able to take Woofa for a walk.
4. She was able to put the rubbish in the bin.
5. She was able to phone her friend.
6. She was able to cook something for supper.
7. She wasn't able to plan her summer holiday.
8. She was able to do her homework.

2b
1. Was Hank Williams able to talk on his spacesuit radio? No, he wasn't.
2. Was Hank Williams able to return to the space shuttle? Yes, he was.
3. Was P.J Kirby able to walk in space? Yes, she was.
4. Was P.J Kirby able to repair a satellite? Yes, she was.
5. Was B. Rogers able to repair the shuttle's computer? No, he wasn't.
6. Were the astronauts able to stay in space after the computer failed? No, they weren't.
7. Were they able to stay in space for six days? No, they weren't.
8. Were the astronauts able to return to the earth? Yes, they were.

Words in action

3a
1. was able to
2. can
3. could
4. was able to
5. were able to
6. could

3b
1. g
2. b
3. a
4. f
5. d
6. e

3c
1. telephones
2. cameras
3. pens and paper
4. rockets
5. telescopes
6. satellites

Unit 8

1a
1. doesn't he
2. hasn't he
3. can he
4. isn't he
5. do you
6. does she
7. aren't I
8. are they

1c
1. aren't you
2. is she
3. isn't it
4. can she
5. hasn't she
6. don't they
7. aren't they
8. do they

2a
1. did she, No she didn't
2. didn't he, Yes, he did
3. did she, No, she didn't

2b
1. wasn't he? Yes, he was.
2. did they? Yes, they did.
3. did they? Yes, they did.
4. didn't they? No, they didn't.
5. didn't they? No, they didn't.
6. was he? Yes, he was.

CHRIS Episode 3

3a
1. hard
2. harder
3. seriously
4. casually
5. friendly

Workbook answers

3b
1. wrote
2. took
3. wasn't
4. met
5. liked
6. has worked
7. haven't seen
8. has just disappeared
9. has left

3c
1. didn't you
2. did you
3. isn't it
4. have you
5. can't you

Consolidation 1

1
1. bought
2. takes
3. stayed
4. received
5. watching
6. talks

2
1. went
2. turned
3. sat
4. began
5. was doing
6. fell
7. looked
8. was looking
9. fell

3
1. Have you ever been, went
2. Did you finish, finished
3. Has Tony cleaned
4. has lost, did he lose
5. Did you go shopping, haven't been shopping.

Unit 9

1a
1. are going sightseeing
2. visiting the scince museum
3. are climbing the Statue of Liberty
4. am going shopping
5. are watching a baseball game
6. are returning to London

1b
1. Are Wendy and her brother visiting the science museum on Wednesday? Yes, thet are. They're visiting the science museum on Wednesday.
2. Are Wendy's family going sightseeing on Thursday? No, they aren't. They're climbiing the Statue of Lberty on Thursday.
3. Are Wendy's father and her brother watching baseball game on Friday? Yes, they are. They're watching a baseball game on Friday.
4. Are they flying home on Saturday? Yes, they are. They're flying home on Saturday.

1c
1. are returning
2. are visiting
3. aren't coming
4. are staying
5. am going shopping
6. are giving
7. are leaving
8. are sailing

1d
Student generated answer

2a
1. I'm going
2. Jason and I are taking
3. Are you doing
4. I'm studying
5. I'm doing
6. Is he doing
7. He's halping

2b
1. see
I'd like to. I really like going to the cinema.
2. go
I'd love to but I'm having dinner at a friends house this evening.
3. take
Sorry. I don't really like animals.
4. play
I'd really like to. I haven't played in a match for years.

2c
1. Would you like to go shopping on Monday morning?
(any accurate refusal)
2. Would you like to come to my house on Sunday?
(any accurate refusal)
3. Would you like to go to a concert tonight?
(any accurate acceptance)
4. Would you like to see a play on Friday evening?
(any accurate refusal)

Words in action

3a
1. is going
2. is not coming
3. is returning
4. Is she doing
5. is going
6. Is she going
7. is not doing

3b
Students choose three answers from the following:
Would you like to go to the swimming pool on Tuesday? Sorry, but I can't. I'm studying for a test.
Would you like to go to see a play on Wednesday? Sorry, but I can't. I'm playing tennis.
Would you like to go to the museum on Thursday? Sorry, but I can't. I'm listening to music.
Would you like to walk in the woods on Friday? Sorry, but I can't. I'm visiting my grandparents.
Would you like to come to a party on Saturday? Sorry, but i can't. I'm going out with my family.
Would you like to visit our friends on Sunday? Sorry, but I can't. I'm staying at home on Sunday.

Unit 10

1a
We eat: crisps, eggs, hamburgers, sandwiches, tomatoes,
We drink: coffee, lemonade, milk, orange juice, tea, wine.

1b
1. eat
2. tea
3. drink
4. plate
5. bean
6. kilos

1c
1. A cup of tea
2. A kilo of fish
3. A glass of water
4. A loaf of breadl
5. A plate of vegetables

1d
1. many chickens
2. many potatoes
3. much rice
4. much bread
5. much olive oil
6. much lemonade
7. much ice-cream
8. many paper plates
9. many plastic glasses

Workbook answers

2a
1 There are too many plates.
2 There aren't enough glasses.
3 There isn't enough lemonade.
4 There aren't enough sandwiches.
5 There isn't enough bread.
6 There aren't enough biscuits.
7 There's too much ice-cream.

2b
1 There are too many people
2 There's too much noise.
3 There are too many vegetables.

2c
1 weren't enough chairs
2 was too much salt
3 weren't enough paper plates
4 wasn't enough food
5 weren't enough cassettes

2d
Student generated answer

CHRIS Episode 4

3a
2 too many
3 enough
4 very few
5 too much

3b
1 are going back
2 are going
3 are you leaving
4 are you getting
5 are catching
6 Are you meeting

Unit 11

1a
1 will take
2 will arrive
3 will have
4 will need
5 will have
6 will make
7 will show
8 will be
9 will get

1b
1 What time will we get to the museum?
2 Will Mr Brown make a video of the trip?
3 Will you give us any homework?
4 What will the weather be like?
5 When will we get back exactly?/When exactly will we get back?

1c
1 We'll get to the museum at (about) ten o'clock.
2 Yes, Mr Brown will take a video of the trip.
3 No, we won't give you any homework tomorrow.
4 It'll be quite cool tomorrow.
5 We'll get back at six o'clock in the evening.

1d
1 She isn't going to go shopping.
2 She is going to wash her hair.
3 She is going to tidy her bedroom.
4 She isn't going to write an article for Brilliant.
5 She is going to phone Jane.

1e
Student generated answer
1 f
2 a
3 d
4 c

2a
1 Could you
2 Would you mind
3 Would you mind
4 Would you mind
5 Would you mind
6 Could you

2b
1 Can you close the window?
2 Could you tell me the way?
3 Would you mind taking/you take a/my photograph?

2c
a 1
b 3
c 2

Check up: Units 9–11

3a
She is having lunch with Steven on Saturday. She's having a guitar lesson at three o'clock on Saturday afternoon. She's playing tennis with Dave at eleven o'clock on Sunday morning. She's going to the cinema with Mary. She is meeting her outside at seven o'clock on Sunday evening.

3b
1 is going to organize
2 are going to check
3 are going to make
4 are going to interview
5 is going to take
6 is going to write

3c
1 she'll give
2 will she have
3 She won't have
4 she'll probably talk
5 she won't disturb
6 she'll leave
7 We'll see

3d
1 There is very little rice.
2 There are a lot of beans.
3 There are very few eggs.
4 There is a little olive oil.

Unit 12

1a
2 They have to start school at 9.00 in the morning.
3 They have to do homework every night.
4 They don't have to go to school at the weekend.
5 They don't have to study in the library after school.
6 They have to work hard.

1b
1 She doesn't have to wear a school uniform.
2 She doesn't have to bring lunch from home.
3 She doesn't have to pay for the museum.
4 She has to do a history project.
5 She doesn't have to write notes in the museum.
6 She has to give her project to Mr Brown.

1c
1 g
2 e
3 f
4 c
5 h
6 d
7 a

2a
1 They couldn't find a hotel so they had to ask the way.
2 She couldn't open the door so she had to climb through the window.
3 They couldn't play outside so they had to watch a video.
4 He couldn't sleep so he had to close the curtains.
5 They couldn't lift the piano so they had to get some help.

Workbook answers

2b
1. I have to do my
2. I didn't have to tidy my bedroom.
3. I had to go to school with my brother.
4. I have to help with the housework.
5. I have to look after Woofa.

2c
Student generated answer

Words in action

3a
1. She has to take Woofa for a walk.
2. She has to take a tape to the video library.
3. She doesn't have to get milk.
4. She has to tidy her bedroom.
5. She has to do her homework.

3b
1. He had to get some money.
2. She had to buy some food.
3. He had to return a tape.
4. He had to buy some new football boots.
5. They had to borrow a book.

3c
2. b
3. b
4. a
5. b
6. a

Unit 13

1a
1. are made from textiles
2. is made from glass
3. are made from paper
4. are made from metal
5. are made from plastic

1b
1. is buried
2. is recycled
3. is used
4. are taken
5. are put
6. is collected
7. is sold
8. is used
9. are made
10. is wasted

1c
1. One bin is used for organic waste.
2. The second bin is filled with the other rubbish.
3. The organic waste is (usually) thrown into the sea.
4. The other rubbish is kept on the boat.
5. The rubbish is separated when we arrive in harbour.
6. The recyclable rubbish is put in a recycling bin.
7. Glass bottles are taken to a bottle bank.

1d
1. Rubbish is sold by SORT.
2. Recycled paper is used by factories to make newspapers and books.
3. Poisonous smog in big cities is caused by car exhaust fumes.
4. Famous old buildings are damaged by pollution and chemicals.
5. Forests are destroyed by pollution.
6. A lot of rubbish is thrown away by people.

2a
1. was built
2. was completed
3. was damaged
4. was sold
5. was owned
6. was bought
7. was put
8. was opened

2b
1. were given
2. was called
3. was read
4. was given
5. were made
6. were used
7. was divided
8. was printed
9. were helped
10. were written
11. were taken
12. was read

2c
1. The news was collected and organized by Helen.
2. (Sometimes) mistakes were (sometimes) made (sometimes).
3. Photographs were borrowed from a local library.
4. An old printing machine was used.
5. *Amazing* was printed on normal paper.

CHRIS Episode 5

3a
1. had to go
2. couldn't work out
3. didn't have to look
4. had to guess
5. had to go

3b
1. When was it built?
2. Who was it built for?
3. Why was it built?
4. Where was it built?
5. When were the Crown Jewels stolen?

Unit 14

1a
1. You should study harder
2. You should use a knife
3. You should turn on the light
4. You should eat a sandwich
5. You should buy a new one
6. You should wear a pullover

1b
1. You shouldn't
2. You shouldn't
3. You should
4. You should
5. You should
6. You should
7. You shouldn't

1c
1. You should rest sometimes
2. You shouldn't study when you are tired.
3. You should study in a quiet room.
4. You shouldn't study while you are listening to music.
5. You shouldn't study in front of the TV.

2a
1. You should put
2. You should spend
3. You should buy
4. You should go
5. You should give

2b
1. I don't think you should eat the hamburger.
2. I don't think you should swim in the sea.
3. I think you should use the dictionary.
4. I don't think you should watch TV
5. I think you should look under the bed.

2c
Student generated answers

Workbook answers

Check up: Units 12–14

3a
1. We had to light candles.
2. She has to practise every day.
3. We don't have to wear a uniform.
4. They had to help do the housework.
5. I didn't have to do the washing up.
6. I don't have to travel far away.

3b
1. is damaged
2. is buried
3. is produced
4. are killed
5. are made

3c
1. called
2. flew
3. was built
4. was called
5. it travelled
6. were built
7. was opened
8. was produced
9. was called
10. were sold

Unit 15

1a
1. so people had to keep food in cold places
2. so people used to send letters
3. so people used to use pens and paper
4. so people used to read books

1b
1. He used to live in a house but now he lives in a block of flats.
2. He used to ride a bike but now he drives a car.
3. He used to listen to the radio but now he watches TV.
4. He used to play with his dog but now he plays tennis.
5. He used to write with a pen and paper but now he uses a computer.

2a
1. used to have
2. used to do
3. used to read
4. used to learn
5. used to give

2b
Student generated answers

2c
1. I didn't use to have extra classes at school
2. Kelly used to play school sports at the weekend.
3. They used to write tests every Wednesday morning.
4. We didn't use to travel far to school.

2d
1. She used to wear
2. She didn't use to have
3. She didn't use to be
4. She didn't use to wear

2e
1. used to play
2. used to worry
3. didn't use to bite
4. used to cry
5. used to be

2f
Student generated answers

Words in action

3a
1. You shouldn't
2. You shouldn't
3. You shouldn't
4. You should
5. You shouldn't
6. You should

3b
loud, friendly, healthy, easy, hungry, dirty, gentle, lucky

3c
1. dirty
2. healthy
3. loud
4. easy
5. friendly
6. hungry
7. lucky

Unit 16

1a
1. Mr Odd might fall off the ladder or he might get a shock.
2. Olive could burn herself or she might start a fire.
3. Ozzy might break the furniture or he might hurt himself.

1b
1. might/could fall into the water
2. might/could put their heads in the sand
3. might/could bite you
4. might/could think you are a visitor
5. might/could lose your job

2a
1. You might make a lot of noise
2. You might be able to climb through an upstairs window.
3. Someone outside could see you.
4. You could need them
5. Someone might rob you

2b
1. to eat
2. to eat
3. drinking
4. putting
5. to do/doing
6. to do
7. to do/doing

2c
Student generated answer

CHRIS Episode 6

3a
1. cover, get
2. putting, damage
3. touch, damage
4. repair, get
5. turn Chris off, lose
6. have, reading

3b
3. They didn't use to use computers
4. They used to go fishing.
5. They didn't used to travel by plane/on planes
6. They didn't use to listen to the radio.
7. They used to write letters on stone

Consolidation 2

1
1. How many, There are a lot of trees in a forest.
2. How many, There are very few elephants in England.
3. How much, There is a lot of sand in a desert.
4. How much, There is a lot of water in an ocean.
5. How many, There are very few space stations in space.
6. How much, There is very little smog in the countryside.

2
1. are they going to paint
2. will pay
3. will buy some
4. won't bite
5. are you going to go home
6. am not going to do

Workbook answers

3
1. She has to travel abroad
2. She has to wear smart clothes.
3. She doesn't have to go to school.
4. She dosen't have to get up early
5. She has to work late

4
1. is drunk
2. is spoken
3. was invented
4. were used

Unit 17

1a
1. don't play the music loudly
2. eat the spaghetti in the fridge
3. call a doctor
4. watch TV or a video
5. use the candles in the kitchen
6. drink something from the fridge
7. tell them to clear it up
8. tell them to go to bed

1b
1. understand
2. run out of
3. make
4. have
5. want

1c
1. If you don't find a bus, take a taxi.
2. If you are cold, wear something warm.
3. If you go out, tell Shelly's mother where you are going.
4. If you need more money, ask Shelly's mother for some.
5. If you want to stay longer, phone me.

2a
1. If you miss the bus, you'll be late.
2. If you run out of money, I'll lend you some.
3. If you don't wear something warm, you'll catch a cold.
4. If you forget a waterproof coat, you'll get wet.
5. If you go to bed late, you'll feel tired tomorrow.
6. If you study hard, you'll be a better student.
7. If you eat too much, you'll feel ill.

2b
1. leaves, will take
2. dives, will hurt
3. eat, feel

2d
1. If you forget your homework, the teacher will be upset.
2. If you draw on the desk, the teacher will shout at you.
3. If you throw paper aeroplanes in the classroom, the teacher will ask you to leave the class.
4. If you study hard, you will learn a lot.
5. If you leave the class without permission, you'll get into trouble.
6. If you do your exercises well, you'll make a good impression.

2e
1. is
2. will go
3. isn't
4. will stay
5. is
6. will visit
7. get
8. will call/phone

Words in action

3a
1. dish washer
2. washing machine
3. CD player
4. key
5. fridge
6. torch
7. video camera
8. telephone

3b
1. police officer
2. stunt double
3. fire fighter
4. photographer
5. life guard

3c
Student generated answers

1a
1. Why don't we
2. How about
3. Let's/We could
4. How about
5. Let's/We could

1b
1. Let's/We could go sightseeing.
2. Let's go shopping?
3. How about visiting/Why don't we visit the museum?
4. Let's go to the zoo?
5. How about eating/Why don't we eat at a local restaurant?

1c
1. How about
2. Why don't we
3. Let's

2a
1. I'd rather stay home and relax.
2. I'd rather stand.
3. I'd rather have spaghetti.
4. I'd rather buy one.
5. I'd rather go to bed early.
6. I'd rather write them a letter.

2b
1. I'd rather ride...
2. I'd rather visit...
3. I'd rather go...
4. I'd rather take part...

2c
1. don't know
2. do
3. going
4. don't
5. go
6. looks/seems/is
7. will
8. have

2d
Student generated answers

CHRIS Episode 7

3a
1. return
2. walk
3. run
4. catch
5. run
6. sees
7. know
8. going
9. follows
10. lose
11. go

3b
2. a
3. b
4. b
5. b
6. a

Unit 19

1a
1. She has been having singing lessons for six months.
2. Her brother has been learning the piano since 1993.
3. They have been practising together for four months.
4. She has been writing songs since last year.
5. They have been trying to record a CD since October.

Workbook answers

1b
1. I've been waiting to see the doctor since o'clock this morning.
2. We've been learning English for three years.
3. Bill has been cooking for half an hour.
4. Kate has been reading that book since Tuesday.
5. They have been playing tennis for two hours.

1c
Student generated answers

2a
1. They have been helping sail the boat since 1993.
2. They have been having lessons on the boat for one year.
3. They have been living on the boat since July.
4. They have been visiting interesting countries for eleven months.
5. Vicky has been writing letters to her penfriends in England for ten months.

2b
1. She's been helping
2. How long have you been studying?
3. Has he been playing computer games?
4. Has he been watching TV?
5. has he been doing
Q. He's been mending his bike.

2c
1. They have been walking in space.
2. He has been doing his homework.
3. The dog has been digging holes in the garden.

2d
2. b
3. a
4. b

Check up: Units 17–19

3a
1. enjoy
2. feel
3. stay/be
4. run out of
5. rescue
6. be

3b
1. have
2. getting
3. phone
4. go
5. go

3c
1. She has been walking in the rain.
2. He has been studying for school.
3. They have been listening to music.
4. She has been working hard all day.
5. They have been having dinner.

Unit 20

1a
1. It can't be a koala bear because it can't climb trees and it doesn't eat eucalyptus leaves.
2. It can't be a camel because it hasn't got a hump.
3. It can't be a kangaroo because it doesn't jump.
4. It can't be an alien because it doesn't come from outer space.
5. It can't be a whale because it doesn't live in the sea.

It must be an ostrich.

1b
1. Alexia can't be, he is out of town on holiday.
2. Alexia can't be, there are no classes today.
3. Alexia can't be, Woofa is in the garden.
4. Alexia can't be, she hasn't got any money.
5. Alexia can't be, her running shoes are in the cupboard.
6. Alexia can't be, her racket is in her room.

1c
1. must be
2. must be
3. can't be
4. must be
5. can't be
6. can't be

1d
1. sofa
2. curtains
3. cabinet
4. armchair
5. cupboard
6. desk
7. chest

2a
1. It can't be, has got thick tyres
2. It can't be, has got small wheels
3. It can't be, has got a large, comfortable saddle
4. It must be

2b
1. She must be an astronaut because she is walking in space/wearing a space suit.
2. She must be a police officer because she is wearing a poice uniform.
3. He must be a cameraman because he is carrying a camera.

2c
1. It must be a city because there's a lot of traffic and air pollution.
2. It must be summer because it's very hot.
3. She can't be staying with friends because she's staying in a hotel.
4. It must be a place near the sea because she goes swimming every day.
5. It can't be Italy because she can't use her Italian phrase-book.
6. It must be Greece.

Words in action

3a
1. singer
2. sings
3. director
4. directs
5. organization
6. organizes
7. robbed
8. robber

3b
1. dangerous
2. friendly
3. success
4. sun
5. crowded
6. stranger
7. comfortable
8. rainy

3c
1. A cool drink.
2. An ancient coin.
3. A long sausage.

Unit 21

1a
1. I would/wouldn't put it in a bank.
2. I would/wouldn't spend it all.
3. I would/wouldn't buy a new bike.
4. I would/wouldn't give it to my friends.

1b
Student generated answers

1c
Student generated answers

Workbook answers

1d
1. survival
2. food
3. sand
4. desert
5. first
6. cooker
7. plant
8. shelter

2a
1. drink something If I was/were thirsty, I'd drink something.
2. ask someone the way If I was/were lost, I'd ask someone the way.
3. not wear a pullover or jacket If I was/were hot, I wouldn't wear a pullover or a jacket.
4. eat a sandwich If I was/were hungry, I'd eat a sandwich.
5. wear something warm If I was/were cold, I'd wear something warm.
6. go to bed early If I was/were tired, I'd go to bed early.

2b
1. If I saw a fire, I wouldn't call the police I'd call the fire brigade.
2. If I found a wallet, I wouldn't take it to the bank. I'd take it to the police.
3. If I saw an accident, I wouldn't call the police. I'd call an ambulance.
4. If there was an earthquake, I wouldn't stay inside the house. I'd stay outside.
5. If I felt ill, I wouldn't see a dentist. I'd see a doctor.

2c
1. wouldn't give, was/were
2. wasn't, would work
3. saw, would ask
4. bought, would be
5. would go, went
6. weren't, would visit

2d
Student generated answer

CHRIS Episode 8

3a
b 1 It can't be Paris.
   2 It must be London.
c 1 It can't be a cinema.
   2 It must be the National Theatre.
d 1 It can't be a skyscraper.
   2 It must be Cleopatra's Needle.

3b
The twins enjoyed their adventure. They found Chris and his computer program.
They were very clever.

Unit 22

1a
1. French
2. China
3. Italian
4. Spain
5. Portuguese
6. Japan
7. German
8. Hungary

1b
1. (no article)
2. (no article)
3. (no article)
4. (no article)
5. (no article)
6. a/-(no article)
7. a
8. the
9. a
10. a
11. (no article)
12. the
13. (no article)
14. the

1c
1. (no article)
2. (no article)
3. (no article)
4. a
5. the
6. a
7. the
8. (no article)
9. the
10. a
11. (no article)
12. (no article)
13. (no article)
14. a
15. the
16. a
17. the
18. the
19. (no article)
20. (no article)

2a
1. to buy
2. talking/to talk
3. helping
4. to talk
5. asking
6. to make
7. to ask
8. to be
9. talking
10. to help
11. talking
12. to leave

2b
1. to be
2. working
3. not to work
4. singing
5. to record
6. doing

2d
Student generated answers

2e
Student generated answers

Check up: Units 20–22

3a
1. (no article)
2. the
3. a
4. the
5. a
6. a
7. the
8. the
9. the
10. the
11. the
12. (no article)
13. the
14. the
15. the
16. the
17. the

3b
Student generated answer

3c
1. forgot
2. decided
3. managed
4. was trying
5. refused

Unit 23

1a
cut–cut, get–got, give–gave, find–found, fly–flew, hide–hid, go–went, cost–cost, feel–felt, send–sent, wear–wore, catch–caught, bite–bit, hold–held, drive–drove, stand–stood, do–did, forget–forgot, have–had

1b
1. was studying
2. arrived
3. made
4. sat
5. were drinking
6. heard
7. looked
8. was lying
9. was getting
10. phoned
11. ran

Workbook answers

1c
1. They drove to the hospital.
2. He phoned his parents.
3. He was talking to the doctor when his parents arrived.
4. She wasn't seriously hurt.
5. No, she didn't have to stay in hospital.
6. Ziggy had to do the test because her teacher didn't believe her story.

1d
1. b
2. f
3. a
4. i
5. e
6. d
7. c
8. h

2a
1. for
2. Then
3. ago
4. this
5. yesterday
6. when
7. while
8. on

2b
1. when
2. When
3. At first
4. Then
5. After that
6. In the end

2c
Student generated answer

Words in action

3a
1. b
2. a
3. b
4. a
5. a
6. b
7. b
8. a

3b
1. last
2. for
3. Then
4. After that
5. Finally
6. at

3c
1. a
2. b
3. b
4. a
5. a
6. a

Final consolidation

1
1. go
2. don't dig
3. will get
4. Don't go
5. don't stay
6. find
7. don't eat
8. are
9. will give
10. don't get
Q. Woofa

2
1. How about
2. Why don't we
3. we could

3
1. Helen has lived in London since 1983.
2. I was on holiday for two weeks.
3. The Odds have lived next door to the Normals for a year.
4. Alexia stayed at the party for three hours.
5. I've been doing my homework since six o'clock.

4
1. What time are you going to leave?
2. How do they go to school?
3. Why didn't he go to school?
4. Who was at the party?
5. What were you doing at nine o'clock?

5
1. lived
2. loved
3. weren't
4. found
5. took
6. felt
7. have been looking
8. have been living/have lived
9. bought
10. have been looking
11. hit

6
1. it might/could be
2. It might/could be
3. it can't be
4. It must be
Q. 1–4 Student generated answers

7
1. went, would stay
2. stayed, would lie
3. lay, wouldn't work
4. didn't work, wouldn't have
5. didn't have, wouldn't be able to

8
1. was collecting
2. was watching
3. seemed
4. made
5. dropped
6. was picking
7. jumped
8. felt
9. started
10. ran
11. slipped
12. was running
13. fell
14. looked
15. was running

Heinemann English Language Teaching
A division of Heinemann Publishers (Oxford) Ltd
Halley Court, Jordan Hill, Oxford OX2 8EJ

OXFORD MADRID ATHENS PARIS FLORENCE PRAGUE SÃO PAULO CHICAGO MELBOURNE AUCKLAND SINGAPORE TOKYO IBADAN GABORONE JOHANNESBURG PORTSMOUTH (NH)

ISBN 0 435 25031 0

Text © Michael Vince 1995
Design and illustration © Heinemann Publishers (Oxford) Ltd 1995

First published 1995

All rights reserved; no part of this publication may be reproduced, stored in a retrieval system, transmitted in any form, or by any means, electronic, mechanical, photocopying, recording, or otherwise, without the prior written permission of the publishers.

Note to Teachers
Photocopies may be made, for classroom use, of pages 253–287 without the prior written permission of Heinemann Publishers (Oxford) Ltd. However, please note that the copyright law, which does not normally permit multiple copying of published material, applies to the rest of this book.

Designed by Gecko Ltd

Cover design by Stafford and Stafford

Acknowledgements
The publishers would like to thank the following people for their help: Julia Tanner, Liz Driscoll, Carolyn Roles and Ross Robertson.

Student's Book acknowledgements
Designed by Andrew Oliver
Cover design by Stafford and Stafford
Cover calligraphy by Ruth Rowland
Cover illustration by John Gilkes
Commissioned photography by Paul Freestone
Picture research by Anne Lyons

Illustrated by: Adrian Barclay pp7, 19, 31, 41, 53, 65, 75, 87, 99; Derek Bishop pp12, 28, 29, 30; Jo Dennis pp10, 13(t), 41, 76, 77, 88; Sue-Dray pp11, 23, 35, 45, 57, 69, 79, 91; Sarah Jowsey pp5, 84, 90(r); Frances Lloyd pp68(r), 77(t), 87; Chris Long pp26, 58, 92; Phyllis Mahon pp8, 9, 16, 24, 25, 26, 43, 49, 51(b), 52, 62, 63(t), 67(r), 68(l), 83, 85(r), 86, 93, 94, 100; Julian Mosedale pp13(b), 14, 15, 17, 18, 27, 33, 34, 61, 63(b), 67(l), 72, 73, 74, 81(r), 82, 95, 98; Rodney Shackell pp20, 21, 99, 102, 103; Simon Turner pp7, 31, 36, 40, 51(t), 64, 89; Shaun Williams pp15, 27, 49, 61, 83, 95; Gary Wing pp6, 38, 53, 59, 81(bl), 85(l), 97; Patrick Wright pp42, 44, 56, 60, 65, 66, 81, 90(l).

Author's acknowledgements
I would like to thank all the teachers in Argentina, Brazil, Egypt, Greece, Jordan, Lebanon, Turkey, Thailand and Uruguay who have used and commented on earlier drafts of these materials, or whose classes I have visited. I would also like to thank everyone at Heinemann who has been associated with this project, and in particular Sue Bale, Sue Jones and Karen Spiller. My biggest thanks go to my editors, Charlotte Covill, Fiona MacKenzie and Carolyn Roles, on all of whom I have depended for so much, and who have made such a great contribution to this project. Thanks also to Julia Tanner, Ross Robertson and Liz Driscoll. Finally, thanks to my sister, Susan Lewis, for keeping me supplied with reading material.

Acknowledgements
The publishers would also like to thank the following for their help: Mr Antoniou, Vicky Barbalexi, Jenny Browning, Linetta de Castle, Katerina Danilidou, Alex Gros and Mrs Spiroglou – Vafopoulou School, Katerina Kostidou, Nafsika Koulouri, Dimitris Lefkaditis, Katherine Lukey-Coutsocostas, Mrs Malliou – Omiros School, Teta Marinou, Peta Nelson-Xarchoulakou, Mary Nicalexi, Betty Orfanidou – Svarna School, Vaso Panayioteli, Dimitra Papadopoulou, Mr Papalexiou, Georgia Papas, Elisavet Plakida, Savvas Savvides, Schools – Cararigas Sa, Darzenta X, Evangelidou and Ananiadou, Mihou Ant, Mrs Stamatopoulou, Chris Stavridou, Joanne Swan-Hazapi, Mrs Tsoe, Eva Tsopanakos-Venizelou, Poppy Vassilakou.

Thanks also to the following for their help in making the photostory: Susanne Bates, Tarek Chueiri, Amanda Clegg, Ruth Egau, Jackie Ely, Ben Harries, Troy Hawkins, Susie and Charlie Healey, Robbie Hedge, Anna McCleery, Alice MacLennan, Seadna McPhail, Niall McWilliams, Rhiannon Matthews, Jessica and Joey Miles, Annette Mngxitama, David Pickford, Marcus Pirou, Robert and Ann Poulter, Matthew Quaralt, Carla de Sales, Ian Simons, Ben Speedy, Emily Traer, Hannah Welch; the Cherwell School; David Miles and the Oxford Archeological Unit; John Hitchins for supplying the metal detector and video camera; Jessops for supplying the telescope.

Text and photograph acknowledgements
The author and publishers would like to thank the following for permission to reproduce their material: extract from Programme for Belize p76, © *Young Telegraph* 1992; extract, p54, from *The Blue Peter Green Book* by Peter Brown, Lewis Bronze and Nick Heathcote with the permission of BBC Enterprises Limited; photographs (except dustcart), p54, reproduced from *Blue Peter Action Book* published by BBC Books @ £4.99. In cases where they have been unsuccessful in contacting copyright holders they will be pleased to make the necessary arrangements at the first opportunity.

The author and publishers would also like to thank the following for permission to reproduce their material: BBC Enterprises, all on p54 except dustcart; Bridgeman Art Library p71; Bruce Coleman Photo Library p13 (balloon: photo Harald Lange), (jeep: photo John Waters), p19(c) photo Gerald Cubitt, p32 (ostrich: photo Mark Boulton), p43 (koala bear: photo Hans Reinhard); Environmental Picture Library p55 (metal skip: photo Amanda Gazidis); Robert Harding Picture Library p13 (camel: photo Christopher Rennie), p75 (photo Bildagentur Schusteer/Bramaz), p78(b); Frank Lane Picture Agency p13 (camper van: photo David Hosking), p43 (whale: photo S. McCutcheon); Ken Lockwood p54 (dustcart); Oxford Scientific Films p19 (l, r: photo Hjalmar R Bardason), p32 (chimpanzee: photo Joe McDonald), (penguin: photo Kjell Sandved), p32 (panda: photo Kjell Sandved) (toad: photo Jack Dermid); South American Pictures p76, (photos Chris Sharp); Eye Ubiquitous p78(t) (photo E J B Hawkins); Zul p53 (photo John Heinrich), p55 (badges).

Produced by Gecko Ltd.
Printed and bound in Spain by Mateu Cromo

95 96 97 98 99 20 10 9 8 7 6 5 4 3 2 1